Football and Colonialism

NEW AFRICAN HISTORIES

SERIES EDITORS: JEAN ALLMAN, ALLEN ISAACMAN, AND DEREK R. PETERSON

David William Cohen and E. S. Atieno Odhiambo, *The Risks of Knowledge*

Belinda Bozzoli, *Theatres of Struggle and the End of Apartheid*

Gary Kynoch, *We Are Fighting the World*

Stephanie Newell, *The Forger's Tale*

Jacob A. Tropp, *Natures of Colonial Change*

Jan Bender Shetler, *Imagining Serengeti*

Cheikh Anta Babou, *Fighting the Greater Jihad*

Marc Epprecht, *Heterosexual Africa?*

Marissa J. Moorman, *Intonations*

Karen E. Flint, *Healing Traditions*

Derek R. Peterson and Giacomo Macola, editors, *Recasting the Past*

Moses E. Ochonu, *Colonial Meltdown*

Emily S. Burrill, Richard L. Roberts, and Elizabeth Thornberry, editors, *Domestic Violence and the Law in Colonial and Postcolonial Africa*

Daniel R. Magaziner, *The Law and the Prophets*

Emily Lynn Osborn, *Our New Husbands Are Here*

Robert Trent Vinson, *The Americans Are Coming!*

James R. Brennan, *Taifa*

Benjamin N. Lawrance and Richard L. Roberts, editors, *Trafficking in Slavery's Wake*

David M. Gordon, *Invisible Agents*

Allen F. Isaacman and Barbara S. Isaacman, *Dams, Displacement, and the Delusion of Development*

Stephanie Newell, *The Power to Name*

Gibril R. Cole, *The Krio of West Africa*

Matthew M. Heaton, *Black Skin, White Coats*

Meredith Terretta, *Nation of Outlaws, State of Violence*

Paolo Israel, *In Step with the Times*

Michelle R. Moyd, *Violent Intermediaries*

Abosede A. George, *Making Modern Girls*

Alicia C. Decker, *In Idi Amin's Shadow*

Rachel Jean-Baptiste, *Conjugal Rights*

Shobana Shankar, *Who Shall Enter Paradise?*

Emily S. Burrill, *States of Marriage*

Todd Cleveland, *Diamonds in the Rough*

Carina E. Ray, *Crossing the Color Line*

Sarah Van Beurden, *Authentically African*

Giacomo Macola, *The Gun in Central Africa*

Lynn Schler, *Nation on Board*

Julie MacArthur, *Cartography and the Political Imagination*

Abou B. Bamba, *African Miracle, African Mirage*

Daniel Magaziner, *The Art of Life in South Africa*

Paul Ocobock, *An Uncertain Age*

Keren Weitzberg, *We Do Not Have Borders*

Nuno Domingos, *Football and Colonialism*

Football and Colonialism

Body and Popular Culture in Urban Mozambique

∽

Nuno Domingos

Foreword by Harry G. West

OHIO UNIVERSITY PRESS ∽ ATHENS, OHIO

Ohio University Press, Athens, Ohio 45701
ohioswallow.com
© 2017 by Ohio University Press
All rights reserved

To obtain permission to quote, reprint, or otherwise reproduce or distribute material from Ohio University Press publications, please contact our rights and permissions department at (740) 593-1154 or (740) 593-4536 (fax).

A substantially different version was published in Portuguese as *Futebol e colonialismo: Corpo e cultura popular em Moçambique* by Imprensa de Ciências Sociais of the Institute of Social Sciences of the University of Lisbon, 2012.

Printed in the United States of America
Ohio University Press books are printed on acid-free paper ⊚ ™

27 26 25 24 23 22 21 20 19 18 17   5 4 3 2 1

Library of Congress Cataloging-in-Publication Data
Names: Domingos, Nuno, 1976– author.
Title: Football and colonialism : body and popular culture in urban Mozambique / Nuno Domingos ; foreword by Harry G. West.
Description: Athens : Ohio University Press, [2017] | Series: New African histories | Includes bibliographical references and index.
Identifiers: LCCN 2017018181| ISBN 9780821422618 (hc : alk. paper) | ISBN 9780821422625 (pb : alk. paper) | ISBN 9780821445976 (pdf)
Subjects: LCSH: Soccer—Mozambique—History. | Soccer—Social aspects—Mozambique. | Soccer—Political aspects—Mozambique. | Mozambique—Social life and customs.
Classification: LCC GV944.M85 D6613 2017 | DDC 796.33409679—dc23
LC record available at https://lccn.loc.gov/2017018181

Contents

List of Illustrations		vii
Foreword by Harry G. West		ix
Acknowledgments		xiii
Abbreviations		xv
Chapter 1	Football and the Narration of a Colonial Situation	1
Chapter 2	A Colonial Sport's Field	21
Chapter 3	Football and the Moral Economy of the Lourenço Marques Suburbs	61
Chapter 4	A Suburban Style of Play	102
Chapter 5	Witchcraft Practices in Football's Symbolic Economy	135
Chapter 6	Sweetness and Speed *Tactics as Disenchantment of the World*	158
Chapter 7	Football Narratives and Social Networks in Late Colonial Mozambique	190
Chapter 8	Embodied History	225
Notes		233
Bibliography		299
Index		319

Illustrations

MAPS

1.1.	Mozambique, 1903	5
1.2.	Metropolitan Portugal and the Portuguese colonial empire (used in classrooms), 1934	15
2.1.	Lourenço Marques and its suburbs, 1907–8	23
2.2.	General plan of the city and harbor of Lourenço Marques, 1926	23
2.3.	Plan of the city of Lourenço Marques, 1929	45

FIGURES

2.1.	Lourenço Marques's Gorjão wharf and railway lines	25
2.2.	The tennis courts in the Public Garden and the Clube da Polana golf course	31
2.3.	Sketch of a modern gymnasium	45
3.1.	Munhuana's native neighborhood—crematorium	70
3.2.	A company of native infantry	81
6.1.	Dominant triangles in the short-pass game	167
6.2.	Dominant triangles in the long-pass game	167
6.3.	Eusébio shooting, Amsterdam, Ajax Stadium, 9 May 1965	189
7.1.	Benfica football team, Amsterdam, Ajax Stadium, 9 May 1965	195
7.2.	Eusébio and Flora; the Benfica team leaving the Netherlands	221
7.3.	Children playing in Chamanculo, 2010	223

TABLES

2.1.	Percentage of black members and mestiço members at sports clubs and associations in Mozambique, 1935–58	50

2.2. Percentage of black members and mestiço members of sports clubs and associations in Mozambique and Lourenço Marques, 1959–64 — 52

2.3. Number of Mozambican sports associations and clubs and total membership, 1930–64 — 54

Foreword

The bigger picture is sometimes best seen in the littlest details. According to Thomas Hylland Eriksen, the importance of anthropology lies precisely in its ability to examine "large issues" in "small places."[1] That is exactly what Nuno Domingos accomplishes in *Football and Colonialism: Body and Popular Culture in Urban Mozambique.*

At first glance, the work is about football as it was played in Lourenço Marques—the largest city and administrative center of the Portuguese colony of Mozambique—in the first half of the twentieth century. The work charts the development of the game from the founding of the first football clubs by British expatriates, to the establishment of satellites of Portuguese metropolitan clubs such as Sporting and Benfica, to the opening up of these clubs to African players including mostly elites of mixed racial heritage, to the eventual creation of an African Football Association whose players were mostly working-class Africans living in the poorer periphery of the city where their matches were mostly played.

Historians of football will, of course, be interested to learn more of the sporting context that produced such talents as Mário Coluna and Eusébio, both of whom made their mark in European football in the mid-twentieth century. And football's claim to be a—if not the—"world sport" will only be strengthened by accounts of the enthusiasm with which urban Mozambicans of varied backgrounds embraced the game so long ago. Domingos's work is, however, far more than a historical account of the spread of a European (if only in its "modern" form) game to an African colony. The bigger picture with which this work engages is the relationship between colonized and colonizer, seen through the lens of that game.

As such, this account builds upon and extends a social science tradition that has produced rich results in African studies in recent decades, namely the study of "popular culture." To date, studies of African popular culture have mostly focused on the arts, including sculpture, painting, music, dance, literature, cinema, and theater. Such work has rendered visible the dynamic interaction of tradition and modernity on the African continent, highlighting the ways in which African forms of expression have engaged with the lived experience of historical processes connecting the continent to a larger world, from colonialism, to revolutionary nationalism, to socialism, to neoliberalism. In the mix, Africans have adopted and adapted European genres of expression to their own ends and, as this body of work has shown, contributed profoundly to the global trajectories of these various forms.

Domingos himself adopts and adapts the "popular culture" approach to his ends in this study. He extends the approach to a realm too often ignored by historians and social scientists, namely sport. By seeing how football was played in urban Mozambique through the conceptual framework of "genre," he dispenses with the assumption that a game—defined as it is by a set of rules—travels unchanged from one social context to another. Like the arts, he shows us, football has been transformed by those who have played it in places like colonial Mozambique. But it is not the transformation of the game itself that most interests Domingos in this work. He is instead most interested in the "larger issues" of how the game of football did or did not transform those who played it in colonial Mozambique, as well as how they were or were not able to use the game to transform the world in which they lived.

What little has been written about sport in colonial contexts has tended to focus on its use as a tool of colonial power. By playing—or, being made to play—the games of the colonizer, it has been argued, the bodies of the colonized have been disciplined and their minds oriented toward new ideas such as "structured competition," "fair play," and "the rule of law." Domingos's work clearly shows that, to some extent, the Portuguese regime conceived of sport, including football, as a means of "civilizing" natives. But as Domingos demonstrates, this was not an entirely successful project. Urban Mozambicans played the game in ways that both expressed and reinforced their own ways of being in the world, even as they played it, in part, to transform themselves in attempts to gain greater access to a world that too often excluded them.

Domingos's use of the writings of the protonationalist Mozambican journalist and poet José Craveirinha—who chronicled football in the "cane city" neighborhoods of Lourenço Marques—affords readers an intimate view of the minutiae of the game as it was played by working-class Africans, including the "littlest details" such as descriptive terms, physical gestures, and moral dispositions that animated players and spectators alike in the many "small places" in which they played. On rough makeshift pitches in the midst of the crowded, squalid urban villages that surrounded the "cement city," humor, creativity, deception, and violence were part of the game, just as they were a part of everyday life for residents of these neighborhoods under colonial rule. Playing the game as they did, urban residents of these "mean streets" simultaneously submitted to the rules of the game and challenged them, while at once resisting colonial power and seeking to capture it. Domingos's recognition and exploration of defining paradoxes like these gives foundation to an account of rich and subtle detail.

In these pages, football is not "just a game," but instead the centerpiece of a vivid tableau whose subjects have heretofore remained underexplored. Accordingly, Domingos's work not only provides missing pieces of the bigger pictures of Portuguese and Mozambican history, not to mention of the history of football, but also offers an exceptionally fine-grained perspective on the lived experience of colonialism in Mozambique—shedding comparative light on such experiences elsewhere—while alerting us to the many and often contradictory potentialities of sport to shape human subjectivities.

Harry G. West

Acknowledgments

The publication of this book concludes a process that had the crucial contribution of various individuals and institutions.

First of all, I would like to express my debt to the permanent, open, and rich dialogue I had with Harry G. West at the Department of Sociology and Anthropology of the School of Oriental and African Studies. I am also grateful to the late John D. Y. Peel, whose work was an important inspiration. At SOAS I would also like to thank my colleagues Paul Hansen, Mao Wada, Alex Verbeek, Mira Moshini, Robert McKenzie, and Dorota Szawarska.

I have benefited from the comments, amendments, and criticisms that I received from Deborah James and João de Pina Cabral during my Viva.

I am particularly grateful to Nelson Teixeira and Miguel Pinheiro for their support during the period I spent in Mozambique. In Maputo, I was fortunate to have the collaboration of Humberto Coimbra, Natu Harilal, Carolina Leia, Teresa Cruz e Silva, Aurélio Rocha, Renato Caldeira, and Fátima Mendonça. I am also grateful to the staff of the Historical Archive of Mozambique, the Ministry of Youth and Sports of Mozambique, and the Eduardo Mondlane University.

I would also like to thank the staff of the National Library of Lisbon and the Imprensa de Ciências Sociais of the Institute of Social Sciences of the University of Lisbon, where the first version of this book was published in Portuguese.

The critical and attentive readings and the suggestions of Bárbara Direito, Frederico Ágoas, Inês Brasão, Isaura Domingos, Jorge Domingos, José Neves, and Rahul Kumar were decisive for the completion of my work.

Most important were the comments made by the manuscript's reviewers and the editors of the Ohio University Press New African Histories series. I am especially grateful for Allen Isaacman's encouragement. I want also to express my gratitude to the people who worked on the book's production at the Press, and especially to Gillian Berchowitz and Nancy Basmajian.

The final version of this book owes a great deal to the skilled work of revision and translation of Miguel Cardoso. I wish also to thank the translation work done by João Paulo Oliveiro for the first version of this manuscipt.

Diogo Ramada Curto kindly persuaded me to research the Portuguese colonial experience abroad, and Salwa Castelo Branco also insisted that I should pursue that enterprise in London.

For many and diverse reasons I'm also grateful to Alfredo Margarido, Ana Estevens, Augusto Nascimento, Clara Cabral, Cláudia Castelo, Diana Costa-Felix, Eduardo Ascensão, Elisa Lopes da Silva, Elsa Peralta, Fernando Domingos, Isabel Pombo, Isadora Ataíde, João Fazenda, José Mapril, José Manuel Sobral, Luís Sá, Marcelo Bittencourt, Miguel Jerónimo, Nina Tiesler, Nuno Dias, Nuno Medeiros, Onésimo Teotónio de Almeida, Pancho Guedes, Paulo Catrica, Pedro Martins, Pedro Roxo, Raquel Borges, Rui Santos, Roberto Chichorro, Sofia Miranda, Tom Herre, Todd Cleveland, Victor Andrade Melo, and Victor Pereira.

This research was funded by a grant from the Foundation for Science and Technology (Portugal).

Without the contribution of all the former players and coaches of Maputo I had the opportunity to meet, this research would not have been possible.

Abbreviations

ACPEFM	Arquivo do Conselho Provincial de Educação Física de Moçambique (Archive of the Provincial Council of Physical Education of Mozambique)
AFA	Associação de Futebol Africana (African Football Association)
AFLM	Associação de Futebol de Lourenço Marques (Lourenço Marques Football Association)
AHM	Arquivo Histórico de Moçambique (Historical Archive of Mozambique)
CPEF	Conselho Provincial de Educação Física de Mozambique (Mozambique Provincial Council on Physical Education)
CUF	Companhia União Fabril (Company Union Manufacturing)
DGEFDSE	Direcção Geral de Educação Física, Desportos e Saúde Escolar (General Office of Physical Education, Health, and School Sports)
DSAC	Direcção dos Serviços de Administração Civil (Head Office of Civil Administration Services)
DSNI	Direcção dos Serviços dos Negócios Índigenas (Head Office of Native Affairs)
FIFA	Federação Internacional de Futebol Associação (International Federation of Association Football)
FNAT	Federação Nacional para a Alegria no Trabalho (National Foundation for Joy at Work)

GALM	Grémio Africano de Lourenço Marques (African Guild of Lourenço Marques)
INEF	Instituto Nacional de Educação Física (National Institute of Physical Education)
PIDE	Polícia Internacional de Defesa do Estado (International and State Defense Police)
RAU	Reforma Administrativa Ultramarina (Overseas Administrative Reform)
SCCIM	Serviços de Centralização e Coordenação da Informação de Moçambique (Mozambique Office for the Centralization and Coordination of Information)
SNI	Secretariado Nacional de Informação (National Secretariat of Information)

1 ◆ Football and the Narration of a Colonial Situation

JOSÉ CRAVEIRINHA'S ETHNOGRAPHY OF SUBURBAN FOOTBALL IN LOURENÇO MARQUES

In 1955, José Craveirinha, a prominent Mozambican *mestiço* poet and journalist,[1] suggested that the distinctive performance of African players from the suburbs of Lourenço Marques revealed a form of intelligence, an "extraordinary and limitless . . . fantasy" of the *indígena* (native) population, which the poet attributed to its "acute sense of malice." *Malice*, usually associated with grave and harmful actions springing from an evil source, was here given a positive spin, as intelligence or cunning.[2]

This was one among a series of articles that Craveirinha wrote that year in *O brado africano*[3] on the kind of football played in the suburbs of Lourenço Marques. In another piece, he addressed the way in which suburban players adopted, adapted, and re-created the game, a European invention.[4] "The indígena," he emphasized, "is ready to adapt to new things but also to transform them or even discover them anew."[5]

The use, in local football, of what he termed "witchcraft practices" was one of the most conspicuous manifestations of this process of adoption. Craveirinha highlighted the influence of "ancient taboos, beliefs, superstitions" in the local adoption of the game. These beliefs had a powerful effect on the players' "reflex system." For years in succession, Beira-Mar, a team from Chamanculo, a suburban neighborhood, won the local championship because, the poet claimed, "before the matches, their athletes drank a special tea at the president's house and, at some point, several black-and-white crows would appear behind the opposing team's goal, to indicate how many goals they would suffer." "Black men and many mestiços," the poet continued, "still entered the pitch with small 'copper'coins inside their boots, and would rub certain 'remedies' on their knees beforehand in order to protect their bodies from the opponent's sorcery." Africans, he noted, "gladly accepted countless impositions and customs from a more advanced civilization but, at the same time, they held on to a series of traditional practices that reflected their 'worldview.'" The interpretation of this topic led the poet to issue a challenge: "these manifestations demand a vast study, which would lead to a greater knowledge of the black man, of his problems, of his clashes with European civilization, in short, to a thorough treatise of useful and instructive ethnography."[6]

As in so many other places, the urbanization process in Lourenço Marques transformed both individuals and groups. In the city, one acquired practical skills but also began to perceive and imagine the world differently. In the capital of Mozambique, this modern phenomenon was shaped by colonialism, and more specifically by the colonial projects that marked this space under Portuguese rule. The development of sporting practices and forms of consumption in Lourenço Marques was underpinned by this colonial situation.[7] From the first decades of the twentieth century onward, both in the center of the "European city" and in the African suburbs, from children's matches taking place in any random plot of land to the more organized competitions, from matches of an informal nature among friends to those following the model of an official competition, football established itself as a dynamic element among emergent leisure practices, and made its mark as a communitarian spectacle. Here, as elsewhere around the world, by becoming a public event, the game no longer had a meaningful existence for the players on the pitch only. Performance was now shared with an audience, with those that witnessed the spectacle in situ as well as with those that gathered information on it through other, indirect, means, either personal interactions or specific channels such as the media. Sports like football were thus transfigured into a medium of everyday individual and collective identification, a secular religion of sorts, a universal language.[8] In those contexts where football became a competitive spectacle, performed for an audience, the effect of competition and of the growing pressure exerted by fans converted football into a "serious" activity, in contrast with the typical image of a "disinterested" amateur practice.[9]

The values and practices shared and praised by football players and public in the Lourenço Marques suburbs, and above all the predominant faculty of malice, will serve as a starting point for an inquiry into the specific nature of colonial domination in Lourenço Marques and the particular culture it fostered. The situated study of players' bodies gives rise to a singular representation of the colonial process. This representation is in stark contrast to the pastoral genre that gave voice to the interests at play within the field of colonial power. In the Lourenço Marques imagined by colonial propaganda, its suburbs were either culturalized or, quite simply, omitted. The city was also conceived by modernizing projects that, from the 1950s onward, were concerned with the way in which the African labor force had been reproducing.

The nature and evolution of the colonial field of power in the capital of Mozambique can be perceived through the way in which the Portuguese state and other agents—local interest groups, companies, religious organizations, nations, and international institutions—conceived the city's suburbs and their populations. The adoption of football in the periphery ran parallel with the struggles for the definition of a suburban social contract. Framed by the indirect rule that characterized the *indigenato* system, and under the thumb of a predatory state, this social contract was geared toward fulfilling the need for the reproduction of the suburban labor force and maintaining the order and racial hierarchy that regulated the relation between the colonizers and the colonized.[10] The existence of a local football dynamic in the suburbs of Lourenço Marques was partially a response to a segregation policy led by the state institutions and translated into the network of sport associations. Sports practices and consumptions were part and parcel of a broader, radically uneven process of exchange, which affected the living conditions of Mozambican populations and their specific adaptation to the environment of the city.

In this work, the malice described by José Craveirinha is not treated as an idiosyncratic trait of culturally framed individuals. The point, rather, is to interpret it as but one aspect of an informal social contract that emerged on the outskirts of Lourenço Marques and that was sustained by the unsettled routines of its inhabitants. In this sense, malice is not an element of a prescriptive notion of "culture" or "identity."[11] Nor, for that matter, is it meant to stand for a form of "national agency," so often invoked in the analysis of colonial experiences.[12] The use of prescriptive identitarian projections is common in the analysis of sports performances. By absorbing external referents (of a national, ethnic, cultural, or political nature), the game style (Brazilian, African, English)[13] naturalizes the very principles of which it is presumed to be a reflex: nation, race, identity, culture.[14] As a feature of a suburban habitus, a malice was inscribed in individuals' strategies and in the responses they gave to the strict conditions that constricted and confined them.

In this book, football performances, translated into a locally meaningful style of play, operate as a laboratory of bodies, senses, and worldviews through which one can offer a representation of the local colonial society, of its structures of power and means of social reproduction, but also of the elements of transformation brought about by historical change and human aspirations.

The game, as a practice but also as a shared popular and mediatized culture, helped the population's integration into networks of interdependence, not only those previously established through ethnic and geographic bonds, but also those shaped by other distinctly urban groups, and which may or may not have replicated those previous belongings: those that gathered in each neighborhood and those that emerged from work relations or the participation in association movements. Organized in the form of performances, played before a live audience, football contributed to the formation of a specific social stock of knowledge.[15] Knowledge about football bred everyday encounters and interactions, cemented identities, and created an idiom of expression and relation for and within the community, but it was also a means of communicating with the world. In the outskirts of colonial Lourenço Marques, football was a vehicle through which local inhabitants aspired to another material and symbolic existence, sport being one of the few fields where Africans could stand out in the frame of a colonial society. This desire for social mobility was reinforced when some black and, most all mestiço players started a professional trajectory that would eventually lead them to major metropolitan clubs. Among the latter are the well-known cases of Matateu, Mário Coluna, Hilário, and Eusébio. Thus, while an analysis of the players' on-field choreography enables us to interpret the structures of a system of domination in the capital of Mozambique, the urban dissemination of football brings to the fore the extent to which the system was unstable and subject to pressure exerted by the desires and aspirations of its inhabitants.

LOURENÇO MARQUES

In the urban history of Africa, colonial cities like Lourenço Marques established themselves, since the last quarter of the nineteenth century, as specific types of social organization.[16] They were focal points in a network of transnational economic relations reliant on decisions made in the metropolitan political centers and in the international commodity markets. These urban colonial societies were regulated by a set of laws and institutions, and their development generally involved military occupation and the employment of coercive means; the implementation of an

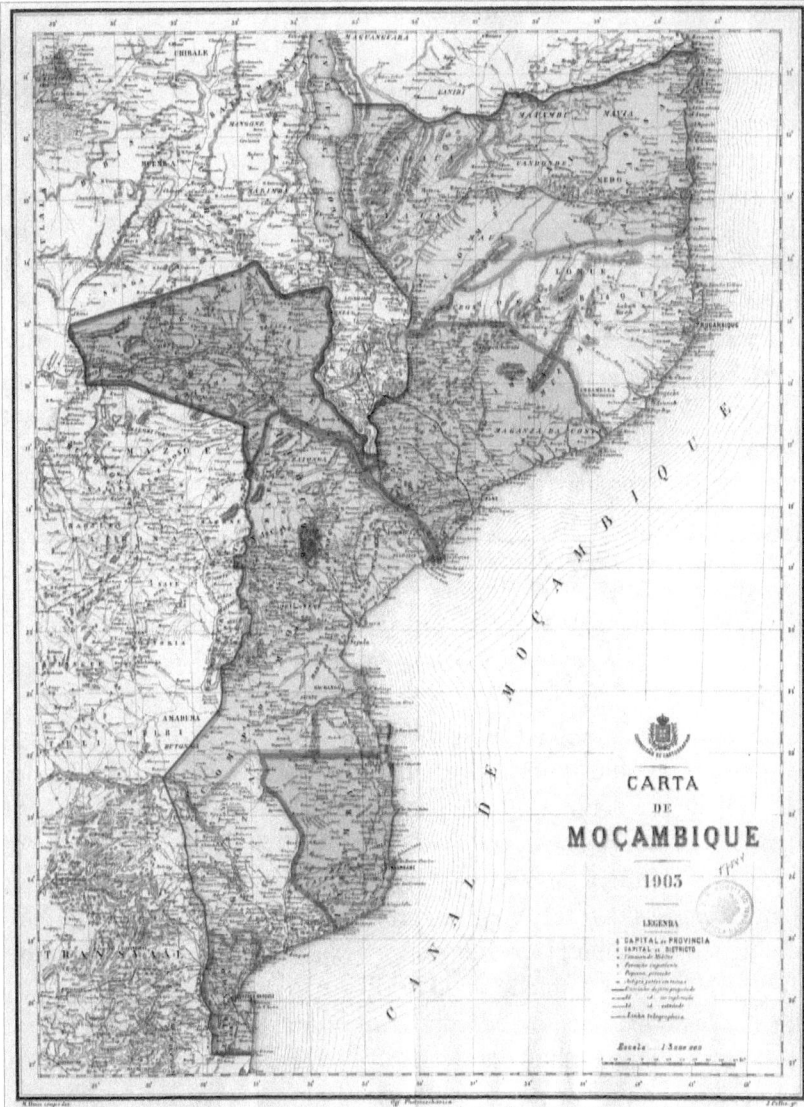

MAP 1.1. Mozambique, 1903. Comissão de Cartografia. *Source:* Biblioteca Nacional de Portugal.

administrative apparatus; the enactment of laws regulating the rights, duties, and movement of the populations; and the establishment of a regime of economic exploitation, aimed at the reproduction of the labor force, which integrated African goods and workers in international networks of production and trade.[17] Colonial cities distinguish themselves by their functional role within a set of commercial and productive relations, their

Football and the Narration of a Colonial Situation ⌒ 5

political framework and degree of state intervention, their social and professional stratification, their demographic structure and ethnic composition. Part of a larger process of social transformation, each colonial city presented its own unique dynamics.[18] As complex and creative spaces of exchange and mobility, colonial cities like Lourenço Marques were defined by processes of social and racial segmentation that led to the creation of segregated urban areas, each with a European center surrounded by African suburbs. After World War II, the African colonial city's functional specialization went through a decisive shift, when the need for cheap raw materials and labor generated a demographic explosion.[19] Many Africans were then introduced to the dynamics of a capitalist economy, becoming workers or servants, but also consumers, participants in a developing urban culture. Facing severe material and symbolic hardships, they went on to occupy a city they had built with their own hands. A site of linguistic, religious, and cultural reinvention, the city, through the specificity of its social and spatial relations, created new patterns of conflict and cooperation, new practices and worldviews.

A symbol of a new stage in Portuguese colonialism in Mozambique, the growth of Lourenço Marques came to represent the advent of this process. Despite the unmistakable signs of fragile territorialization and lack of capital, knowledge, and human resources, in other words, the relative weakness of the state's infrastructural power, in the sense used by Michael Mann,[20] the projects developed in Portuguese colonial territories did not significantly contrast with the general trends that define European colonial rule in Africa, and with which they were connected. Portuguese colonialism was no exception.[21] Lourenço Marques, which became Mozambique's capital, replacing the former capital in the Island of Mozambique (Ilha de Moçambique) in 1898 (although legally only in 1906), had singular features. The new Mozambican capital, served by an important deep-water port, would become one of the axes of a regional economy nurtured by South Africa's precocious industrialization, funded by British capital and based on gold and diamond prospecting. The train connection between Mozambique's main cities and its neighboring regions, between Lourenço Marques and Transvaal Province and further north between Beira and Rhodesia, defined the city's economic role, within the frame of a "transit and emigration economy" that characterized the southern Mozambique economic system.[22] A focal point of commercial relations, Lourenço Marques became the center of one of the most important regional labor markets. The Portuguese government made several worker transfer agreements with its neighboring regions. These agreements were one of the main colonial sources of income. Each year, thousands of Africans were sent to South African mines. The migratory-work phenomenon affected the more underprivileged populations, especially those whose rural life structure was shaken by the "colonial encounter," by tax exaction and compulsory labor.[23] The transfer of workers to the Transvaal was negotiated under a monopolistic regime in exchange for the passage through the port of Lourenço Marques of a parcel of southern African imports and exports.

The construction of the suburbs of Lourenço Marques is inseparable from the colonial system's need to reproduce the labor force necessary to sustain the city's economic activities, but also, particularly in the first decades of modern urban formation, those of the flourishing South African regional industry. The Portuguese occupation removed the indígenas from the city center, pushing them to the periphery, where many others would join them from the countryside. Successive labor regulations punctuated the various stages in the formation of a symbolically differentiated space in Lourenço Marques, composed of more or less limited zones of interaction, subject to distinct rights and duties. Suburban dwellers, with no rights to land or to ownership of the houses they had built, were forced to rent them. The rental market in the suburbs drew the contours of a hierarchical space in which residents were distributed according to their possessions. A profitable business, the private exploitation of plots of land and houses persisted, stimulated by the lack of urban planning. As with much of the urban built space in Africa in the wake of nineteenth-century colonialism, in Lourenço Marques a large portion of the population inhabited a sprawling periphery, in the fragile condition of occupiers, at the mercy of all kinds of arbitrary acts.

The prevalent economic model in the Portuguese colonial system—mercantilist, barely industrialized, and lagging behind in the employment of capitalist processes[24]—prevented the local growth of an extensive proletariat,[25] despite the increase in economic activity in the late colonial period, when the populations of settlers and Africans grew significantly. Although it was a modern colonial city, Lourenço Marques did not share some of the characteristics of other African cities, whose economic structure was built around large-scale industrial infrastructures. Many of the workers returning from the South African mines, and coming through Lourenço Marques, went back to their villages, a seasonal mobility that contributed to minimizing the effects of proletarianization.[26] The labor insecurity of those who tried to settle in the city helped maintain close connections between the city and the countryside, the latter providing a last resource of social security, based on the extended family, in a context defined by the state's feeble intervention.

The site of the reproduction of a cheap, disposable, and unskilled labor force, which the state regulated in a discretionary manner and where domestic servants made up a large portion of the population, the suburbs of Lourenço Marques showed the pattern of development of a servile society forced to adjust itself dramatically to modern structural processes. The institutions of the colonial state, ruled from 1926 by a metropolitan dictatorship,[27] sought to shape this urban environment, adjusting their particular concerns to the evolving and at times contentious interests of the colonial forces. The constant struggles that traversed the colonial field of power help us interpret the singular development of the urban structure in Lourenço Marques and the role played by the state in this process.

LEISURE AND FOOTBALL IN THE COLONIAL CITY

Urban formations such as colonial cities—spaces of social interdependence enhanced by the various routes opened up by business, trade, services, the sprawling state apparatus, and the growing labor market—created the conditions for the development of the spectacle of football as part and parcel of urban popular culture.[28] The expansion of sport in Africa, dependent on the colonial process as a whole, was the result of a dynamic of heterogeneous dissemination, often not reliant on the initiative and control of economic or state institutions. Even in English colonies, where the sway over cultural apparatuses was relatively more far reaching, sports dissemination did not quite follow a linear script. Football, for example, was not a part of the traditional elite games (cricket, polo, and even rugby, but also tennis, squash, or badminton) included in the curriculum of the colonial cadres educated at Cambridge or Oxford. As noted by Harold Perkin, footballs did not so much travel in the suitcases of diplomats, administrators, and missionaries as much as in the luggage of soldiers, small businessmen, railway workers, and teachers.[29]

Craveirinha's articles reveal how the game was more spontaneously appropriated in the Lourenço Marques suburbs. He even suggests that the suburban player's humor ("reflected in the way he enjoys the game, in the theatricality of his feints and dribbles, and in the expressions he employs to belittle the player who has just been tricked: 'pysonho,' 'psyêtu,' . . . onomatopoeic expressions that are only employed here") was one of the features that distinguished it from other conceptions of the sports activity: "these colorful gatherings become inebriated with the practice of the sport but not with the latter's role as an activity for physical improvement;

they even appear oblivious to this restrictive concept."[30] According to his description, local leisure went against some of the characteristics that defined the sports movement of a nationalist, hygienist, and pedagogic (occasionally premilitary) nature that had begun to spread across Europe in the nineteenth century and took its mold from organized models of physical reinvigoration.[31] The creation of physical education schools was also stimulated by the imperial expansion and by the need to form colonial cadres, but this ideology of the body was also present in the local colonial institutions, such as schools and military forces. In Mozambique many Africans were introduced to gymnastics through their compulsory insertion in Portuguese military companies.[32]

Research centered on leisure practices and consumptions has enabled us to understand how leisure and sport simultaneously define and defy the boundaries of colonial society.[33] Monographic works by Phyllis Martin on colonial Brazzaville, Laura Fair on Zanzibar, Peter Alegi on South Africa, and Bea Vidacs on Cameroun[34] have shown how much the study of sports practices and consumptions has to add to research on African colonial and postcolonial societies.[35] These research works demonstrate how a modern practice, whose urban adaptation some authors associate with the influence of traditional practices,[36] was adjusted to deeply stratified societies; how, in extremely segregated contexts, forms of modern popular culture, sometimes creatively interlinked with previous traditions, have generated urban bonds among subaltern populations;[37] how, despite being the object of surveillance and political co-option by state institutions, religious and economic actors, sports associations promoted practices and consumptions, mobilized people and enabled urban encounters and, in some cases, were even converted into sites of organized resistance; most important, how spectatorship and body practices, which are specific arenas of individual and collective struggles, become empirical grounds for the research of historical processes.[38] Much like these studies, research into football in Lourenço Marques fits into analyses of colonial processes focused on recovering the strategies of subordinate groups as agents of their own history and on interpreting how they transformed and tested the existing structures of domination,[39] even if their actions most of the time did not imply a project of organized and formal resistance.

FOOTBALL'S SPECIFICITY

The role played by football in the construction of the suburbs of Lourenço Marques was anchored in the game's features as a form of popular culture. A particular social process transformed the players' performances, the basic cells of a sports activity, into shared knowledge.[40] Football knowledge (a player's name, the memory of a certain special play, the list of scores) was managed according to the interactional situations individuals found themselves in.[41] Through a singular process, a specific sporting capital was converted into social capital, given that the team, its victories and defeats, represented the individual in a variety of everyday situations. In the colonial city, leisure practices contributed to the development of these more or less widely spread "specific bodies of knowledge."[42] Individuals related to this knowledge according to their social position and trajectory and, in the case under analysis, along gender lines. Football in Lourenço Marques was mainly a performance by men, and for men's consumption. For young African men the game was not only an athletic performance but also a means to achieving a certain status within a local urban environment that defied previously established hierarchies.

One of the most salient features of the process of accumulation of this specific knowledge was the way in which the information produced by the game, regardless of its scale, was organized by means of a narrative texture disputed by those who appropriated and transformed it.[43] The recursive nature of football competitions ensures the temporal continuity of these "football narratives."[44] In Lourenço Marques, apart from informal neighborhood matches, which generated a grassroots knowledge, three institutionalized narratives with varying degrees of dissemination were prevalent, emerging out of three distinct competitions: the "European city" championship, the "African suburb" championship, and the metropolitan championship, covered by the local media. A dimension of "the presentation of self in everyday life,"[45] club affiliation was the structuring element of local football narratives, the position from which individuals manage their football knowledge in the course of their social interactions.[46] While allowing individuals to communicate and establish bonds, this specific knowledge became an "interaction repertoire."[47] During interactions individuals used their knowledge through rhetorical apparatuses—shared expressive techniques—creatively adjusting their dramaturgical agility to the social situations where they are involved: at school, at work, or in leisure relationships.[48] The rhetorical use of narrative enabled the development of personal interpretations on a range of facts that in turn may be shared, or not, with others: teams and players' histories, competition results, trophies.[49]

Sports identifications have become, in many instances, a means to express social struggles and frontiers, enhancing the strength of identities and occasionally generating radical breaks.[50] Integrated within social relations defined by the existence of what Max Gluckman has called "multiplex ties,"[51] sports narratives are able to operate as elements that reinforce the practical and identitarian frontiers of human groups organized according to specific ethnic, religious, class, or spatial bonds (a shared regional past, a new life in the urban neighborhoods), strengthening the self-identification of the group in a context of interaction with groups of different backgrounds in an urban space, for instance. In Lourenço Marques, where the development of sociabilities was conditioned by a system of domination inscribed in the urban space and in the existing social stratification, the circulation of knowledge, the acquisition of techniques, habits, and schemas for the interpretation of the surrounding world was subject to a variety of social enclosures and favored the development of belongings and identities, bonds activated to respond to a host of practical everyday issues.

However, football knowledge, as an interaction repertoire, also facilitated the creation of bonds against the background of nondysfunctional conflicts. In these cases, the conflict, as noted by Coser, was a means of recognizing difference and agreeing upon a relational lowest common denominator.[52] Regardless of the capacity to cement previous identifications, sports narratives, woven into a growing popular culture, were able to assist in interactions between individuals that did not share any other filiation or even a social or spatial proximity other than that of belonging to a stratified urban community. This specific knowledge, then, helped the creation of what Mark Granovetter has termed "weak ties."[53] In the context of intense urbanization, where people of different backgrounds found themselves interacting with each other, the creation of a common knowledge and common ways of acting was a key principle of coexistence. These weak bonds were fragile but nonetheless essential bridges that allowed for interknowledge among individuals of different backgrounds who were compelled, in this context, to interact.[54]

The way in which these football narratives are transformed into a relational resource, facilitating participation in everyday encounters, points us toward a wider interpretation that will be critical in the history of football in Lourenço Marques. The manipulation of information in interactional situations is the ground for the formulation of arguments, the justification of opinions, the participation in debates, emotional expression and sharing and the production of moral and aesthetic judgements.[55] Being in possession of football knowledge, which in the colonial city was far more democratized than other bodies of knowledge, individuals use it as a mechanism for personal and gregarious affirmation before others, which can either be part of their closest circles or socially more distant. The manipulations of football narratives, then, meets the need for differentiation that results from the urban collective dynamics itself.[56] Thus a specific public space takes shape. This is critical because by means of the manipulation of a sports narrative, commentaries on other spheres of reality are being produced. These comments do not imply the manifestation of an opinion on a particular political, economic, moral or religious issue, although they may also function as a means to judge these matters. In a mediated and implicit manner, the production of aesthetic and ethical judgments on events within the sports practice itself offers a set of reference points that legitimate or invalidate forms of agency and worldviews and that manifest the strength of a reason molded by local practices.

STYLES OF PLAY

The emergence of a local style of play was an element of the construction of this specific public space in Lourenço Marques. With Craveirinha's help, football's language could become the foundation for a historical inquiry. Norbert Elias and Eric Dunning note,

> The observation of an ongoing game of football can be of considerable help as an introduction to the understanding of such terms [*social configuration* or *social process*] as interlocking plans and actions. Each team may have planned its strategy in accordance with the knowledge of their own and their opponents' skills and foibles. However, as the game proceeds, it often produces constellations which were not intended or foreseen by either side. In fact, the flowing pattern formed by players and ball in a football game can serve as a graphic illustration not only of the concept of "figurations" but also of that of "social process." The game-process is precisely that, a flowing figuration of human beings whose actions and experiences continuously interlock, a social process in miniature.[57]

The practice of football is defined by a set of elementary conditions that delimit the performance: the maneuvering of the ball and the relation established with a given space for a given period of time. The rules that organize the match, in turn, mediate the choreography of modern football. The universalization of modern sports formats, governed by preordained rules, was a fundamental element in what Elias calls "sportization process," the phenomenon of the regulation of pastimes.[58] These norms are not neutral: they convey a certain ethics. For instance, they establish a principle of universality: everyone is subject to the same law. Rules seek to curb situations deemed prejudicial to the game, such as the violent incidents that are commonplace in physical performances involving constant interaction. The elaboration of a body of rules, originally delineated in 1863 in the context of sports competitions between English public schools and overseen since 1886 by the International Football Association Board (IFAB),[59] gave rise to an orthodox game model, the Football Association, distinct from a wide variety of popular versions based on unshared local conventions, which tended to disappear.[60]

Football rules subjected players to a code and thus constrained their individual action, and yet they did not determine the greater portion of gestures nor the general dynamics of the game. The dissemination of modern football through the world from the second half of the nineteenth century was not linear. The game established itself as a situated and historically embedded practice, producing gestures inscribed within constellations of local meanings. These performances, Elias and Dunnning have argued, were small-scale historical laboratories. From a set of homologies, the examination of sports practices allows us to discern long-term shifts in and through the players' bodies. In turn, these allow, for instance, for an analysis of the dissemination of certain behaviors, of the individual embodiment of principles of practical action and worldviews, of the degree of tolerance toward violence and to relate this with the increased complexity of the social division of labor, growing social interdependencies, state centralization, and a greater degree of individual, externally conditioned self-restraint, as a means of curbing impulses.[61] Although in a singular manner many of the modern structural changes that Elias linked to the modernization process were part of the colonial social configuration in the twentieth century, namely in major urban centers like Lourenço Marques.

Football styles of play result from a particular relation between, on the one hand, the features of an evolving language—shaped by an ethics intrinsic to the official regulations and, progressively, by a specific tendency toward body rationalization, which molds individual and collective movements with a view to achieving greater efficiency[62]—and, on the other hand, structural and contextual historical trends. It is also the outcome of a series of struggles between diverse agents within a specific field of activity—players, coaches, the audiences, journalists, and other intermediaries—over the definition of what would be the most "appropriate" movement, the more spectacular performance, or the most efficient route to victory.[63]

In the contexts where modern football was more developed, the game's language became increasingly interpreted by professionals, because only a professional with a learned training routine and bodily grammar could interpret the match with the necessary rigor and efficacy, as well as meet the demands intrinsic to the "representation" of the will of the fans, neighborhoods, cities, and countries. The command over football's language was obtained by means of predetermination of the individual and collective movement carried out through the progressive development of tactical thinking. Within the frame of the modern tactical rationalization, the "pass," for example, became the center of the game's economy, which meant a subalternization of other gestures, such as the dribble, now subject to a more calculated use. The specialization of players' roles and positions, in turn, attributes to each position on the pitch a particular task, whereby the proportion and types of movements depend on the performance of a specific function, which is also associated with certain physical and performative traits of the athletes (tall center backs, fast wingers, etc.).

Such rationalization of football's language, which is always contested and adjustable within the universe of professional football, imposes a bodily *hexis* on the professional player, or a *motor habitus*, defined, after Bourdieu's conceptualization, as a specific motor translation of trained bodily disposition during performative situations.[64] However, where the conditions for the constitution of a competitive body were fragile, as in the case of the Lourenço Marques's suburbs, the specific struggles for the definition of a style of play gave rise to multiple and heterodox genres, performed by motor habitus less shaped by this hegemonic rationality. As an empirical site of historical research, the game could operate as a barometer for gauging the expansion of structural and procedural tendencies in the long term and be the observatory of the local moral aesthetics that mimicked, recreated, subverted, or resisted, and thus fostered "other footballs."[65] The movements of Lourenço Marques suburban players, whose practical and symbolic reason was described by Craveirinha as malicious, were a specific example of how the game, when locally embedded, becomes defined by local economies of symbolic exchanges[66] that produce a singular, but contested, moral economy: this moral performance expresses contradictions and is a space of negotiations, challenges, and subversions that are ultimately translated into the language of the game.[67]

The football choreographies enacted by the players from the Lourenço Marques suburbs expressed a physical orientation that was also a social and ethical orientation put into action by a specific libido that underlay the movement.[68] Filtered by a formal language, this condition and these moralities also turned into a specific aesthetics. Individual and collective movements were the key signifying elements of that language and the embodied record of a specific historical process. Collective movements were

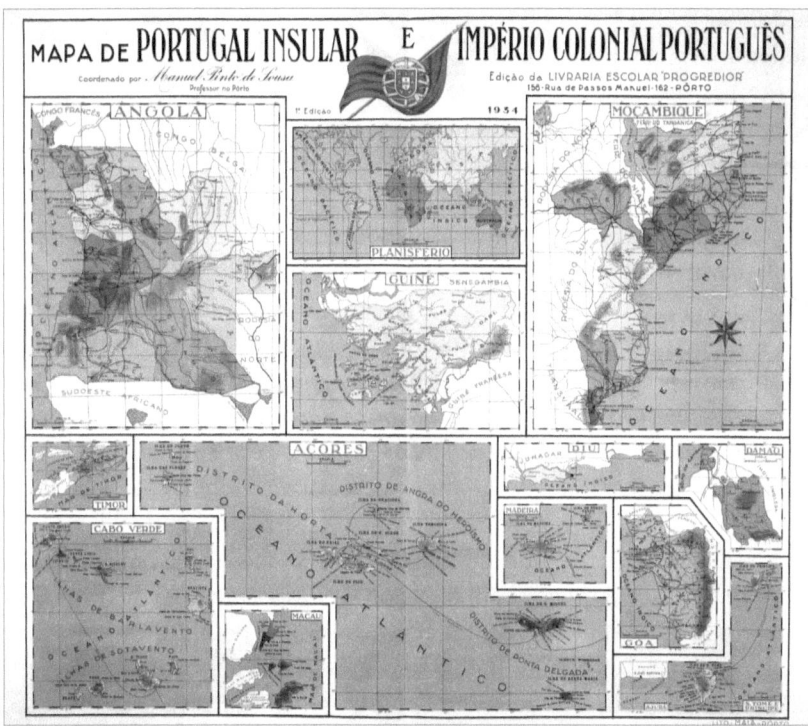

MAP 1.2. Metropolitan Portugal and the Portuguese colonial empire (used in classrooms), 1934. Manuel Pinto de Sousa, Porto: Livraria Escolar "Progredior." *Source:* Biblioteca Nacional de Portugal.

not random. Expressing the existence of an order, an "interaction order,"[69] the game was shaped by specific conventions and norms that were locally meaningful and defined a performative arena: a "space of stylistic possibles."[70] The cells of these interactions were the gestures and movements that defined the players' "motor repertoire," their bodily techniques, in the sense Marcel Mauss lent to this term.[71] The moral and practical meanings inscribed in these movements are the gateway for the study of Lourenço Marques's singular suburban social contract under Portuguese rule.

GENDERED PERSPECTIVES, METHODOLOGY, AND CHRONOLOGIES

The present research was based on archival work, both in Portugal and in Mozambique, on newspapers and magazines of the period and a set of interviews with some of the protagonists of the time, key elements to retrieve a sense of the dynamics of the game of football as it was practiced in the suburbs of Lourenço Marques. To the important descriptions of the history of football in these parts and in this period, these accounts have added information that sheds light on some of the features of the sports performances. This book aims to look at a historical process through the lens of a particular activity and, more generally, through the experience of suburban inhabitants, so as to offer a perspective that is mostly absent from the archival documents and written sources.

This partial view of the historical process can certainly be found in the "colonial archive," even if it often reveals lines of fracture within the Portuguese power structure. Out of these conflicts and the ramification of interests around the state and its institutions there emerged a variety of viewpoints on the city's peripheral spaces and on their populations. However, from the "African side," by which I refer to the press in particular, the suburbs were still represented all too narrowly. In the way they critically described Portuguese colonialism in Mozambique, newspapers such as O *africano* and O *brado africano* are indeed rare and precious historiographical sources. And yet, while their accounts do bring to the surface some of the dynamics of the historical processes in the capital of Mozambique, their analyses play down, and even exclude, other processes and points of view, namely of those that did not share the social status of this African elite, or their economic position, their religious beliefs, or their status vis-à-vis the state. One of the challenges of the present book was to avoid drawing a general portrait of the suburban experience through the gaze of these individuals, diverse and contradictory as it was. It could not fail to take into account their singular experience as an important historiographical source, but at the same time it also needed to avoid magnifying the information and interpretations they offer us.

The gathering of narratives on the local sports scene and on the itineraries of suburban football players was an attempt to remedy the near-absence of accounts of life on the edges of the city. Mostly provided by players with stable sports careers, these accounts do not faithfully represent the diversity of suburban experiences throughout the period under study. Be that as it may, their words help us identify dominant practices and norms that were expressed, first and foremost, by means of a specific style of football play. This style then functions as a laboratory that opens onto a wider field of analysis of the conditions in which the colonial periphery developed. In retrieving a sense of this suburban life it was also important to include the data produced by the colonial regime's own institutions, namely the monograph of the colonial cadre António Rita-Ferreira (*Os africanos de Lourenço Marques*, 1968). When placed in the context of its production, which implies a critical distance from its intents and conclusions, these data yield information that ensures a richer frame for understanding the urban situation in the capital of Mozambique.

The local society portrayed by the game of football was almost exclusively composed of men. While in many ways suburban men shared with suburban women a similar urban experience, framed by the unstable local social contract that we wish to survey, the game was primarily a dimension of the masculine experience, adaptation, and performance. As one would expect, football's local institutionalization reinforced gender discrimination, as sports clubs were structurally unequal. Recent work by Jeanne Marie Penvenne on female workers in cashew factories in Lourenço Marques between 1945 and 1975, published when this book was nearly completed, examines the gendered perspectives of the urbanization process.[72] Addressing the same spatial context, Penvenne lifts the veil from the dramatic living conditions of the population of the suburbs of Lourenço Marques and thus retrieves the working and urban experience of these female workers, by bringing them into the fold of historical narratives—of the proletariat, of migratory processes—from which they had been excluded; she reveals the singularity of their survival strategies and how adaptation to an urban environment was bound by prior conditions for which the city was a space of struggle and transformation.

Informal women's matches did take place in the suburbs of Lourenço Marques, but football, maybe alongside boxing, was the ultimate frontier in terms of gender discrimination in sports. Football clubs, both in the suburbs and in affluent, all-white cement city, did not have female teams, though there was an active women participation in other sports activities. In the suburbs the mestiço elites promoted gymnastics for women, as well as athletics and basketball teams, later on. Women's participation in sports was also influenced by the way in which gender discrimination translated into the Portuguese official sports' policies. In the metropole the creation of the Mocidade Portuguesa Feminina (Feminine Portuguese Youth), in 1937, institutionalized a sexual separation and a distinction between the types of exercises appropriate for each sex.[73] The same categorizations were present in school syllabuses. Both in gymnasiums and outdoors, classes for men and women were separated. Physical education should provide men with "opportunities to assert a virile personality in displays of disciplined energy, loyal competition and the sublimation of fighting instincts," and lead women "to a fertile family life,"[74] as women needed to be "protected from the great muscular and masculinizing efforts of athletics, a feminine aberration that went against this sex's sensitiveness and woman's natural role as a future mother and educator."[75] School syllabuses marked this

Football and the Narration of a Colonial Situation ⇒ 17

distinction between the woman, seen both as mother and educator, whose physical activities expressed control over the domestic realm, and the athletic man, ready to defend the nation. The development of sports beyond the sphere of the state in Lourenço Marques took place within the frame of such gendered official conceptions, which were deeply rooted in the Portuguese colonial system, namely in the indigenato system.[76]

The central argument of this book is that the game of football in Lourenço Marques, by absorbing the main traits of the local colonial society, became an embodied representation of a historical experience. The appropriation of a modern activity, as a performative practice but also as a medium of everyday relationships and a ground for the creation of social networks, offers a unique point of view on the formation of a system of colonial power with distinctive features, thus revealing, at the same time, the way in which individuals reproduced and transformed the system. This representation of local life runs counter to the culturalist and exotic visions of the periphery promoted by the regime's propaganda, but also counter to modernizing views that, by diagnosing the suburbs as an urban pathology, explained their misery through the self-exclusion of Africans.

The relation between football and colonialism in the capital of Mozambique, between the game's embodied language and the structures of colonial domination, became crystallized through a process of dissemination and institutionalization that I attempt to describe in chapters 2 and 3. Appropriated by a variety of urban populations, the game organized itself along the lines of, and indeed reproduced, existing social differences, namely those imposed by a colonialism of an increasingly racialist nature. Once disseminated and accessible, football was the ground for specific performances but also for the creation of associative structures that shaped urban identities that the state tried to organize, control, and use to its own advantage—not always successfully. In the city's suburbs, where a particular social organization was imposed, the process of the game's appropriation by the local populations forged a unique performance, a local style of play that had its own moral economy, plainly linked to the urban and labor policies of the colonial state and the key role these policies played in the formation of a suburban habitus.[77]

In chapter 4, I attempt an archaeology of this style of play and outline its main features, paying particular attention to the way in which football became a medium for negotiating the grounds for the construction of an informal social contract that could organize, however precariously, the life of those that lived in the periphery of the city. The descriptions by José Craveirinha of this malicious game, as well as the accounts of former suburban players, are the foundations for this archaeology of the local style of play. By retrieving the game's language, the chapter proposes an alternative narrative of the suburbs, its structures, practices, and convivial norms, one that brushes against those accounts that idealized it, culturalized it, or reduced it to a social pathology. This effort of narrating the suburban life continues in chapter 5, now on the basis of an interpretation of the links between the game of football and a series of local traditions that were being adjusted to the colonial city environment, such as witchcraft and faith healing. Healers and witch doctors, just like the best interpreters of the local style of play, were the performers of these informal rights, aspirations, and desires, and their heroic feats were narrated in stories that have survived to this day.

This changing world had multiple points of contact with the outside world. For the local style of play, regardless of its unique traits, the rules of modern football remained a reference point, and the local game was far from impermeable to other ways of playing. The game was likewise appropriated by local fans, who brought football into their everyday lives, as an identitarian trait and a means of relating to a wider universe, as the game had spread throughout the globe. News of its practice in the metropole, in Europe, and across the world reached the suburbs. Chapters 6 and 7 address this process of transformation and the way the suburban populations, while constrained by the colonial system, connected and related to the world. An aspect of the ongoing negotiation of the suburban social contract, this process manifested itself in different ways. Chapter 6 exposes how the players that abandoned the suburban style of play so as to pursue a professional career felt the effects of that change in their very bodies, in the form of a self-conditioning, a disenchantment, as if they had let go of who they were. However, it was precisely under the sway of the modern game and its constraints that some suburban players began their professional and social mobility trajectories, by means of which they became key figures in the game and an inspiration to the populations of the suburbs of Lourenço Marques. Modern football had created its own space of stylistic possibilities, based on a specific use of time and space, with singular symbolic exchanges that shared traits with other modern activities, namely those that implied a complex division of labor. By rewarding the merit and talent of African players, modern football placed itself at the service of a desire for justice, but it also disrupted the local style.

It was also in the course of this process that football became an idiom of social contact. Through football, one also expressed the desire for a different social contract. In this demand, the game served as a foundation for the establishment of a particular public space, one structured by rules, rights, and opportunities. This universe opened up the possibility of belonging to worlds of signifying constellations and to spaces for the creation of commonalities, a practical and symbolic egalitarianism that offered instruments of public representation in a world where they were scarce. Chapter 7 aims to reveal how football played its part in the process of urbanization of suburban inhabitants on the basis of a singular phenomenology that converted knowledge into narratives embedded in an interactional everyday. Suburban fans' admiration for Portuguese clubs, where some of the most distinguished local African players displayed their talent, is testimony to this appropriation of the possibilities afforded by the modern game and its competitions.

2 ⁀ A Colonial Sport's Field

THE development of a field of sports practices and consumptions in Lourenço Marques was shaped by the organization and evolution of a colonial power structure, replicating its forms of social closure. Simultaneously, however, the dissemination of sports created specific autonomies that had the power to defy existent structures of domination. The social and political role played by local sports associations and clubs, and the importance of emergent forms of urban popular culture in reinforcing identities, promoting new bonds, and backing individual and collective aspirations, were among the aspects that defined the introduction of modern sports in the colonial city.

LEISURE, FOOTBALL, AND THE BIRTH OF THE COLONIAL CITY

The construction of a penitentiary in 1782 was the first step toward the formation of Lourenço Marques's fragile urban mesh.[1] The first settlers, arriving in 1825, laid out a disordered cluster of primary streets. A dynamic slave trade to Brazil developed in this period. In the same time frame, a small community of Indians from Daman and Diu was established. In 1850, Lourenço Marques had six hundred inhabitants, confined to the coastal area. Portuguese authorities were had to deal with local kingdoms and were closely watched by English fleets that oversaw the slave traffic. In 1875, Portugal won the right to govern Lourenço Marques Bay, which was being disputed by the British, after a decision by French president Marshal MacMahon, who was mediating the disagreement.

When it became a village, in 1876, Lourenço Marques already had a small administrative and commercial center. After the arrival, in 1877, of a public-works expedition led by engineer Joaquim José Machado (who later became governor of the territory), the process of draining the marshland surrounding the small urban area began, thus allowing the city's expansion. In 1887, Lourenço Marques was incorporated as a city. An urban expansion plan, devised by engineer António Araújo, was approved in 1892. Resorting to military-engineering techniques, Araújo proposed the construction of an orthogonal urban structure, whose geometry reflected modern building methods. The colonial city's growth led to a series of expropriations. In 1891 local populations were dislodged from the central area of Maxaquene and moved to the Mafalala, Munhuana, Hulene, and Chamanculo neighborhoods.[2] An outbreak of bubonic plague, which hit the city in 1907 and 1908, led to further social segmentation.[3] The question of property established itself as one of the elements of the "illegality" of the colonial suburban space.[4] A situation with wider contours, this "illegality" signaled, in Lourenço Marques, the exclusion of this population from the institutional spheres that handled administrative, judicial, and labor issues and that catered to the "civilized." As early as 1890 the freehold concession to Africans was limited.[5] According to the regulations on the ownership of urban plots of land approved by Joaquim Mouzinho de Albuquerque in 1897, property owners had to prove their ownership in writing and to build a house within six months—a bureaucratic scheme that, together with the lack of capital, systematically excluded the indígenas.[6] The regulations for the concession of state-owned land of 1918, in force until 1961, established a class of plots of land, reservations, for the exclusive use of the indígenas: they could occupy land but not own it.

The Lydenburg Road, which began to be built in 1871 and served as a connection to the Transvaal, became a focal point around which the suburbs organized themselves and grew. The inauguration of this road— named after Lydenburg, a region in Transvaal where gold seams were discovered in 1874—marked South Africa's labor market's influence on the growth of the suburbs of Lourenço Marques.[7] The city's outskirts, which also included the Malanga, Malhangalene, and São José de Lhanguene neighborhoods, were made up of roads and paths that recognized and respected local mobility needs.

In Lourenço Marques, where various types of spatial and social stratification coexisted, the main border was the one separating the so-called cement city from the suburbs, also called the *caniço* (lit., reed—the building material of most suburban houses). The *circunvalação* (ring)

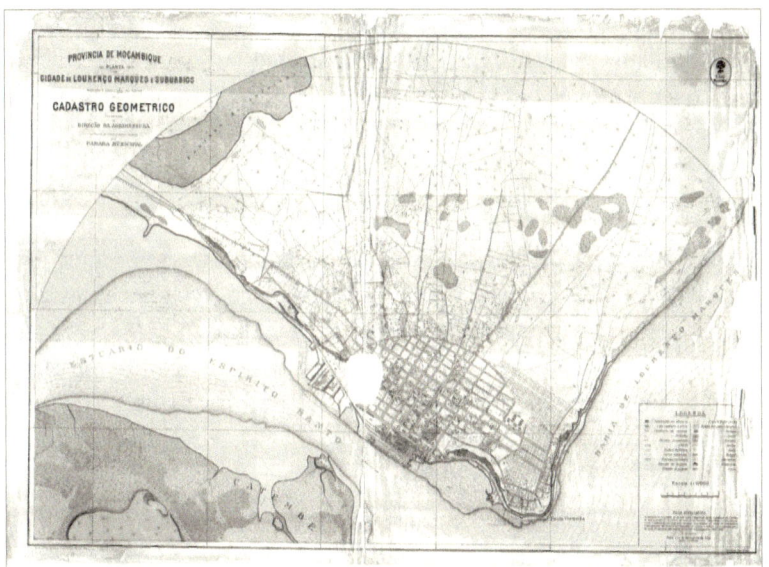

MAP 2.1. Lourenço Marques and its suburbs, 1907–8. This is one of the first representations to include both the cement city and its periphery. *Source:* Centro de Estudos Geográficos. Instituto de Geografia e Ordenamento do Território.

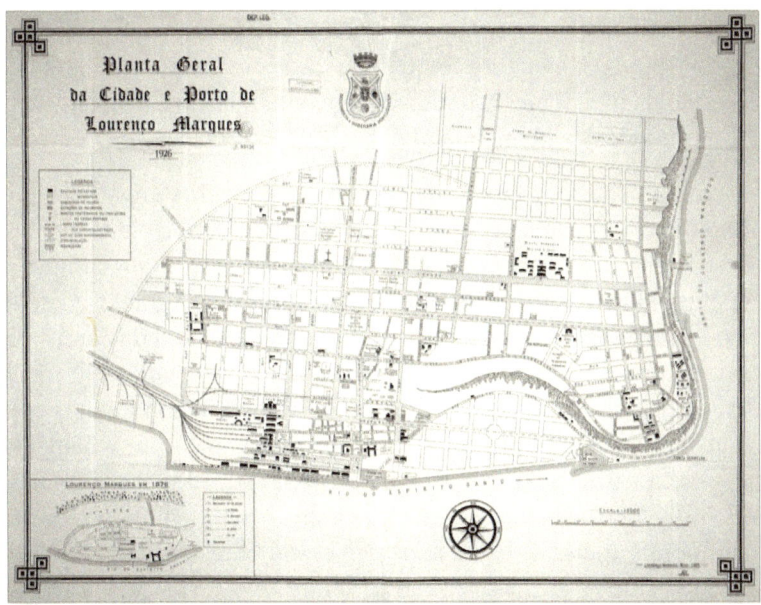

MAP 2.2. General plan of the city and harbor of Lourenço Marques, 1926. This map shows a more common representation of the cement city's modern structure, considered by the colonial mind as the "proper city," the one made by the Portuguese—the "civilized" city, with its rational design and geometry. *Source:* Biblioteca Nacional de Portugal.

road, built in 1903, represented this line of demarcation both physically and symbolically. The urban structure imposed by Plano Araújo determined how the city would grow, something that is noticeable even in the early twenty-first century.

In 1971, Mozambican architect "Pancho" Guedes described the main characteristics of the caniço:

> Every city and small town in Mozambique is surrounded by *caniços*. They are the towns' out-buildings—the places where servants and laborers live. The word *caniço* means reed; in southern Mozambique reeds are the traditional building material most frequently used for walling and screens whenever they are available in the rural areas. . . . The *caniços* range from villages scattered around small towns, to vast slums and shanty towns made up of many quarters surrounding the larger towns and cities. In the small towns the *caniços* adjoin land where maize, manioc and other crops and fresh vegetables are grown. The sites they occupy are as close as possible to the town. Some are even located within the towns themselves, occupying land which has not been developed because it was low-lying and subject to flooding, or because of its irregular or steep configuration. In Lourenço Marques some of the *caniços* occupy the edges of an old lagoon; they are subject to floods and heavy rain, and are quite close to the main part of town.[8]

Coming from the countryside, a great portion of the population built their houses with traditional techniques, using tree trunks, branches, bamboo, grass, and various fibers and clays.[9] Technologic innovation improved the quality of the housing. The poorer population and migrant workers occupied fragile huts, which were built with burlap bags and tin cans.[10] This kind of construction was replaced by better-equipped houses. Near the end of the colonial period, when more than two hundred thousand people lived in the larger suburbs, most houses (88 percent) were rectangular, covered with zinc, "with reed or wattle walls, daubed or bare, or made of zinc or cement blocks, houses with yards surrounded by reeds with a kitchen porch, the bath fence and latrine and other rudimentary facilities."[11] At the time, the masonry houses (a mere 6 percent) were owned by the local privileged class.

The city was the symbol of a new era of Portuguese colonialism in Mozambique. In the final quarter of the nineteenth century, Portugal's sovereignty over the territory became clearer. The definition of borders,

FIGURE 2.1 Gorjão wharf and railway lines, Lourenço Marques. The photo provides evidence of the economic role that the city had in the regional economy, led by the industrial development of South Africa. Photos mainly by H. Graumann and I. Piedade Pó, void of copyright as collective work. Scan of original book from Memórias d'África e d'Oriente, Aveiro University. *Source:* Wikimedia.

traced during the Berlin Conference of 1884–85 and ratified in 1891, was a result of the balance of power that emerged out of the conflicts between the main colonial actors. Portugal's role in this new stage of colonial expansion was inevitably hampered by its structural condition. During the 1890s, unable to effectively set up a local administrative apparatus, it surrendered a great deal of the Mozambican territory to large foreign capital companies (*companhias majestáticas*). Controlling native labor became the main colonial goal, something that was in line with a history of occupation that had been sustained by the commercialization and exploitation of slave labor.[12] A succession of labor codes (1892, 1899, 1911, and 1914) categorized the types of work to which Africans were subjected: forced, voluntary, correctional, due to vagrancy, due to law infringement. "Native" labor was regulated by institutions such as the Intendência dos Negócios Indígenas e Emigração (Superintendency of Native and Emigration Affairs), which worked in liaison with the governor general from 1903 onward and would, in 1907, become the Secretaria dos Negócios Indígenas (Office of Native Affairs). A disciplinary control model flourished, enacted by laws imposing IDs, as well as residency, labor, and travel permits, upon native people.[13] Failure to abide by these procedures brought the imposition of forced-labor regimes, locally known as *chibalo*.[14] Chibalo sustained not only state initiatives but also private enterprises, both of which benefited from the political and economic protection of the power structure. These means of recruitment were used to engage factory workers as well as the great mass of domestic servants that worked in the city center. High-ranking colonizers soon criticized the large number of male African domestic servants in Lourenço Marques as a sign of economic underdevelopment, which demonstrated the Portuguese incapacity to exploit the African working force in a rational manner.[15]

Beginning in the 1870s, criticism directed against Portuguese liberal legislation's[16] notion of egalitarian assimilation reflected the need for the

A Colonial Sport's Field

domination stage to come to be framed by new ideological, political, and legislative instruments. Based on a set of social-Darwinist principles, the control and categorization of the native population changed the indefinite category of *selvagem* (savage) to the more manageable *indígena* (native).[17] The "civilizing mission," which ideologically justified Portugal's presence in Africa, was based on a set of laws that distinguished the rights and duties of the indígenas from those of the "civilized." Portugal's colonial regime also admitted the existence of a third category of individuals, known as *assimilados* (assimilated), those who, having proven their adaptation to European civilization and "Portuguese culture," began to enjoy the rights of the "civilized." In Mozambique the first law that defined who would be classified as an indígena was published in 1894 and aimed to regulate the application of penalties of compulsory labor in public works.[18] In 1909 a decree regulating land concessions introduced the "color variable," meaning nonwhite, as a feature of the definition of *indígena*.[19] In 1917 an edict by Mozambique's governor general passed into law the distinction between *indígena* (native), *não indígena* (nonnative), and *assimilado* (assimilated).[20] This edict established the prerequisites to obtain a document (*alvará do assimilado*) that would serve as proof of a new status. A less rigid version of this law was approved in 1927.[21] Until 1961 the administrative management of the Lourenço Marques suburbs fell upon the traditional administrative authorities, divided into four hereditary ruling councils, turned into *regedorias*: São José (which included the areas of São José, Chamanculo, and Malanga), Munhuana (Munhuana and Zixaxa), Fumo (Fumo, Polana, Mavalane, Chitimela, and Infulene), and Malhangalene (Malhangalene, Mafalala, and Lagoas).

Portugal's colonial system, reliant on a supposedly evolutionist conception, did little to create the economic, educational, and social conditions that would make "assimilation" possible.[22] The failure of the educational system in Mozambique, which served mostly as a rhetorical trope,[23] contrasted with the permanence of a colonial practice focused on the reproduction of a cheap working force. In Lourenço Marques, the social segmentation excluded indígenas from accessing cultural activities in the city; more broadly, it excluded them from any citizenship model set out by the colonial state.[24] The Portuguese colonial policy delineated from the late nineteenth century onward, exacerbating nationalistic and racist conceptions, endangered the position of the local petite bourgeoisie,[25] composed mostly of mestiços, who had achieved important positions within public administration and in commercial circuits from the beginning of the nineteenth century.[26] Facing greater colonial repression and stronger professional competition following the growing numbers of settlers, members of this petite bourgeoisie developed a political and social protest dynamic, assuming the defense of the rights of indígenas. The Grémio Africano de Lourenço Marques (GALM), created in 1908, became the institutionalized center of these protests; its basic principles were spelled out in publications such as O africano (est. 1908) and O brado africano (est. 1918). The group around the GALM, educated and culturally identified with European colonial society, had an active role in denouncing colonial abuses, thus fighting for citizens' right to equality, especially indígena people's access to education and the Portuguese language as crucial instruments for their social mobility.[27] Embracing the "African" cause, and influenced by the international Pan-Africanist movement, by metropolitan political associations, and by the South African political process, the GALM was very active until 1926.[28] This protest was made not along anticolonial lines but rather in the name of a more humane and modern economic colonialism in which, for instance, African labor would be better handled—housed in organized compounds and in well-designed suburban neighborhoods, protected from the harm caused by wine made easily available by the metropolitan producers—instead of being used in the development of South Africa's mining industry. As the colonial system became more repressive, a certain African elite was able to confront the colonial administration's policies in an increasingly euphemistic register, which in many instances took on an integrationist slant (e.g., "we also deserve to be part of the Portuguese nation").

The military dictatorship established in Portugal in 1926, which gave way in 1933 to the Estado Novo regime led by António de Oliveira Salazar (r. 1932–68), set about updating the previous legal framework of domination. Even before the military coup of May 28, 1926, João Belo's government issued the Estatuto Político, Civil e Criminal dos Indígenas de Angola e Mozambique (Political, Civil, and Criminal Statute of Angolan and Mozambican Natives), the original basis for the indigenato system,[29] fine-tuned in 1929, when the Estatuto Político, Civil e Criminal dos Indígenas (Native's Political, Civil, and Criminal Statute) was approved. According to these statutes, civilizational status of the indígenas did not entitle them to constitutional rights, and they were thus subjected to a specific legal regime, based on their custom and usage, which the colonial administration would formalize. Portugal promised to gradually integrate indígenas through work and education. The diplomas they earned would complement the basic laws that defined the place occupied by the colonies within the Portuguese nation. The 1930 Acto Colonial (Colonial Act), as well as the 1933 Carta Orgânica do Império Colonial Português (Organic Charter of Portugal's Colonial Empire), alongside the Reforma Administrativa Ultramarina (Overseas Administrative Reform), set up the centralizing policy imposed by the Portuguese state on its colonial domains. In 1928, reacting to the international pressure that arose after the publication of the Ross Report, in 1925, denouncing the continuation of compulsory forms of labor regimes in Portuguese colonial territories, the government approved the Código de Trabalho dos Indígenas das Colónias Portuguesas de África (Portuguese African Colonies' Native Labor Code), which excluded forced labor.[30] However, various exception clauses foresaw the use of chibalo as a law enforcement method. The ambiguity of this law and the inoperativeness of any type of control allowed for the continuation of semi-enslavement practices by public and private interests, sustaining a weak production structure based on intensive labor practices.[31] The 1929 Diploma Orgânico das Relações de Direito Privado entre Indígenas e Não Indígenas (Organic Diploma of Private Law Relations between Natives and Nonnatives) completed this legal framework. Placed outside the corporative order imposed by the Estado Novo regime in Portugal, which was extended to the colonies on 5 March 1937, the indígena had a specific labor status.[32] He also benefited from a separate education. After the 1926 Estatuto Orgânico das Missões Católicas Portuguesas de África (Organic Statute of the Portuguese Catholic Missions in Africa) had recognized the role of the Catholic Church in the indígenas' education, the Acordo Missionário (Missionary Agreement) of 1940 and the Estatuto Missionário (Missionary Statute), approved the following year, gave the church the de facto responsibility for setting up segregated schools. The educational role entrusted to the Catholic Church aimed at countering the "denationalizing" effect attributed to the influence of Protestant missions, which, from the end of the nineteenth century, as a reflex of South Africa's influence,[33] were active in the Lourenço Marques region.[34]

After the end of the Second World War, although at a hesitant pace at first, the indígena question was reframed, which explains the appearance of a euphemistic rhetoric in many official documents as well as in the general language we now find in the archives. The process of euphemization of the exercise of power reached its highest level in 1951, when the Portuguese government replaced the terms *empire* and *colonies* with *overseas* and *overseas provinces*. Portugal was *uno e indivisível* (one and indivisible). A few years later, the lusotropicalist theory devised by the Brazilian sociologist Gilberto Freyre was a political legitimating tool, based on the principle of the exceptionality of Portuguese colonialism.[35] During this period, the regime was laying the groundwork for a new stage of economic exploitation of its African territories.[36] Still, the increasing state control over African labor, put in place by laws like the Regulamentos dos Serviçais Indígenas (Indígenas Servant's Regulations) of 1944 and 1949, continued to foster the conditions for the formation of an institutionalized discriminatory society.[37] According to these regulations, which essentially aimed at regulating social life in urban spaces like Lourenço Marques, the indígena was generally defined as a servant whose urban existence was dependent on a labor activity that the state, through the Curadoria dos Negócios Indígenas (Native Affairs Curatorship), tried to discipline through fear, intimidation, and punishment. The coercive formation of a labor market imposed a certain moral economy in which paternalism and violence become the ground of a wide social contract.

The elaboration of the Planos de Fomento Económico (Economic Development Plans), which also served to accommodate private capital's growing business interest, marked a new era of expansion.[38] As argued by Gervase Clarence-Smith, in spite of the discourse on Portugal's civilizing mission, the Portuguese Third Empire in fact reinforced its economic vocation.[39] The state's investment in infrastructure but also in the production of specialized knowledge, to face the multiplication of colonial science's spheres of intervention, sought to accommodate the internationalization of Mozambique's economy and the influx of capital, which was concentrated in large metropolitan economic groups and in foreign companies. Historian Adelino Torres defines the Portuguese strategy in Angola as a "second colonial pact."[40] On the basis of the formation of an imperial economic space, Portugal tried to maintain sovereign control within a context of economic internationalization. In Lourenço Marques, during the late colonial period the economy became less dependent of South African demand, but colonial revenue captured by the taxation of the migrant workforce continued to be decisive for the equilibrium of the trade balance.[41]

Lourenço Marques was inhabited at the close of the 1970s by at least one hundred thousand Africans.[42] This population grew at an average rate of twelve hundred individuals per year between 1940 and 1959, and sixty-five hundred per year between 1950 and 1960. After the end of the indigenato, with the slackening of restrictions to circulation and residence, entries increased.[43] Dependent on entering the symbolic space of "the cement" to survive, suburban dwellers built their own life territory, beyond the city's social and racial dividing line, in the absence of state urban planning.

The concentration of workers in the cities, the adaptation to a life regulated by modern social institutions, the monetization of exchanges, and the loss of traditional bonds became causes of potential instability. In the African colonial context, considering the nature of the working masses, the problems arising out of the "social question" were grouped, by colonial policies' theoreticians, under the term *detribalization*, a term that described the process of social, cultural, and economic adaptation to an urban and industrialized context. Although the "detribalized" indígenas did not enjoy the rights afforded to the "civilized," living in a context that Brigitte Lacharte designates as "apartheid laissez-faire" they integrated the urban culture they had indeed built.[44] Sports practices and consumptions were part of this urban dynamic at least since the beginning of the twentieth century.

Leisure Practices in the Cement City

Within the framework of a system of social segregation, Lourenço Marques's dynamic economic activity in the transition to the twentieth century placed Mozambique's new capital at the center of the territory's development, as a port of call for various economic interests, traders, workers, and numerous public and private activities, transforming the city into a cosmopolitan place where there was a permanent flux of people and goods. Among the various national groups living in the city, the British community stood out due to its power and influence.[45]

As in many other regions of the world, the existence of a British community was decisive toward the introduction of sporting practices in Mozambique, namely in Lourenço Marques. Besides founding association-type clubs, such as the English Club (est. 1905), the British Club or the Caledonian Society (1919), British people set up their own sports clubs, such as the Lourenço Marques Athletic Club (1908). They also contributed toward the foundation of elite clubs, like the Lourenço Marques Lawn Tennis Club (1908), Club de Golf de Lourenço Marques (1918), or Club da Polana (1923). Part of the Portuguese colonial bourgeoisie of Lourenço Marques joined these sporting social circles. In the first two decades of the twentieth century, the British Athletic Club was one of the main promoters of sports practice, especially football. Newspaper articles from this period suggest that football matches were part of a set of mundane activities and were meeting spaces for the colonial ruling classes, in which athletes could exhibit an amateur ethos.[46] The sophisticated sportsman, whose ethics and gestures represented the modern embodiment of a privileged condition, was also present in the colonial world. In many ways the European hunter in Mozambique was the forerunner of the local modern sportsman.[47] The expansion of sporting practices in the

FIGURE 2.2. The tennis courts in the Public Garden and the Clube da Polana golf course. Tennis courts and golf courses were spaces used by the local English elite, as well as by some Portuguese members of the city's upper classes, to entertain themselves. These appropriated spaces were also conquered landscapes in which hegemonic social projects were singularly situated. Passive and barefoot African golf caddies were an expression of this project. Photos mainly by H. Graumann and I. Piedade Pó, void of copyright as collective work. Scan of original book from Memórias d'África e d'Oriente, Aveiro University. *Source:* Wikimedia.

early twentieth century in Lourenço Marques followed the elective affinities of a "ruling class" composed of high-ranking state administration officials and the colonial bourgeoisie, both Portuguese and non-Portuguese, which explored the business opportunities opened up by an expanding regional economy.[48]

Among the sports introduced in Lourenço Marques from the beginning of the century, football became the most widely practiced. One of the first records on sports activity in Mozambique, written in 1931 by a Portuguese army captain, Ismael Mário Jorge,[49] indicates that football matches were being organized as early as 1904.[50] The crews of ships anchored in Lourenço Marques often formed teams that challenged local groups. The growing number of settlers, some of whom had played the sport in the metropolis, contributed to the game's development. At the beginning of the century, several clubs emerged, projects that, albeit brief, expressed a growing associative mindset.[51]

Football matches integrated a set of spectacles promoted by urban life—the leisure activities of a burgeoning community.[52] Teatro Variéta, inaugurated in 1912, featured opera performances and cinema, and included a dance hall. In 1913 Teatro Gil Vicente opened with theatrical plays, but it also doubled as a cinema. By 1916, Lourenço Marques already had thirty bars and pubs.[53] The 1912 census of the city counted 13,353 inhabitants, including 5,324 Europeans, of which 1,299 were non-Portuguese. The city's

A Colonial Sport's Field 31

outskirts had 12,726 inhabitants.[54] During this period, public buildings, commercial establishments, leisure areas, banks, and hotels were built. The Polana Hotel, still the most sumptuous hotel in Maputo, was inaugurated in 1922 in the eastern part of the city, an almost deserted area whose grounds had been allotted to private investors.[55] There, before the hotel existed, the British community had built a field where football and nine-hole golf could be played.[56] Downtown, near the penitentiary, the English Club improvised a cricket field where members of Clube Indo-Português (a Goan association founded in 1921) also played.[57]

Lourenço Marques grew from the coastal area, site of its initial urban street network, toward the interior. The vast majority of the native population, arriving in the city from the country, went only as far as the suburbs or, in fewer cases, impoverished transitional neighborhoods such as Alto Maé or Alto de Maxaquene.[58] Downtown and the central part of the city were dominated by commerce and administration. The industrial area was west of the city, bounded by the railway. Part of the working population was employed here, in the railway, port, national press, civil construction, tram, or metalwork industries. Each residential area reflected its inhabitants' class, national origin, and ethnic differences. The European population concentrated in Ponta Vermelha and Polana, especially the ruling class. The Central neighborhood, more heterogeneous, mostly housed Indian traders.[59]

The line tracing the beginning of the modern city was an avenue that cut across it, parallel to the coast, almost from one end to the other.[60] The football pitches of the most popular clubs in town were built along this avenue. These are the clubs that today still exist in Mozambique: Sporting de Lourenço Marques (est. 1920, presently Maxaquene), Grupo Desportivo de Lourenço Marques (1921), and Clube Ferroviário (1924). Given their location, these clubs became known collectively as *clubes da baixa* (downtown teams). The hierarchy of the football game moved, from the top to the bottom of the pyramid, from downtown to the suburbs. 1.º de Maio, a club founded in 1917 by a group of railway workers, completed the quartet that for a long period monopolized official competitions.[61] Grupo Sportivo Indo-português (1921) was one of the more active participants in these early competitions and one of the chief promoters of cricket. Football's growth in Lourenço Marques justified the creation, in 1923, of the Associação de Foot-Ball da Província de Moçambique, which in 1926 became the Associação de Futebol de Lourenço Marques (AFLM, Lourenço Marques Football Association), an institution affiliated with what was then known as the União Portuguesa de Futebol (Portuguese Football Union).

The new association promoted "association football," as stipulated in the rules of the International Board.[62]

In 1924, in the suburbs of Lourenço Marques, another football association was created, the Associação de Futebol Africana (African Football Association). Gathering a significant group of clubs, the AFA organized its own competitions, which became elements of a vigorous urban life growing on the outskirts of the city. The existence of two football associations exposed processes of discrimination also manifest in the distribution of football fans in the downtown stadium. Born in 1929, Mário Wilson, one of the first Mozambicans to play in the metropole, recalls that Africans "could watch the game but they had to be in a specific section for Africans . . . and, for those that were down-and-out, not even that was possible."

These venues were only one among many urban spaces where a policy of social segregation was in place. Indígenas were barred from many areas of the cement city after certain hours: leisure spaces (beaches, cinemas, theaters, cafés, gardens), state institutions (administration, courts, the mail, schools, and hospitals), public transport (trains, trams), even its very streets.[63] Colonial racism affected not only the indígenas but also all people that had been subject to racialization in the capital, such as Chinese, Indians, and assimilated mestiços.[64]

While tennis, sailing, and motorsports continued to be restricted to Lourenço Marques's colonial bourgeoisie, football became more popular, though its expansion, albeit still limited, did not drive away Portugal's colonial elite from the sports associative movement. Clube Ferroviário, although founded by a group of workers, was controlled by the heads of the railway administration. The directors of Sporting Clube de Lourenço Marques, associated with the colonial military and police power, came from the various organs of the colonial administration.[65] Desportivo, founded on the initiative of civil servants and traders, was sponsored by local notables, becoming the most representative among those supported by the "old settlers."[66] Sponsorship was prestigious to the clubs; likewise, the associations' popularity improved the reputation of these local figures. The management of sports clubs by notables, such as industrialists, civil servants, traders, lawyers, and bankers, established itself in much the same way it had previously in other colonial contexts.[67] As the Portuguese associative movement grew in Lourenço Marques, English influence weakened.[68]

Downtown Associations, Clubs, and Players

The formation of football clubs benefited from an associative dynamic, which arose in Lourenço Marques during the first decades of the century.

This was particularly prominent in the period of the First Portuguese Republic (1910–26), when class associations, cooperatives, mutualist associations, savings banks, and other associations were created.[69] The associative network facilitated the social integration of settlers, many of them poor, having arrived in Africa without a penny to their name. The welfare and mutualist associations sought to socially integrate the urban populations. In a different and more impromptu manner, recreational and sports associations enabled the settlers to come into contact with organized personal networks, which often reproduced a metropolitan sense of belonging, especially, within this context, of a regional nature.[70] On the other hand, some sporting clubs became delegations of Portugal's main football clubs. Grupo Desportivo de Lourenço Marques was affiliated with Sport Lisboa e Benfica (est. 1904);[71] Sporting de Lourenço Marques was affiliated with Sporting Clube de Portugal (1906). In the following decades, delegations of these clubs would spread throughout the territory.[72]

Clube Ferroviário had a different origin. Formed in a period of intense labor unrest[73] among a group of railway workers, it was sponsored by the railway company, a powerful industrial enterprise whose expansion went hand in hand with the formation of a regional network sustained by South Africa's economic growth. The company's bureaucratic organization and the control it tried to exert over its employees' spare time (among other things, by assembling a music band and setting up a library), turned Clube Ferroviário into an example of industrial paternalism, a way of managing the working force typical of contexts where relations of production are more developed. This type of management, common in Europe since the end of the nineteenth century,[74] was later employed in some regions of sub-Saharan Africa, mainly in South Africa's industrialized areas.[75] Throughout the Portuguese colonial world, the use of sports as an instrument of labor management emerged across various contexts. Ferroviário, along with the network of delegations it founded throughout the territory, became the most precocious and relevant example of the relationship established between football clubs and public and private companies in Mozambique. Changes in the colonial economic infrastructure during the period following the Second World War strengthened the connection between sports practice and businesses' labor policies framed by a private corporatism sponsored by the state.[76] In many ways the use of organized leisure as an instrument of social integration was pioneered by public and private companies and not directly by the central state.

AFLM teams, the sources of the spectacularization of football in the colonial city center, were mostly composed of settlers and other European players, though class ties enabled some players from old native families, namely mestiços, to play in the downtown championship. When the young Guilherme Cabaço (b. 1919), a settler who at the time was starting what was to be a long-lasting career in the colonial civil service, joined Grupo Desportivo de Lourenço Marques, in 1926, the black and white of the team's official shirt represented for him the two worlds that existed Mozambique. In the 1920s and 1930s, this old colonial civil servant reported, Desportivo had white and nonwhite athletes, mostly mestiços, such as the Bento brothers. Except for Sporting de Lourenço Marques, where only white players played, "in the other teams people mixed." This "mix," however, happened within the strict confines of a circle of interests close to the local "ruling class." 1.º de Maio, further removed from this circle of relations, was, as he recalls, a "club for workmen and suburban people."

During its first decades in Lourenço Marques, the spectacle of football within European society never ceased to be a class-bound practice. The search for talented players, however, granted opportunities to some settlers from lower social groups, who arrived in town and gradually integrated into the professional labor system, as workmen, especially in the railway, but also in small commerce and the civil service. Football's transformation into a competitive public spectacle, which promotes rivalries, led the clubs to look for the best players. This phenomenon, already noticeable in the 1930s, led to the gradual formation of a market.[77] The football player would secure his own status; he was admired for his performative abilities and for the fact that he represented a socially identifiable collective, linked to neighborhood communal experience, for instance, against opposing collectives.

The continuous arrival of Portuguese settlers heightened the social differences within the European population, as the administration and labor market became more specialized. In 1930 the settler population was 17,842; 27,438 in 1940; 48,213 in 1950; and 97,245 in 1960.[78] In 1974, a year before Mozambique's independence, this population reached two hundred thousand people.[79] Sports associations, accompanying the city's growth, were organized in the neighborhoods, establishing an umbilical connection with these places of sociability. As such, clubs like Malhangalene, a settler neighborhood previously inhabited by the native population, and Clube do Alto Maé emerged, founded in 1934 and 1937, respectively. In the 1950s and 1960s, other neighborhood clubs appeared, such as Carreira de Tiro, in 1950, and Clube de Futebol o "Central," in 1951.[80] In the following decades, others followed the same pattern, with clubs always representing a sense of social and spatial belonging.[81] The activities of small sports associations allowed for the simultaneous reinforcement of close regional networks and the introduction of their members into larger networks of relations, which operated as a mechanism of social integration. Despite the differences between the small clubs and the powerful downtown teams, which was also an indicator of the social stratification among the settlers, the sports movement in the cement city, even after the political overture in the sixties, was mostly a way to reify the European origin of its members; as a locus of sociabilities the clubs were agents of what Dane Kennedy identifies as "islands of white."[82]

According to Cabaço, football, in its first decades, expressed—through the effort of those who founded the clubs, organized matches, and erected pitches—the heroism of the pioneers who built the city. As he recalls, the actual match ball, in that era of conquest, served as a metaphor for the hardships of this period:

> It was terrible, pure agony, because it was made of leather and inside it had a piece of rubber that had to be air-pumped, and at the opening was a leather string. We thought twice before heading the ball. When you headed it, you lost some of the skin on your forehead. The string was prominent and it was horrible, even for goalkeepers. If the ball came sideways and the guy touched it with his hand, he lost most of his skin. Not today; nowadays it's more like a toy, like those small rubber balls I used to play with at home.

Football as Urban Spectacle

In the first decades of the century, football became one of the most popular organized leisure activities in Lourenco Marques. Clubs promoted themselves through meeting and sharing centers, spaces of communitarian mobilization and organization. Practice pitches, which were originally very precarious, regularly hosted the first competitions. Newspapers began to follow the game more closely, reporting on the main matches. In 1922 the first specialized newspaper, A *semana desportiva*, was published, lasting only one year and briefly returning in 1932. In 1938, *Eco dos sports* was the first sports newspaper to succeed, becoming an important instrument for the dissemination of the game as well as a standard-bearer for the sports community's demands before the state.[83] Newspapers were a fundamental means of promoting the game. The press turned rivalries into copy and into the raw material for readers' identification and imagination. Football press narratives were a particular dimension of what Benedict Anderson calls "print capitalism."[84] Football's presence in the newspapers, marked by the calendar of the competitions, was like a never-ending soap opera, which the reader followed passionately. The organization of the first Mozambican football championship, in 1956, one of the first public events to gather representatives from the various Mozambican provinces, was made possible, above all, through the persistent work of the local sports press.[85]

Prime media moments were those in which a selection of Lourenço Marques's best players, from the AFLM, played against visiting teams representing other regions, particularly South African teams, such as Northern Transvaal and Southern Transvaal, but also metropolitan, English and Brazilian teams, as well as teams from other countries.[86] Visits from the metropolis, quite common after the 1940s, also served to renew national ties and had a festive, nostalgic component: they provided opportunities for settlers to demonstrate their vitality before representatives of the empire's ruling center.[87] This was all the more significant since these matches featured the so-called Lourenço Marques home-born team, a group composed exclusively of players born in Mozambique, the sons of settlers.

A source of local pride, sports often served as a ground for making demands, and a vehicle for an autonomous consciousness that, although limited in scale, occasionally translated into proto-autonomist positions.[88] The most persistent demand was perhaps that of taking part in competitions that included representatives of all Portuguese territories, from which the settler clubs were excluded, a demand voiced not only through the press[89] but also through official interventions and institutional relations.[90]

After newspapers, radio would also play a decisive role in promoting the game. In March 1934, the defeat of Portugal's national football team by its Spanish counterpart in Madrid was broadcast by Estação Emissora do Grémio dos Radiófilos, through loudspeakers placed in the head office of one of the most important local newspapers, *Notícias*. This broadcast, a novelty in the city, took place "before a huge crowd."[91] The match report reached Lourenço Marques with a two-minute delay, which was close to nothing for people who were used to getting the news several days later, in the newspapers. This technological novelty inaugurated a different relation with football, in which a new kind of mediation enabled the fan to accompany and imagine a distant event in real time through an oral report that could be shared. Following a match no longer depended on going to the stadium. The broadcast was also a social event. Technological evolution would bring about the gradual privatization of radio reception, something that never stopped broadcasts from becoming an opportunity for meeting in the public space, not just in the cement city, but also in the suburbs.

Over a relatively short time, football ceased to be an activity experienced by a small number of individuals; it became a regular and public display organized by clubs and followed by large groups of fans. Club identification grew and expanded. The game became a source for the creation of a specific stock of knowledge, a generator of local narratives that were then reproduced through daily interactions. Even though football practice in the cement city was mostly confined to a white universe of relations, as a type of knowledge mediated by popular culture it could be much more widely disseminated. This allowed for its expansion beyond the line of social segregation and into the suburbs of Mozambique's capital. But this did not happen merely with the information that came from the downtown competitions. A narrative of metropolitan football, promoted by the settlers, by the media, and by the various tours the metropolitan clubs made in Lourenco Marques, gradually reached the suburbs, becoming shared knowledge. As an element of an urban popular culture, football, an architect of bonds and identifications, broke, not arbitrarily, with the social closures that also constrained the dissemination of information in a divided urban area. In the actual practice of the game, however, things were different.

SPORTS AND STATE POLICIES: SEGREGATION, REGULATION, AND PROPAGANDA

The manner in which the colonial state and other colonial powers intervened directly in the process of sports dissemination and adoption in imperial contexts was addressed by research studies focusing the role of sports as an instrument of cultural domination, mostly inspired by the English colonial experience. The formation of a "cultural bond," the result of an imperial socialization based on colonial culture, would have affected "indigenous cultures," political relations, and the way in which the governed perceived the rulers and vice-versa.[92] Sports were central to the curriculum that contributed to the formation of colonial cadres in English public schools. Their role was that of a school of character building and virile virtues. In the colonial milieu, they were introduced to the local elites through the school environment and religious missions; sports became an instrument of socialization and domestication of bodies and contributed to a growing hegemonic domination.[93] This perspective, underpinned by the principles of indirect rule, is in line with the study of hegemonic forms of domination, discipline, and regulation of bodies and minds that permeated the cultural venture of colonialism and that complemented the forms of economic, political, religious, and military power.[94]

In Lourenço Marques this association between colonial policies and colonial culture was far from being linear. State intervention in the realm of sports was internally diverse and had to respond to distinct demands that sometimes were contradictory. Moreover, state institutions were not able to control the social effects of associative sports, especially when organized sports began to develop a specific market based on spectatorship and labor protoprofessionalism.

The participation of suburban players in the downtown championship depended on the clubs' boards' decisions and the AFLM's policy. The number of nonwhite athletes playing in this competition was, until the end of the 1950s, minimal. The downtown transfer market, sustained by the growing influx of settlers, rarely involved suburban players.[95] Some footballers, however, managed to achieve this promotion. In 1938, Vicente, from Beira-Mar, and Américo, from João Albasini, started playing for Desportivo's team.[96] In 1941, *O brado africano* wrote that Laquino had embraced a professional career and would be earning between MZE 40 and MZE 50 per match.[97] According to the newspaper, this was a deplorable situation: "What has African neighborhood football come to, when you play for money and not for the love of the sport."[98] Desportivo and 1.º de Maio were the first clubs to open their doors to nonwhite players.[99] According to Mário Wilson,

> In a somewhat racist context there was the Associação de Futebol de Lourenço Marques, where racial mixture was rare. Racial mixture only took place within the elite, the privileged. Every now and again a person of color appeared. There was racism . . . there was a period where the possibility of mixture wasn't even there, even if the door was not closed shut. Then there were guys who played on both sides, but only those that belonged to the two races, to the mixed races . . . there would be one or two that stood out from the pack, but they were few and far between. That was the way of things in Desportivo, in Ferroviário, in Sporting. I don't know if it was written down or anything, but that's the way it was. I recall that it was common for some to be pushed out, not because of their football performances but because it just wouldn't do. . . . I played in the elite championship, I came from one of the privileged families, the Wilsons.

The possibility of African teams playing alongside downtown teams was not even considered before the Second World War. In 1943, Joaquim Augusto Correia, also known to his readers as Jack, a Portuguese settler writing for *O brado africano*, started a campaign for the inclusion of Beira-Mar in downtown competitions.[100] Shortly after this initiative, *O brado africano* announced his dismissal, following an AFLM communication accusing him of writing "articles that are inconvenient to the sports cause and to the native policy followed by this nation's government."[101] *O brado africano* protested[102] several times the fact that the few black and mestiço players playing downtown were excluded from the teams representing the city, something that happened whenever they traveled to South Africa or when they received South African teams.[103] The dispute, in defense of the positions of the local mestiço petite bourgeoisie, often challenged the regime's assimilationist rhetoric.[104] From the 1950s, the journalist and poet José Craveirinha, writing for *O brado africano* and *Notícias*, regularly defended the right of African players to play in the downtown league. Black athletes' performances, especially North American ones, from the achievements of Jesse Owens in Berlin to the idolized Joe Louis, revealed the value of the "race" despised by the European.[105] Praising these athletes was a way of demonstrating, within the general frame of the debate on the value of races, the political importance of "black pride."[106] Sport was an effective arena of contestation. For most of inhabitants of the cement city, the universe of suburban football was an unknown reality, merely another piece of a spatial puzzle drawn by prejudice and stereotype.

The Legitimation of State Discrimination

As can be seen clearly from the epic description of the development of physical education in the territory of Mozambique in the 1920s that Ismael Mário Jorge presented at the 1931 Paris Colonial Congress, the state fostered the separation between educational and associative sport, exclusive to settlers and "assimilated," and the disciplinary practices indígenas were subjected to, as part of their integration into Portuguese military structures and schools. The Estatuto Político, Civil e Criminal Indígenas (Natives' Political, Civil, and Criminal Statute) did not grant the indígenas any political rights within European institutions.[107] Further, the 1933 Reforma Administrativa Ultramarina (Overseas Administrative Reform) barred them from forming administrative corporations. These normative resolutions also excluded indígenas from the right to form associations, including sporting associations. The Carta Orgânica do Ultramar (Overseas Organic Charter), approved in 1929,[108] and the RAU gave the colonial administration powers to oversee associations' activities, to approve statutes, budgets, and administrative bodies, and, if necessary, to put an end to them.[109] This supervision was exercised by the Direcção dos Serviços de Administração Civil (DSAC, Head Office of Civil Administration Services), which devoted part of its services to the Agremiações Regionais de Recreio, Defesa, Desporto e Estudo (Regional Leisure, Defense, Sports, and Study Associations). Each sports club had a file in the DSAC. While indígenas were not permitted to lead associations, their participation in the activities of some African clubs, as members and athletes, meant that the clubs came under the supervision of the Direcção dos Serviços dos Negócios Indígenas (Head Office of Native Affairs), equally represented by a section devoted to Agremiações Regionais de Recreio, Defesa, Desporto e Estudo (Regional Leisure, Defense, Sports, and Study Organizations).[110] The DSAC and DSNI launched enquiries into some African clubs, whenever they suspected a possible foreign involvement, which was testament to the degree of political control exerted over the field of sport. Later, the Serviços de Centralização e Coordenação da Informação de Moçambique (SCCIM, Mozambique Office for the Centralization and Coordination of Information), created in 1961 by the Overseas Ministry but directed by the local governor, increased the surveillance over associations and sports clubs.[111]

In 1930 the charter that organized the indígena education system in Mozambique, dividing it into "rudimentary," "professional" and "normal" teaching—the latter dedicated to the training of teachers—included the discipline of physical education.[112] However, when the Mocidade Portuguesa de Mozambique (MP; Portuguese Youth of Mozambique), the first institution devoted to the promotion and regulation of sports activities in the territory, was created in 1939, it was directed exclusively at the "civilized" population. A premilitary youth organization, Mozambique's Mocidade Portuguesa, modeled on the metropolitan Mocidade Portuguesa—which in turn was inspired by the Italian fascist Balilla and the German Hitlerjugend (Hitler Youth)—was created in 1936 by the Estado Novo within the scope of the Reforma da Educação Nacional (National Education Reform) carried out in that same year.[113] The MP's mission carried on the Estado Novo's commitment, in line with previous concerns and policies, to the use of physical education as a means of moral, hygiene, and military education.[114] During the 1930s, after a period in which the institutionalization of physical education was a slow and convoluted process,[115] the regime thus pursued a Europe-wide movement of institutionalization of gymnastic models which, in their various configurations, responded to the pedagogic, hygienic, and premilitary needs of modern nation-states.[116]

The importance of physical education in the formation of colonial cadres, prominent in the French and, to an even greater degree, in the

British cases, was also echoed, albeit more feebly, in Portugal.[117] The Sociedade de Geografia de Lisboa (Lisbon Geographic Society) was one of the first Portuguese institutions to organize, in 1930, a physical education course aimed specifically at colonial cadres.

A Portuguese Body

The Estado Novo's model of physical education was promoted as a push toward the "regeneration of the race." This "race," however, a national race framed by a sovereign state, did not include the African population, whose sports habits were considered to be "natural" and "pre-modern." In the metropole the Estado Novo intervened in the sports practice of students and workers,[118] and in 1940 it founded a training center similar to the civil and military specialized schools that had been established in several European countries[119]—the Instituto Nacional de Educação Física (INEF, National Institute of Physical Education)—and created an official structure that coordinated and supervised all sports activities organized outside state control: the Direcção Geral de Educação Física, Desportos e Saúde Escolar (DGEFDSE, General Office of Physical Education, Sports, and Scholastic Health). Control over sports associations was one dimension of a wider plan that sought to regulate the associative movement in Portugal.[120] Trained in foreign schools, the men who established the theoretical and practical bases of the Portuguese model of physical education were military officers, such as the notable Celestino Marques Pereira and António Leal de Oliveira.[121]

During the Estado Novo regime, football matches were among the few mass public demonstrations taking place in Portugal. The national football league was created in 1934 and definitively institutionalized in 1938. Football was seen as an inadequate exercise by the state. In 1932, a decree was issued, within the Ministério da Instrução (Ministry of Instruction), the Direcção dos Serviços de Educação Física (Head Office of Physical Education Services), which considered sports games as the "antithesis of all education" and a vehicle to "physical deformation" and "moral perversion." The high-school physical education regulation, approved in 1932, forbade "Anglo-Saxon sports and athletic games, and all competitions in general, namely football matches, as their educational value was nil and their dangers obvious."[122] Furthermore, football's professionalizing tendency, which stimulated processes of social mobility, challenged an official corporative framework that was based on the principle that class relations should remain stable.[123] The success of players from a working-class background, in an activity with a powerful media impact, sent the "wrong" message about the existing social organization.[124]

The official ideology of the body was also an ideology of the place occupied by gesture within everyday social life, which was clear from the critical commentaries, emblematic of this model of physical education, on the modern city and the habits that thrived in it. Physical education, a scientific and rational discipline, contributed to the return of "bodily naturalness" and regulated the individual's adjustment to his new social milieu.[125] This science measured and systematized movement on the basis of knowledge about mechanical and physiological principles. But as movements were triggered by emotions, physical exercises should be "executed in line with established norms and intentions . . . in harmony with other means of moral and intellectual education."[126] The emotions that trigger movement, according to Leal de Oliveira, should be the result of the "existence of morality, religion, education, and civilization."[127] This Portuguese model of physical exercise was sustained by moral principles that synthesized Christian thought, Latin historical heritage, and modern corporative ideas.[128]

The Portuguese researchers in physical education wanted to develop a strategy that could sustain the application of a state model.[129] If in a premodern context this physical activity, although instinctive, was part of a natural order, in the artificial environment of an industrialized city, the socializing framework underpinning these impulses was artificial. Modern physical education needed to control such "inherited and involuntary motor techniques," and "innate reflex movements."[130] For this rationalization process to be effective, body movements would have to be predetermined, in view of the "intellectual and perhaps moral meaning of a conscious goal."[131] For Leal de Oliveira, the concept of ideomotor stood for predetermined movements: "Movements springing directly from an idea are called ideomotor movements, an idea that is integrated within an instinctive tendency that, in turn, mobilizes and articulates reflex actions."[132] Every deliberate movement was ideomotor. Its execution was "conditioned by a power or personal will, which provides reflexive consciousness along with the faculty to execute the movement or not, and in a specific way."[133] Bodies whose movements did not correspond to a predetermined impulse were considered potentially harmful: "noneducated impulses," responsible for heterodox and impure gestures, should be eliminated.[134]

The movements deemed adequate for preparing the bodies of the Portuguese were those of the Swedish gymnastics method.[135] Segmented movements were fundamental (suspension, support, balancing, walking, running, rising, and transporting movements, as well as throwing and jumping). Cadenced movements, quite common in gymnastics, "facilitated collective work because rhythm represented an order, a natural discipline conducive to the harmony and concordance of partial efforts and to their union."[136] The idea of cadenced rhythm, of ordering, was common to numerous educational practices during the Estado Novo, namely those that involved the use of music.[137] Natural exercises such as "walking, running, climbing, balancing, throwing, rising, carrying, swimming" were, by definition, useful and correct, "when executed in a manner that preceded any changes brought about by civilization."[138] Symmetry was the basic feature of the exercises prescribed by this gymnastics method. On the contrary, according to Leal de Oliveira, asymmetrical exercises could hardly become a habit because they "require the dissociation of symmetrical coordination fixed by habit. Human attention has to divide itself between the two homologous parts of the body, through which corresponding impulses and ideas immediately follow in the mind."[139] In his view, the dissociation of attention, the possibility of choice and the confusion between ideas were perverse qualities and led to an ill-defined body. Leal de Oliveira pointed out that a movement's aesthetics rested on its usefulness, adding that "rectilinear movements," typical of gymnastics, "express calm and determination," whereas "curvilinear movements," present, for instance, in sports such as football, reflected "indecisiveness."[140]

The careful tailoring of each movement to the age and sex of the participant was one of the basic principles of the Ling method. The creation of the Mocidade Portuguesa Feminina (Feminine Portuguese Youth), in 1937, institutionalized a sexual separation and distinction between the types of exercises appropriate for each sex.[141] Thanks to the ability to categorize students according to a specific biotype, the kinds of movements more appropriate for each individual would be determined, thereby improving physical performances, correcting the bodies' postures, preventing illnesses, and guiding youths in their professional life.[142] A specific training space was necessary for the proper teaching of this orthodoxy of movement. The modern gymnasium, which since the late nineteenth century had gradually become more common in Europe, represented the space where the relationship between teacher and student could be regulated through a set of norms and hierarchies. It was a closed domain, measured and organized according to the intersection of straight lines. By taking individuals out of their social environment, this domain became a laboratory of bodies and ways of being and acting, argued Leal de Oliveira.[143] The socializing function of this kind of total institution,[144] inspired by the Greek gymnasium, had been adapted to modern times. According to the first commissioner of the *Mocidade Portuguesa*, Francisco Nobre Guedes,

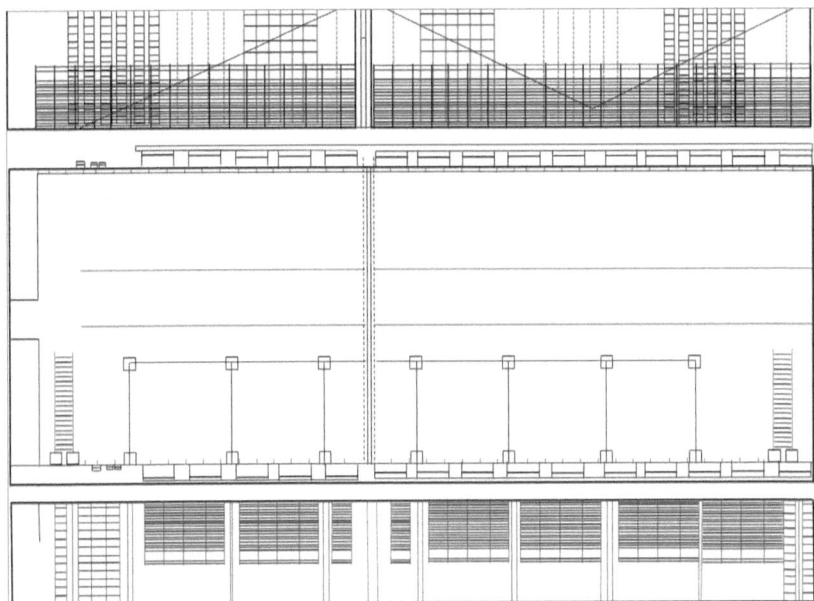

FIGURE 2.3. Sketch of a modern gymnasium. Author: Ana Estevens. *Source:* Adapted from Celestino Marques Pereira, *A educação física na Suécia*,163.

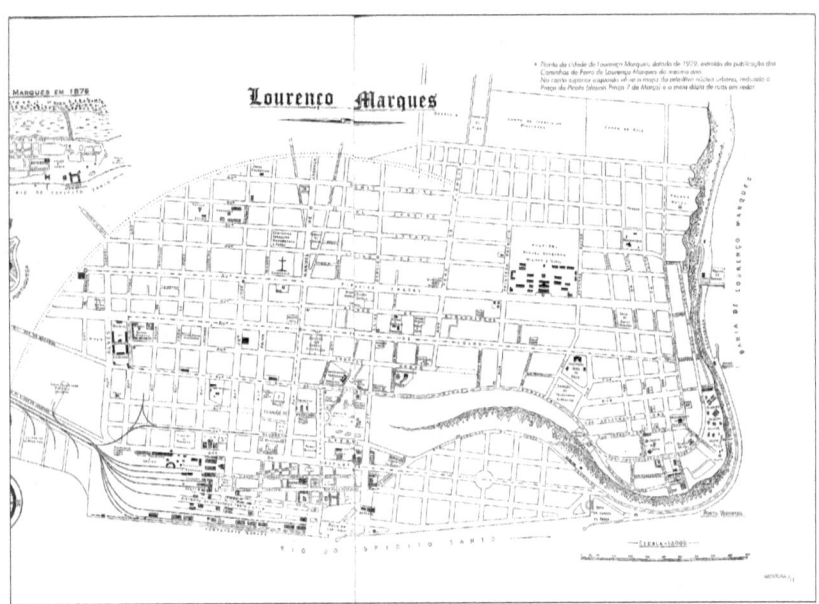

MAP 2.3. Plan of the city of Lourenço Marques, 1929. There are obvious similarities between the structure of the modern gymnasium shown in Pereira's 1939 original sketch and the principles behind the geometric layout of Lourenço Marques's cement city. In a way, both these spaces were conceived as modern, confined, and organized spaces where life is produced. Caminhos de Ferro de Lourenço Marques. Source Wikimedia.

inspired by Pierre de Coubertin's ideas, "You must protect the gymnasium from the twofold danger represented by the proximity of school and sports society. Both, were they to penetrate its walls, would lead it astray from its objective and neutralize its main action."[145] The chaotic city, where football thrived, was described in 1928 by António Faria de Vasconcelos, a psychologist and educator, in a text where the purifying benefits of the Ling method were praised: "We need only look at our own life, its zigzags and jerking curves, its haphazard rhythms, a fleeting flame of will and work, sometimes ablaze, sometimes slumberous, shifting from enthusiasm to despondency at a stroke, a life, in short, lacking spirit, balance, control, and discipline."[146]

Movements molded by unregulated spatial contexts, such as sports associations, football grounds, and school playgrounds, had a negative impact on the teaching of symmetry.[147] Schoolteachers were also to take part in this control of space by monitoring breaks between classes, on the playground, to "avoid excesses and deviations in children's spontaneous activity," especially in the course of "very dynamic games."[148] More dubious, from an educational point of view, were the movements executed in spaces such as football pitches, where players competed, in a more or less institutionalized way, before an audience. The football field had proven to be an unregulated space, not easily controlled by the state.[149]

The practical implementation of this model did not depend solely on the actions of state institutions vis-à-vis state-sponsored activities but also on their ability to regulate sports activities promoted by private associations, to change their principles, and to convert them into instruments of a "proper education." The moral principles once prevalent in amateur sports matches had been corrupted by the growing popularity of those activities. For the Portuguese physical education theorists, body movements associated with popular games such as football reflected an urban space that was unhealthy, unpredictable, prone to conflict, hesitant, filled with disordered actions: daily movements executed by individuals who left the steady pace of country life for the uncertain rhythm of the city; individuals who lived in insalubrious houses and attended subversive associations and spaces where politics were discussed. The structural problem of sports games, according to Marques Pereira, rested in the acknowledgment that the movements they generate have a "utilitarian purpose," an "ill-defined" trajectory, and are asymmetrical.[150] This utilitarian purpose was connected with their competitive nature. Individual movements, syncretic (and synthetic), were driven by the intent to beat the opponent. Because sports games were interactive, specific gestures could not be predetermined, nor could they become the rational outcome of an ideomotor principle, as defined by Leal de Oliveira. The game's structure relied on immediate experience and empirical knowledge, which meant that its technical progression emerged out of an "experimental basis."[151] A product of a school of vices, outside the scope of state pedagogy, this alternative motor habitus did not fit into the project of a respectable citizen, educated by a nationalist school, the Catholic Church, and the corporative system.

Although ambitious, this educational project was not very effective, especially when translated into the colonial context. Policies on the colonial ground highlighted the potential benefits of a control over sports associations, a cheaper and more effective form of ruling. Basic institutional structures of social life that provided a structure for social participation and identification, sports associations maintained an ambiguous statute: they could be loyal servants of indirect-rule policies but, when not properly surveilled, could turn into hubs of anticolonial resistance.

In Mozambique

In Mozambique the Mocidade Portuguesa became responsible for overseeing the statutes of all associations whose activities entailed youth participation.[152] In 1942 a new decree integrated "within Mocidade Portuguesa's educational centers all school associations, canteens, school funds, excursion funds, secondary school philanthropic funds or associations, professional schools, farming schools and agricultural management schools."[153]

The principle of exclusion inherent in the activity of the Mozambique MP persisted in the 1956 law for the reorganization of overseas sports activities, the first piece of legislation (drafted after a research mission[154]) that sought to bring all sports practices, generally speaking, within the fold of the state. The 1956 law and the subsequent legislation that established Conselhos Provinciais de Educação Física (Provincial Boards of Physical Education) for each region, drew inspiration from DGEFDSE regulations: 63 percent of the content of the 1957 Mozambican law replicated this document.[155] The colonial legislation defended the use of private associations to promote the state model of physical education. Associations and clubs were expected to organize gymnastics classes, otherwise their athletes would be excluded from all competitions.[156] This law disapproved of sport-as-spectacle; competition was acceptable only when under the tutelage of the state.[157] The opinion issued by the Câmara Corporativa (Corporative Chamber),[158] and written by the prominent Portuguese physical education theoretician Celestino Marques Pereira, suggested the need for the state to swiftly find a frame for the problem of indígena sport:

> The physical education of the indígena populations in the overseas provinces is a current problem that has a significant impact on the future and progress of these territories. The excellent results attained in previous efforts by some private and official entities indicates that a gradual resolution of the problem is likely. The câmara considers that this is a matter of great importance in the much wider issue of the indígena's welfare and believes that various sports entities serving the economic life in the overseas provinces may contribute effectively to the resolution of the problem, if only the state, through its own organs, helps them with the necessary guidance, stimulus, and support.[159]

The new Conselho Provincial de Educação Física de Moçambique (CPEF, Mozambique Provincial Council of Physical Education) was entrusted with the elaboration of "plans and solutions for the gradual integration of native gymnastic and sports activities in the current diploma's regime."[160] In the discussion that took place in the Conselho Legislativo (Legislative Council), Governor Gabriel Teixeira expressed the view that, despite the enthusiasm among indígena athletes, "even in the furthest corners of the bush," there remained the "impossibility of, given their cultural state, [their] adaptation to the rules created by the civilized."[161] Although the law on the right of association published in May 1954 did not discriminate against indígenas, the fact that they did not possess any political rights contravened that legal disposition.

Managing Exclusion

In Lourenço Marques, the approval of the statutes of suburban football clubs by the colonial state—for the most part in the thirties—brought about a situation where official recognition was made along discriminatory lines: in local competitions, settlers' clubs were separated from African clubs. Gradually, however, local authorities would adopt a policy of reaching out to populations discriminated against within the field of sport. This was a slow process defined by tensions and indecisions within the colonial state and its institutions, which were permeated by conflicts such as the one that opposed a metropolitan state struggling to demonstrate the nonracist character of Portuguese colonialism and a local settler community largely resistant to any such form of openness. The activities of the Mocidade Portuguesa, by excluding the indígena populations, and the resistance of a large portion of settlers and their elites to any political outreach, clashed with the goal of social integration, which was particularly pressing in urban contexts.

The need to tailor a new official model of physical practice to the specific challenges that defined the period from the mid-1950s onward highlighted the state's inability to impose its conception of a proper education of the body. The political effect of segregation preoccupied the colonial rulers; the case of sport was especially troubling because of its capacity to bring people together, to cement identities, and to raise consciousness. The postwar political scene, namely in terms of the multiplication of the processes of independence in Africa and the eruption of armed conflict in Angola in 1961, in Guinea-Bissau in 1963, and in Mozambique in 1964, called for other ways of addressing the indígena issue. Furthermore, the context of postwar economic modernization, albeit deficient, meant that the state framework had to be reconfigured with a view toward the stabilization of the African labor force. These structuring elements in the evolution of the colonial field of power spilled over into sports practices and consumptions.

In 1947 the Catholic Indo-Português club was integrated into the AFLM. The following year the Portuguese state allowed athletes' transfers between the colonies and the metropolis.[162] In 1949, the SNI's leader, Captain Montanha, when answering a request by the Associação Africana de Inhambane, stated, "We have been recognizing for long that it is a good policy to support indígena associations, giving them all necessary help, with the main objective of creating an associative spirit among the indígena masses and, simultaneously, to take those associations to cooperate with the government's colonizing and civilizing work. In my opinion, it is through this process that we will achieve a slow and useful assimilation."[163]

In 1952 the creation of a second division of the AFLM, composed mostly of a second line of settlers' clubs, also included two teams organized by mestiços: Atlético de Lourenço Marques and Vasco da Gama. The fact that the latter club came from the AFA prompted a long debate within colonial institutions. The DSAC advised against the inclusion. They were afraid that the registration in the AFLM championship of a team composed almost entirely of "nonwhite" players could give way, through football's actual competitive logic, to a public-order management problem.[164] The governor general, Gabriel Teixeira, on the contrary, supported the inclusion. Still, this openness was indeed an attempt to reach out to mestiço elites.[165] The new competition, besides having granted these clubs access to "downtown football," stimulated the circulation of players between the AFA and the AFLM. The number of athletes that shifted from one association to the other was hardly meaningful, but their performances, on the one hand, and the fact that transfer virtually meant getting a job, on the other, raised football's value as a vehicle of professional integration.[166] The establishment of a second division was also a response to the growing dissatisfaction among the boards and the supporters of a few settlers' clubs, who felt discriminated against by the notables that ruled over local football. This aspect of integration highlights the fact that social management was not confined to the dichotomies indígena/civilized or white/nonwhite but stretched across an ever more complex class system.

The integrationist intentions behind the 1956 and 1957 colonial sports law contrasted with the persisting local discrimination. The percentage of black members at sports clubs and associations in Mozambique decreased over time (table 2.1):

TABLE 2.1.

Percentage of black members and mestiço members at sports clubs and associations in Mozambique, 1935–58

	Black Members (%)	Mestiço Members (%)
1935	15	8.7
1940	14.3	12.1
1945	10.4	9.
1950	6.6	9.3
1955	4.1	9.4
1958	4.7	9.2

Source: Based on data from *Anuário estatístico de Moçambique* (1935–58)

On the other hand, the percentage of mestiços was stable over time. If we take into account that membership in all sports clubs increased significantly, we can conclude that the growth of sports associativism in the central areas of Lourenço Marques excluded the black population.[167]

During the discussion in the Conselho Legislativo on the creation of the Conselho Provincial de Educação Física (Provincial Council on Physical Education), the governor general of Mozambique pointed out that, although indígenas were not covered by the law, it was important to find solutions for their gradual integration within the sports field; this should be carried out with "a degree of flexibility, so as to allow for experimentation, trial, and error."[168] The uncontrolled consequences of the football market, which help create new African heroes, would put this "policy of flexibility" to the test, more so even than the state itself.

In 1957, when African players such as Matateu and Coluna were already showcasing their skills in the metropolis, Carreira de Tiro, an AFLM club, asked the newly created Conselho Provincial de Educação Física (Provincial Council on Physical Education) for information regarding the registration of indígena players. The CPEF was faced with questions for which the law had no answer. Tacitly legitimated by the social-organization model, racism in sport became a public matter only when those discriminated against belonged to a small African petite bourgeoisie with access to newspapers. Carreira de Tiro's request triggered a decision-making process[169] that revealed the nature of the strategies of euphemization that strove to conciliate persistent racist actions and policies with the new lusotropical face of Portuguese propaganda, as well as with the wider issue of urban social control.[170] Under the cover of a discursive façade, state agents acted strategically, seeking to balance a politically correct rhetoric with the existing interests among the settler community.

The skewed rhetoric of Fernando Olavo Gouveia da Veiga (the CPEF's president) as he strove to sum up the problem and produce doctrine, can be seen as a metaphor for Portugal's colonial policy during this period. Racist policies were not inscribed in the law, since it did not distinguish between indígena and nonindígena players. The decision to employ them was left to the clubs. In Lourenço Marques, some did. The CPEF's president pointed out the possible political gains in "integrating the indígenas." To delay integration would have "harmful effects . . . in more advanced indígena circles, as sport is one of the main vehicles of passion, something that isn't always easily controllable." In line with the international image the country was trying to promote, discrimination was "contrary to the higher principles of our constitution, all the more so since it goes against our mentality and governing practices, guided by integration and assimilation principles." Integration should not, however, upset "nonindígena circles," which would only "reluctantly accept the random registration of indígenas as players for our own clubs and associations." To reconcile the deep-seated local racism with the need to create laws that enabled the integration of indígenas, their sporting participation was legalized, although it was left "to the clubs' judgment" the possibility of blocking the indígenas' access, by invoking sports and associative internal regulations. This solution would be, the CPEF's head concludes, "a demonstration, even within the international field, of a real indígena integration policy employed in our social system." In a note in this same document, the SNI's acting director agrees with the registration of certain elements, but adds that the registration of teams composed exclusively by indígenas should be studied with care.[171]

In 1959 the colonial administration decided to abolish the African Football Association,[172] integrating some of its clubs in the AFLM's third division, which had been created for this purpose.[173] In the same year, African clubs had to remove from their statutes words that hinted at any type of racial discrimination, although terms like African had become commonplace and were employed consciously as a reaction to colonial racism.[174]

This integration strove to put an end to various situations that gradually revealed the hypocrisy of the Portuguese assimilation system.[175] When, in 1959, the AFA clubs moved to AFLM's third division, they did so under very specific circumstances. Matches were played in downtown pitches, which offered the best setting for the game, in the hours that remained free from matches involving clubs from the two upper divisions—in other words, almost always early in the morning. In the first year, the possibility of the third division's champion moving to the upper division was not even considered. This situation would later be rectified.

Said Mogne, who started playing football in the AFA championship toward the end of 1940, made a link between these changes and transformations in the political situation:

> The Associação Africana de Futebol was created with a specific intent, that of segregation. There was the Associação de Futebol Africana, on the one hand, and the Federação de Futebol de Lourenço Marques, on the other. There was no common ground between them. When the "smoke" of independence began to rise up then there was an effort toward approximation . . . and the idea emerged of, one way or the other, merging the two clubs. Those that had the good fortune of being integrated survived. . . . The question arises because of existing political pressure. There had to be a coming together because separation in the AFA was a racial issue.

In the 1960s, official statistics indicated a greater degree of inclusion of nonwhite members in Mozambican sports clubs and associations. Between 1959 and 1964 the number of black members of sports clubs and associations increased across the territory (table 2.2):

TABLE 2.2.

Percentage of black members and mestiço members of sports clubs and associations in Mozambique and Lourenço Marques, 1959–64

	Black Members		Mestiço Members	
	Mozambique (%)	Lourenço Marques (%)	Mozambique (%)	Lourenço Marques (%)
1959	5.89	–		
1960	–	7.7	10.5	10.9
1961	–	9.1		
1962	–	8.5		
1963	–	10.6		
1964	19.7	11.6	9.5	9.7

Source: Based on data from *Anuário estatístico de Moçambique* (1959–64)

It is likely that these statistics included African clubs that had not been previously surveyed. The inclusion of their members in these figures puts the notion of openness in perspective.

THE INEFFICIENCY OF THE PHYSICAL EDUCATION MODEL

Even when it came to the segment of the population included in its activities—that is to say, the nonindígena population—Mocidade Portuguesa proved largely inoperative. Reports sent by its Comissariado Colonial (Colonial Commissariat) to the governor general between 1949 and 1951 reveal a difficult situation, characterized by an inability to act outside district capitals[176] and by a permanent lack of funds, material, and employees.[177] MP had to recruit specialized civilian teachers, even though these teachers and technicians often declined the post since they would earn less than what they received from the clubs.[178] The development of official sports policies in the final period of Portuguese domination, given the lack of direct investment, depended on the income generated through sports competitions, such as the football championships. Part of the budget of Mozambique's CPEF came from the Fundo de Expansão Desportiva (Sports Expansion Fund), whose revenue was gathered by collecting 5 percent of sports competitions' ticket sales.[179] In 1966 the introduction of a sports betting competition in the territory, Totobola,[180] raised the funds that would be channeled to sports.[181] This led the state, at a time when the war effort was already eating up a great portion of the budget, to reduce direct investment in this area even further.[182] Official reports from meetings taking place between 1959 and 1967 reveal that during this period a great deal of the CPEF's work had to do with the resolution of problems related to federated competitions. One example is the validation of footballers' transfers following requests from the respective clubs and associations.[183] Although filtered by social and racial divides, the football market managed to create its own means of labor integration.

The disciplinary instrument, which aimed to regulate and impose a new logic on the activity of associative sports, namely football competitions, was held hostage by the actual system it strove to control. Failing as an agent that aimed to "produce" acceptable sports practices and consumptions, the state sought to regulate activities, oversee them, avoid political appropriations, and, as far as possible, to use the specific social power of associative sports to hold on to their control over the city's populations.

In the metropolis, given the inability to curtail the popularity of football, a sport that led young people away from schools and workshops,[184] the regime acknowledged, in the 1953 law that reformed "national physical education," that sports associations promoted "a physical culture that, although lacking control and practice, had the virtue of uniting groups of people who enjoyed competition or exhibition. Here, they found a complement to an increasingly demanding social life."[185] In 1960 the Estado Novo recognized professionalism in football, cycling, and boxing[186] so as to distinguish amateur sports, sponsored by state institutions, from professional sports, which were pedagogically and morally reprehensible.[187] This law was extended to colonial territories in 1963,[188] when it was already obvious that football had become, in cities such as Luanda or Lourenço Marques, a powerful social force.

Even though it was not considered a good practice by state specialists, in Mozambique's capital, in the cement city, and in its suburbs, football mobilized young men and adults, practitioners, and spectators of a popular culture that established itself as a basis for ample sociability. The number of clubs and associations constantly increased, as did their total membership (table 2.3):

TABLE 2.3.

Number of Mozambican sports associations and clubs and total membership, 1930–64

	Number of Mozambican sports associations and clubs	Total membership
1930	19	2,911
1935	23	5,579
1940	36	6,157
1945	52	10,531
1950	62	17,401
1955	95	28,664
1960	193	49,602
1964	196	56,252

Source: Based on data from *Anuário estatístico de Moçambique* (1930–64)

Maintaining its criticism of the irrational and unedifying character of competitive games, the regime saw them from a different angle. Government experts considered now that football had an escapist effect; it created an arena for the manifestation of conflicts in a political context where the channels for public protest were virtually closed. In the colonial world these transformations are inseparable from the debate on the indígena question, as well as from imperial propaganda and urban social-management policies.[189]

During the 1960s the number of transfers, instigated by the rise in the number of settlers and by the end of the indigenato, reached an impressive tempo, although the state attempted to delimit this market.[190] For example, it stipulated that athletes wanting to compete should have a minimum level of schooling.[191] This policy prevented many players from competing. Despite such restrictive measures, football's primacy—as a promoter of sports movements in Lourenço Marques, repeated in informal practices, and consumed as a dominant leisure activity—was imperious. Even if they were politically controlled, clubs and associations continued to promote an antipedagogic "movement policy" and became the key nuclei of football narratives deeply embedded in popular culture. The "game's gestures" were replayed in the neighborhoods, in schools, on beaches, and in organized competitions, and then were echoed in the media, read, and listened to.

In the closing years of Portuguese power in Mozambique, the colonial state sought to use sports policies as a way to invert its role as the legitimating ground of a deeply hierarchical and racialized society. To that effect, a number of interrelated factors proved crucial: (1) the propagandistic exploitation of sports, (2) the implementation of social policies, particularly in the major cities, but also (3) the specific and relatively autonomous dynamics of a specialized field of physical education teaching and theorization that gradually abandoned the semimilitarized model of the MP in favor of a teaching system that, although integrated within the regime, had been subjected for some time to influences from more progressive traditions.[192] It was only after 1967, when José Maria Noronha Feio, formerly a director at the Instituto Nacional de Educação Física (INEF) in Lisbon, was appointed leader of Mozambique's CPEF, that sports policies, welfare, and urban-inclusion policies finally came together more efficiently. Noronha Feio managed to break with the semimilitarized practice of the MP, whose members still exerted influence on the CPEF.[193] Regarding his action as a policymaker, Noronha Feio stated that his priority was organizing "educational recreational activities that promoted the gregarious spirit among the less-developed populations, in spheres such as hygiene, human relations, and land settlement." This action, he continued, "represents one of this nation's government's greatest concerns—*the integration of the populations.*"[194] Within the Portuguese state apparatus the need to integrate populations was rhetorically used by interest groups that had different opinions and pursued distinct objectives. Access to sport in the suburbs of Lourenço Marques became one of Noronha Feio's main projects, integrated in a vast social intervention plan titled Plano de Beneficiência da Área Suburbana de Lourenço Marques (Lourenço Marques Suburban Area Improvement Plan).[195] Noronha Feio would leave Moçambique in 1973, when he was elected *director geral dos desportos* (general director of sports). The "integration of the populations" thus became a discursive device that legitimated forms of intervention on the ground. The regime's interest in integrating the populations, to avoid social and political upheaval and to stabilize an urban African labor force, generated the necessary conjunctural conditions for a handful of agents on the ground to initiate a policy of democratization of sports practices, which allowed the field of sports, which was structurally discriminatory, to open up to some degree.

Imperial Narratives

The attempts to instrumentalize sports for social and political management, presenting it as an example of social integration, were at odds with the discrimination that prevailed on the ground. While this situation persisted, a propagandistic imperial narrative that exploited the success of a few African athletes in the metropolis was developed. To a degree that would merit closer scrutiny, this discourse drew on the powerful penetration of the football narrative in a mediatized urban popular culture so as to invest in a wide-spectrum and widely disseminated lusotropicalist rhetoric, which became even more effective when mediated by the seemingly neutral prose of specialized media outlets.[196] This situation revealed the need, among those who held key positions within the colonial field of power, to take into account the social influence of popular culture.

The presence of African players, the most prominent of whom came from Lourenço Marques, in popular metropolitan clubs, and in the national team promoted a "banal lusotropicalism" that was adopted by the Portuguese government, especially when the Benfica club of Eusébio and Coluna won the European Cup in 1961 and 1962,[197] and when the national football team came third in the World Cup in 1966.[198] The induction of Eusébio in the Portuguese army in 1963, widely reported by the media, and his participation in campaigns in support of Portuguese soldiers organized by the Movimento Nacional Feminino are only some of the examples of the political exploitation of the popularity generated by football.[199] In the context of the war, the campaigns run by the Gabinete de Acção Psicossocial (Office of Psychosocial Action) were also built around the presence of a metropolitan football narrative among the African populations.[200] Spurred on by a powerful associative impulse and supported by the local authorities, the various tours of Portuguese clubs to the colonies reinforced these imperial conceptions of nationality.[201] The propaganda efforts undertaken by the Portuguese from the 1950s onward, which translated into a process of euphemization of the pervasive racism in the colonial spaces, opened up a split between events in the colonial terrain and an official and persistent historical narrative based on the romanticized accounts of these African players' sports narratives.

Before the participation of the Portuguese national team in the 1966 World Cup, journalists were already referring to a "Euro-African" game style, which was a vehicle for political metaphors and cultural prejudices. Media narratives often registered the naturalization of an imperial motor habitus,[202] the synthesis of a lusophone body created by the Portuguese gest. The style of play was included as part of a discourse of propaganda and control that will have had its identitarian effects, shaping the imagination of the population both in the colonial territories and in the metropolis. The bodily movements of the national team players expressed, from this point of view, a singular identity, distinct from any other national football style. Vítor Santos, a journalist for *A bola*, a metropolitan sports newspaper, emphasized the influence of the "'technical touch' executed by the players from tropical and subtropical areas" in the "lusophone football 'model'": "the result of this miraculous mix of a natural technique, relaxed and swinging, typical of tropical and subtropical players, with the methodical preparation conducive to seriousness and to the achievement of an ideal performance, which is the product of the studiousness that, in some way, defines 'northern people' from this Old continent with a long history and tradition."[203] The discourse was similar, in many ways, to Gilberto Freyre's lusotropicalist narrative, here adapted to football. For Freyre, in the many pages devoted to the unique features of the bodily practices of the Brazilian players, football was the manifestation of a national identity, a non-European one, of course.[204]

African players' performances in Portuguese teams also led to various political and nationalist metaphors.[205] After Benfica won its second European Cup, the director of *A bola*, Silva Resende, a man linked to the Estado Novo regime, talked about the benefits of having African players, such as Eusébio and Coluna, playing for Portuguese teams. These players, who had the "feline appearance that sets colored men apart," introduced to the "game an element that was new to the habits of a public that perhaps had not realized that Portugal, without losing its intrinsic nature, was a multiracial nation."[206]

Sports and the Colonial Field of Power

The process of sportization promoted from the early twentieth century in Lourenço Marques reified the main dividing lines that traversed the colonial system: class practices, racial divisions, and gender inequalities. The colonial situation thus helped to structure a segregated sports sphere of activity. The dissemination of sports, essentially promoted through the practice and consumption of football, took place, to a large extent, outside the state's direct action, through the initiative of the network of associations and clubs that created regular competitions. The relation between the state and the private sports dynamic was ambivalent and must be interpreted in the context of the ambiguous territory of indirect rule. The leaders of clubs and associations within the settler's universe, especially among those that had more influence, came for the most part from the dominant colonial classes. These leaders used sports as an instrument of clientelist and patronage relations, which granted them local prominence and also gave them, in the sphere of commercial and industrial development, the means for managing workplace environments, which proved useful in terms of achieving social peace and economic productivity. Although under political control, clubs and associations fostered competitive sports that officially were thought to have no pedagogical purpose and that gathered crowds that were fed misguided conceptions of the role of sports. Given that they could not impose, all the way from Lisbon, the official project of physical practice, set up in the 1930s, the state ended up trying to use sports popular culture, promoted by a federated associativism organized across transnational networks, to cement a wide social domain, both in terms of a policy of social integration and for propaganda purposes, by means of the creation of imperial narratives. It was only in the last stage of the Portuguese dominion over Mozambique that sports was included within a belated social policy program driven by the state. Although theoretically relevant, the division between private sports and state sports, the latter promoted by the colonial power itself, has obvious limitations, as both had their political field of performance, sometimes complementary, other times contentious. Such tensions and conflicts steer us toward a more adequate interpretation of the state's action, beyond its laws and discourses. Hence, the untimely concern with the integration of indígenas, in the 1950s, forced the state to attempt an opening of the sports field, more in line with the lusotropicalist propaganda than with the reality on the ground. It was only in 1959 that legislation was passed to end the split and racialized football organization in Lourenço Marques.

The project of social transformation and political tutelage that pervaded the regime's physical education policies and that took the athlete's body as the site for the reproduction of the social and political order, proved unable to structure the field of sports. In this context, the state tried to develop its model of indirect rule, much dependent on the dynamics of local society and on the strategies of several agents in the colonial terrain. While presenting dimensions of informality that were often not picked up in the documentation, this model adjusted to the political cycles and to the changing needs of social regulation felt by the colonial system, that explains for instance the relation between segregation and political overture. But this model was also forced to respond to the development of the sports field, which by creating a specific market based on spectatorship and professionalism brought about new problems of regulation. While recognizing that African associative elites could reinforce the indigenato rule ("integrated but separated"), from the late fifties onward it was crucial to reconfigure this framework so that the image of a multiracial community bound by lusophone culture could emerge. While the sports field seems to not have posed a direct threat to the regime's stability, it would develop potentialities and powers of its own, appropriate for agents that used sports practices and consumption as a means of pursuing private interests, of expressing and enjoying themselves, a means to forming bonds and sociabilities, of reinforcing social identities and political causes. The emphasis on the instrumental uses of sports as creators of bonds can overlook the way in which sports can promote horizontal ties that nonetheless, for the most part, exclude women.

As conceived by the physical-education theorists of the Estado Novo, movements that could not be predetermined, either through the natural order of the world (the expression of a pastoral idealization) or through physical-education science (applied to a political and social utopia), were not useful. The unpredictability of athletes' trajectories during a football match, with their inconstant movements, reflected a disordered society. The match's events, its rhythm, exposed life's irregularities. Craveirinha, as he observed the gestures of players in the suburbs of Lourenço Marques, was looking at a whole different scenario: the game revealed Africans' creativity, intelligence, and culture. It proved that Africans were not "doomed" to practice a premodern "natural sport," supposedly consistent with their civilizational state. In the informal neighborhood matches and in the more organized competitions, the heterodox movements of suburban players, in the context of a singular historical and social experience, challenged a totalitarian vision of the body. Far from the practical institutionalization of politically driven ideomotor movements, these football matches expressed a socially embedded practice as well as the emergence of a situated motor habitus defined by a malicious motor repertoire. Their interpretation demands, however, a return to the process of construction of the suburbs of Lourenço Marques and to the way in which football was integrated within the economy of local practices.

3 ⸺ Football and the Moral Economy of the Lourenço Marques Suburbs

VISIONS OF THE SUBURBS

The suburbs of the capital of Mozambique, where football was played from at least the early years of the twentieth century, were represented in various ways. The epic narratives of conquest, focused on the agency of the colonizer, did not take them as an object except as an informal space that was somewhere beyond the bounds of the real city and where African political structures, almost always thought of as the enemy, organized.[1] Later, the propagandistic and touristic lusotropicalism would represent the capital of Mozambique as a natural and cultural paradise. While for the most part the suburbs were overlooked in these representations, it sometimes appeared in the form of a folklorized space. In the same period, developmentalist economic discourse projected a modern and productive future for the city. However, unlike lusotropicalism, modernizing discourse was a response to a more pressing will to intervene, grounded in the old goal of economic exploitation, but now renewed by the science of productivity. The modernizing sectors, increasingly active in the colonial field of power, demanded a more qualified labor force, state investment, and a new social contract. While lusotropicalism imagined a culturally harmonious society managed by a mechanic solidarity, in the Durkheimian sense, the discourse of modernization deemed this organicity, supported by indigenato, unreliable. It was urgent, rather, to create other forms of social cohesion, grounded in a labor interdependence that could sidestep class or race consciousness. In this sense, the critical discourse of modernization, while it did not cross swords with the lusotropicalist façade, considered the suburb an unbalanced space that state planning should redress. The modernizing diagnostic, which was quite critical toward suburban society, in the end explained the origin of the problem in terms of a cultural adaptation, or lack thereof, to modernity. And yet the economic backwardness of the suburbs was the ground on which the local colonial field of power was built, to the benefit of a wide set of interests. The analysis of the dissemination of the game of football in the suburbs of Lourenço Marques allows us to generate an alternative representation of this peripheral space.

Colonial Pastorals

In 1971 a promotional book on Mozambique written by the colonial historian Oliveira Boléo and edited by the Agência Geral do Ultramar portrayed Lourenço Marques as

> a beautiful seaside city with wide avenues with plenty of trees, with beautiful gardens, hotels, theaters and cinemas, museums, monuments, viewpoints, bullfight arenas, swimming pools, fields for the practice of various sports, a hippodrome, libraries and archives, an international airport, in short, a modern cosmopolitan city, where black, white, yellow, and brown and mixed [*mistos*] mingle in the streets, always visited by numerous foreigners. . . . The public health, welfare, and school services are exemplary.[2]

After the Angolan war broke out, in 1961, the Portuguese state reinforced the idyllic representation of colonial societies as a harmonious blend of progress and cultural diversity. From academic works to profusely illustrated touristic brochures, from the commission of films to the production of newsreels that were screened before commercial feature films in both the metropole and the colonies, a variety of media were used to publicize an African pastoral. Lourenço Marques was often represented in line within the frame of this benign version of colonialism.[3] The publication, in 1966, in both Portuguese and English, of the autobiography of the great Mozambican player Eusébio da Silva Ferreira, in the wake of his extraordinary performances in the World Cup in England that same year, is an example of the wide variety of ways of producing this banal lusotropicalism. In its very first pages, we are introduced to a zealous, well-behaved African student, properly brought up by his mother, Elisa; he was a man who learned to play football in the humble, yet dignified, harmonious, colorful, exotic, and traditional environment of the suburbs of Lourenço Marques.[4]

In 1968, *Os Africanos de Lourenço Marques*, a monograph about the city by colonial anthropologist António Rita-Ferreira, had painted a scenario that was strikingly different from these lusotropicalist pastorals. Mozambique's capital was not a harmonious space. It was structurally divided, and existential insecurity defined the urban experience of the large periphery.[5] According to this account, most suburban inhabitants lived with an uncertainty about remaining at their current address. The occupation of private lands, which they rented, exposed them to cursory evictions. Heavily policed and removed from easy access to civil courts, their means of protest seemed narrow. Besides the recurrent floods, which affected a large portion of the constructions in the periphery, in the reed world fires spread quickly and easily, started by candles, oil or petrol lamps, and bonfires.[6] Other natural dangers, such as falling tree limbs lightning, or landslides, further increased the risk of this arduous everyday existence. Besides being exposed to natural disasters, the suburbs were also the laboratory for a host of human phenomena. According to the monograph's author, the loosening of the grip once exerted by the family and the tribe[7] explained the moral dissolution brought by prostitution, alcoholism, corruption, gambling, illegitimate offspring, crimes against property and persons, and the abandonment of one's home and children.[8] The suburban population was terrorized daily by gangs of criminals, most of them young: it was estimated that 80 to 90 percent of cases of crime prevention presented before the juvenile court involved African youngsters in the suburbs.[9] Thefts and robbery of homes and shops, made easier by poor construction materials and the absence of public lighting, became commonplace, as did physical assaults.[10] Given the absence of institutionalized means of punishment, public lynchings were common.[11]

Local diets, heavily based on the consumption of corn, sorghum, cassava, and sweet potato, encouraged malnutrition. The lack of vegetables and fruit meant a poorer diet when compared to rural consumption habits.[12] Only 13 percent of Rita-Fereira's interviewees had three meals a day, 76 percent had two, and 11 percent ate only one; 83 percent claimed to eat less than they needed, and only 3 percent consumed at least a kilogram of meat in a week. The wage workers' dependent family members found themselves in an even more precarious situation.[13] In a suburban neighborhood 99 percent of the population did not have electricity and 89 percent had no running water; 99 percent had set up their kitchen on the porch, 76 percent used a latrine in their backyard, and fewer than 4 percent had a septic tank.[14] Stagnant water, where children often played, teemed with rats, mosquitoes, and all kinds of diseases.[15] Respiratory problems and intoxications flourished. To fight an ever-growing number of afflictions, suburban dwellers resorted to traditional medicine. In 1964 seven times as many Africans died as Europeans, although the two populational universes were about the same size.[16]

Rita-Ferreira's impressive account was not propagandistic as such, but neither did it offer any anticolonial invective. On the contrary, his report emerged from within the colonial scientific vanguard. But unlike Oliveira Boléo's lusotropicalist pastoral, for the anthropologist and civil servant the suburb was primarily an economic and political issue, and its populations were conceived as economic and political agents. The critical description of life in the city's outskirts responded to problems raised by modern developmentalist projects, which demanded the fixation and qualification of the labor force, and by their interchange with the consolidation of political management at a time when the war had spread. The quick turnover of workers in Lourenço Marques's labor market harmed economic activities that required a greater degree of worker specialization and for which a training period was necessary.[17] Malnourishment led to exhaustion and a weak psychomotor activity.[18] Between 60 and 75 percent of the budget of the individuals interviewed by Rita-Ferreira was spent on food;[19] nonindígena families of Lourenço Marques put aside nearly 34 percent of their budgets for that same purpose, close to the average percentage (30) in developed countries.[20] Complaints by some economic sectors on the feebleness of the local "human capital" were related by Rita-Ferreira and would be heard further on.[21]

Workers' dependence on their extended families as a social and economic support network brought along a set of obligations inherent in gift economies grounded in kinship (attending family rituals—weddings, christenings, funerals; assisting the sick and minors; lending a hand in building a house). Such obligations collided with the schedules imposed by work regimes, generating situations of recurrent absenteeism and quick turnover that reduced productivity. The uncertain and dangerous conditions of this urban labor market, inadequate for individuals to plan their futures, left open the option of returning to the safer and more stable environment of the countryside.[22] When he published *Os Africanos de Lourenço Marques*, Rita-Ferreira registered the existence in the suburbs of what he called a "cultural hiatus."[23] In Lourenço Marques there grew a structurally young population, educated in the city and freer from its ties with rural society, managing their own movements and desires: "many urbanized Africans live in marginal and transitional areas, and even immoral and broken, environments where there are no new values to take over from the old ones."[24] Empirical evidence clearly demonstrated how the suburban social contract was not a reliable framework for regulating the production and preservation of social peace.

These studies acknowledge that the colonial state's incapacity to fill this void could lead to the emergence of a dangerous national consciousness.[25] Even if South African labor agencies continued to operate in Lourenço Marques, unemployment among young educated Africans grew, and with it a resentment of the lack of opportunities, which made them potentially dangerous in the eyes of the colonial apparatus.[26] Their position within the social structure, their educational level, and their contact with sources of information made them more sensitive to discriminatory processes, which persisted well after the end of the indigenato.[27] The situation of racial conflict in neighboring South Africa made these fears all the more vivid. Such dangers were enhanced by continuous discrimination. In 1967, out of the 1,069 marriages celebrated in the city, only 52 joined people of different ethnic groups; only one involved a white person and a black; and 21 joined whites and mixed-race people.[28] In that same year, of 5,499 births, 522 resulted from "mixed" relationships, and 254 were illegitimate children.[29] In 1968, 8.3 percent of the city's population was the result of a "racial mix" and the trend seemed to point toward a decrease in these numbers.[30]

The biographical memories of former football players who were born out of relations between Western men, mostly Portuguese, and African women, bear clear testimony to this basic inequality. Mário Wilson talked about the origins of his privileged situation:

> My grandfather was an American, Wilson, who snatched a black woman, just because he wanted his problems sorted out. He crossed over to the other side of Lourenço Marques, Catembe, and on one of his walks he spotted the daughter of a régulo that had the shapely body he was looking for, and he said, "That one's mine." He crossed the river again, back to Lourenço Marques, and made her his wife. Because he was an American he might well have been racist through and through, but he still had child after child, six children, and he raised every one of them simply because he could afford it, [and] sent them over to study in South Africa. The two eldest sons were sent to boarding school straightaway. . . . Across the whole of Africa, all the Mandelas were born among the African elite. The African part had their own culture, their social gatherings and festivities, their sporting representations, but all of these things were marked by racism, a rejection that individuals themselves internalized and accepted as natural.

The story of Hilário da Conceição (b. 1939), a Portuguese international raised in Mafalala who played for Sporting de Lisboa, is rather different. He thinks of himself as a "second-rate mulatto," the typical condition of children not recognized by their white fathers:

> My mother is a Chopi, tribal, one of those that have tattoos on their faces and belly. . . . I never knew my father. My mother came from Manhiça to the city. . . . she was a very pretty and sweet girl and she didn't know anyone there. . . . To this day I don't know who my father was. That happened sometimes, you know? In this kind of relationship, the father was almost always Portuguese, and then he'd take off. And why did he take off? Because often the Portuguese would go from Portugal to Mozambique but had a wife back home, or else the wife was here and they had children, a married life, but they had fun with the African women. But then when there was some responsibility . . . if they had got a woman they were seeing pregnant, then they'd cut and run.

Rita-Ferreira's research also demonstrated how the indigenato was still operational after its legal end.[31] Although the administrative division of Lourenço Marques approved in 1969[32] did not make any reference to traditional powers, the state continued to delegate certain functions to it.[33] Beyond the day-to-day management, the state delegated a host of official duties to these authorities: information on local issues, resolution of cases of private law, and identification of individuals wanted by the law.[34] Reports on the "social situation" sent by the local Portuguese governors to the SCCIM in 1965, which were based on a centralized inquiry, revealed how traditional authorities were chosen, co-opted, and permanently surveyed long after the indigenato was abolished.[35] The transference of Africans, in 1969, into the framework of common law did not solve the problems of a population that for the most part remained unregistered or unidentified by the administration[36] and that lacked the educational, financial, and bureaucratic means to access justice or file complaints about urgent matters: property rights, rent disputes, labor law issues, and questions of social rights or family law. The construction of provisional shelters and houses in the suburbs also depended on the acquiescence of traditional administrators.[37] The suburb dweller continued to be subjected to institutions that were increasingly inadequate to handle the disputes that emerged out of the everyday urban experience. Given the legal vacuum and the frail legitimacy of the traditional institutions in the resolution of conflicts and problems, suburb dwellers increasingly resorted to the services of the emergent "witchcraft market" as a means of defending their rights. Many of these practices broke with the standards of the weakened customary law. The need for protection was consistently invoked by former football players when they mentioned witchcraft. Daniel Matavela (b. 1952), one of the first black players to play in the Mozambican branch of the Portuguese football club Académica de Coimbra, in 1968, noted,

> Each people have their own ways. The African is superstitious. Religion tried to educate us, so that we would stay clear of witchcraft, but it's just a reality. In Africa people live in backyards, not apartment blocks. There are a number of ways to protect your backyard. The Portuguese and the European did not take kindly to it: "you and your superstitions." I don't believe it myself . . . in fact I don't like witchcraft, but the fact is it exists.

Legislative changes, such as the end of indigenato, were of little use without a new urban social contract shaped by a more detailed and modern state intervention. While in the metropole there was on ongoing debate about a reformation of corporatism, a model that was not efficient within the framework of postwar economic projects, in the colonial context a segregated corporatism proved even more obsolete.[38] Outside the corporative system, indígenas were excluded from the legal framework for labor relations, passed in 1956.[39] According to the 1962 Rural Labour Code, only individuals considered urban workers, who were mostly white, could join unions. After the end of indigenato, the unionization of Africans was still extremely low.[40]

Other colonial powers addressed the urban question in Africa much earlier.[41] National and international institutions[42] shared policies and techniques and promoted empirical studies that aimed to back social policies usually announced under the banner of "social promotion" or "rural welfare" when aimed at the placement of rural populations.[43] In the Portuguese context, concerns with detribalization—the social integration of the urban, "evolved" indígena, the monetization of exchanges, the loss of traditional community bonds, the stabilization of the labor force, the dangers of proletarianization in the wake of state and private investment[44]—were recognized by state colonialists such as Marcelo Caetano, Joaquim Silva Cunha, and Adriano Moreira.[45] But in the colonial terrain, urban management continued to depend mainly on the old methods of co-optation, violence, intimidation, and surveillance.[46] Organized by Adriano Moreira in 1956, the Centro de Estudos Políticos e Sociais (Center for Political and

Social Studies) was the most serious effort toward modernizing the official social-management structure.[47]

Late empirical diagnoses of the urban situation in Lourenço Marques like Rita-Ferreira's monograph should not damage the lusotropicalist narrative, which was increasingly promoted by state agencies and occupied with political propaganda and with the affluent local tourism industry. Suburban misery, it was argued, did not result from Portugal's colonial action but was the outcome of an unbalanced modernity that promoted cultural isolation and self-exclusion.[48] The urban segmentation was kept because "so many evolved and highly paid Africans" would not trade "the ease, conviviality and prestige they enjoyed in the suburbs for the restrictions, impersonality and anonymity that they would experience in the large and modern apartment buildings."[49] The euphemization of discrimination by way of paying compliments to a suburban culture supposedly prone to isolation, did little, however, to tackle the problem of the labor force's productivity or political and social unrest.

Progressively inoperative, the suburban social contract, which established a set of minimal principles of sociability and conviviality among groups with diverse backgrounds and habits, was seen in the eyes of the modern planner as a space of marginalities, fostered by a cultural and social anomie that for a long time proved useful to the colonial-exploitation model promoted in the region: that contract benefited suburban land proprietors and homeowners, private and public businesses that exploited the permanent stock of African workers, as well as the vast number of settler families that could easily have had in their houses and commercial spaces a large number of domestic servants.[50] Despite the existence of distinct strategies to face the urban malaise, which expressed how state institutions were permeated by different rationalities, urban plans, as well as the few concrete interventions in the suburbs of Lourenço Marques, in fact increased the policy of social separation. This situation facilitated the persistence of a cheap reproduction of the labor force, based on a policy of high taxation, low salaries, and reduction of the managing costs of the suburban space: it was up to Africans to build their own existential territory and their social welfare networks. Suburban football grew out of this forced autonomy.

Housing, Work, and the Creation of "Suburban Autonomy"

The aim to organize indígena neighborhoods in the periphery of Lourenço Marques, already present in the plan devised by Araújo in the early twentieth century, would only be achieved later. The nearby experience of South African compounds were the inspiration behind the plans in the capital of Mozambique. In 1916 a committee put together by the Câmara do Comércio (Chamber of Commerce) and by the Administração do Concelho do Porto e Caminhos de Ferro (Port and Railway Council Administration)[51] visited Durban to assess the municipal housing experience and the workers' food regime, so as to apply a similar system to the four thousand indígenas that worked in the port of Lourenço Marques.[52] Between 1918 and 1921, near the market of Xipamanine, the administration built a small social-housing project. The high cost of rents meant the thirty-three brick houses ended up in the hands of the black and mestiço bourgeoisie.[53] The journalist João Albasini visited the neighborhood in 1921 and painted a dark picture: it had no running water, electric lights, sewage system, or roadways and had only a single cesspit.[54] In 1922 a decree authorized the government of the colony to take out a loan for the construction of hostels or indígena neighborhoods.[55]

The 1922 police regulations for servants and indígena workers, besides imposing a mechanism of registration, identification, and permanence and contract authorization, forced these Africans to settle into hostels.[56] The capital for the construction of these facilities, gathered through a fund financed by the compulsory registration of Africans arriving in the city, ended up being diverted to indígena-labor inspection services.[57] Large companies that hired and transported workers to South Africa, as the Witwatersrand Native Labour Association, the Railways, and Delagoa Bay, built provisional neighborhoods on the outskirts of the city to accommodate migrant workers.[58] A 1926 ordinance required all male indígenas over fourteen to carry an identification and job carnet: the labor contract determined not only the permanence but also compelled holders to have a place of residence.[59] It was only at the end of the 1930s that the fund for the construction of houses for the indígenas was reestablished. Using cautious language, the discourse of the Law by Decree of 1938, which regulated the construction of new indígena neighborhoods, suggested an interest in separating populations under the pretext of a controlled adaptation to urban space.[60] In 1939 the first expropriations took place, close to Angola Avenue. In 1940, after the areas destined for indígena neighborhoods had been established,[61] the first houses of the neighborhood of Munhuana began to be built. Justified by matters of "health, public order, and morality," the project, inaugurated in 1942 and whose responsibility fell on the Repartição Técnica (Technical Division) of the Câmara de Lourenço Marques (Lourenço Marques Municipality), was inspired by South African models.[62]

FIGURE 3.1. Munhuana's native neighborhood—crematorium. Author: A. W. Bayly and Co. *Source:* Arquivo Histórico Ultramarino.

The 1942 Regulamento de Identificação Indígena (Indígenas' Identification Regulations) and the 1944 Regulamentos dos Serviçais Indígenas (Indígena Servants' Regulations) maintained the existing mechanisms of control over permanence and mobility, under penalty of correctional labor.[63] Forced labor was applied to other misdemeanors: change of job without prior consent, self-employment without permission, casual unregistered work, absence from the municipal area without prior authorization, instigation of colleagues to give up their occupations, failure to register within three days after your arrival.[64] By the end of the 1950s, fines began to replace forced labor,[65] and before the end of the indigenato regime, the new identification regulations issued an identity card to "evolved" indígenas who showed good behavior, which afforded them a greater degree of mobility.[66]

The logic of social closure continued to define the city's growth plans developed by the Gabinete de Urbanização Colonial (Office for Colonial Urbanization)[67] in the early 1950s. Plano Aguiar (1952–55), devised in 1947 by the architect João Aguiar for the Gabinete de Urbanização, foresaw the organization of various indígena neighborhoods, which included a set of public facilities. It separated these neighborhoods from the cement city, and proposed an intermediate landscaped area that would operate as both a physical and a social buffer.[68] The project did not come to fruition, but Plano Aguiar continued, up to 1969, to direct the city's growth. Aguiar, head of the Gabinete de Urbanização, was responsible for the elaboration of the *planos de urbanização* (urbanization plans) of numerous cities in Portuguese colonial Africa. As registered in one of the key documents that defined Portuguese colonial urban policies, the land use in these projects stressed the fundamental distinction between the spaces for Europeans and those for indígenas, even though the distinction between the two was now more subtle.[69] Aguiar defended ethnic discrimination among the indígena population and, even within the European population, he distinguished among the various types of Europeans, from colonial clerks to the poorer settlers, whom he in fact called settler-workers (*colonos-trabalhadores*).[70]

When, in 1958, the Fundo para a Construção de Casas Destinadas à População Indígena (Fund for the Construction of Houses Destined for the Indígena Population) was created, urbanization plans gave priority to the construction of public facilities, schools, sports fields, gardens. In 1961, in the newspaper *Notícias*, José Craveirinha protested against a form of urban planning that worked against the integration of the indígena.[71] He felt the policy of promoting neighborhoods that "represented clusters of stability for intrinsically tribal cultural forms," was only attenuated by the presence of poor settlers: "the precarious houses of the so-called 'reed-and-tin neighborhood' in the suburbs of Lourenço Marques are not an asocial sign of local exoticism but rather a universal particularism of the large populational clusters, nor are these neighborhoods we speak of destined solely for African residents since many metropolitan families live there."[72]

Several suburban players spoke of this poor milieu, where a few whites stood out among the local population. Hilário called them "black-whites":

> Poverty was normal, we had our wood-and-zinc houses, ate flour and rice and fish and prawns . . . that's what was available, in nature. I mean, misery did not get to the point where, how can I put it, we would starve. No, we lived within our means. . . . In the suburbs there were people with very diverse origins, some came from Zambezia, others from Manhiça, others yet from Inhambane, and there were also different religions; there were Muslims . . . it was a rather diverse world in that sense . . . there were bricklayers, carpenters, fishermen, mechanics, a little bit of everything. . . . Then there were mulattoes who lived in the city. First-class mulattoes . . . There were very few whites in the suburbs. The tradesmen owned the place, the shops, the canteens, they had daily contact with lots of African people. I mean, they were black-whites. . . . In the neighborhood schools there were no whites; a mulatto might possibly go to a white school, but not the blacks.

Mário Wilson's description shows football as a particular laboratory of the wider urban situation:

> There were very few spaces where whites and blacks could play football together, only in what we used to call friendly matches, in neighborhoods where, given the scarcity of players, Europeans and non-Europeans had to mix, driven by their passion for football, by its magic, and so kids would play with each other.... It was only the poorest among the Portuguese that would do it ... there was this coincidence, the fact that it was only the poorest, because the elite were channeled onto other neighborhoods ... the poor Portuguese were a decadent bunch, because they came from less well-to-do families, and less exclusive places, and so they had no choice, they had to play and embrace whatever pleasures came their way.

Approved in 1962, the Código do Trabalho Rural (Rural Labour Code)[73] — which, in accordance with postindigenato policies, did not establish any form of "cultural" or "ethnic" distinction among workers — aimed at accommodating "economically fragile workers." These terms, used to designate the individual's position within the economic system, replaced culturalist and racialist classifications, all the while avoiding the politicized language of class. Among those deemed "economically fragile" were workers classified as "rural"[74] but also all those who, performing a variety of activities, were classified as unskilled, their work reduced to "simple labor services." This last category included many workers that lived on the periphery of cities; these workers, as well as those in "domestic service" and those involved in "labor relations established between labor providers and people in their families" (both falling outside of the scope of the code), made up a large portion of the urban working population — African for the most part.[75] This law further established the difference between permanent and casual workers. The latter were workers "hired for the day, week or month, with no continuous or long-term prospects and whose habitual residence is located in the vicinity of the workplace." By putting an end to racial distinctions, the transformation of the legal apparatus would reclassify social categories, bringing to the fore the contrast between the qualified, permanent, unionized worker, almost always white, and the "economically fragile," temporary, and unqualified worker, almost always black.[76] Allowing for a new representation of society, the "disappearance of the indígenas" and the emergence of the "worker" was signaled by the creation of the Instituto do Trabalho Previdência e Acção Social (Institute of Work Welfare and Social Action) and by the elimination of the

Direcção dos Serviços dos Negócios Indígenas (Head Office of Native Affairs).[77] These shifts in labor legislation tried to reconcile the need to adjust to the political changes brought by the end of the indigenato system and the desire of certain economic sectors, namely industries with a presence in urban areas, for more flexible labor regulations.[78]

Urban Plans for Economic Fragile Workers

Once indigenato was over, the indígena housing construction fund became, in 1962, the Junta dos Bairros e Casas Populares (Popular-Neighborhoods and -Houses Board). In 1963, in an article titled "The Sick City," architect Pancho Guedes spoke of the drama of the "reed belt," which bordered "another city where more people live than all the people in the city—the city of the poor, of servants and manservants."[79] These people lived far from the center, in dire hygienic conditions and in precarious and unsound houses where children starved. Then, he pointed his finger at the way in which the cement city had swollen, the lack of planning and the proliferation of real estate businesses, thus proposing the creation of a construction plan aimed at bringing these two cities closer together and reaching "a genuine social integration—or are the 'blacks' fit only to stand in kitchens and lobbies?"[80]

"There were lots of people who came into the city from the countryside," says Matine (b. 1947), raised in Chamanculo, a black athlete who moved to Lisbon's Benfica in the 1960s. "I remember all too well that to the south of the Save, the Save river, everyone went in search of a livelihood in Lourenço Marques. Most of them would find a job sooner or later. They had their homes and started living in those suburbs, had their jobs."

According to Hilário,

> The worst thing that happened was that when the colonial war broke out people who lived in the countryside fled to the city, empty-handed, and had no place to live, so they took over any land they could grab and built their shacks there, with no sanitation. The empty spaces where we played football were gone. Then the war pushed people out of the countryside and that was it. Whatever space was there in between the shacks or the houses, we used it to play football, even if it was five-a-side, or six-a-side, and in the larger spaces we would play eleven versus eleven. Gradually that [football games] faded away.

In 1963 in Lourenço Marques a working group was put together to think and offer solutions for the problem of the city's suburbs. Led by the psychiatrist Sousa Sobrinho, the so-called Grupo Central de Trabalhos (Central Working Group) gathered technicians and suburban inhabitants, namely a group of nurses that were part of the Caixa de Socorros dos Enfermeiros Nativos (Native Nurses' Assistance Body).[81] A series of meetings, accompanied by the press and the information services, resulted in the elaboration, in early 1964, of a survey that was then handed to the Câmara Municipal de Lourenço Marques (Lourenço Marques Municipality), which the group accused of inaction. The misery in these spaces, which were home to 150,000 to 200,000 people and were "incompatible with the most rudimentary concepts of housing hygiene,"[82] reinforced the effects of insalubrity caused by the recurrent floods ("breeding ground for mosquitoes," "municipal dung heap") and epidemic diseases (such as hepatitis). In the "reed" there was only one first-aid post, and there was no post office or gardens, playgrounds, roadways, electricity, or sewers.[83] Unhappy with the response on the part of the municipality, the working group carried out a vast urban renewal study entitled "Housing Problem among the Economically Fragile," grounded in the application of the public right of expropriation and in the construction of various sorts of housing projects.[84] Concerned with the living conditions of the African population, the group reproduced modernization's purifying logic, representing the suburbs as an abscess that needed to be lanced.[85] At the same time that it claimed to be the most intelligent intervention from the point of view of colonial interests[86]—undertaken in the name of a harmonious cultural coexistence necessary to avoid possible political and social dangers[87]—the plan was justified by the need to integrate the suburban populations into the city, to regulate the entry of "rurals," all the while avoiding segregation.[88] In this plan, the African population's access to private property was seen as an important instrument of social stabilization.[89] Revealing the existence of a small public space where housing in Lourenço Marques could be discussed, this rift served as proof of the lack of interest on the part of state authorities. Accordingly, the signatories suggested that the necessary process of expropriations and urban renewal did not move forward simply because they threatened the revenue of the owners of suburban plots.[90]

The intervention of the Câmara Municipal of Lourenço Marques during this period was intentionally feeble, despite the late effort to organize garbage collection, install drinking fountains, and a sewage system.[91] The creation, in 1964, of the Gabinete de Urbanização da Câmara de Lourenço Marques (Lourenço Marques City Hall Urbanization Office), constituted a reaction to this state of affairs. Then, official urbanism finally attempted to promote new urban-planning methods, articulating them with the principles underpinning the lusotropicalist inversion of the Portuguese colonial ideology, embodied, in the particular case of the organization of the populations, in the defense of multiracial settlement.[92] The prophylactic action of modern urbanism, as it faced these social management problems, had been developed in Lisbon by the Direcção dos Serviços de Urbanismo e Habitação do Ministério do Ultramar (Overseas Ministry's Head Office of Urbanism and Housing Services).[93] The elaboration of new studies, such as the 1966 Plano Regulador de Ocupação do Solo de Lourenço Marques (Regulatory Plan for Land Occupation in Lourenço Marques), yielded no practical results. The failure of official urbanism was more acutely felt during this period, when large-scale economic projects and the need for political regulation lacked effective methods for the management of the working populations. After the construction of the Munhuana neighborhood, only a four-story block was inaugurated in that same site, two blocks (thirty-two households) in the Malhangalene neighborhood and four hundred houses in the industrial zones of Matola and Machava. Given the rate at which the population was growing, these efforts fell short of the mark.[94] Urbanism's adaptation to the fresh face of Portuguese postindigenato colonialism was still far removed from any de facto inscription in the suburb, even if the Lourenço Marques city council had indeed shouldered some of the responsibility for some new infrastructures.

In 1969 the Gabinete de Urbanização e Habitação da Região de Lourenço Marques (Office of Urbanization and Housing for the Region of Lourenço Marques) is created, reporting directly to the General Government. New technical studies are then carried out.[95] Based on the results of preliminary inquests conducted by the General Government in the reed, the decree that created this office made this new entity responsible for "vast urban renewal operations" whose "key goal was to improve the conditions of the interested populations and provide them with the necessary collective facilities, thus avoiding, whenever possible, any major displacements of the current dwellers." It was crucial to find a permanent address for those who came to Lourenço Marques every year looking for work, lured by the "strong magnetism of the city, by the port-railway complex and by the industrial centers of Lourenço Marques's neighboring regions." This required the construction of new "urban structural units" that would cater efficiently to the clusters of productive activity, and where several categories of the population would live, with no "inconvenient social segregation."[96] Devised by the engineer Mário de Azevedo, the new Plano de Urbanização (Urbanization Plan), approved by the Lourenço Marques Municipality only near the end of 1972,[97] sought to achieve the stated goals. This plan already incorporated the concern for a more efficient integration of the peripheral city, in a convergence between social concerns and modern theories of neighborhood urbanism.[98] "Caniço" was now promoted to a "traditional housing area," where precarious, "spontaneous," "undisciplined" dwellings were located, and where the "economically fragile" populations lived.[99] Urban renovation in Lourenço Marques, an urgent matter for political and labor management, now also piqued the interest of a host of investors. The hypothetical construction of satellite cities and the elimination of the reed, as defended in a 1969 study,[100] created an extraordinary business opportunity. While fixation of the labor force was among the incontrovertible goals of these plans, there was no agreement as to the way it was to be achieved.[101] The organization of the Plano de Beneficiação da Área Suburbana de Lourenço Marques (Plan for the Improvement of the Suburban Area of Lourenço Marques), in 1971, just before independence, would become the most ambitious intervention project. It was, however, much too late.[102] In the 1970s the growth of the cement city, which spread toward the industrial areas of Matola and Machava, triggered a wave of evictions.[103] The process was over in a short time and the compensations offered to tenants were meager. While modernizing diagnoses defended state intervention to address the problem of the suburbs, the history of the construction of the periphery of Lourenço Marques demonstrated the active role of state institutions in the creating the problem in the first place.

The Suburban Moral Economy

The many continuities between the two moments that caused a structural shift in the Portuguese colonial system brought to light the practical limits of the end of indigenato, as well as the failure, despite the official propaganda, of the construction of even a blueprint of a common citizenship. A space split into different symbolic zones, Lourenço Marques was ruled by a social system of ecological segregation against which laws—such as the one that in 1961 prohibited discrimination in public spaces—were of no avail.[104] Suburb dwellers learned to adapt their behavior to the spaces through which they circulated, to accommodate their bodies and devise strategies adjusted to the forceful contingencies they were exposed to. The minimization of obstacles to the circulation of suburban dwellers after the end of the indigenato did not impact the interactional meaning of the suburban's presence in the "cement," a hyperregulated space, the entrance to which depended almost exclusively on the performance of a work duty. Of the 21,904 Africans that lived in the cement city in 1968, most were domestic servants or doormen who lived in special annexes built within the houses they worked in: a further means of reproducing the system of separation. In turn, the 9,288 Europeans registered in the suburbs belonged to a poor segment of the settler population, one that seized on the labor commercial opportunities that emerged in the transition areas between the two parts of the city.[105]

The precarious indígena was now the economically fragile worker. In the terrain there were no conditions for the suburban worker to give up the old social contract. In the sixties, manual workers who worked in stowage, construction, storage, or mechanical transportation were still subject to a daily contract.[106] The same labor uncertainty affected workers in the proletarized third sector: janitors, shoe shiners, security guards, servants, and street vendors. The introduction of a minimum wage for industrial workers (MZE 550 per year) was not only not honored, as a rule, but fell short of the basic needs of African workers, especially since they had to support their immediate families as well as help their extended ones.[107] Racial discrimination continued to characterize the postindigenato labor market. Besides the precariousness of the contracts there was wage discrimination, even though it was less emphatic in the city than in the fields.[108] Even in the privileged world of public servants, discrimination was severely felt.[109] Assimilados, whose status guaranteed them certain wage benefits, were affected by the competition of settlers for the most qualified jobs, to the point where some wished to lose their status as "civilized" so as to gain access to other areas of the labor market.[110] Complementary activities were a common strategy for supplementing income, particularly small trades (tailors, shoemakers, seamstresses, cabinetmakers, carpenters, quilters, traditional artisans, basket weavers), personal services (barbers, shoe shiners, automobile washers, food and beverage vendors), or small retail, in which thousands of women were involved, spread among official markets but even more among the numerous spontaneous ones.[111]

The tradition of using coercive practices for securing the necessary labor force, namely chibalo, generated a deep-seated distrust of employment contracts among workers.[112] Seeking to avoid longer and poorly paid contracts, workers embraced the risk of casual, often illegal, work, thus exposing themselves to the danger of forced labor.[113] The "informal job," a common means of subsistence, was illegal and persecuted by the authorities.[114] Labor strategies, risky by definition, forced these workers to carry out a continuous assessment of their possibilities and to adapt their behaviors—learning, through their interactions, which behavior was the most likely to bear fruit. To play the role of the "good boy" or the "good girl" might enable them to find a "good boss," one that would respond to their demeanor with a patronizing paternalism and, with any luck, refrain from using violence. As noted by Penvenne, there was nothing to be gained in challenging the city.[115] The presence of the suburb dweller in the prevailing interaction order in the cement city was determined by an intrinsic subordination, against which cunning offered a possible form of resistance, given the dangers of an open confrontation.[116] Obedience, deference, and solicitude were best adjusted to the demands of that particular space.

This public transcript, marked by the physical and symbolic violence of the state and employers, by humiliation and paternalism, was not reproduced in the relations between the inhabitants of the suburbs.[117] There, specific principles of interaction developed, and they were not necessarily harmonious. Decentralized competition for resources turned the suburbs into risky places. The local inhabitants had to develop bodily abilities to deal with these difficult interactions. While demonstrating how suburbans were engaged with a city they were erecting, such faculties explained the logic of construction of a suburban society and defy the culturalist folklorized visions proposed by lusotropicalist representations and the pathological views of modernists' ambitions. For decades on end both the colonial state and private investors reaped the benefits of this "suburban culture," now chastised by modern thinkers and colonial researchers. "Dysfunctional" social pathologies became one of the key elements in the process of reproduction of a cheap labor force. Prostitution, regulated by the colonial regime itself, mitigated the social effects of the uneven ratio of men and women.[118] Petty theft was part of a wider strategy of survival. Alcohol consumption, to the delight of local vendors—the *cantineiros*—had been promoted by the colonial state and the big metropolitan producers, who depended on the African market as an outlet for their surplus production.[119]

From the point of view of the populations, this suburban "marginality" was their life. From within an extreme precariousness, suburban populations developed cooperation and safety networks and endorsed the behavior models that best fit their most vital necessities. Among those inhabitants there were dock workers, railway workers, and construction workers, alongside workers under the threat of chibalo and other forms of labor exploitation, newly arrived rural populations, servants and domestic servants, street vendors and artisans. As Craveirinha summed it up in 1955, the inhabitants of the neighborhoods of Munhuana, Xipamanine, and Chamanculo faced the housing crisis with their own labor.[120] A large portion of the African city was constructed through local initiative, by self-organized and more-or-less formalized groups that sought to build a common space, not only houses and streets, but commerce, collective assistance networks, religious, recreational, and sports activities, and, to a large extent, the whole social organization. Chaotic descriptions of this universe, so common in modern functional perspectives, fail to interpret its logic and dispositions. Step by step, newcomers, at first housed by family or friends, built precarious and temporary dwellings with whatever materials were at hand—a place to sleep, cook, and keep their scant belongings. Subsequently, they would move to a traditional hut.[121] The construction process mixed old techniques with the imaginative use of materials that circulated through the city. Cardboard boxes, plastic products, and other disposable materials were creatively combined with traditional techniques re-created in the suburbs.

FOOTBALL IN THE SUBURBAN SOCIAL FABRIC
The Dissemination of Sports Practices

Leisure time, sometimes organized by local associations, became sites of urban adaptation, arenas of identitarian construction but also spaces for a wider communitarian sharing. Football matches, both in the neighborhoods and in AFA competitions, absorbed a set of features that defined the urban milieu; alongside other activities that were part of a popular culture whose presence was felt in everyday relations, was a space for the expression of shared practices and values.[122] This history of the process of institutionalization of football in the suburbs opens up another point of view on the periphery of the colonial city. This alternative view of the suburb will be unfolded, not only in terms of a process of urban institutionalization but also through an examination of the practices of its inhabitants. Told from the point of view of a bodily representation of the conditions of urban construction, perceived through the bodily strategies and their moralities, shared by the wider community, the narrative of suburban football provided a different account of the suburban social contract, by drawing on the memories and experiences of those who lived through it, as well as on the ways in which they imagined, and acted on, their everyday lives. The genealogy of a suburban habitus, which was the practical projection of a historical experience that transpired into the bodies, is simultaneously a genealogy of the colonial system managed by the Portuguese.

In the second half of the 1920s, the first references to suburban football matches—between African teams—appear in *O brado africano*.[123] In all likelihood, however, the game had been played, informally, on improvised pitches, since the first decade of the century. The practice of football, in the suburbs as elsewhere, was part of the process of urban structuration. A protohistory of suburban football registers, in the early 1910s, the presence of several sports groups, such as the Mashakeni Football Backing Club,[124] the Buranga Club, Clube Esperanto,[125] the Grupo Universal de Football, the Zebra Club,[126] and the Espring Book Club.[127]

The game's dissemination occurred through the convergence of various elements, with no single key factor. Despite urban segregation, the contact lines between "downtown" and its periphery led to a spontaneous and organized emulation of leisure practices. Although it was not included in Catholic missionary repertories,[128] school curricula, and official military methodologies, there is evidence that football was also promoted through these Portuguese colonial institutions. A simple mode of congregating a group of individuals and of instilling in them rules and values, the game was endorsed by native military battalions in Lourenço Marques between 1927 and 1932.[129] In the suburban neighborhood of São José de Lhanguene, the eponymous Catholic mission put together a football team in 1930.[130] Though not integrated in official syllabuses, the game was played in schools, as recalled by former African players, whose first memories of the game often evoke pitches adjoining educational establishments. Even if it was not explicitly included in any colonial "modality of control,"[131] the game of football was nonetheless spread by religious, educational, and military representatives, who probably had contact with the game in the metropolis and found it a crucial element of sociability and education in the colonial environment.

For a sharper interpretation of this process of dissemination, one needs to pull back from Portuguese colonialism's more immediate area of influence. The system of circulation of workers, commodities, and capital between the region of Lourenço Marques and the neighboring regions of South Africa became the axis for numerous exchanges. It was between Zixaxa Road and Lydenburg Road (which led to the South African mines), in the Munhuana, Xipamanine, and Chamanculo neighborhoods, that suburban football grew. These were also the most urbanized suburban neighborhoods.[132] The road to Transvaal, a corridor for thousands of workers, was one of the foci of transmission of values and new ways of life. This road also served as a passageway for objects, new consumer habits, and a number of leisure practices.[133] In South Africa, football was played from the final quarter of the nineteenth century and became, during the first decades of the twentieth century, the most popular sport among

FIGURE 3.2. A company of native infantry. Many Mozambicans were introduced to modern physical exercises while serving in the Portuguese army. Although they were properly equipped and had their bodies disciplined and aligned, they were still barefoot. Photos mainly by H. Graumann and I. Piedade Pó, void of copyright as collective work. Scan of original from Memórias d'África e d'Oriente, Aveiro University. *Source:* Wikimedia

the urban black population.[134] Protestant missions, whose presence south of Lourenço Marques, from the end of the nineteenth century, followed this flux of emigrant workers, also became hubs of the game's practice.[135] The consolidation of networks of local associative relations, tied to the main South African cities, would become the major force behind the institutionalization of its practice. Even before this process was completed, football had already set foot in the suburban neighborhoods.

Neighborhood Matches

Fostered by a number of agents, football became an integral part of the daily life of Lourenço Marques's suburbs. Its original performance arenas were neighborhood matches, which became elements of the suburban landscape from the first decades of the century. Played with bare feet and balls made up of socks, these *peladas de bairro* (neighborhood matches) generated a sense of spatial belonging and became an occasion for socialization for children and adults whose families had settled in the city. The basic cells of the practice of football, these matches heightened the neighborhood's importance as a way to structure social relations and to generate enthusiasm and solidarity. Spatial identification was also promoted by acknowledging the borders separating one suburban neighborhood from another. Therefore, the representation of this difference contributed toward imagining a communitarian space made up of different pieces. Mário Coluna (b. 1939), a *mestiço*, a major figure in Mozambican football who would eventually become captain of the Portuguese national team, spent his childhood playing in the Chamanculo neighborhood, where local teams challenged groups from other neighborhoods, betting cans of cashews, and where "whoever won took the lot." In those "barefoot times," he recalls, "there was no clock and whoever scored the first four goals won." The former Portuguese international Vicente Lucas (b. 1935), brother of the famous Matateu, one of the first Mozambican footballers to play in the metropolis, remembers playing alongside Coluna in 1951 on a neighborhood team called Acrobático. Sponsored by João Albasini, one of the most prominent clubs in the Associação de Futebol Africana (African Football Association), Acrobático's members were allowed to use the team's head office to organize parties and dances. With the money raised in these events, they would buy cans of cashews to bet on subsequent neighborhood confrontations.

Issufo bin Haji, locally known as Issufo Batata (b. 1934), who played in and managed several suburban teams, started playing football during the 1940s in the Mafalala neighborhood, where "people played everywhere. If it wasn't a school day, after the *mata-bicho*,[136] we ran out to play football." The most popular game was *mete a três* (get three goals): "We built a goal with reed posts and no crossbars, occasionally with a string, and each of us kicked to that spot. Whoever scored three would go in goal." Issufo played on the streets, in the local courtyard, and in school with a "small tennis ball," afterward with a "small rubber ball" and only later with a crude leather ball. Hilário describes the group of friends with whom he played during his childhood as an assortment of kids

> from poor neighborhoods suffering from a variety of deprivations. Whoever was better off would get a Facobol ball [a brand from a local rubber factory]. If you couldn't afford one you'd grab a sock, fill it with cloth, make a sock ball and start playing in the neighborhood. They weren't championships as such. We would invite a club from another neighbourhood. And we would play for money. That was an old tradition, playing for money. We would get a referee. And we respected the referees; sometimes fights broke out but we did respect their decision as to whether it was a goal or not, for instance. The goal did not have a crossbar, it was just a string; if the ball hit the string and went in that was a goal, and the guys respected that.

Issufo remembers these matches in the Chamanculo neighborhood, in Campo da Glória, and at the São José pitch, organized by the mission housed in the church square. Neighborhood teams, with local sponsors (*madrinhas*), often played for money, which indicates that life in the suburbs, even in its leisure moments, incorporated the main forms of economic reward established in the colonial city. This became more common after the Second World War, when more money was in circulation. Augusto Matine describes the process:

> These matches were played for money. We put it together. At the time, each [player] contributed one *escudo*. We gathered ten *paus*[137] and the other team also contributed ten paus. After one team scored two goals, the teams changed sides and whoever scored four goals won. Two changes, four [goals] wins. There was no time limit then; only goals mattered.

In the neighborhood, especially through impromptu matches played on vacant lots, football became an initial performative space, a suburban spectacle acted by local performers for the benefit of a nonorganized local audience. It was from these practices that the first codification of movements arose, translated into rudimentary choreographies and later consecrated through narratives of matches or particular plays. These stories, which circulated within small networks, spoke of the first heroes of the suburbs, of those whose gestures pleased their fellow players and spectators the most. It was also in this formative period that rivalries with bordering neighborhoods developed. Suburban football became part of a common life for individuals who, despite their different backgrounds, were thrown together and had to develop ways of relating to each other. In these neighborhood matches, the primary context for the creative adaptations that Craveirinha was so keen to analyze, suburban football fabricated its own brand of morality.

Although these matches were deeply enmeshed in local sociability, from the 1940s and 1950s the names of neighborhood teams revealed that other football narratives had arrived in the suburbs. Issufo remembers teams such as Águias da Mafalala, created by supporters of Lisbon's Benfica, or Botafogo, in homage to the eponymous Brazilian club. Hilário da Conceição started playing in his neighborhood on a team called Arsenal, in homage to the London club that someone had seen playing in a short film at a suburban cinema. Eusébio da Silva Ferreira, the most famous Mozambican player and a major figure for Benfica and the Portuguese national team, was nicknamed Nené when he played barefoot in the Mafalala neighborhood, at the end of the 1950s. This was the name of a Brazilian player. In those days, his idol was Real Madrid's star Alfredo Di Stéfano, about whom there were plenty of stories in the local newspapers.[138]

The Institutionalization of Suburban Football

Football in the African suburbs, while never casting off the dynamics of neighborhood matches, assumed nevertheless a more organized appearance, sustained by the activity of clubs and of the Associação de Futebol Africana. The process of institutionalization was crucial for the development of a specific knowledge, providing the raw material for a suburban football narrative that was part of a growing urban popular culture. Together with musical groups,[139] religious bodies, and labor organizations, sports associativism enabled the strengthening of ties among the local inhabitants, thus cementing a community in the making. Institutionalization further created the conditions for the emergence of a public, who learned to share a set of principles of appreciation of this urban spectacle. A leisure habit, the consumption of the game thus became an everyday interaction resource, employed in a variety of contexts.

This institutionalization began in the early twentieth century but had its key period in the 1920s and 1930s. Founded in 1915 within the scope of the welfare and educational work carried out by an association of black Muslims (the Anjuman Anuaril Isslamo) who came from the Comoro Islands,[140] Grupo Desportivo Mahafil Isslamo was the first club in the suburbs of Lourenço Marques to be more than an ephemeral project.[141] The association was created in 1912 in the Xipamanine neighborhood and served as a contact platform between the various Muslim communities in the city.[142] Some suburban neighborhoods like Mafalala had strong Muslim communities that had moved from Macua territory, in the north.[143] The football club was a means to promote these relations, within a religious context where racial divisions were becoming stronger, separating recently converted black Muslims from mestiço Muslims, usually of Indian descent.[144] Shortly after the club's founding, a football pitch was built, with money gathered through subscription, in the Kokolwewne-Minkadjuíne area, in Zixaxa Road, a route connecting the poor neighborhood of Alto Maé to the Xipamanine market.[145] Between 1915 and the end of the 1930s, nearly two dozen clubs would be created in the suburbs of Lourenço Marques, most of which with statutes approved by the colonial administration. As in Mahafil's case, African clubs founded in the suburbs of Lourenço Marques functioned primarily as spaces in which interest groups were reproduced, as nodes in knowledge and solidarity networks and as gateways into urban life.

The decisive step to football's institutionalization in the suburbs was the creation, in 1924, of the Associação de Foot-Ball Africana (AFBA), which shortly afterward became the Associação de Futebol Africana. The AFA's creation was deeply influenced by the South African sports movement. Mohamed Sicândar, president of the Victoria da Malanga club, returning from a trip to the neighboring territory, decided to create a competition along the lines of South African ones. He spoke with Samo Matafene, a director in Clube Internacional (which later became Sport Nacional Africano) and with Castigo Miglietti, Tigre Gulama's president—which later became João Albasini.[146] Together, they created the AFA. In 1925 the first official championship took place and was won by Victoria da Malanga. In 1926 this club changed its name to Primo Rose, probably a derivation from Primrose, a city in Transvaal with significant mining activity where many Mozambicans worked.[147] In 1929, Primo Rose became Beira-Mar.[148]

One of the features of South African competitions, which greatly interested Mohamed Sicândar, was the fact that teams fought for a trophy and not just for money or a can of cashews.[149] Changing the nature of the reward was very significant indeed. The monetary award was only given to team members, although victory could be a source of local pride. The trophy, however, did not belong exclusively to the players, not even to the clubs, as these, whenever in the pitch, represented the public, club members, and residents from the neighborhood. Through this representation, a responsibility arose. Collectivized, rivalry ceased to be limited to a contest between two teams and became something experienced by a wider group of people. Suburban football had created the conditions for it to become a public spectacle, capable of mobilizing people, through associations and clubs that congregated individuals and strengthened preexisting identifications but that could also foster other forms of identification and belonging, namely the feeling that, differences notwithstanding, they all belonged to a new urban collective.

This particular capacity of football did not go unnoticed by the members of a politicized native elite who strove to unite a population segregated by the colonial regime. Until the beginning of the 1930s, *O brado africano*, the standard-bearer of this elite's sensibilities, had shown little interest in suburban football; it was placed at the bottom of a news hierarchy dominated by political intervention and protest against the colonial situation. The few news items that addressed football matters were descriptions of "downtown" clubs' matches, in which some mestiços, elements of an African petite bourgeoisie, took part. Suburban matches would merit the occasional notice but were covered in a section written in Ronga/

Landim, the main African language in the Lourenço Marques area. However, changes in Portugal's colonial system during the transitional period from the 1920s into the 1930s prompted a change of attitude. In the face of the local administration's tougher stance, associations became a means through which the local movement reorganized itself.

The first newspaper references to football activities in the suburbs reveal the existence of a close relation with the associative dynamic whose main support was Lourenço Marques's Grémio Africano. As Grémio's newspaper, *O brado africano* emphasized the connection between football's institutionalization in the suburbs and its own activities. The importance of *O africano* and *O brado africano* to understand the suburbs of Lourenço Marques in this colonial period, as some of the rarest and richest of written sources one may have access to, can have the effect of downplaying other lines of research, not so well documented. In the case of suburban football, for instance, the master narrative in *O brado africano* does not does give enough recognition to the crucial role played by Muslim communities in this process.

Grupo Desportivo João Albasini, which was founded in 1920 as Tigre Gulama, had its name changed in homage to the most prominent figure in African associativism, João Albasini, a mestiço who for a long time was *O brado africano*'s main writer and a patron figure of the Grémio Africano (GALM).[150] The influence of the GALM's members was also noticeable in the formation of Grupo Desportivo Beira-Mar (est. 1920), originally named Victoria da Malanga, founded by students who lived in Malanga, near Lourenço Marques. In 1922 the GALM would host a "sports commission."[151] Clube Internacional (1921), which later became Sport Nacional Africano, was close to Congresso Nacional Africano (African National Congress), the GALM's first dissenting faction led by black Muslims and Protestants, inspired by Marcus Garvey's pan-Africanism and linked to the Partido Nacional Africano (African National Party), founded in Lisbon in 1921.[152] It was also during this period that Luso-Africano was created, a football club close to the Luso-Africana Church, the strongest independent messianic religious organization active in southern Mozambique—the Igreja Episcopal Luso-Africana de Moçambique, which was also associated with the GALM, and resulted from dissension with the American Methodist Mission.[153]

In April 1930, *O brado africano* gave wide coverage to the beginning of the AFA's football championship, a regular competition with weekly fixtures, in which Mahafil Isslamo, Luso-Africano, Grupo Internacional, and Beira-Mar participated. This original nucleus was extended by Nova

Aliança, a club founded in 1924 by a Catalan priest—which explains why the team's football kit sported the colors of FC Barcelona; Vasco da Gama, a mestiço club with close ties to the GALM, founded in 1932; Sporting Clube Munhuanense, popularly known as Azar (bad luck),[154] founded in 1928 in the popular suburban neighborhood of Munhuana;[155] and Atlético Mahometano, a Muslim club created in 1929, in the wake of a split in Mahafil Isslamo.

In March 1931, during the AFA championship awards ceremony, presided over by Miguel da Mata, the AFA's president and a prominent member of the GALM, several speakers reflected on what the "practice of sports in an African milieu" represented.[156] Francisco de Haan, the GALM's official representative, recalled the association's engagement as a "bastion of the defense of our sacred political and civil interests" in a "sports movement that day by day becomes more globally present in our milieu." The following day, at the party given by Mahafil, the AFA's champion, for its players,[157] Francisco de Haan told both the clubs and the AFA about the need to have their statutes approved by the colonial administration, thus gaining an official status, something that only the ceremony's host had achieved. African sport, organized in and through associations, would become a unifying and civilizing instrument, fitting the "African evolution" program defended by the GALM.[158] The ceremony's consensual mood was upset by a speech given by Francisco da Silva, Beira-Mar's president, denouncing divisions between black and mestiço representatives, which still existed within African associativism. António Ceita, a GALM member and Grupo Internacional's president, answered, "sport does not recognize religions, castes or qualities, in short, sport is a physical and moral education that quells the enemy's need for justice."[159] The need for a consensus, which sports associations—"schools of urbanity, loyalty and chivalry," in the words of Jorge Albasini, the AFA's secretary, during the first ceremony—would help materialize, was, so it seemed, a long way off.

The existing internal clashes, which were a prominent feature in the formation of the local petite bourgeoisie, did not, however, put an end to football's increasing popularity. On 1 August 1934, the AFA was recognized by the colonial administration, following the approval of its statutes. With its head office in Zixaxa Road, it was constituted by representatives of its associate members. The elected president, Mário António Pereira, was a leading member of the GALM.[160] In comparison with the teams that took part in the 1930 championship, there were three new clubs in the 1934 season: Alto Mar Nhafoco, from Inhambane (which became Inhambanense in 1936—originally founded in 1930), and Beirense, from Beira, both representing the populations native to these two Mozambican provinces. The third, São José de Lhanguene, was the Catholic mission's club.[161] Outside of the founding group, there remained some teams playing in the suburbs of Lourenço Marques, such as Zambeziano and Victória Gazense, whose members came from, respectively, Zambezia and Gaza Provinces. Establishing themselves as nuclei in the organization of interest networks in the new urban environment, clubs identified by their regional bonds reflected the heterogeneous composition of the suburbs of Lourenço Marques.[162]

At the beginning of 1935 the construction of the new AFA pitch started in Xipamanine, an initiative undertaken by the two Muslim clubs, Mahafil and Atlético Mahometano. In a period of economic crisis, this demonstration of financial health revealed the commercial-interest networks behind these clubs. Concurrently, Beira-Mar announced the construction of its pitch, in the popular neighborhood of Chamanculo. In fact, the pitch was built by the Associação Afro-Maometana (Afro-Mohammedan Association), which was an association of black Muslims created in 1934. Mohamed Sicândar, who was an active member both at the club and in the association, was behind the deal that allowed Beira-Mar to use the field in exchange for half of the ticket revenue.[163]

Reflecting on this collective enthusiasm, Estácio Dias, a major figure in the GALM's history and one of its founders, wrote an editorial in O brado africano, celebrating the birth of an African associative spirit.[164] This enthusiasm, mostly present in sports associations, was, according to Dias, a sign of civilization. The African had reached a "rational consciousness, leaving behind the drinking establishments for gatherings where political life was debated and regeneration through sport was discussed." The movement, he said, still lacked cohesion, but people had to be patient.

Political Control

The chances to politicize the sports movement in Lourenço Marques were quite meager in the mid-1930s. Estácio Dias's discourse attributed to the suburban sports movement the role of civilizational educator, in a manner not too dissimilar to the notions of physical reinvigoration expounded by the regime and which now, under the GALM's initiative, had to be democratized. The colonial administration imposed rigid supervision over African associations, in an attempt to circumscribe their formation and activity and to co-opt their members. The creation of Instituto Negrófilo (Negrophile Institute), in 1932, an association of assimilated black men, was supported by the regime and arranged with local businessmen and with the South African labor recruitment company the Witwatersrand Native Labour Association (WNLA).[165] The promotion of a black petite bourgeoisie contributed to the breakup the associative movement, exploiting racial and social divisions already present in the sports field.[166]

"What did the Portuguese—not the Portuguese, the colonizer—what did he do?" Issufo asked me. "What he did was to make the blacks oppress other blacks. He created division. The mestiço oppressed the other mestiço. We had the Associação Africana, which integrated mestiços and blacks as assimilados. That was what politics was about. . . . The Chinese had a Chinese club, and while they didn't play football, they had their own associations. The Portuguese had their fraternities as well, the Casa do Algarve or the Casa das Beiras. There were these divisions. The Indians had the Hindus and the Pakistani section, each with their own separate lives."

Unable to mobilize any type of collective protest, far removed from the political arena and, more pressingly, from the labor sphere, the center of the Portuguese domain, this African elite was gradually driven away from indígena interests, of which it claimed to be a representative.[167] Political surveillance over the clubs' activity also increased. During the process that led to the approval of its statutes, Grupo Desportivo Beirense was investigated by the DSAC. This investigation was driven by fears that some members of these clubs were linked with Protestant churches,[168] something that had already been the cause for the vetoing of other associations' and clubs' statutes.[169] Although there was nothing suspicious about Beirense's founders,[170] the approval of the club's statutes was successively denied in 1942, 1949, and 1950. The council administrator, upon consultation by the DSAC, argued that there were too many clubs, "given the colored population in the city and suburbs." Vitória Gazense was investigated on account of a hypothetical connection of its members to the Wesleyan Church[171] and to the União dos Negros Lusitanos da Colónia de Moçambique (Union of Portuguese Black Men from Mozambique), an association that had its statutes approved in 1936 but that would be dissolved a year later, for having "changed its objectives." A complaint alerted the DSAC to disputes and political discussions taking place on the African native languages in the general assemblies of the União dos Negros Lusitanos.[172]

Renamed the Associative Center for Mozambican Blacks, in 1937, the Instituto Negrófilo (Negrophile Institute) was closed down by the colonial administration in 1965, on suspicion of political infiltration. The links between the center and the AFA team Sport Nacional Africano were brought up by some suburban players, as was the case with Abissínia Ali, an Atlético Mahometano player and one of the first African sports journalists, at the *Lourenço Marques Guardian:* "The thing about Sport Nacional Africano is that it had a political element. That's why when the war broke out in Africa these clubs started being targeted . . . by the former political police, the PIDE." The state surveillance apparatus, which was gradually redefined and reinforced over time—namely, since the creation of the Gabinete dos Negócios Políticos (Cabinet of Political Affairs), in 1959, and the Serviços de Centralização e Coordenação de Informação de Moçambique, (SCCIM) in 1961—would always be vigilant of the activities of sports clubs and associations in Mozambique. However, these were clearly not the primary focus of their concerns.

The Assimilation Mechanism

The employment of these coercive surveillance mechanisms, which were particularly attuned to external interference, became a way to complement the mechanism of social control intrinsic to the system of assimilation, which aimed to divide the African associative movement and to create a kind of urban indirect rule. A space of privilege, a gateway into the European world, and a means of seducing the local leaders, assimilation brought about an ambiguous social territory.[173] The difficulty of conceiving of a common project in the suburbs can be attested in the wording of the statutes submitted by African clubs for approval by the colonial administration. Run by African members, following the exclusion imposed by European associations, local clubs could not find a common definition of "an African," a matter that gave rise to racial, regional, and ethnic schisms. Escaping the "indígena condition" epitomized the social aspirations of the assimilados, as well as those who thought of themselves as being close to achieving this category, a symbolic stumbling block to the organization of more effective resistances.

In 1935, Xipamanine's pitch, a bastion of African football, was inaugurated in the presence of Sul do Save's governor general, the mayor of Lourenço Marques, and the AFLM's president.[174] Although represented at the highest level, the colonial administration did not contribute to the pitch's construction. The governor was once again present when Beira-Mar inaugurated its playing field, in the following year. On these occasions, the AFA, the GALM, and the Instituto Negrófilo's representatives were entitled to make a speech.[175] The presence of African associations at official ceremonies, thus securing a place in "colonial life" for an "African petite bourgeoisie," confined them to a subordinate position, with little room for open protest. In 1932, when Armindo Monteiro, the *ministro do ultramar* (overseas minister), came to visit, there was a great sports party in which a match between AFA teams preceded another one between Ferroviário and a selection of local players.[176] In 1939, when General Carmona, president of the Portuguese Republic, visited Mozambique, this ritual was repeated.[177] These rituals of subordination,[178] occasions when the social hierarchy was represented, revealed the position occupied by the African associative movement. Toward the end of the 1930s the lack of associative involvement led the Associação Africana (African Association, previously known as the GALM) to circulate a letter requesting the return of former members who had left, disillusioned with the association's course.[179]

While the presence of members of an elite in leadership positions at many Lourenço Marques African football clubs reinforced their position as intermediaries with European society, this status also had an impact within the borders of the local society. The leadership of sports associations legitimated the hierarchies present in the social structure of the suburbs. To acquire a status in the suburbs of Lourenço Marques gradually came to depend on certain individuals' abilities to deal with the power structures imposed by colonialism, as indeed was the case in other neighboring African contexts.[180] Football clubs and associations, "modern" institutions whose operation required the mastery of bureaucratic instruments and official procedures, became fields of activity in which educational resources, command of Portuguese language, integration in the labor market, adoption of a European lifestyle, and participation in associations recognized by the colonial power were valued qualities.[181] For the majority of players I talked to, taking a political stand also depended on possessing this kind of capital. The players' indifference to the terms used to discuss politics and take political action does not imply, however, that they do not hold an opinion as to the situation in which they were placed: "It was only a matter of club rivalry, there were no politics in those days," according to Coluna. "We were indifferent to politics, all we cared about was football," Issufo said. And he added: "There was politics in the AFA, but only for the select few, it was not for everyone . . . but that would only come much later anyway. Most of them were members of the Centro Associativo dos Negros. That's where you see some young men appear that would then go to Tanzania in search of independence. In these parts people were mostly out of it. Even in the Centro dos Negros, it wasn't your average man in the street, but doctors, hand-picked from a community that had a completely different status from the rest of them." According to Hilário, "Craveirinha got involved in politics because he had a cultural baggage that was out of the ordinary. And for that reason anything Craveirinha said was sacred to us. If Craveirinha had wanted us to . . . that whole Mafalala gang would join FRELIMO and go to war. But that wasn't his thing, he didn't want us to get involved in it, he wanted us to stick to sports . . . and he pulled it off."

The community accorded these notables a local status, often achieved through the fact that the individual was a spokesperson, gatekeeper to the colonial world, promoter and vehicle of habits and consumptions. In Lourenço Marques, this prominence was regulated by the assimilado's condition. These notables operated within a framework of political action that was constrained by their singular social condition, resulting both from their role as intermediaries of the colonial system, even though they were socially discriminated, and their contingent position of leadership in the peripheral society of Lourenço Marques. Observed only through a political lens, these figures, placed along a narrative thread leading directly to the independence of Mozambique, are underestimated in their role as elements of cultural and social transition, bridges between the centers and the peripheries, nodes in growth networks and components of a precarious social cohesion.

The Spectacle by the Suburb, for the Suburb

In 1943, Mozambique's governor general, José Tristão da Cunha, in a report sent to the Ministério das Colónias (Colonial Ministry), stated that Mozambique's cultural activity, concentrated in Lourenço Marques, was poor and only included, for the most part, what he called "culture for whites."[182] Only in sports, he added, was there a place for the indígenas. In the cultural universe that the governor referred to, defined along erudite and socially situated lines and cherishing the activities of theaters, museums, and some cinemas, the scenario was bleak; associative dynamics, on the other hand, flourished: "In the colony, there are many associations of all kinds, cultural, economic, regionalist, sporting, recreational, welfare, and charitable. This associative fever even reaches the actual indígena. There are fourteen associations run by black men spread throughout the colony, almost all of them pertaining to sports, with football, which is much liked by the indígenas, as its main sport.[183]

The political inconsequence of the sports associative movement did not weaken football's strength as a community-building instrument. In the suburbs AFA competitions stood out by their symbolic significance. An organized suburban spectacle, football matches gained a status of their own, as a result of being the basis of a modern calendar-based leisure activity, where groups representing the growing community faced each other. AFA matches were also the only suburban football competitions to benefit from news coverage, though at first only by *O brado africano*. The news coverage immortalized the spectacle, leaving a version of the events for posterity, one that would be discussed by a community of readers that, although small, disseminated the information through their contact networks, thus consolidating an ever-growing football narrative.[184] Teams played before the local population, following football association rules, overseen by a referee, in paid spectacles, something that, in an impoverished milieu, lent it some gravitas. These matches differed from the basis of suburban football, the peladas de bairro (neighborhood matches) organized in a more haphazard manner, with teams that at the time were made up of a variable number of players, on improvised fields or on AFA pitches, with variable lengths and often specific sets of rules and local adaptations. The adoption of performance modalities closer to the orthodox version of football had an impact on the local game patterns but did not wipe out the performative principles and classifications that legitimated the movements that suburban players had brought from neighborhood matches. Subject to a set of rules that constrained the players' performance, the brand of football played by AFA players did not cut its ties with the informal football being played in improvised suburban pitches.

Suburban competitions were an integral part of the community's leisure activities: they were a spectacle organized by the suburb, for the suburb. Newspaper articles from the early 1930s describe numerous spectators in Xipamanine, extolling the presence of "girls, with their new dresses, as well as ladies, children and gentlemen."[185] Spectators tried to accommodate themselves the best they could, as there were no stands at the pitches. Saide Mogne recalled that some people, in order to sit down, "brought a box from home," while others brought their own chair; whoever brought a chair "already had a certain status." Kids, he remembers, tried to get into the pitches any way they could, and often succeeded—by carrying a player's boots or towels, for instance. According to Hamido Nazimo, a former Mahafil Isslamo player, neighborhood supporters gathered, organized excursions, and traveled to the pitch where the match took place. The spectators enlivened the spectacle with "songs, drumming, and dances." Hamido Nizamo (b. 1943), who played for Mahafil Isslamo during the early 1960s and who grew up playing in the suburban neighborhoods, described some of these games:

> It was beautiful football. It was a joy to watch those matches. So the grounds were full, the Mahafil one and the Beira-Mar one alike. These grounds would be full every time; there were even organized excursions. People would be divided into groups, they

would sing and dance and there were these girls that would go round with these ribbons to collect donations, anything to help out . . . there were traditional songs, *batucadas*, everyone would cheer . . . the associates would contribute through fundraising bazaars, that's how you got the revenue to keep the club going. Sometimes someone from the club's board would prepare soup in their own home. Players would go there before putting on their kit and they would eat some soup before the match. Another one would offer some snacks and the whole kit was washed in somebody's home, a board member's home.

The best players became local heroes. Going to a football match, as mentioned by Phyllis Martin when describing the game's ritual in colonial Brazzaville, "was to be at the heart of a city experience. Nowhere else could one encounter drama on such a large scale and share it with old and new friends."[186]

Meeting the requirements of the "football association," in a spectacle that was conceived in accordance with the modern game's rituals, demanded not just that players follow the rules but that they present themselves neatly, with a full kit, boots included, or at least some kind of footwear. The statutes of some African clubs, besides introducing a set of administrative and protocol procedures, imposed a strict dress code for athletes and associates, when representing their club. This was a symbol of public respectability and of the adoption of European custom and usage, which was also a condition for achieving assimilation status, instigating the use of Western clothes as a means of connecting to and belonging to the urban world.[187] Spectators at AFA matches were mindful of these matters of presentation, all the more so in moments of communitarian sociability.

From a legal viewpoint, at the AFA, as noted by Issufo Batata, and contrary to what happened in the practice of football in the cement city, everyone was accepted "without distinction . . . no documents were demanded, and it did not matter if you were an *indígena*, *assimilado*, or white. Whoever wanted to play, played." During our conversation Hilário confessed that he did not recall ever seeing a "white man playing in the suburbs," but then he remembered an exception: "There was only one player that wanted to play in African football. He played for Sporting Lourenço Marques. His name was Paiol, from Madeira. He was the only white man I knew and he came because he was my friend. Because I played with him at Sporting and then at Xipamanine. And so this Paiol fellow wanted to play . . . I can't recall right now whether he did play, in the end. But he was the only one." Abíssinia Ali vows that, except for Mahafil, and even in clubs with religious ties, such as Atlético Mahometano and São José, there was no discrimination: "socially, everyone was accepted."

Internal Stratification

Access to sports practice and consumption in the suburbs of Lourenço Marques did not take place on a level playing field but rather expressed the internal divisions in that part of the city. The need for a kit, and especially footwear, was a way of narrowing the players' selection. In this context, in 1943, Beira-Mar's players' jobs reveal a moderately privileged professional status: five of them were printers and one a newspaper binder, five worked as locksmiths (most of them in the railway), and there was also a driver, a shopworker, a pharmacy employee, a bookbinder, an upholsterer, and a typist.[188] Saide Mogne confirmed that "not everyone could play football." Most of the players were "the sons of somebody or other, a homeowner with his own business." Almost everyone had a job, but most belonged to relatively stable families, which allowed them to "buy a pair of sheepskin boots, knee pads, shorts." Only "rarely, very rarely," he adds, "would a destitute individual show up." Some of the poorer individuals saw their talents rewarded by being sponsored by a trader or a club owner. Possession of footwear marked the transition from "peladas de bairro" (neighborhood matches) to AFA matches, which was a social promotion of sorts—a promotion that required talent, but also some money. When he started playing for Mahafil's reserves, Issufo Batata started wearing boots. Club owners, Mogne says, paid for their registration and the issuing of an AFA card: "Everything else, boots, socks, and shorts, was bought by the players themselves. They only were given the club shirt." The obligation to play in boots, as pointed out by Matine, was a problem for some players, who were used to playing barefoot and would never get used to it: "Many were lost, great football players that were lost along the way."

"All neighborhoods had some good players and most of them played barefoot," Matavela told us. "I often played barefoot, up until 1969. Then I would play in trainers, because they were cheaper. The suburban teams would often play in trainers because boots were expensive. Some of those who played downtown would steal boots from the clubs they played for and take them to the suburbs. Some played better when they were barefoot. . . . We had no idea where we got our strength from, we just played on and on."

"In the suburbs the game was tough, nobody had boots," Vicente confirmed. "You wouldn't play barefoot, but there were no proper boots. Any shoe would do. Downtown they had boots. If someone fell and hurt himself, he would just get off the pitch and drink a *uputo*. Do you know what that is? A uputo is something you prepare in a clay jar, you use flour and throw a whole bunch of stuff in there, let it ferment, and that's it. It gives you strength. You'd find it on every corner. All the establishments sold it. They would drink it before and during the match. That thing went to your head. Uputo is made from corn stuff, mixed, and boiled for a couple of days. It's good, it's really good. That was our stimulant."[189]

The social distance between an AFA player and what Mogne terms a "down-and-out individual," one who only seldom appeared in these competitions, stretched across a wide set of social conditions. These conditions became progressively more complex as the social division of labor became more diversified in the city, but also as football spread more widely among the suburban population. Lourenço Marques's labor structure had little order to it and included several occupations, many of them of a so-called informal nature. A territory built by its own inhabitants, the suburbs could hardly be compared to the organized South African proletarian suburbs.[190] Some of these inhabitants were on the move to the South African labor market, a trend that was responsible for the proletarization of a large number of Mozambicans. This migrant demographic gradually decreased, making up 15 to 16 percent of city dwellers in 1968.[191]

Most men worked as "servants" or unskilled industrial workers. At the end of the 1960s, in Lourenço Marques, of the 130,000 Africans that official statistics counted as active, 30,000 (23,000 men and 7,000 women) held jobs—as servants, tutors, valets—that fell under the category of "personal services."[192] "Manufacturing industries" employed 19,500 workers (12,500 men), "public works," "transportation, storage, and communications" employed 11,000 African workers, and 12,000 held posts in "commerce, banking, insurance" (7,000 men).[193] Women, underrepresented in the statistics, also worked to complement men's salaries. At the end of the 1960s, there were 27,500 women classified as "domestic," who worked in family farming in the outskirts of the city, harvesting, or in small-scale trade. Grupo Desportivo Beirense's founders, for instance, despite having steady jobs, mostly in proletarized services, did not come near the professional standing of the local elite, predominantly constituted by civil servants, traders, printers, specialized laborers, and qualified and semiqualified workers in the railway and other public and private companies. Among Beirense's founding members, there was one fish trader, two shopworkers, three drivers, seven caretakers, one lifeguard, one dockworker, one ticket collector, and five servants." Not all its founders and directors were assimilated.[194] It is likely that Beirense's players, like those of other clubs, reflected their leaders' social standing. Most of Clube Vitória Gazense's players were workmen in Fábrica Vitória.[195] Hilário da Conceição talks of suburban football players as "guys who lived in the neighborhoods, in huts, shall we say—wood-and-zinc houses" and worked in "factories or petrol stations, in the docks or the railway."

The AFA championship, run by local elites (namely, assimilados), also involved semiqualified workers, carpenters, shoemakers, and even, though fewer, workers from less well paid jobs, such as masons, stevedores, or construction workers. The ones who played were those who, with greater or lesser professional stability, and with or without the club's or some benefactor's help, met the minimum requirements to compete. Some clubs maintained rigid selection policies, while others were open to individuals from lower social ranks. Football, through its competitive logic, sustained by the search for talented players, created its own conditions for social and professional mobility. Talented players began to be coveted by the best clubs and to be rewarded for their participation. Hilário remembers the promises made by the directors of some African clubs: "if you win [one match], you get a case of beer; if you win everything, you get a demijohn of wine." Other motives, related to the dynamics of suburban life, led to a greater circulation of players: a change of neighborhood, a wedding, the athlete's wish to play for a different club.[196] The social network grew during the filiation process of groups of supporters and associates, identified with their neighborhood club or united by some other bond. These clubs attracted, through various local activities, an increasingly larger number of individuals. These initiatives contributed to strengthening these supporters' ties with their neighborhoods and with a wider suburban space consolidated through the shared practices and references that popular urban culture helped shape.[197] The associative dynamic contributed to the creation of networks of social bonds that broke free of the closed social circuits grounded in their members' regional origin. While they did neutralize the strength of ethnic and religious ties, an enduring element of social reproduction, popular culture, and sports in particular, helped lay the ground for another form of urban interdependence, already fostered by other phenomena.

In neighborhood matches, played barefoot in deserted fields, there was a greater social diversity among players. Matine remembers that in these neighborhood peladas, especially in the poorer neighborhoods, which had populations from Lourenço Marques's surrounding regions, there were a lot of "carpenters, masons and various apprentices, some who ironed clothes in a family house, some who washed clothes in the suburbs, in the river . . . some who were cotton pickers." These people played even further into the suburbs, for ten paus, twenty paus. This collective, created in contrast with the universe of the cement city, was itself stratified, something that became gradually more conspicuous as new populations arrived in the city. Thus, the practice and consumption of football in the suburbs helped differentiate among the local inhabitants. Devoid of urban habits, the newly arrived populations were less engaged in sports activities and in other modern leisure practices. Social distinction also operated at other levels. The playing field, the athletes' kit, the chance to earn money, and compliance with the norms and regulations of association were among the features that granted football the power to draw a clear dividing line between types of players and football spectators.

New Sociabilities

The growth in the practice and consumption of the game was not the only means through which sports membership generated new urban ties. Clubs in the neighborhoods enlivened communitarian life. Among the activities they promoted was the regular organization of parties. The parties of Vasco da Gama or Atlético, a mestiço club that never played in the AFA, adopted the European precepts, influenced by the exclusive dance balls promoted by English clubs. Gala balls with formal suits and dresses, where jazz bands played, reproduced the spirit of the time in a cosmopolitan city in which bars and night clubs abounded.[198] The lower social groups, on the other hand, opted for street parties, in which Western musical genres were played alongside traditional drumming and dancing.[199] In many of these parties, as mentioned by Hilário, there was no band, so people danced to records played on a gramophone. Organized in a relatively informal way, these parties took place near the "cantinas" nuclear spaces in the suburbs, usually managed by Indian and Portuguese tradesmen, where alcohol was sold alongside other commercial products.[200] In 1933, *O brado africano* described the atmosphere surrounding football in Munhuana, a neighborhood whose main club was Munhuanense Azar, a team whose membership included "the entire elite from the surrounding areas" and the club with the most "impressive" group of supporters, which celebrated even defeats with "rockets, clapping and . . . drinks." "There is no need to tell the reader," concluded *O brado*'s reporter, "that as we are writing this article, an itinerant vending van loaded with drinks is being driven around Munhuana, to properly celebrate Azar's victory."[201]

The more solemn festivities, usually to mark an association's anniversary, had as their main event a tournament organized with teams from

South Africa. At night, after the match, Saide Mogne recalls, a ball was organized; several girls went round with a box to collect donations; each individual offered "one escudo, two escudos and fifty cents." As was the case with football in the cement city, the suburb developed, from the 1930s, a series of regular contacts with South African associations and teams.[202] Paradoxically, long before it was a nation, Mozambique, through football, competed in matches known as internationals, both in the suburbs and downtown. In the AFA this interchange was limited to relations with South African associations and clubs. The AFA developed a close relation with the Transvaal African Football Association and the Johannesburg African Football Association as well as with their clubs, and even had a representative in the region. Beira-Mar may have been the first suburban club to "become international," by visiting South Africa in 1933.[203] In 1936, Johannesburg's All-Blacks Football Club played against a selection of AFA players.[204]

The formation of a selection of local performers, contemplated in the association's regulations, strengthened "African football's" identity and became an essential mechanism to, in Benedict Anderson's words, "imagine a community."[205] The process of imagining was anchored in the daily handling of a specific knowledge, produced by football competition and translated into individual and collective narratives that were then discussed. Discussions regarding the criteria for selecting the best local players were rife with accusations of favoritism. These arguments, revealing the importance of racial, neighborhood, and religious identities, ended up legitimizing a communitarian consciousness. *O brado africano* amplified the discussion, placing it in importance above daily conversation.[206] When AFA teams traveled to South Africa, groups of supporters gathered and, with the colonial administration's permission, rode in a bus that accompanied their team. Mogne took part in some of these trips. South Africans, he says, "managed to establish a blockage system through which no white man entered the pitch." These "international" matches were privileged moments where it was possible to compare match styles and assess the strength of the local clubs before the onlooking public and press.

The interchange between AFA clubs and clubs from outside the territory contrasted with an almost total absence of relations between Lourenço Marques's African clubs and Mozambican clubs from outside the capital.[207] The same was true of the AFLM championship. This confinement revealed the fragility of economic social, cultural and linguistic ties between the various regions of the Mozambican territory, as well as the inability of the Portuguese colonial state to consolidate a de facto sovereignty. The growth of football competitions in the colonial capital, a sign of the evolution of the process of economic and political integration, was essentially an evidence of the dynamics of a localized urbanization process and its relation with South African modernization. These networks of economic relations helped to shape a singular colonial territory, whose actual configuration did not match the one established by political treaties or by cartographic projections as truthful representations of reality.

A Frontier

In a context where the social structure was deeply affected by the racial conditions, the suburban community emerged as a parallel social structure with its own hierarchy and logic, although these were derived from the relations established with the colonial power structure and, above all, within its labor market. Sports practices and consumptions translated the internal diversity of these suburbs. Within the space of the suburb, a social organization with its own norms, values, and power relations, there emerged a universe with its own relatively autonomous forms of mobility, recreation, and sociability.[208] However, this mosaic made up of neighborhoods where different interest groups coexisted, had a primordial frontier, the line that divided it from the cement city. The formation of a field of sports practices and consumptions expressed the concreteness of this frontier, the ambiguities of the Portuguese "assimilation" system and its racialist nature. The colonial system, as stated by Issufo Batata, classified the landowner as an indígena, thus taking away his rights. The indígena "could not be out at certain hours of the night, could not go to the cinema or to the theater." For the Portuguese state, the institutionalization of football in the suburbs created a cheap mechanism of social integration. However, this network had to be surveilled.

When, still during the 1930s, due to the bad condition of Xipamanine's pitch, some AFA tournaments were played on the fields of "downtown clubs," the suburban community lost interest, as if leaving their own space, the place where they grew up socially, culturally, and affectively, was in itself a form of violence. It was difficult, as *O brado africano* noted, to take "people out of Munhuana."[209] Although the newspaper celebrated this "contact" as a way to advance the African and take him out of the suburb, a kind of antechamber to the civilized city, suburban football belonged to its own space, where daily life was built collectively. The various borders that persisted in the suburb, places of dispute between different interest groups, were still less rigid than the one separating the suburb from the colonizer's world. In the cement city, the interaction order imposed upon suburban inhabitants a basic inequality, one that was nonnegotiable.

Vicente Lucas recalls that people "were afraid to go downtown. We avoided going downtown; what would we do there?" In his opinion, the influence of the South African system was felt: "the Englishmen came from over there on Friday to spend the weekend in Lourenço Marques. The black must be separated, the white on the right, the black on the left, and that had to happen in Lourenço Marques also." South Africa's ascendancy over Lourenço Marques was used as a recurrent trope to justify local racism. The circulation of Africans from the city suburbs into the colonial center was virtually restricted to paid duties, a situation that would remain unchanged until the end of the Portuguese colonial power.[210]

According to Hilário da Conceição, Mafalala was a "border" between the cement city and the suburbs, and if "a guy was born there, he would die there, and there was no need to leave." When, in 1953, Hilário accepted a job offer and moved from his suburban club to Sporting Clube de Lourenço Marques, until then composed exclusively of white players, his friends in Mafalala would ask him, before they finally cut off any ties with him, "So you'll be playing with the jackals now?" *Jackal* was the name given to white South Africans:. "When I signed my contract and got back to the neighborhood I told everyone straightaway, 'Hey, I signed a contract with Sporting!' 'What, you signed a contract with that bunch of racists?' 'Hey, I need food on my plate, I need to support my mum, and my brothers and sisters, and I have no money, I'm not rich. I signed a contract because they got me a job.'" This fundamental divide, which defined the contours of a split citizenship grounded in a racial ecology, did not, however, cancel the effects of the singular urban experience to which football was necessarily tied.

4 ~ A Suburban Style of Play

Anthropologist António Rita-Ferreira attributed to the game of football, as it is played in the suburbs of Lourenço Marques, an unruly and almost illogical character: "Many youngsters form spontaneous groups in the suburbs" and "in the scarce vacant lots, in their leisure time, they practice a brand of football devoid of any rules."[1] However, contrary to what is implied here, the performance of football players in the suburbs of Lourenço Marques, whether in the neighborhood matches described by Rita-Ferreira or in the more institutionalized competitions, organized by the AFA, did not spring from a series of random and arbitrary actions. The present chapter carries out an archaeology of the style of play in the suburbs of Lourenço Marques and begins by registering how the hopes that an African petite bourgeoisie pinned on the educational and civilizational virtues of this modern game faltered in the face of a local appropriation that brought into the game all the dramas and contradictions that traversed the construction of the periphery of Mozambique's capital. By zooming in on some of the features of the performative structure of the local game, namely those gestures among the motor repertoires that were valued the highest, the glossary of the movements specific to suburban football published by the poet José Craveirinha in *O brado africano* contributed to reconstructing this local performance. His description gives us access to some of the practices that defined a particular exchange, establishing a starting point for interviews with the players that took part in such matches and for the interpretation of the meanings they attributed to their own actions.

ON THE LAW OF FOOTBALL, VIOLENCE, AND DISEASE

In the suburbs of Lourenço Marques, the growing number of neighborhood matches reflected the close ties between football and the urban construction process. In the vacant lots between the reed houses, football was played under several different guises and local moralities. In this context, betting, whether with money or cans of cashews, was an important motivational tool for the sporting performance, and it spurred neighborhood rivalries. Football's transformation into an institutionalized suburban spectacle, within the bounds of AFA competitions, gave the game a different meaning. The regular spectacle, with paid admission and run by local notables, established itself as a focal point for the community to gather around. It was this growing importance of football, noticeable in the suburbs at least from the 1920s onward, that led some members of the local elite to idealize the game as an educational tool, promoting African unity under the banner of respectability. The AFA championship would provide proof of Africans' capacity for assimilation, consecrating the effort of its organizers: regenerators of the suburb, agents of modernity, and, as such, privileged mediators with the colonial power. The game's practice, translated into the players' gestures, would become a school of civilization.

To achieve this goal, the game had to be played according to the laws laid out by the centers that codified the "universal" version of *football association*, the International Board, and FIFA.[2] AFA rules reproduced the International Board's regulations, as adapted by the Johannesburg African Football Association (JAFA), which meant there were a few specific adjustments to be made.[3] The official rules of the AFA, approved in 1934,[4] set a minimum standard for the movements of players,[5] by defining which gestures were legitimate and which were ruled out.[6] The rules' existence in writing fixed the norm, granting it a specific authority, in the sense given to this term by Jack Goody[7]—a verifiable authority, abstracted from particular situations and with the power to encompass a vast and inclusive community of exchanges and beliefs. To coordinate and supervise its application, an organizational and bureaucratic structure was created, similar to the sports associations that represented the colonial power. Excluded from the football association organized by Europeans in the city center, African clubs, under colonial legislation, could establish a parallel body with identical functions, promoting the same activity and obeying the same rules, a procedure that was not extendable to other areas of colonial life where the law, also fixed in writing, was an exclusion factor. The adoption of football's universal law placed Lourenço Marques's suburban football, despite segregation, within the "world dynamic." The adoption of association rules allowed African teams, at least theoretically, to play against teams that followed the same norm. The employment of football's universal rules also enabled the basic exercise of assessing the comparative value of different performances. By showing that the African player could perform according to football's universal law, his ability to be integrated in other spheres of social life was demonstrated.

In order for the correlation between sports practice and the claim for citizenship to prove consequential and fruitful, as a practical political element, the football pitch was expected to represent a space of relations in which compliance with the law was manifest and where the players' movements expressed the emergence of a "proper" behavior, thus enunciating the new historical condition of the suburban community.

Since the abstract democracy of the football pitch, as the basis of an idealized "bodily ethos," depended on the strength of the law, the AFA statutes paid a great deal of attention to the figure of the referee. The referee, who represented the written law and was responsible for enforcing it and penalizing whoever transgressed it, for determining the fairness of on-field movements and interactions, had to evaluate the outcome of any interaction on the pitch, circumscribing the symbolic significance of gestures by framing them within the intrinsic morality of abiding by the law: the referee, as the arm of the law, thus helped shape a fair and egalitarian "reality." Anchored to the interpretation of the law, his subjectivity instituted an "objectivity": "a foul exists whenever the referee spots it."[8] In 1935, in the rooms of Grémio Africano, there were lectures on some of the principles of association, namely addressing the "referee's authority" and the offside rule, one of modern football's basic tenets.[9] The regulation of the game's space and time was established as one of its grounding principles of organization.

The AFA regulations, published in 1935, spelled out the conditions under which the performance was to be placed.[10] The regulation of the game's space and time was rendered through basic organizational principles. The pitches had to be "properly marked" and have "nets, posts, and flags in their proper places." The document stipulated the match's duration, sixty minutes, divided in two equal halves with a five-minute break, as well as their regularity, creating a kind of "football time," with its own schedule, inscribed within a leisure time that, in turn, was defined through its relation to labor time.[11] The referee controlled the game time with a whistle, a kind of sonorous extension of the clock. The whistle, which served the order set by the clock, signaled the beginning and end of football time. The AFA players were identified by a card, which had to be presented before the beginning of each game.[12] The card certified the player's inclusion within a community of practitioners and established a set of rights, specially the possibility of taking part in the game, as well as a set of duties. The AFA thus became a minisociety of sorts. Whoever failed to abide by its rules incurred a penalty.

The gate receipts served to cover organizational expenses, such as ground security and pitch maintenance, as well as to offer financial aid to injured players, a specific welfare function that expressed, on a small scale, the need for local forces to take into their own hands the role of providing social assistance, one they fulfilled earnestly, even if rather imperfectly.

A space for the affirmation of communitarian ethics, the game was also expected, given the role sports played in some Western countries, to have a regenerating effect. It should, so the reasoning went, be a way to fight against the modern world's perverse effects, which now, worryingly, were reaching the suburbs. In 1938, Guidione Vasconcelos Matsinhe, the AFA's secretary, pointed out, in a tone close to the official speeches by some of the key public voices within the Portuguese regime, that sports prevented the "withering of the race," plagued by urban diseases such as syphilis and tuberculosis.[13] Matsinhe had written a book, published in one of the local native languages, on the need for morality in daily life. In the above-mentioned newspaper article, he took a stand against "clandestine prostitution," "unsanitary conditions," "bad nourishment," and "public dance balls." At urban balls, he wrote, "youngsters plunge their lungs into whirls of dust teeming with germs of all kinds, in small rooms with no ventilation, drowning themselves in cold drinks that are served in glasses washed in that very same germ-filled water."[14]

The ability of suburban football to establish itself as a regenerating activity depended little, however, on the wishes of AFA leaders or their moralizing rhetoric. The intention to regulate the dominant interaction order in the local game was grounded in the belief that the regenerating morality of the rule and the law, as laid out in the book, would impose itself on reality. Time would prove them wrong.

VIOLENCE

In Lourenço Marques, since the first decades of the twentieth century, not just in the suburbs but also in the cement city, there was a clear contrast between football conceived as a regeneration mechanism and the football that was actually played on the fields. The players' motor habitus, instead of expressing itself through movements that fit the values of honor and respect for the laws of the game, gained a performative power that constantly challenged those laws and their morality. One of the most frequent transgressions to take place on the football pitches of Lourenço Marques was the execution of gestures that were deemed violent and were punished with a foul according to the official law. The penalty for these infractions, the foul, signaled the violation of a sports rule that, simultaneously, operated as an interactional convention with a wider everyday meaning, expressing the need for social regulation of the level of violence.

The phenomenon was observed in Lourenço Marques, already in the early 1920s, in the context of local European society's mundane activities. In 1923, shortly after winning the Lourenço Marques championship, the English Athletic Club played against Desportivo for the Taça de Honra (Honor Cup). The *Lourenço Marques Guardian* pointed out that Desportivo "employed plenty of violence and more than one deliberate trip was noticed."[15] The bilingual newspaper, directed at the community of British traders living in the city, added a few comments in its English-language version of the article: "It is regrettable that the spectators could not control their feelings at some of the decisions given by the referee who, on several occasions was forced to reprimand a section of the crowd."[16] The following year there was another match between the two teams at Desportivo's stadium. Once again, the *Guardian*'s reporter was far from pleased. The game, "a school of dedication," was turned into a "carnival" in which many *sportsmen* played alongside "other creatures who perverted everything, putting all shame aside to stoop as low as to throw themselves upon the propaganda of disorder and aggression," and the following words could even be heard: "break his shins."[17] Within a small milieu, where the "English practice" remained an example, some behaviors on and off the pitch were not considered proper: players' violence, their protests against a decision by the referee, the rowdy complaints of the crowd. In short, anything that did not fit the idealized notion of the "gentleman-player" or the "gentleman-spectator." At the time, referees were recruited from among the players and more often than not they were renowned sportsmen—which meant their impartiality was indisputable.

In that remote eastern coast of Africa one could witness a reaction to the popularization of football that had emerged decades earlier, against the historical backdrop of nineteenth-century England. The persistence of attitudes showing a lack of respect for the amateur ideal was reported by Mozambique's governor general, Tristão da Cunha, in 1943. "Football is the main sport, played with as much enthusiasm as in the metropolis and with a lack of discipline and sporting spirit that is most likely identical, here and there, judging by the number of sanctions handed out to the players and reported in the press."[18]

In the suburbs, some of the amateur ideals typical of the "English practice," even though they were not among the founding principles of the game, weighed heavily on the establishment of a local African sports movement, namely in the documents that stipulated how the AFA would be organized. The importance given to the law and to the figure of the referee was an attempt to mend behaviors that had been taking place with a worrying regularity.

In November 1930 the Vasco da Gama players walked out of their match against Munhanense Azar, held in Xipamanine, which triggered the public's anger and led to a series of violent clashes. A month later, the club's board justified their attitude in *O brado africano*, pointing out the difficulty of playing in Xipamanine, a field where brawls were commonplace.[19] Throughout the 1930s a number of newspaper columns included accounts of violent scenes during matches.[20] The approval of the AFA statutes and regulations, which announced the rebirth of football in the suburbs, was insufficient to put an end to these incidents. In September 1935, during a match between Mahafil and Vasco da Gama, supporters invaded the pitch and fights ensued.[21] In August 1936, Mahafil's players assaulted the referee, and a member of the public would be chosen to replace the one initially appointed. Violence against the keeper of the law had become so common that AFA-appointed referees often failed to appear for matches.[22] In the same month, Tayub Tricamo, a Mahafil director, wrote to *O brado africano* that it was "rare to watch a football match that did not involve boxing scenes or other violent spectacles" and there were often "punches, chases at the end of matches, broken legs." He concluded that "players should employ their technique rather than violence."[23] Two months later, the newspaper's reporter that usually attended AFA matches pointed out that, at that time, there was not a single match day that did not register some kind of clash.[24] In October 1936, *O brado africano* announced that the International Board had forbidden the use of metal plates in the players' boots.[25] The bodies that oversaw the rules of the game introduced changes to halt the pervasive violence, and local associations were entrusted with enforcing these rules.

In 1937, following a few more violent match days, with scenes "worthy of a battlefield,"[26] the AFA issued an unofficial note that stated that disorderly clubs would face severe penalties. The association guaranteed that from that date onward, regulations would be strictly observed.[27] However, the invocation and imposition of the power of the book—that is to say, of the power of football's orthodox model—demanded an institutional structure that could oversee and ensure its application. The AFA was unable to create such a structure. The success of this normative inscription depended on an adjustment between the values implicit in the norm and the bodies of players on which it was imposed. At the end of that year, *O brado africano* announced that the football tournament it had organized had ended in a scuffle.[28] The 1938 championship's second match day was "rife with accidents, broken legs, fighting scenes, and lousy refereeing."[29] Shortly after, at the end of a match between Atlético Mahometano and Mahafil Isslamo, referee Paulo Albasini was beaten up.[30] In July 1938 the match between Luso-Africano and Gazense had an equally sour end. *O brado africano* called it "the worst match ever played in Lourenço Marques."[31] Onfield violence spilled over to the stands of Beira-Mar's pitch, which was the second most important suburban venue. The boards that supported the stands were ripped loose and thrown as weapons. At the end of the battle, the stadium had been damaged beyond repair.

Assaults on referees persisted as a common feature in the development of African competitions. In 1942 the referee Custódio was repeatedly beaten.[32] In the following year it was announced that several referees were going to quit their position, citing repeated physical assaults.[33] In 1945 the AFA's new board of directors decided to "impose a set of rules and instructions on the clubs, in order for them to deal with certain abusive and undisciplined acts on and off the pitch."[34] The AFA wanted the paying spectator to see "actual football" and not "spectacles that more closely resemble boxing matches and barbaric fights."[35] This initiative did not put an end to the problem. In 1949, in the critical view of *O brado africano*, AFA matches were still tainted by "fighting scenes and bad refereeing."[36] In that same year, the newspaper stated that "incompetence, biased judgment, and the referee's inability to impose discipline are ruining the only sport practiced in the African milieu."[37] In 1953 the *Guardian desportivo*, in a report on the match between Beira-Mar and Atlético Mahometano, highlighted the amount of "unsporting plays, completely outside the rules of the game."[38]

DISEASE

The abundance of violent incidents during matches, involving both players and public, did not affect football's popularity in the suburbs. On the contrary, the game became an increasingly central spectacle in community life. The passionate relation between the public and the game, where conflict was rife, put players under enormous pressure and impacted their behavior. The terms according to which the game could establish itself as an educational factor were inverted. The ideal context, where the player's gesture, in accordance with the book, would become an instructive example to the public, was in stark contrast with a situation where the latter's militant devotion put pressure on players to act outside the law.

In the grip of passion, the fan was described as "sick" or "diseased," a common epithet both within the frame of settler football and in the African milieu. The football-stricken, or ball-stricken (*doente da bola*, "ball" being a common synecdoche for the game), was the description of an individual who, in this particular everyday sphere, had lost his sanity or balance.[39] The diseased condition explained their irrationality, the way in which, when it came to football, they would suspend their "normal" values in the throes of a passion so one-sided and all-consuming that it pushed aside all decency and respect, placing a disproportionate importance on an activity that many summed up, disparagingly, as that game where "eleven men run around chasing after a ball." While some may have perceived this condition as picturesque or even amusing, for those who saw reality as the ground for the realization of political and civilizational principles, the "football disease" was evidence of a process of degeneration. A large number of sick people together in one place, such as those that gathered in Xipamanine, would form an unruly, feral, dangerous mob, seemingly devoid of belief or purpose:[40] an affront to the petite-bourgeois and assimilationist morality of the local elite as well as to the discipline upheld by the colonial state. The figure of a diseased football fan became the more or less acceptable example of abnormal behavior—passionate and irrational, and seemingly beyond comprehension.

In 1936 in O *brado africano*, a tribune for the local public sphere, black journalist José Cantine, a member of the GALM and a teacher in the Sá da Bandeira school for indígenas, referred to the role of football in the construction of the suburban community and to its value within the frame of an ongoing debate among the local petite bourgeoisie—the debate on African evolution.[41] Cantine argues that something had gone awry in the African's assimilation process.[42] From the "European civilizing stream," the African assimilated only "its material elements, namely clothes and amusements, some of which do nothing but contribute to our stagnation and annihilation." Within the context of this negative assimilation, football was singled out: "the civilized and evolved among us do nothing but eat, drink, smoke, and ... kick a football around."[43] Football had become so central that suburban associative life seemed to be reduced to it: "We discuss football, we gather around football, we organize dancing soirées to promote football, and waste huge sums of money in maintaining football pitches. Bloody football."[44] Football, alongside "dancing and drinking," was part of a model of hedonist assimilation that precluded the implementation of an emancipatory project sustained "by the more ennobling qualities of white society": "There is something more important than fun and games—evolution, progress, fighting for our survival, education, bringing up our offspring."[45] He added that "to the majority of our people, civilization means simply to be fluent in some European language or other, to wear nice clothes, dance, kick a football, and nothing else."[46] The game was infected, one of the most notorious hosts of the "urban" sickness, a negative dimension of the colonial presence in Lourenço Marques.

SPORTING PURIFICATION

Football's decadence, reflected in the players' belligerent motor habitus and in the public's *disease*, elevated the practice of other sports, which better fulfilled a pedagogic role and conformed rather more to the "acceptable body." Athletics, introduced in the suburbs in the 1930s, became quite popular locally. Its internal logic was tied to the notion of bettering oneself, of setting and breaking records, and of establishing points of comparison: the ideal activity for the African athlete to display his qualities, like the celebrated Jesse Owens in Berlin's 1936 Olympic Games. While track and field served more assertive purposes, gymnastics became the model for the affirmation of respectability, an antidote against the corruptions of modernity, which contaminated a "new generation devoted, heart and soul, to the sports of dancing, smoking, and cinematographic poses."[47] According to Cantine, this generation was "physically useless, lacking pride or fighting ability." As an antidote to this state of affairs, gymnastics made it possible to assimilate the "best qualities of European civilization," constituting itself as a purifying element performed in a gymnasium, a closed and controlled environment, less exposed to external influences.[48] The Associação Africana team became a repository of the African gymnast's qualities. The athletes, "hard workers, upright and so often brilliant" showcased "the gradual coordination of movements and the gymnast's predisposition for intellectual development."[49] The Associação Africana tours in the metropolis, celebrated by the local media, especially by *O brado africano*,[50] attested to the African's ability to excel in more complex human activities that were scientific and aesthetically legitimized by the actual hierarchy imposed by the colonizer's official sports model. Gymnastics' motor habitus, which manifests itself through the execution of predetermined, predictable, and rational gestures, brought to the fore an image of purity and regeneration.

As symbol of assimilation, the practice of "respectable" sports, close to the values of a local petite bourgeoisie, authorized some members of the local African elite, whose worldview was framed and determined by the condition of the assimilado, to spurn the "obscure practices" that surrounded the development of football, a sport that spread across social and cultural barriers. Suburban football still displayed the symptoms of a certain "Africanization" or, even more significantly, an "indigenization"; it was a vehicle for witchcraft, for healers and sorcerers, symbols of the backwardness of Africans, of their practices and traditions. As the suburbs grew, there was, according to this point of view, ever growing evidence of a subverted assimilation. Social gatherings, such as the balls organized by Associação de Trabalhadores Indígenas (Native Workers Association), were described by J. L. J. Simango in *O brado africano*, as "contributing to a mental, moral and social backwardness"; he claimed that melodies lead to "vertiginous dancing where all consciousness is lost." These practices should be banished because "the worker needs rest" rather than "impertinent drumming." How would it be possible, the author wondered, for the suburban dweller to "feel like going to mass"?[51] Still, despite these worries, football was increasingly part and parcel of the world of the "perverted" suburb, moving ever further away from the universe of the best European practices, of which the game was not by any means an example.

FOOTBALL AS A SOCIAL PROBLEM?

The acts of public indiscipline and disorder in football also affected the matches in the cement city. The vicissitudes that accompanied football's growth in Lourenço Marques were not ignored by the colonial administration. After the Second World War, the increasing complexity of the urban situation, alongside the exponential intensification of activities and exchanges, led the state to try to exert a more effective control. To uphold public order, there was a need to put an end to acts of violence at football grounds. In 1950 the Comando da Polícia de Lourenço Marques (Lourenço Marques Police Command) issued a letter concerning the "indisciplina nos campos de jogos" (indiscipline at sports fields) in which it declared its willingness to put an "end, once and for all, to the constant disturbances of public order, as well as the players' and the public's indiscipline."[52] Under the sway of state definition, football, far from being a paragon of civilization, had turned into a social problem. The game's definition as a social problem, as a consequence of its association with acts of public violence, also showed how violence, in certain urban social contexts, had become less acceptable, despite its visible presence in other spheres of colonial life: "football matches constantly threaten to generate public-order disturbances, thanks to the improper behavior of some players who, perverting the main goal of sports, assault and try to neutralize their opponent through forms of violence that are condemned by the game's laws." Spectators, on the other hand "obsessed with a fairly undignified club spirit, which is the product of an erroneous interpretation of the objectives to be accomplished through the practice of sports games and of a poor civic education, are used to hurling at players and referees, during sports practices, disloyal and incorrect suggestions as well as insulting words that usually offend morality!"[53]

Given this scenario, law enforcement officers working in the fields would have the power to arrest and send to trial, "for bodily injury," a "player who assaults another or provokes an injury that prevents the other from playing, so long as it can be attested that this action was done with the intent of neutralizing his opponent." Police authority should replace the referee as the law enforcer (and the state take the place of the associative movement), not just to protect public order but also to prevent work absenteeism that resulted from frequent injuries. Police officers also had the power to arrest "any individual who insults the players and referees, who offends public morality with obscene words or gestures, who triggers public-order disturbances or purposefully damages the venue or any items in it."

In the matter of sporting violence, as in so many others, the suburb was a world of its own, and the presence of the state was scarcely felt beyond the process of labor force recruitment, tax collecting, and the regulation of the circulation of dwellers in their travels to the city center. In the periphery, football was not a social problem. In the suburbs, during AFA matches, there was still no police presence, which was all the worse for some referees. As long as violence in suburban football, an index of the weakness of the laws of the game as an element of organization of the on-field interaction order, was limited to the suburbs, there was no reason, as far as the authorities were concerned, to intervene; except when the levels of violence might lead to serious work absenteeism. In a context where an unstable, cheap, underqualified, and relatively disposable labor force was predominant, the issue did not merit a great deal of attention. Only later would the question of the reproduction of a labor force more adapted to new economic projects lead to a more thorough effort to identify "social pathologies" in the suburbs. Alcoholism, prostitution, or delinquency, as well as, in its own specific scale, football, only became "real" problems when their effects had an impact on the productive system or otherwise interfered with the rhythm and flow of the colonists' sociabilities.[54]

INTERPRETING VIOLENCE

The process of football's conversion into a social problem was based on the idea that the game, corrupted by an "urban affliction," ran counter to the rules of sociability. The state, the actual sports movement, educators, and moralizers were charged with the responsibility for creating a framework that would normalize football. From this moral perspective violence was a deviation that had to be eliminated. Violence became the measure through which football players' movements, as well as the public's amoral behavior, were interpreted and condemned.

The reduction of part of football's performance to a common—barbaric, crude, and unwholesome—denominator was not, however, the only criterion used to scrutinize football players' gestures. José Craveirinha, as he interpreted the game in the suburbs of Lourenço Marques, argued that the gestures of some suburban athletes, a few of which were considered violent, should be subjected to a more in-depth analysis—in short, that evil and malice should not be conflated. With this goal in mind, the poet would describe and express in the glossary published in O brado africano a number of movements that were regularly executed in the suburban pitches, both in neighborhood matches and in AFA competitions. Craveirinha's interpretation, which does not dwell too much on the violence associated with the movements, puts a rather different spin on the nature of some of the gestures that were part of the motor repertoire of African players in the suburbs of Lourenço Marques:

> *Pandya* (pronounced "pandja"): While in Portuguese there is no word that expresses the moment when, as they dispute the ball, the players kick it simultaneously and produce a sound that is distinctive of this type of collision, the African sportsman created the word *pandya*, which, translated literally, means to crack or to burst! This expression became a part of the local Portuguese jargon; *Beketela*: The player who anticipates the opponent's action and places his foot on the ball in such a way as to provoke a clash that quite often causes serious injury to the player who kicks it and almost always leads to his falling over. It translates as to put. Beketela is used viciously, by placing one's foot slightly above the ball in such a way that the leg (the ankle and shin area) will hit the heel of the foot placed on the ball. There is the *Beketela henlha*—to put in the air—and *Beketela hansi*—to put below; *Wandla*: To purposefully slow down the play so that the opponent manages to kick the ball first, but, carried by his own momentum, he violently grazes his shin area against the

top of the [opponent's] raised boot. Translation: to bark; *Tyimbela* (tchimbela): To shoot the ball directly at the opponent with as much force as possible so that he is intimidated in later plays, so that advantage can be gained simply by threatening to kick, something that almost always makes the target turn his back to the ball, allowing the player to pass him by very easily.[55]

Despite Craveirinha's interest in presenting the suburban football of Lourenço Marques as the epitome of African cultural adaptation, the gestures he describes do not suggest the establishment of a unique cultural and performative construction. It is essential not to turn them into something folkloric. The existence of moments in the game when various types of clashes, of diverse origins and plasticity, is typical of a sport in which, by definition, players and ball are constantly interacting. The difference with Lourenço Marques's suburban football was that these performative acts received specific designations—something that, as Craveirinha mentions, did not happen in the metropolitan or English sports jargon. The creation of unique expressions, shared by the players and public, to designate specific performative actions, shows that these gestures were increasingly important within the context of suburban matches and also reveals the way local languages adapted to new activities. Furthermore, it shows that they did not occur by chance, as so often happens within a performance like a football game, but rather intentionally, being acknowledged and interpreted in this way by both players and public. Craveirinha was interested in exploring the meaning of this intentionality, a mark of its reflexive and strategic nature. As meaningful performative acts, they were an ingenious artifice devised by the players to gain an edge over their opponents: they did not come about fortuitously, but neither were they the result of a violent instinct.

The poet was more interested in looking into the dynamics of this strategy than in identifying a possible infringement of the laws in these movements. Playing mental games on the opponent, and using a variety of tricks and ruses, showed that the African player was not a "physical and instinctive being," as was claimed by prejudice, but someone who interpreted the game's actions and thoughts in such a way as to gain an advantage over a rival, even when this procedure led to strategies in which violence played an active role. It was within the frame of this interpretation that Craveirinha invokes the word *malice*, tying it to "the extraordinary and inexhaustible . . . fantasy" of the *indígena* population. For Craveirinha, football—like music, dancing, gastronomy, and oral stories—was an activity in which the importance of *cultura indígena* (indigenous culture) was highlighted. The struggle for suburban football's recognition as a cherished and significant cultural practice was part of a wider struggle being fought by Craveirinha. This was fought not just against the colonial administration, with the goal of gaining equal rights and acknowledging difference, but also in opposition to elements of a local African elite, who had a spiteful disdain for "the influx of African-based cultural currents, in an ignorant somnambulism that ha[d] been going on for too long."[56]

Not sharing the state's preoccupation with public order, not even the concern of some members of the local elite with problems associated with African evolution and respectability, José Craveirinha interpreted the question of violence otherwise. To the gestures many deemed violent and illegal he attributed a meaning that went far beyond both the legalist classifications ensuing from a conformity with the rules of the game, or from a morality that measured individual behavior, in this case the gestures of athletes, against the ideal of social integration. In this sense, he opposed the idea of respectability fostered by the assimilationist discourse of the colonial administration. In practice, this respectability was imposed coercively by the logic governing the interaction order imposed on Africans whenever they entered the cement city. Within this frame, marked by very asymmetrical power relations, the suburban dweller had little choice but to develop other strategies, such as playing the role of the "good boy," as described by Penvenne.[57] This cunning of the weak, in James Scott's sense, was geared to protect the worker, not always successfully, from the arbitrary use of power on the part of both authorities and employers. In suburban football, however, as will become clear, there was no room for nice boys. The strategic and malicious appropriation of qualities that designated the polar opposites of malice—kindness, earnestness, innocence, naiveté—in social performances in the context of their interactions with the colonizer was not repeated in the interaction order that defined suburban football. Here, malice took on a wholly different shape.

The weight that Craveirinha's analysis puts on the value of malice, by challenging a reductive representation of violence, suggested a contrasting interpretation of the players' performance, one that would reconstruct their actions and purposes, simultaneously circumventing both naturalist and culturalist notions, for which the traits of the African body and of their ancestral culture were the principle of causality.

THE RECOLLECTION OF THE PERFORMANCE

The expressions described by Craveirinha, coined in the African suburbs, were quickly identified by Saide Mogne, a former AFA player: "*Beketela* is to put your foot. When someone is about to kick, the other puts his foot on it and that is called beketela." He added that *"tymbela* is to put the foot on the ball. You do not touch the ball and when the other player is about to kick it, you also kick it. *Wandla* is to purposefully slow down a play so that afterward . . ." Mogne also added the expression *tchimba*, which means to tie up: "tie that guy up."[58] Issufo Batata corroborated these meanings: "*Beketela* is to stop. Someone wants to kick the ball and you prevent him from doing that. *Pandya* means to tear. *Wandla* means to peel (off). *Tchimbela* means to kick the ball against the opponent. To kick against him."

Ângelo Gomes da Silva (b. 1942), a railway worker, although he never participated in the AFA championship, started playing football in the suburban neighborhoods and border areas, such as Malhangalene, where he grew up listening to and employing the terms listed by Craveirinha. He spells out the meaning of *beketela* in great detail: "it's like stepping on your opponent. As he is about to make a move, it's something we do to harm him, even injure him. As he is about to make a move, I reach over with my boot, stretching my leg so that he clatters against the sole of my boot. And that's when the pain really hits him." According to Ângelo, *pandya*, "to break, tear, tear him" has a similar meaning to *wandla*. To better explain the actions associated with these gestures, Ângelo turned these expressions into verbs: "*pandyar* is to break; *wandlar* is to tear, *tchimbelar* is to purposefully kick the ball against the opponent." Augusto Matine points out that expressions such as *beketela* were employed in other everyday situations. "For instance, if we are in a given situation and a group comes toward us, we say *beketela*, stop it, *beketela*." *Wandla*, to peel, can be used when talking about fruit: "peel that piece of fruit." During the game, the expression refers to peeling the opponent, skinning him.[59]

These gestures were part and parcel of the suburban game, both in neighborhood matches and institutionalized competitions, according to Matine:

> From very early on we learned how to play without a referee, but still followed the rules that everyone went by. . . . We didn't know the seventeen laws of football, but we knew the key ones: a hand on the ball is a handball, if you foul it's a foul. Then, to organize ourselves across the pitch, the eldest one would say, so and so cannot come out of the penalty area; all he does is defend. We invented the law, obeyed its principles by looking at the law itself, even without knowing what it actually said. That was just the way of things in the neighbourhoods where football was played. . . . Yes, there was always some bickering, because a

lot of us knew the rules, but the one who knew it best would pick the ball up and say, it's a foul against you. Everything referees did we did as well, or tried to, we kind of winged it.

In AFA matches, these gestures' recurrence within the game's economy attested to the competition's violent reputation. Ângelo decided not to play in the AFA when, in Beira-Mar's pitch, he saw his brother Julinho, a slender individual who played for João Albasini, "fly off like a bullet" following a foul by the opposing team's ferocious left back. At that moment, Ângelo, whose social standing already placed him, in many ways, closer to life in the cement city, thought, "No, I won't have anything to do with this kind of football."

Former players who had lived in the suburbs and played in peladas de bairro (neighborhood matches) and in AFA competitions, recognized the expressions and described them in very similar terms. While not sharing Craveirinha's cultural agenda nor employing the same terms, such as *malícia* (malice), these former players, like the poet, never saw these gestures, central elements of their performance, as violent. As a principle of classification of performances, Saide Mogne distinguished toughness, a positive element, from violence, which was deemed negative: "We should not mistake violence for hardness." The suburban game was tough but not violent. Although lacking the political intent that lay at the center of Craveirinha's discourse, former players' descriptions of their own movements gave them the same strategic function the poet had singled out. The gestures that Craveirinha had called *intimidatórios* (intimidating) were part of the local game's intelligence, axes of a specific symbolic exchange.

The valorization of intentional gestures, whose local meanings (e.g., tearing, breaking, cracking, tying, putting someone in order) confirmed that the suburban players' strategy was based on a motor repertoire that challenged the laws of the game, seeking to reconfigure them, to shift their sense, to rearrange them, as indicated by the term *beketela*. The challenge to the game's official laws, as well as to all those to whom observance of regulations reflected a civilizational attitude and an acceptance of the values of respectability, was one of the key features of the gestures described by Craveirinha. The referee's precarious status in suburban matches, an indication of the official law's fragility, was confirmed by former players: "the referee," says Mogne,

> had to be an accomplished high jumper. When he was about to whistle at the end of the match, he looked for the busiest area and once the match was over he would put his foot on the first

beam and run for his life. He would look for the easiest escape route. Afterward, he would put his foot there and off he went. That happened in almost every game. He had to run, otherwise he would be beaten up and there was no police there.

The referees did not have proper training, and, quite often, players or even members of the public had to referee the matches: "If the match went well, there were no problems, but if there was a disallowed goal, in which case the public would be enraged at the referee, then he would be in trouble." "The referee's job," says Matine, "was tough. He often had to run away. In suburban matches, the referee was not respected as a judge, as a competent person, the one all of us should look up to. He was not respected." "During the match," he continued, "sometimes there were older people, locally respected, who would say, I'm going to punch that guy." These actions "incensed the public, and they would follow what the older man may have wanted to do. The public always argued about what was right and what wasn't." "The referee was always protected," Mataleva says, "there was always a whole committee there to protect the referees, but sometimes there were brawls, the referee had to be protected properly."

THE PUBLIC AS AN ELEMENT OF COLLECTIVE PERFORMANCE

The referee's powerlessness to enforce the official regulations became one of the conditions within which the gestures identified by Craveirinha were produced. The players resorted to the official law and interpreted whatever happened according to their own viewpoints. The argument would immediately spread to the public. The audience's rhetoric also had an important role in these negotiations. Mogne recalled that when one of these gestures occurred, they immediately generated numerous discussions, arguments as to what degree the game's laws had been broken. The match, he points out, "was always being interrupted." The abstract model of democracy ideally represented by the game, in which a central and fair power protected equality by enforcing the law, was superseded by a decentralized negotiation, sufficiently open to legitimize the movements that broke the law. The gestures that Craveirinha called *tácticas intimidatórias* (intimidating tactics) offered some form of protection for the players within a local interaction order that, given the law's weakness, allowed for a decentralized violence.

In 1937, Vasco da Gama, a mestiço team, started arriving at AFA matches with incomplete teams, often failing to appear at all. The club's president, Mário António Pereira, a prominent member of the GALM, stated that this was not a decision made by the board but rather by the players themselves. He also added that, although it was true that some athletes were "wasting themselves at parties," the main reason for their nonattendance was their "fear of the violence" that took place during matches, as well as of what he called the "persecution of mulattos."[60] Given their social standing, the latter players were the ones more in tune with a respectable definition of the game and those who stood to lose the most in case of a generalization of violence.

The suburban football spectacle was not judged by uniform criteria. The diversity of classification principles registered the differences in social origins, standings, and trajectories of both players and public. The negotiation of boundaries that characterized suburban football's style of play continued to expose the struggle between distinct worldviews, between idealized conceptions of the practice of this sport, that projected contrasting social standings and aspirations. While the lack of unanimity in the appreciation of the spectacle, especially with regard to the legitimacy of the gestures, may have driven away some players and a segment of the public, it did not cut the ties between the game and the community. Recognizing the right to break the law, a common principle of conflict regulation was put in place. That was the site for the proliferation of malicious strategies, spurred on by the public. Ângelo remembers how the public enthusiastically asked for a beketela, a "raised foot," a gesture that is forbidden by football's laws. The public "enjoyed it and incited the players."

Some athletes were singled out for praise, due to their exceptional skill in executing the gesture. Whoever was unwilling to throw himself into a game with these specific performance conditions—such as the mulattos of Vasco da Gama or Ângelo, who soon realized this brand of football did not suit him—would steer clear of the competition, just as a certain segment of the suburban public favored other leisure activities, more in tune with their refined lifestyle.

Issufo Batata is sure that all the terms listed by Craveirinha were "coined by the public." These expressions, he insists, were not part of a strategy devised by the manager to demoralize the opponent. Saide Mogne recalled that "even the organized supporters issued orders. This vocabulary was used among the players and even among the audience . . . the audience asked and the players executed." Much like in a boxing match, the public incited violent clashes: "Some players used knee pads, and people in the stands would shout, 'Hit him right there on the knee.' The guy already had an injury and another was expected to take him out of the game." Hilário recalls, "We were thrilled by a dribble, a tough tackle, beketela, which was not mean-spirited, it was foot against foot and the ball in the middle, and both players fall, and people are thrilled."⁶¹

"There was this player who came from [the district of] Mozambique—Dinis—who used to be called 'frolic in the sand,'" Hilário recalls. "They love that sort of player in Africa, the Garrincha type. To play without dribbling and swerving, with no skill, just running around and shooting, simply didn't cut it; you needed to know how to stop the ball and dribble past the other player, that's what gets the public going. In Spain and in Portugal when a guy dribbles past the other, they yell *olé, olé*, but in Africa, it's *ééééééééé, éééé, éééé*. Everyone loved watching Garrincha play. But when a guy comes along and plays a simple game, moving the ball along at the first touch, playing accurate passes, no one really appreciates it."

THE FEAR FACTOR

The public in AFA matches incited certain actions, while condemning others, and constantly debated over their legitimacy. Players recognized and shared the ethical and aesthetic standards of spectators, behaving in accordance with the boundaries that demarcated these expectations and that simultaneously circumscribed the space of stylistic possibilities. The players' bodies thus interacted within a locally devised convention, which did not result merely from the interactions among athletes but also between them and the public; they all brought to the game a wider and looser moral code that helped shape the performance style. Out of the subversion of the official law of the game there emerged a "parallel law,"⁶² which lacked a standardized model, such as a textual existence, that would grant it a degree of objectivity. The symbolic value of each gesture depended on its capacity to challenge the official law of the game. At the same time, these gestures legitimated the rules of the game as a condition of possibility for the performance, as well as a source of authority that provided, even if in rather indefinite terms, a form of guidance for the players. The instability of this "local convention" spurred the athletes to employ performative strategies that were situated somewhere along the boundaries of the game's official law, a territory that was ambiguous enough to open up a negotiation about their legality.

In these performative conditions, malice was a priceless capital, an elementary faculty in the management of the athletes' motor repertoire and in negotiating the law's boundaries. The players on the pitch learned to anticipate their opponents' gestures, knew their strategies and tricks, incorporated ways of moving across the field, of reading their colleagues' movements and a whole set of cunning actions, malicious gestures, and tricks to deal with the law and to circumvent it. Intimidating tactics, which were crucial elements of the suburban player's motor repertoire, defined how he experienced space. His motor habitus underpinned his perception of the space of physical movement. There was a constant measuring of the rule's boundaries, of what was possible and impossible, an evaluation of the nature of the performance and of when a gesture could be seen, or not, as being "acceptable." The suburban players' motor habitus, on account of the instability of the convention that organized the local game, had to subject itself to constant adaptations and to devise more-or-less creative strategies. The best "authors" of this spectacle were its most malicious interpreters.

As this performance depended on the game's official law, any effort to enforce that law meant that the player would have fewer possibilities to execute strategic actions such as the "intimidating gestures" described by Craveirinha. Issufo Batata was critical of the way in which a strict interpretation of the laws of the game had wiped out a host of performative strategies: "Of course players were afraid. But not today. It's all about the rules of the game. Maybe they were told that Maradona should be spared. He should be spared because princes and kings wanted to see him play. That's not right. He is not there to be spared, he is a player just like any other. But that's what happens nowadays." The efficacy of the fear factor, a founding principle of the on-field interaction, depended on the official law's permissiveness. In suburban football no one was spared; everyone was placed on a level playing field, and it was on that common ground that they revealed the genius of their malicious habitus. For this "suburban democracy" of the football match to work, the referee had to square his actions with a common sensibility, to have a firm grasp of the limits of the interpretation of the laws of the game. "A good referee," says Issufo, "lets it flow. He should only blow his whistle for a foul once the ball starts rolling again." When a player insisted on a play such as beketela, says Matine, the referee should be careful not to signal a foul every time: "if the referee whistled for three fouls, that was already too much, even if the player was actually fouling every time."

When the referee's interpretation of the law was too far removed from the criteria imposed by local convention, it led to "those situations when the referee had to run off at the end." If the referee whistled too often, showing an "unreasonable" respect for the law, the fear factor would no longer define the art of movement. The referee himself was "schooled" by the game's morality, refereeing not only the match itself but the social situation as a whole. To survive unscathed, he needed to develop a keen practical sense, a sensibility that would enable him to manage interactions between players while at the same time meeting, within certain limits, the public's expectations. In the end, the referee's job, traversed by this permanent tension, permeable to pressure and often permissive, was at the service of the convention that ruled over the local game.

The ambiguous status of the movement before the law of the game was also the basis for the public's rhetoric and for the way spectators interpreted the narrative of local football. Hence, the suburban game was filled with constant rhetorical challenges. The opinions and arguments about the nature of the performance took place not just within the context of the match. Their social existence reached much further, extending itself into arguments that took place outside of the here and now. Controversial game plays, often involving gestures named in the local terminology, by giving rise to rhetorical devices, became a defining part of the actual game's narrative structure. The players' and public's arguments and opinions about these performative game plays, usually reliant on each person's club preferences (which almost always reflected a neighborhood belonging), transformed this knowledge into an interaction repertoire. In these everyday encounters, the discussions were furthered through arguments in which the gesture was evaluated through moral and aesthetic judgments. The dramatic structure made possible by the game's features was the ideal basis for a number of discussions. Malice, especially, was not just an important faculty employed during the performance on the pitch. It was essential in the discussions that involved players, the public, and referees, as well as in the way the public managed information beyond the game's here and now: a malicious management, employed in everyday social performances in which popular culture operated as a shared idiom, a lingua franca. Those who showed the greater skill in manipulating the narratives of local football would win these rhetorical stylistic exercises, filled with statements that constantly drew on everyday values.

A performative and symbolic capital, malice was a product of the conditions of production of a socially situated sports practice, which established a relationship between players and public. An elementary faculty of the spectacle of local football, malice was not determined by the players' natural or cultural traits, nor by a "deviant" form of exclusion, framed by the state as a social problem, but rather from a strategic sense adapted to particular space of possibilities. The faculty of malice also manifested itself in a second set of performative gestures in Craveirinha's glossary. These movements open up a more subtle interpretation of the rationale of the interaction order in the suburban game as well as a better definition of the specificities of a space of stylistic creation.

MALICE'S SECOND NATURE

This second group of actions described by José Craveirinha entailed the execution of virtuoso gestures by the athletes, celebrated with satisfaction and humor by a public conquered by the interpreter's talent and ruthlessness in outfoxing his opponent. Craveirinha interpreted these gestures within the scope of his valorization of Africans and of how Africans had adopted football, adding a hedonist dimension to the game. This second set of gestures compiled by the poet allows for a more detailed appreciation of the motor repertoire of the Lourenço Marques' suburban football player, of the features and meanings of his performance, and of the latter's relation with the economy of practices and symbolic exchanges behind the local game pattern.

> *Hpfa*: the exact moment when the player has just dribbled and still hasn't regained his balance, or the exact moment when the following happens: the ball touches the net, the sound of boot against boot, etc.
>
> *Psêtu*: is used to poke fun at the opponent in a play, just after he is beaten. It has an onomatopoeic origin.
>
> *Pyonyo*: when the play just mentioned is repeated or when its execution takes its time; in this case the translation means: to finish the player off.
>
> *Wupfetela*: the name of the play in which the player targets the goalkeeper with the intention of tiring or demoralizing him by continuing this action. The expression is derived from a term for seasoning food and it means to season the goalkeeper by tiring him. There is, as can be seen, a great deal of psychology involved in this action.[63]

Some of these expressions designated the execution of technical gestures that took place in the face of one's opponents, namely the dribble, an action that in other geographic contexts is associated with dancing.[64] The superiority of a movement that gives the performer an edge over his opponent—either because the opponent has been left in his trail or has lost his balance and has fallen over—turned into, as pointed out by the poet, a moral superiority, the outcome of a psychological strategy. These expressions classify actions in which two players are involved and one overcomes the other, something that was already present in the description of interactions under the category of "intimidating gestures." Both forms of interaction, intimidating and malicious, broken down into individual actions, revealed a specific construction of a collective identity. Technical execution was a central element of suburban football. The virtuoso gesture established an immediate line of communication with the public. In this symbolic exchange, such movements generated a particular set of meanings.

According to Hamido Nizamo, the dribble "was always the best thing." If the player "could beat three, four guys, he was a great player." Mogne talks about the "dribbler" in AFA matches, as the public's hero, as "everyone's hero," the player who, when the match came to an end, was carried shoulder high. In neighborhood matches, the dribble was an instrument of individual exhibitionism, a means of earning a reputation. "All players are individualist by nature," Issufo said. "Then there are those who obey and those who disobey, and the one that disobeys often does it because he's overcome by tiredness and holds on to the ball for too long, falls down, gets kicked around even more. When it comes to the crafty ones, the players and coach either allow it or don't. He has to use his skills, his natural gift. Those are the ones that make a difference." In the words of Matavela: "The game was tough but very technical, since players were born with that natural technique, even without any training; people simply had football in their feet."

Hpfa, confirmed the interviewees, described the "instant," "the moment," when the player was beaten on the dribble. That instant, perpetually anticipated, produced the wonder the public was craving. The "dribble" was the "joy of the people," an expression that designated, within the context of Brazilian football, the feeling aroused by Garrincha's movements, the great dribbler with bent legs. Garrincha was the "joy of the people."[65] Mogne invoked the great Brazilian player when he stated that "any individual with bendy legs was dangerous. An individual with bent legs, and there are some in the suburbs, has a greater chance of troubling any defense." Bent legs, a physical disability, a detour from normality, explained the charm of the dribble, as if it was something supernatural rather than a fitting part of the order of things. In this sense, the dribble and the dribbler possessed the charismatic ability to challenge order. Once more, the communicative power of the dribble was not a peculiarity of the suburbs of Lourenço Marques. However, its local relevance manifested itself in a number of designations that not only named the execution of certain gestures but defined their timings, their pauses, and the meanings produced by each of the movements, segmenting this economy of symbolic exchanges and isolating their time frames. This kind of grammar of movement revealed the strategic and malicious use of the dribble.

The dribble, within suburban matches, had a similar value to the one epitomized by a goal. The dribble belonged to a specific aesthetic universe, whose autonomy challenged the gradual pressure imposed on game movements by the principle of efficiency. According to this principle, the goal is the basic evaluative yardstick of a performance. By gaining autonomy, by producing its own set of specific meanings, where the illusions generated by the virtuoso mark the narrative of events, the dribble became an end in itself, separated from the remaining movements executed on the pitch. The public's support granted a unique status to the dribble virtuoso, who resisted the will of those who wanted to tame him. Nizamo talks about the powerlessness of managers to discipline some players' dribbling, a revealing instance of the local aesthetic and of its classification principles. "What could a manager do," asks Nizamo, "become angry? This was a part of the player's temperament, there was nothing to be done." The "player's temperament," however, answered to the public's pleas.

The public waited for the athlete's movements with bated breath, hoping for something extraordinary. The individual gesture was the most immediate way to communicate the game's enchantment. The great performer, in football, was like an illusionist; an enchanter who pulls the unexpected from out of the ordinary, who breaks with the game's normality, subverting it. When well executed, the dribble is celebrated as the victory of technique and intelligence over a deceived body. The great dribblers were also called *malabaristas* (jugglers or tricksters). The virtuoso was like a conjurer, a magician, always willing to surprise the audience with an unforeseen gesture. The game conjured by the trickster was appreciated by being a circus show of sorts. The public awaited the trickster's gesture, knowing that it was something rare that might not even come to be. Unlike a circus show, where the unexpected came to be expected, in football the unexpected was more fickle: one could only hope for it. One of the meanings attributed to the word *malice* was precisely the ability of those who master illusion.

The game's competitive nature, where the trickster's victory meant the opponent's defeat, added a deeper layer of meaning to the virtuoso gesture. The importance of the trickster's gesture was the result of its relation to risk. The dribble was an individual confrontation. Its outcome would determine the performer's immediate status and that of the opponents closer to him. Among the public's performative repertoire, which included gestures, words, dancing, and chants, the act of laughing, often in a mocking way, had a crucial role in relation to the dribble. These acts were a specific element, with corrosively humorous effects, of a social capital invested in the daily performances of the supporters.

Mogne states that the immediate meaning of a dribble, to whomever had just been faked out or passed by, was "almost a defeat," a moment of dramatic loss. Craveirinha pointed out the psychological effect of these gestures, how *pyonio* meant the elimination of a beaten opponent. There was a specific designation for the unfortunate player who was often dribbled—*psonho*—something the suburban athletes could be anything but proud of. Some of the gestures present in Craveirinha's glossary suggest this mocking and humorous dimension. *Psétu* was the expression used when a player, during the match, made fun of his opponent. Matavela describes it as "making fun of you through a feint."[66] Ângelo added the expression *Xipanana*, which other interviewees also recalled. It designated a nutmeg, the act of passing the ball between the opponent's legs, an instance of supreme humiliation, partly explained by the movement's sexual connotation.[67] The dribble's power of humiliation produced strong reactions. The player who dribbled past three or four opponents knew, Nizamo points out, that "if he tried that again he would be punished." As noted by Vicente Lucas: "Back then, if you tried to use any trickery, you'd pay for it. If you tried to nutmeg other players, they would beat you senseless. You'd dribble a guy once, and leave him sitting on the ground, then you'd wait for him to get up, dribble him again, but then if you tried it a third time you could be in for a beating."

This expectation, which added complexity to the "illusionist's" art, emphasized the interactional role of the fear factor; an element, as noted by Issufo, to which all suburban players were subjected. In a context where the interpretation of the official rules was filtered through the influence of "local convention," the dribble was a risky gesture that could trigger swift punishment. The trickster would go past his opponent and stop; he would look back and repeat the gesture. The moments of pause, which dictated the movement's execution, were essential for the enjoyment of the moment and the modest victory it brought. Mogne compared the gesture of dribbling to the virtuosity of the rider in a bullfight: "The guy passed, the other stopped and then another one came at him like a bull. That football was pretty lively."[68] In a bullfight, whether one is on foot or riding a horse, there is also this dialogue between cunning turned into gesture, on the one hand, and strength, represented by the bull's instinctive power, on the other; the spectator's pleasure is focused on the act of deceiving, on the ritual representation of human victory over the animal. Nowadays, the evolution of the collective sensibility to violence tends to condemn this representation of intelligence, thought of as inhumane. Unlike the bull, the player who was deceived by the dribble and became a victim of the public's corrosive humor could react maliciously and thus display his humanity. Violence ceased to be a purely instinctive act, placed as it was within a network of local meanings. The public's humor governed the athlete's gesture and became the supreme celebration of the gesture's meaning and also, in itself, a punishment for his victim. The importance of skillful gestures in the suburban player's motor repertoire was proof of the principles presiding over the local style of play.

A small segment of the social space, the suburban game consecrated the value of malice as symbolic capital, on the basis of which both players and public defined a space for the production of bodily movements. The dynamics of this spectacle revealed a symbolic exchange that included negotiated infringements of the official law of the game, attacks against the individuals who represent authority, the performance's exposure to risk and to the fear factor—its defensive and bewitching strategies.

AN ETHOS WITHIN AN ETHICS AND AN AESTHETICS

Football players' choreographies were not a dramatization of reality, as in theatrical, cinematic, or literary scenes, constructed by an author conscious of the representational devices and purposefully employing metaphors and other tropes to suggest an interpretation of the real. Players' gestures, guided by a motor repertoire where defensive and spellbinding movements prevailed, were also not haphazard, nor could they be reduced to the superficial and normative interpretation that simply classified them as violent.

The suburban game embraced *association* rules as a precondition of modernity and performance; however, the moral economy of equality and respectability inscribed in the rules of the game did not shape the behavior of suburban players. Instead, the players brought into the game a set of sensibilities, practical senses, and strategies that undermined the principles of that ethical code. From this clash there emerged a style of play. More tolerant of violence, which was conceived, within certain limits, as the ground for legitimate strategies, players favored the employment of defense strategies that were well known to them, and valued, in their everyday lives. The latter were deemed more effective in facing up to the challenges of the game, and achieving its goals. These defense mechanisms, albeit individualized, did not spring from individuals' singular features but rather from the established collective rights: in a way, players were not breaking a law but enforcing it. It was the view that emerged from the morality inscribed in the rules of the game that turned legitimate rights into illegitimate actions. Although weakened, the rule was nonetheless fundamental in establishing the grounds for the performance. In this sense, players' strategies should strike a dialogue with the morality of the rules of the game. That is why violence was expressed through a malicious code that, although subversive, did not discard the law as a principle, one that was not only valid but indeed necessary. By establishing itself as a space in which socially recognized defense and coping strategies confront a performative model that aimed at universality, the game of football created an arena for the practical negotiation of the suburban social contract. While the rule seemed to inflict violence on the bodies, it also adjusted itself to a social world such as the one emerging in the suburbs of Lourenço Marques, where there was a clear pressure to produce spaces and norms that could sustain encounters and interdependencies among people with distinct backgrounds.

The local systems of classification rewarded the bodies that were best able to handle risky situations. Risk was the grounding condition for the acknowledgment of the aesthetic and moral qualities in the players' performances, the foundation of the local style of play. Intimidating gestures challenged the law within the limits set by the local negotiation of its parameters. Violence was subjected to a symbolical revaluation, becoming acceptable and even celebrated when employed with enough malice to subvert the morality of the law. Practical senses and categories for classifying the world were reinterpreted in a specific bodily practice that, in turn, became its own classification system. In the suburbs of Lourenço Marques, the dispositions that defined a particular social condition turned into an ethics that manifested and represented itself through an aesthetics.[69]

The players' collective movements and the most common gestures in their motor repertoire created a specific narration of the colonial process in the city. It allowed to be recognized, as Craveirinha acknowledged, the "innumerable daily worries" and "distressingly heinous psychological problems" that deeply unsettled the suburban inhabitants.[70] Intimidating gestures exalted the individuals' ability to defend themselves against a decentralized violence and to assert themselves before the local society. Running the risk of playing a game where safety was not guaranteed, individual defense strategies were better suited for both players and team. Thus the game, as described in newspapers and in the memory of its participants, was defined by a performance where the various elements were not very interconnected and where the division of labor on the pitch was precarious. The local style of play was nonetheless placed under certain practical coordinates: the display of talent, strength, courage, and social standing, namely that of young men before an urban community in transformation.

"To peel," "to break," "to tear," were the meanings of some of the terms listed by Craveirinha. "Cut him off, beketela," as Matine phrased it. Personal protection was a right guaranteed by the neighborhoods in the suburbs of Lourenço Marques. As Matavela put it, "In suburban football, there were no police. Protection was offered by the neighborhoods, by their fans." Defending the team was almost always the same as defending the neighborhood. In the words of Hilário, "football was tough because there were many rivalries, between neighborhoods, between territories, and between regions." "The neighborhoods," continues Hilário, "were a boundary. In order to enter Chamanculo I had to know people there. This did not mean I couldn't go in, only that it was tougher." What defined the boundary, he adds, "was one having been born there, having one's hut there, having a place to listen to music, talk about football, to form a team to play in another neighborhood." The drawing of the frontiers of sociability, crystalized in the urban neighborhood experience and in the formation of small spaces of safety and routine, was also carried out through the reification of other borders, articulated through family, regional, religious, labor, and educational belongings, but also through one's position within the system of power relations legitimated by the colonial system, such as the conventions that separated the blacks from the mestiços, the indígenas from the assimilados. In football, as acknowledged by Matavela, "guile was the stock-in-trade of skillful players. But guile also comes in handy when you need to defend yourself against those who want to harm you, against those who were naturally gifted. So they had to fend for themselves. *Beketela* means that—to keep, to protect." "These cunning actions," he added, "weren't exclusive to football. The African has his way of acting and needs to be protected . . . from other people's envy." One of its constituent rights gave the players' bodies the opportunity to subvert the laws of the game and to defy its equalitarian and abstract ethics, which did not solve the problems posed by the dynamics and tensions that traversed the performance on the pitch. Hence, malicious defense strategies were legitimated, being more effective in dealing with everyday demands.

By also valuing the players that dodged this dangerous interaction, that escaped its power, the local style of play rewarded a talent that opened up space for autonomy and freedom. Risk also defined the space of action of the skilled player, the one able to trick.[71] The virtuoso gesture, with a destructive symbolic power, faced a hostile territory, whose dangers he tried to dodge. The trickster (or juggler) did not rely on *association* rules to protect himself; he was subject to a parallel norm that granted his opponents the choice of using an intimidating motor repertoire as a defense against the magical moves of the virtuoso. His charismatic powers were not only a defense strategy, but the grounds for a mesmerizing rearrangement of the world. The crafty gesture, facing the risk of a decentralized violence, was a formula, a decoder key that cleared a path. The power to trick or deceive, to interrupt a pattern of imposition of ways of being and doing, was what could enchant the game. The trickster's skill gave the game a new meaning; his magic gift was able to symbolically reorder the game. This natural condition, this gift, meant a kind of power that was also shared by the "witchcraft practices" to be addressed in the next chapter.

While the gifts of these extraordinary players could be locally interpreted as a product of occult powers translated into charismatic properties, through its mastery of a universal trade this talent was acquired a universal currency. The possibility of football becoming the vehicle for individual aspirations and the imagination of another community intensified when some suburban players moved on to play downtown and later in some of the biggest clubs of the metropole.

As in the interaction order prevalent in the suburbs of Lourenço Marques, in the suburban game malice defined a practical, intelligent, and creative sense that managed the body's sensibility. Simultaneously, the valorization of a habitus adjusted to everyday situations was transformed into a principle of evaluation of performances, a classification schema that was ratified by players and audience alike. These shared principles of appreciation did not imply unanimity as to the fairness of a particular strategy, or the legality of a certain malicious gesture. Rife with conflict and traversed by rhetorical devices, the spectacle of football also generated a context for the discussion of the terms through which a local football style was defined, a context that simultaneously imposed itself as a space for debate on the basic principles of the suburban social contract. The transgression of the laws of association was negotiated among the confronting parties in the course of the match, with the permanent intervention of the audience. Since the style of play was formed through tacit complicities, the movement dynamic led to unending debates, which involved players and public, on the status and legitimacy of a given gesture. These discussions, held during the course of the performance but also in subsequent convivial contexts, organized a specific public space that allowed suburban inhabitants, in spite of their differences and specific interest networks, to express their views and participate around a common topic. In these debates, which included the conflictual definition of principles of justice and ethics, of individual rights and principles of collective governance, a "suburban democracy" came into play. The rhetorical capacity of the speakers suggested a transposition of malicious strategies onto these verbal matches. In this context, overall performances, the merits of individual, and collective defense strategies and cunning actions were interpreted in various and conflicting ways. Thus a particular form of citizenship was expressed, whose protagonists were those to whom the colonial state had denied virtually every right.

BUILDING A COMMUNITY

In suburban football's interaction order, where malicious violence prevailed, the trick, the act of dazzling and deluding, did not spring from a political, ideological imagination or a social ideal but rather from a society made flesh, transmuted into a symbolic interaction. The moral economy of the suburban game was at odds with a variety of blueprints for a "community" (or a social configuration) that thought that the game should be a pedagogical space, the embodied version of an ideal, an ideology, a group of social relations organized by a "rational" urban grid or a religious doctrine. Projected by a local elite as an emancipatory space, the football pitch was conquered by the economy of practices and symbolic exchanges that governed the suburbs of Lourenço Marques and that had spilled over into the bodies themselves. The representation of the world created by the football performance reenacted the confrontation between the abstract democracy proper of a game where everyone operated under the same rules, and the principles of action of a motor habitus, educated through a practical and symbolic exchange that legitimated the subversion of the law, thus consecrating wider principles of existence and, more specifically, a malicious practical sense. In the everyday life of the suburb and in the contact between its inhabitants and the world of the colonizer, there were no signs of a fair and evenly applied law—a key factor of appeasement and of the internalization of self-restraint, which Elias linked to the development of the modern state and to the institutionalization of conflict.

The ongoing instability of local life validated defensive behavior patterns, best suited to respond to unpredictable situations. Being excluded from citizenship and in the face of the plurality and fragility of the institutions that organized the material and spiritual life of the suburb (customary, religious, familiar, professional), local inhabitants valued the right to adjust to a world defined by its fluidity. In these particular circumstances, they developed a set of faculties and skills that they strategically used according to contextual social situations. In order to navigate this space one needed specific bodily competences, urban bodies prepared to respond to everyday demands, to the contingencies of labor instability, to temporary work, to the violence of the state and employers, to precarious housing, malnutrition, insecurity, and risk, to the specific suburban conflicts that opposed people separated by their spatial, religious, and ethnic belongings, by their material and statutory conditions. It was thus that process of adaptation to the colonial city that created fluctuating habitus,[72] consecrated the value of malice, understood as a form of everyday cunning, a streetwise means of survival, but also a condition of possibility for creating a new world. Malice was a defense mechanism of a society that was built under a specific set of circumstances. Its role being tacitly acknowledged, malice established itself as a chief characteristic of an individual and collective suburban social contract. As a primordial symbolic capital, it promoted strategies tailored to the surrounding social spaces and situations. In the suburban neighborhoods, it protected the individual from an insecure and uncertain interaction order, subject to a host of negotiations and cunning strategies. In the cement city, where the contours of the interactional situation condemned suburban inhabitants to a predetermined subjection, this cunning, less free and enterprising, triggered a subaltern performance, employed to gain small advantages and to open up clear spaces of negotiation.[73]

As a bodily representation of the suburb, the local style of play contrasted with the idealization of the body put forward by the theoreticians of the Estado Novo. The gestures of suburban players, in light of these ideological points of view, were the producers of a social and political immorality that was not only tolerated by the local conventions but in fact presented before the suburban community as the representation of an everyday cunning, a theater of subversion that expressed an alternative reading of the world. In the grammar of movement suggested by that physical education ideological model, the trickster's dribble symbolized an indeterminate, unpredictable, and instinctive movement. The Estado Novo's physical education theoreticians had warned against the political dangers of an "ill-defined" movement. Indecision was typical of curvilinear movements, of choices made in the here and now, ignorant of the moral and motor principles that sustained it. The dribble celebrated irregularity, illusion, the act of dazzling and deluding the other. In order to correct such an abnormality, the nervous impulse that stimulated the body to move in a certain direction and to execute certain movements should be associated with the transmission of moral and ideological principles. In the case of the suburban player, however, this impulse depended on the conditions determined by a situated symbolic economy that defined a local interaction order, a collective construction unaware of its goals, defining a space of stylistic possibles in which bodily strategies were reproduced.

Being the site of a "reverse" pedagogy, on the suburban football pitch one was instructed in the value of malice and of the negotiation of the law, thus defining a morality that challenged the colonial system's modernizing projects, based on an idealized and predictable African worker. The emergent individualism of this "illegal" suburb was at odds with the need to stabilize the labor force that was gathered on the outskirts of the city. The radical precarization of living conditions and the absence of institutions of social support, associated with the expectations generated by urban culture and its lifestyles, stood in the way of the goals of increased productivity and political regulation. The suburban game pattern, a tangled choreography was a metaphor for the city where the rationalities of the state and of the modern economy had still not penetrated, where urban plans that meant to create a rational, ordered, and stable life did not leave the project phase; a city made up of twists and turns, a map of a labyrinthine and precarious whole where individuals had learnt to orient themselves through malice. The idealization of life in the suburb, evoked by images of internal cultural harmony and by a culturalization of poverty, was not to be found in the terrain of cultural fatality, but rather in the conditions of its reproduction.

The prevalent style in the suburban football game had this rebellious potential, materialized in malicious, violent, individualistic, and cheating gestures; it challenged the public order and the regime's societal conception, founded on the idealization of a stable and hierarchized society, where everyone respectfully knew their place and worked toward a common purpose. It legitimated subversive strategies and inscribed them into an urban popular culture that was voiced and shared through countless narratives. The social contradictions expressed in this interaction order did not constitute, just yet, a political problem. The most common gestures in this style of play that expressed decentralized violence and tricksters' illusions, were essentially defensive strategies and forms of symbolic attack, enunciating struggles not only between conflicting views of the world but also between different dispositions and practical reasons. Still, these small arenas of struggle were not without their victories.[74]

The community in itself was still not a "community unto itself," in the sense of having a political organized agency. The ritualistic representation of suburban dominant social values in football reified the principles of an alternative suburban citizenship, a society of rights and duties, of exchanges and negotiations. However, despite its strong ties to the suburban space, the modern game created a unique performance that allowed the community not only to build itself as such, but also to project itself beyond its own boundaries. The game provided a language in which the unstable logics at work in the construction of a suburban social contract were represented; it lay the foundations for the discussion of this contract in a local public space, which was precarious but lively; and it allowed for the proficient and imaginative adoption of a universal language, as the ground for the enunciation of aspirations and hopes, which shattered the parochialism of the suburb.

The local football narratives celebrated this style of play, these matches, gestures, and heroes, key interpreters of the game of dissimulation and self-preservation, the best keepers of a collective memory. One of the fundamental rights of the suburban game was the use of what José Craveirinha called "witchcraft practices."

5 ⌇ Witchcraft Practices in Football's Symbolic Economy

In the context of the unsteady everyday life of the suburbs of Lourenço Marques, reliance on traditional practices to deal with livelihood issues was among the rights afforded by the suburban social contract; a right that was indeed reinforced in the face of the absence or obsolescence of other means and institutions that could assist in solving these problems. The use of witchcraft practices mentioned by José Craveirinha was deeply tied to malicious acts. In several African contexts, the "production of malice" could not be separated from magic powers and sleight-of-hand trickery.[1] The demands of the urban environment posed questions to these forms of knowledge for which they did not seem to have the answers. And yet the new stimuli spurred traditional forms of knowledge to adapt, bringing to the fore the plasticity of beliefs in the face of a precarious urban experience, and to change through their relation with new activities, offering a worldview that aimed to restore the world's logic. In suburban football the "witchcraft practices" referred to by Craveirinha were part and parcel of the game's symbolic economy. Affecting the players' actions, they were portrayed as a creative invisible hand, the hidden author of the players' movements as well as a creative incentive to the local style of play.

In 1966 several metropolitan newspapers argued that the work of the many metropolitan football managers employed by Lourenço Marques's football clubs was badly affected by the proliferation of *cuche-cuche* and by the action of the so-called *doutores da macumba* (macumba doctors). Suburban players, who played for cement city teams, following the dissolution of the AFA, in 1959, and the end of the indigenato, in 1961, brought their traditions to European football. In these clubs, according to the complaints voiced in Lisbon newspapers, the manager, an increasingly important figure in modern football, responsible for the game's rationalization, was replaced in his role as motivator of the players' actions by pagan practices rooted in "the black man's superstitious nature."[2] This fact signaled a perverse reversal of the assimilation mechanisms that were being widely fought and denounced by Portuguese colonial ideology and that found expression in legislation and in the codification of native custom.[3]

Fréchaut Neto, in a series of articles in *O brado africano* titled "O 'Cuxo-Cuxo' e as perplexidades da ignorância" (Cuxo-Cuxo and the perplexities of ignorance),[4] outlined an answer to these developments and attempted to "rationally" translate the meaning and logic behind the use of *cuxo-cuxo*—and not "cuche-cuche," as it was sometimes spelled, the author noted.[5] The author defended this custom against "Lisbon's intelligentsia." He began by distinguishing cuxo-cuxo[6]—which was executed by the *coscuxeiro*, "someone who throws small bones, divining hierophantic pieces, and belongs to southern Mozambique's Bantus"—from *macumba*, a Brazilian practice with African roots but that also possessed Catholic and spiritist elements.[7] The coscuxeiro was, above all, a fortune-teller, but he was also a healer and a sorcerer.[8] The belief in the efficiency of a "magical thought," he said, rely on the belief that the "coscuxeiro" could influence the "course of events, subjugate people's will, influence things, kill, harm, beat, etc., the enemy, the opponent, a person or more you disliked."[9] This faith was based on the idea that "there are forces that can be controlled by the sorcerer's will, through the secret use of certain words, dance steps, ritual gestures, drugs, pacts with personal and impersonal spirits."[10] The cuxo-cuxo had a strong psychological power. Within the scope of this motivational frame, Neto insisted, it was not a fraudulent practice.[11] "In football these players require nothing more than a tight group unity and playing with the thought that victory cannot escape them"; "they free themselves of their fears" and gain "an extra moral power."[12] "The cuxo-cuxo," he continues, "was akin to the general's speech before a battle, to praying, to the effect of religious constructions"; "both white people and black people need moral energies."[13] Cuxo-cuxo was not an obscure superstition, but rather a local strategy to deal with the needs of a sporting performance.

The employment of cuxo-cuxos in solving problems resulting from urban life, Fréchaut Neto guessed (prematurely), would give rise to an inevitable decline in tradition. The coscuxeiro was "an employee of an ancient social organization" undergoing a disintegration process.[14] Cuxo-cuxo had been used by the populations "according to schemes dictated by ethnic, kinship, linguistic, regional, and even religious affinities," thus contributing to social stabilization in a new relational space and helping people "face, with the greatest possible security, the needs and demands of city life."[15] People tried to adapt through a "moral reorganization based on traditional bonds." He concludes by stating that "the fragmented African social groups sense their weakness in the face of a ruthless urban mechanism and, as such, the various regional boundaries are reduced or extinguished (ethnicity, group, costume) to give way to a solidarity typical of an emergency, instability, or imminent risk situation."[16] The cuxo-cuxo acted within this unstable territory. Maliciously.

THE VOVÔ

What led José Craveirinha to start looking into Lourenço Marques's suburban football universe was the generalization of what was then termed *práticas feiticistas* (witchcraft practices). The adaptation of these ancient traditions to football aroused the poet's interest. Although he thought these customs were "atrasados" (backward), Craveirinha argued that it was imperative to study them.[17] They also revealed the creative aspects of how the African had adopted football. Traditional beliefs, he suggested, had a direct effect on "players' reflexes," influencing the way they played.[18] This powerful influence was a basic premise toward the execution of their movements, a principle behind their efficiency and intensity.

The employment of these traditions in football was a consequence of the urban diversification of an ancient practice and of its adaptation, as stated by N. A. Scotch in one of the first articles devoted to the theme, to social activities not covered by custom.[19] Cuxo-cuxo's adaptation to the resolution of problems created by the urban experience, such as getting a job, the consumption and possession of goods, the individual and collective status within a growing community—where an individualism that destroyed belief patterns and principles of action, and generated new inequalities—gave it a central role within the organization of ways of living and surviving in the suburbs of Lourenço Marques. Its relation with football signaled the game's growing importance in communitarian space. A universe of social participation, a means of achieving a certain status, where ethic and aesthetic judgments are at stake, where you win or lose, football raised similar questions to those affecting the suburban population's daily life.

For the colonial administration, these beliefs represented the most negative aspects of indígena customs and contradicted the logic of the assimilation system. Above all, they challenged Catholic missionary work, its rituals, and its religious and civilizational worldview. This censure grew stronger when these traditional practices approached the European city and were employed in transitional urban areas. The assimilation process forced the indígena to reject these beliefs in order to attain the "necessary presentation and customs toward the full application of Portuguese citizens' public and private law,"[20] which was a way of showing their eligibility to join the European's world.

For the former suburban players, cuxo-cuxo was almost always called *vovô*, a name that could be applied both to the actual practice of witchcraft and to the individual responsible for it. This practice was usually called *preparação* (preparation). The expression *vovô*, a diminutive of the Portuguese word *avô* (grandfather), sounded, in the players' mouths during the interviews, like *vuvu*, a word that in western African tradition is used to refer to the "spirit of the dead."[21] In her study about the use of these practices in Tanzania, Anne Leseth alludes to the expression *juju*, which is a synonym of witchcraft, traditionally used in dancing competitions (*ngoma*).[22] She describes it as a word derived from the French Creole *joujou* (plaything or toy) or, most likely, from the name given to protective ornaments and amulets. She also alludes to a possible Muslim origin, in Quranic words such as *yajuju* or *majuju*. The Mozambican player Saide Mogne, a Muslim, even described the "vuvu/vovô" as *diabo* (devil), which fits the "Muslim hypothesis" Leseth put forward, which describes *juju* as the "evil spirit."[23] In several sub-Saharan African regions,[24] *juju* is the name for an amulet, a bewitched object, a fetish, a talisman, which has the power to act upon reality, after being "prepared" by a specialist. In Macua, one of the main languages in northern Mozambique, a region under a strong Muslim influence, *juju* is the "name of a small drum."[25] In Ronga, one of the main languages in the Lourenço Marques area, the drum, as in many other sub-Saharan regions, is called *ngoma* (or *ngomana*, if it is small), a word that, as Leseth mentioned regarding the Tanzanian case, is used to designate dancing competitions. In Ronga, according to Sá Nogueira's dictionary (1960),[26] the words *vuvu* and *juju* do not exist.[27] If *vuvu*'s transformation into *vovô* resulted from giving a Portuguese form to the expression, the origin of the first expression is less clear in this Mozambican context. Muslim influence in Lourenço Marques's suburban football is an important lead. In another sense, cuxo-cuxo practices in the city's suburbs often meant that the healer had to act on objects or spaces associated with the game—such as the ball, the shirt, and the goal—which brings this practice close to the description of *juju* as an amulet.

The descriptions of *vovô* either refer to the healer (the vovô) responsible for the preparation, usually an older man, an avô (grandfather), whose wisdom was tried and tested,[28] or to the actual nature of the preparation. The vovô's power, Daniel Matavela points out, was reaffirmed every day by an expression that associated his words with the inevitability of various events: *vovô disse* (the vovô said). Issufo points out that *vovô* is the same as *cuxo-cuxo* and that "each one uses the expression they prefer." Abissínia Ali adds that *vovô* was usually employed as a "synonym for witchcraft." He assured, however, that when "*vovô* was used in relation to football matches, it came closer to the healers' art." The vovô seemed to play, simultaneously, the roles of fortune-teller, healer, and even sorcerer, which is in line with the characterization of *cuxo-cuxo* put forward by Fréchaut Neto and by the poet and writer Luís Polanah.[29] In other cases, the word *vovô* designated, more directly, the actual practice of witchcraft. As noted by Hamido Nizamo, vovô was employed in intimidation strategies that took place before the match: "We have vovô and we will use it." But Nizamo himself used the expression when he referred to "the person responsible for the preparation." The stories about the vovôs in suburban football describe an activity whose field of action is that of a healer and a sorcerer. To have an external intervention on the game's outcome and to counter the influence of the opponent team's vovô, required consulting a specialist. As football was a new activity, with specific features, it is only natural that this domain should be open to various specialists. In this chapter, the terms *vovô* or *cuxo-cuxo* will be employed when referring to this practice, as they were the terms used by the interviewees. Its practitioner, following once again the interviewees' own discourse, is designated as healer or sorcerer, its function linked to the status it was given in the course of the narratives they told.[30]

THE VOVÔ'S ART

Saide Mogne recalled that in his time "no one entered the pitch without having been prepared." The preparation meant submitting the players to the knowledge and procedures of a healer. The preparation, he adds, almost always entailed "lighting and burning certain objects, and we had to cover these up and inhale the smoke." Afterward, the healers administered "liquids," Mogne continues, attempting to find a clearer analogy for the benefit of his interlocutor, "very much like vaccines": "they vaccinated us." "The healers would offer vaccines to goalkeepers, for instance," Matavela told us.

> Goalkeepers who made these really acrobatic leaps would get the monkey vaccine. There were sorcerers that would work on the football itself or the shirts. When the opposing team entered the penalty area, their shots would always go wide. There were

also healers or sorcerers that gave vaccines to strikers. When he took a shot you'd see two balls, and you'd go dizzy. Some healers would go to the pitch at night, prepare something, and then they would say, "When you get onto the pitch, you might as well sit in a chair next to the goal, because the ball won't cross the goal line either way." This kind of thing was then gradually brought into city football as well. There are a few secrets that I can't reveal, but it is a reality. Africa has that magic.

The "preparation" was the most common procedure, but Mogne assures us "there were thousands of different things." In some cases "we had to take all the rubbish associated with our preparation along with us and, when dawn came, to bury it in the sea. There were things like this. Things we tied to our wrists and feet. We put coins to fight our opponent, and salt." These preparations served to "protect ourselves from the opponent's disease," that is, they were so as not to be affected by the vovô's contaminating effect. In this sense, the healers offered several forms of advice to the players, creating a series of prescribed and forbidden actions: "to put water in one's mouth, not to look back, not to shake the [opponent]'s hand, to put salt in his boots, to put a coin inside them." Issufo remembers a healer called Pombal. His technique was unique: the game's outcome depended on how many pigeons (Craveirinha mentioned crows) flew over the field where the game was played. Issufo recalled his words: "If my pigeons are flying over the field, you should count them and that's the result you'll get." But if you "get to the field and the pigeons are on the ground, then our team will lose." According to Issufo, the powers of men such as Pombal remain a "legend," a "mystery."

Often, as Mogne says, the healer worked from the club's head office during the game, playing "with little sticks and smoke and any of various other things, ordering the ball as if he could transport it to a certain place, just like that, automatically." Mogne exemplifies how things worked: "We were losing 2–0 and the guy would come and say, 'You keep on playing and I will play from there, from the head office.' The healer would go to the club's head office and would start intervening with his 'smoke.'" The game's outcome, as presented in Mogne's example, rested on two contrasting performances. On the one hand, the players' field of action. On the other, the vovô's territory, an "invisible realm."[31] Stories about cuxo-cuxo in Lourenço Marques's suburban football describe the vovô's power in influencing the game's course of events and the outcome of the players' movements. The healer had his own field of action, through an ability to act upon a space ruled by a logic that existed outside the "concrete" order of things. Issufo Batata, a Muslim, stated that each club "was associated with its own vovô." The vovô's involvement did not contradict the players' and club directors' religious beliefs: "religion had nothing to do with it." The religious leader and the vovô, he explained, intervened upon different universes. The religious leader was someone with power over the community, with an influence over the "concrete" organization of life, over "things of the world," a description that attributes a very specific role to organized religion. The vovô, in turn, was someone who intervened within the scope of belief, with powers to manipulate the occult: a wise man with unique powers, someone who, in his own words, "mastered the knowledge of the woodland."

The healer's art revealed what Issufo termed *capacidade ilusionista* (illusionist ability). Like the football trickster, who had the ability to enchant, the healer had the power to subvert the "game's concrete order." His power, of a malicious nature, like the mysterious talent of the virtuoso player, solved problems that appeared to be unsolvable, by the will that dictated the performers' movements. The game's outcome and its causal relation with the players' gestures and movements did not depend, then, on the players' free will but rather on a will under the spell of external forces. From this we can gather a description of life as a process regulated by forces that escape individual will, like the forces of colonialism's power. This withdrew the responsibility for the game's outcome from the gestures and movements of the players that took part in it. In this sense, the vovô's greatest power was that of absolution. The players' action, reliant on the manipulation of the occult, absolved the actual interpreters from being responsible for their performance. The vovô's intervention thus became an intrinsic element of local football's symbolic economy. His powers, by absolving the players, protected their gestures and movements from events within the game, from the dangers provoked by the opponents' performance, which were materialized in malicious gestures. A creative force, the vovô was thus an element of the performance itself, intervening on the disposition of the players, an ingredient of the local style, an element that defined the space of stylistic possibles.

THE IMPACT OF BELIEF ON THE PLAYERS' BODIES

Ângelo guarantees that suburban football players relied heavily on the healer: "If you don't go to the healer you won't play any good and you'll lose the game." António Cruz, a mestiço who played football in the city of Inhambane before coming to Lourenço Marques, talks about vovô as "a disease, an obsession." Through the vovô's action, a "guy becomes greater than he is, he believes he has an extra power." The belief in the vovô had a direct effect on the athletes' motor habitus, on the cerebral impulse that dictated the body's movement. Without him, as Hilário observed, the "player cannot play."

By agreeing to tell their own stories about the vovô and by doing so with obvious relish, most former players place themselves in a somewhat ambiguous position toward the mechanism of belief, that is to say, as to how their bodies were or were not affected by the strength of these powers. Though everyone employed the vovô and played under his spell, in some cases this outcome was not due solely to the players' own efforts but partly to the team's preparation. During the interviews, players spoke of the vovô as something that had a psychological effect. According to this conception, the vovô's intervention had to do with a "consciousness" of the effect it had over the players. The belief was a stimulus that freed human faculties. Viewed in this light, the power resided in the player and not in the acknowledgment of the strength of an occult force. The context in which the interviews were conducted created an environment that contributed toward this kind of rationalization of belief. To these former players, in a conversation that focused on their relation with football, the most important thing was to talk about talent and individual worth, to offer an account as to how the game was played, to interpret events and to recall important moments. It was especially important to talk about "football matters," as if this was a self-referential universe. The interviewees, some of them with a professional career that put them in contact with more institutionalized forms of football, had a rather detached discourse on vovô. The legitimacy of their careers as football players depended on the acknowledgment of a talent that was scrutinized by the football community. In general, almost everyone said that they believed the game depended on talent, work, and merit.

However, this rationalization contrasted with the importance attributed to belief in the stories they told about the vovô's action in Lourenço Marques's suburban football. This process of putting vovô's power into perspective disappeared in the course of their narratives. Within the regime of causality present in these accounts, vovô clearly had an enormous efficacy. The pertinence of its actions was thus acknowledged. During one of these fantastic stories Mogne asserts that the healer "is a doctor" with "a science" acquired through experience. At the time, "the guys who did this work were honest, straight guys, who had their own lives." Today, he regrets, "there are no honest people. Not anymore. Whoever he is that appears today, you best be skeptical"; today it is, above all, a matter of "business." Mogne's opinion toward what we might call the liberalization of the healer's craft is similar to his views on contemporary Mozambican society and the way in which it fell short of his expectations. Issufo, in turn, assured us that he "always trusted in his work." Talent as a player and manager was a crucial element to explain the course of events on the pitch. It was powerless, however, to influence the "process off the pitch." The game played outside the pitch depended on the work of the vovô. In this arena, his usefulness was undeniable: "I saw, and with concrete evidence, that there are competent vovôs." Those who "work behind trees, roots, and other things." He ended by asserting that "these things cannot be proven, but they exist."

Hilário da Conceição, who claims "to be against vovôs," returned to Mozambique after its independence, to manage Ferroviário. At that time he had to accept the vovô. If you do not accept him, he concludes, "you're better off not managing in Africa." This seemingly strategic consent gave way to a different engagement. Hilário admits that, at a certain point, "the guy convinced me psychologically how I should guide the team." If this happened to him, says Hilário, "imagine how it influenced the players. It is incredibly strong, all these traditions are incredibly strong." If "your vovô says so," continues Hilário, "you do not come in through that door because that door is booby-trapped, that is, it has pieces of dust and magic stuff. If you go through it, your legs will become stuck and you will lose the game. How do we enter the field, I asked? Jump over the wall." Hilário jokes: "Can you imagine, eighteen guys jumping over a wall? Can you imagine Hilário, forty-odd years old, fifty, jumping over walls. Because if you go through that door, then . . . you lose. These traditions," he concluded, "are tough and we have to accept them."

The reflexive distance that was created, which relativized belief, transforming it into a psychological stimulus, existed alongside narratives where the reality of these traditional forms of wisdom was proven, through stories of personal belief. The truth of the discourse, subject to conditions of production that privileged this distance, appeared to be weak in the face of the strength of these traditions, grounded in personal experience. In that precise context, just before a match, it was crucial to believe. This obedience to belief was not the product of a conscious strategy to attain certain specific goals, as seems to be suggested by some of the answers given by the interviewees, but belonged, rather, to a shared "practical reason," it belonged to bodies, their senses and dispositions. While hinging on this "truth" of practices, belief confirmed the "truth" of these worldviews; it was not the result, then, of a discursive worldview or an autonomous mental schema inherited through a cultural indoctrination, one the colonial power would classify as "uncivilized." In football, as in other areas of the colonial city's daily life, the vovô had truly proven his efficiency. His art offered an explanation for the game's contingencies. The actions of players, managers, directors, and of the actual public in the community, attested to the truth of these forms of knowledge, considering the nonexistence or the weakness of any another principle that could define the order of things or that had a coherence that manifested itself in practice. As an instrument toward understanding the world, the language of sorcery was employed to solve the relevant moral, ethical, and practical issues associated with the football game.[32] Football narratives thus became an instrument for reading and interpretation, and a script on which to base one's actions, a ground for creative strategies. The interviewees' reflexivity, their discursive distance, did not counter the veracity of these practices, especially because their logic lived on in their bodies and experiences.

THE VOVÔ'S MARKET: SPECIALIZATION, RIVALRIES, AND EFFICIENCY

The growing problems in the daily life of suburban people in Lourenço Marques contributed to the reconversion of the healers' work. The focus on football's problems, a vigorous communitarian activity, which led to the adaptation of some "ancient preparations," gave way to a creative process in which some new practices were invented. Some healers specialized in matters associated with the game. Ângelo vows that a football team was not taken care of by "just any healer." There were those who, although they treated other problems, had a special "talent" for football. Others, however, when teams approached them, said, "I don't want anything to do with football, you'd better find someone else because my stuff doesn't have any effect on that." In this context of adapting the healer's art to the football universe, the most common procedure, as pointed out by Mogne, was that of the "vovô's preparation of the ball and the equipment"; the players "could not use the equipment before it had passed through the door of his house. He brought his stones, all those things." In the course of his "preparations," the healer imposed an organization on the players' lives, a sort of guide to daily practices. In Ângelo's words, "Before the game, the healer would tell us that we could not do this, we could not do that. You buy the equipment and have to keep it and take care of it, and only get it on the day of the match. Everyone has to inhale some smoke and some roots and to have a bath."

Hamido Nizamo highlights the importance of "preparing the ball." Each team brought a prepared ball "and the referee would then choose. It was a serious matter." In some matches, the supporters of one of the teams, taking advantage of the fact that the opponent's ball had gone out of the pitch's bounds, would puncture it, so that their team's ball, properly prepared by a healer, could then be used. These supporters, who were aware of the dynamics involved in the preparations, tried to annul the vovô's power over the ball; to expurgate the "disease" caused by the preparation of the opponent's healer. It was as if the ball, influenced by magical powers, was no longer round but had gained a will of its own that would inevitably benefit one of the teams. In each match, the "preparation" had to be repeated. If the outcome was not positive, the club would look for a more effective healer. Often, the healer's success would spur the attention of opposing teams who would try to poach him. Issufo remembers a healer named Neru who was hired by Ferroviário, and who called himself "the king of India." The healer himself placed an advertisement in the newspaper stating that he had received fifty escudos so that the railway team would beat Desportivo. In the next match between these two teams, it was Desportivo's turn to pay the amount asked by Neru. On that occasion, Issufo recalled, Desportivo was able to beat Ferroviário: "That is achieved through spirit. Today there are none, or, if there are still some, they are very few and demand millions."

The competitions' development led to the formation of a real "healers' market." Mogne acknowledges that, much like today, witchcraft was also a business back then: "Superstition in the AFA was something extraordinary, something terrible. A lot of money was spent." The widespread use of preparations in the suburban championships, their diversification and adaptation to the football game, the growth of a market of healers who were in constant demand, which is an indication of the local importance of this suburban spectacle, reflected the gradual centrality of success and increasing social differentiation. The prominence the game afforded its participants would be converted into communitarian capital, not only for players but also for heads of associations and even the public, who used their teams' victories as interactional capital within the expanding urban community. Spurred by these growing rivalries, the vovô's market instigated the process of sportization: "The problem," says Mogne, "was that people had this euphoria, this desire. Let me tell you something: if you are my opponent, I will not speak to you or extend my hand before entering the pitch. It's a psychological matter." The will to win, according to Mogne, was responsible for the fact that every player, regardless of his beliefs, "took part in the scheme": "when you want to win, often you're instilled with something that you can't actually analyze. Personally, I would say, man, what's this?" However, the "will to win" would lead even the more skeptical among them to "take part in the scheme." The "scheme's" strength became an orchestration of wills, a collective legitimization of belief. Mogne recalled his relation with belief: "If you did not do it and you lost, your conscience would weigh on you. You would say, If I'd only done this, I'd have won." This weight on one's conscience was the materialization of a guilt that no one wanted to bear. This guilt, both in the context of the game and in other spheres of suburban life, legitimated collective belief, and an individual's right to believe. The will to win justified these preparations: "You go with the wave, as the Brazilians say. Everything those guys say, you accept, even to have a bath wherever they tell you to. The important thing is to win the game." Nizamo remembers that often those responsible for the teams, the managers and directors, in order to get the best out of the players, would lie to them and assure them that they had gone to a vovô. The player then played more at ease even if no preparation had indeed taken place. On other occasions the players would ask the manager if "there was something," and he would answer, "Man, there is nothing today." Conclusion: some players were already defeated as they entered the pitch. Their heads "were no longer working properly."

Employed in this context, vovô was also a malicious practice, an instrument used to put pressure on players, to goad them into adhering more intensely to the style of play, an antidote against the fear factor. As in other spheres of suburban life, in football vovô was an answer to the efficiency problem, to the need to achieve results.

THE VOVÔ NEVER FAILS?

As the outcome of a game left little room for subtleties of interpretation, considerable pressure was put on the vovô. The enlisting of his services aimed at achieving victory: the "sorcerer's" arts had no hand in modeling the aesthetic level of the performance, which was down to the malicious arts of the players. Still, the creativity of the preparation, the strength of his performativity, could indeed legitimate the efficacy of belief, thus freeing the bodies. The healer's work was subjected to a constant and objective evaluation. When the preparations appeared to have failed, the vovô argued that there had been imperfections during the ritual he had devised, and those were the responsibility of the players, managers, and directors. Ângelo explains that the healer is always right, even when he loses:

> You know what is the problem with healers in football? The healer has this particular strength. If we go there and we win, all is well. But if we lose he will say: you failed in everything I told

you; one of you failed, that is the only reason. You failed to do something. If we lose again, we say that healer is a cheat. Then we don't go back to him, we look for someone else. They have this advantage and don't return the money they receive. There are others [healers] who say: go and play, if you win you can pay me and if you don't then you don't have to pay a thing. In the old days, this was how it worked.

Hilário confirmed that the "vovô never fails." He recalled, "If a guy says you can't have sexual intercourse. Or you can't drink alcoholic drinks or some crap like that. And the guy did his spell and we lost, then he would say, Someone has failed." He said, for instance, "you can't come in through that door" and I had gone through it. Did I not tell you not to go through there? The manager did. He made you lose. The guy is always right."[33]

The vovô's arguments were not, however, sufficiently persuasive to protect his position in this particular market. The lack of results by the team would lead to the healer's replacement. The increasing importance of efficiency in suburban football led to a growing rotation in the hiring of vovôs, something that allowed for a greater number of people to enter this market. The ruthless logic of getting results did not make life easy for those, managers and healers, to whom an enthusiastic public looked for satisfaction when the results did not go according to expectations. There was a clear clash between the strength of traditional belief and the basic values presiding over a new order of things, where the principle of efficiency reigned supreme.

The healer's loss of status did not shake the overall status of belief. The fact that it was impossible to find a completely victorious vovô did not put the importance of the "preparations" at stake. Cuxo-cuxo was a communitarian good, one whose usefulness continued to be felt. Whoever put themselves on the outside, whoever questioned the vovô's virtues, threatened the actual belief system and everything that it meant as a representation of ways of conceiving the world, thus threatening, in the final instance, the structure of the performance. When Matine, after Mozambique's independence, became the national team's manager, he tried to fight the vovôs' influence in order to defend football as a profession, regulated by methodical principles that, in the final instance, were responsible for the game's outcome. "I am a football professional and I can't play around with football, because if I play around with football, I'm in trouble." Before a match against the People's Republic of the Congo, Matine faced the local vovôs' power, asked them to guess not only who would win but who would score the goals and when. The manager left Mozambique's national team after he was defeated in that match. A vovô, paid by the national team's directors, assured them they would win, and yet they failed. The manager did not consider the possibility that someone had failed to properly execute the vovô's requests, had failed to execute a procedure, had misinterpreted a ritual. According to him, the actual belief was at stake. The belief had become a business and not an art. The solution, as foretold by Hilário in his words on those who wish to manage in Africa, was to leave.

A COMMUNITARIAN RIGHT

Ângelo, who believes that football is won by being played on the field, still values belief: "Well, we believe. Even today, we believe. Why shouldn't we believe?" To believe was, Mogne concluded, "the best medicine a doctor could prescribe. You've got to believe. If you don't believe, it doesn't have any effect. The body won't accept it, the body won't receive it. Any reaction, you contradict yourself, because there is a problem with the medicine." If someone says that "he will have a go at it, then he'll really have a go at it and fight for it."

Within the context of football, as in other areas of activity in the suburbs of Lourenço Marques, the vovô was basically a "right," a malicious right established in an unwritten law. For the right to be invoked by the local population it had to be credible, people had to believe in it. The clubs, and players, much like the members of the community, regardless of their social standing and regional or religious affiliation, had the right to employ the vovô. As an agent in the resolution of practical problems, it seemed more effective than the rights pertaining to the social and political system imposed by colonialism, which were no less malicious, at times inexistent, or scarce, ambiguous, and often perverse. Deemed by the Portuguese colonial administration as a backward and superstitious cultural practice, this suburban right was part of the community's tacit social contract. The competition for scarce resources and the seemingly unjustifiable and growing inequalities within the community stimulated a specific market. Whoever benefited the most from the new social organization, as underlined by Daniel Matavela, needed protection: "Protection is needed when you start to thrive. . . . Spells protect you, that's a fact; you need protection." Protection helped whoever prospered in the community to defend themselves against those that resorted to sorcerers to fight against this unevenness among equals.

The intrinsic logic of football provided the grounds for the translation of that unevenness: the search for results, the pressure that placed responsibility on the individual for his performance. At the same time, the game had a high degree of uncertainty, filled with intangible elements: the ball that simply did not go in, the one that hit the post, the penalty that was scored or missed, the trickster's magic play. The vovô's performance acted upon an uncertain universe that was inherent to the way the football game was played, helping explain the many chance events that ended up determining the game's outcome. "Cuxo-cuxo's law" benefited from the weakness of alternative principles that could clearly explain how the game was ordered or the reason behind the outcome of the players' gestures and movements. Occult powers justified defeats and victories, good and bad matches, injustices but also incongruities, individual fragilities, appeasing the players' doubts and uncertainties. The vovô's law proved fairer and more reliable.

The underlying principles of the local football style were not challenged by the vovô's actions, even in terms of a subversion of the game's rules or of its implicit moral principles. Alongside the tricksters' movements and intimidating gestures, it was an element of the malicious strategies that defined suburban football. It shared this status with tricky performances that managed fear and risk and were thus able to enchant the game and challenge its mechanisms. The recurrent employment of the vovô, confirming the values that accompanied the process of communitarian adaptation under colonial rule, showed the strength of the principles that regulated life in the suburbs of Lourenço Marques.

THE VOVÔ AS A SOURCE OF LOCAL NARRATIVES: THE WATCH STORY AND THE MANIPULATION OF MODERNITY

Stories about the vovô, one of the most important sources of football narratives in the suburbs of Lourenço Marques, exalted the capacity of local belief to subvert the strength of a given power. The narrative moral of these stories almost always attests to the effectiveness of the vovô's power. The healer rarely embodies the figure of the villain, even to the players and teams who suffered at the hands of his art. Whoever was deceived could not help but acknowledge the mastery of the person who deceived him, which was in fact the only way they could account for their own faults. The performative dimension of the vovô's art was an integral part of these narratives. The healer's mastery was described in these narratives, alongside the creativity associated with the preparations, the process, the mechanism, and the ritual's creation. The description of these details heightened the enchantment of the football narrative. The vovô was also a virtuoso.

One of the most well remembered stories, even today, in the suburbs of Lourenço Marques, a major myth in the vovô's narratives, is the story of the watch. In the local Muslim clash, opposing Mahafil Isslamo and Atlético Mahometano, a powerful healer was able to manipulate the clock, a symbol of the modern world, a regulator of urban life, of its rhythms of production and leisure.[34] In the morning, Saide Mogne met the rest of his team in the house of Atlético Mahometano's president. At that point, he recalled, "a man came to do his work, as usual, and because to us this was the usual, we did not pay much attention." Still in the morning, between eleven thirty and noon, some Mahafil players walked through the neighborhood's streets, fully kitted "with trousers, boots, and socks." Someone from the Atlético team then warned them that Mahafil's players had got back from a place where a "terrible healer lived." Mahafil, claims Issufo Batata, had gone to get Ambrósio, the "terrible Ambrósio, the one who wore a suit and tie." Ambrósio was an old healer who "arrived at the field" wearing a "suit and tie," so that "no one knew he was the healer." The disguise operated as a curious reversal of the exoticism usually associated with these practices, dribbling masterfully past the prejudice of the colonizer and using his clothes as an added legitimation, of a modern and sophisticated nature.

That afternoon, not long before kick-off, the Atlético team left in a truck for Beira-Mar's field, where the game was to take place. When they were approaching the pitch, "just before the final bend," as Mogne recalls, the goalkeeper "remembered he had left his shirt at home." "The club's directors," continued Mogne, "looked at their watches and noticed there was still plenty of time." The truck turned back and they went to the goalkeeper's home, where he got his missing shirt. On their way back to the field, one of Atlético's directors decided to check the time. It was then that he noticed, bewildered, that his watch had stopped. Even more extraordinary, the watches of all Atlético's directors had stopped.[35] When the team arrived at Beira-Mar's pitch, the hour at which the game was supposed to begin had long passed, Mahafil had left the field, and Atlético had lost on account of "nonattendance." Mogne, who was in Atlético's truck, attests to the veracity of this story: "It is true, it happened, I lived through it. It was much spoken of over here." Among the "incredible things" happening in the AFA, Ângelo recalls the "story of the watch" quite clearly, which is "spoken of even today": that of the healer with such magic powers that he was able to set back the opponent's watches. Ferroviário's present director, during the interview, tried to find, with little certainty, a logical explanation: "Even to this day I wonder how this happened. Could it be that only one person had a watch? And maybe that person had got the hour wrong and no one else was asked?" The outcome was not, however, negotiable. To find another reason meant to start an argument about belief: "Until today, no one has said anything else. They only say that that healer was able to set the opponent's watches back so that the team lost on account of nonattendance." When legend becomes fact, print the legend.

The victory of the vovô's powers over "clock time," a triumph of the community over the symbol representing the new system of relations imposed by colonialism, had, however, a limited reach. This manipulation of modernity ended up benefiting the morality imposed by the clock on daily life. Atlético's defeat was justified by compliance with the law that dictated that the suburban game should be ruled by a fixed schedule, that of an organized leisure time, much like workers had to subject themselves to a work schedule. The occasional manipulation of time achieved by the healer's power was a partial subversion of the game rather than a challenge to its foundations. Much like the intrinsic logic of the local style of play and the gestures and movements that composed it, the vovô was employed as a defensive strategy. Local cunning, in its attempts to reorder the meanings of modernity (themselves of a malicious nature), was powerless to stop it.

HEROES OF THE COMMUNITY

The vovôs were major characters in stories about suburban football. They shared their place as heroes in these narratives alongside the great performers, the virtuoso tricksters, and the more "virile" players. All these became the main heroes in this malicious interaction order, those who better managed its practical morality. In this sense, they were not respectable individuals, faithful servants of the game's regulations. Their popularity, much like that of the communitarian outlaws discussed by Eric Hobsbawm, was defined by their ability to subvert the powers that were generally inscribed in a law that was considered ineffective or unfair.[36] The Portuguese colonial ideology saw all these local heroes as despicable figures. The vovôs represented pagan irrationality, anti-Christianity, obscurantism, the practice that truly defined the indígena's backwardness.[37] The gestures of the virtuoso trickster embodied the art of deceitfulness, of inconsequent action, of easy exhibitionism, the lack of any notion of the collective, the absence of religion or ideology. The movements produced by intimidating strategies showed the lack of order, the nonexistence of a central power, the absence of a state policy, things that were tolerated in the suburbs but regarded as unacceptable behavior in the "cement zone." The interpreters of these gestures were outlaws; their acts, as seen by the authorities, had turned football into a social problem. This spectacle, which celebrated such local heroes, was acclaimed by a misbehaving public, a public of "diseased" people. Like the social pathologies identified by power—alcoholism, prostitution, delinquency—football developed in the space where a cheap and disposable labor force lived, or survived—the labor force that for such a long time sustained Portuguese colonialism. Subject to these conditions, suburban heroes were singled out by their art of interpreting local protocols. Before the community, they displayed the cunning needed to survive under adverse conditions. The employment of the vovô was part of these strategies.

Suburban football narrative fixated these stories, thus allowing for the description and reinterpretation of the feats of these individuals. They praised the vovô who stopped the watch, the trickster who solved the game by using his inherent gift, an enchantment of sorts, the tough players who did not dodge a fight and could "take out" their opponents by walking on a thin line, a boundary where they were allowed to do so, and one that was negotiated in each game, between the teams, the public, and the referee. Given the absence of images, these gestures are remembered orally and are enthusiastically described, as indeed was the case in the interviews with former players. These community heroes were the best interpreters of the local moral economy, the ones who were more proficient in their use of the weapons of malice and whose strategic sense, turned into bodily intuition, best defined a gesture with a deep local meaning. Celebrating these heroes also amounted to praise for this peripheral community and for the way in which it organized its everyday life.

THE PERIPHERY INVADES THE CENTER

When suburban players started to gain a steadier access to the downtown football market, especially from the 1960s onward, and to jump more effectively over the strict borders of discrimination, they brought along with them the traditions that had proven beneficial when they played in the suburbs. The vovô's powers did not lose their importance and effectiveness when they entered the field of European football. On the contrary, the fact that the ability to play a sport was, within the context of late Portuguese colonialism, a condition toward landing a job, gave a greater sense of urgency to the vovô's services, and, paradoxically, placed suburban football's malice at the service of this system. During the period when there were more lines of contact between the cement city and the suburbs—benefiting from the transfer market's expansion—"woodland knowledge," adapted to the conventions of the suburban community, established itself within the football game dominated by Europeans. The mechanism of social segregation did not prevent a number of exchanges between the center and the periphery. Suburban football, for instance, absorbed information on styles of play and tactical systems (see chapter 6). Passed on by the media or by privileged informers, knowledge about other forms of playing—the Brazilians' touch, the Italians' intensity—was incorporated, in an improvised way, into the style of play and into the organization of the players' gestures and movements.

This exchange was not, however, a one-way street. The concerns of metropolitan newspapers regarding the profusion of cuxo-cuxo in Lourenço Marques football, mentioned by Fréchaut Neto in his series of articles for *O brado africano*, pointed toward the dissemination, in the cement city, of practices present in the everyday organization of the suburbs. Guilherme Cabaço, an old settler, acknowledges that "sorcery, magic stuff," which "is more associated with the black population" also ended up "affecting Portuguese players and managers." When "the African started to join these clubs, he brought his beliefs with him." In Alto-Maé, a club from a neighborhood bordering the suburbs, there was, remembers Cabaço, "a small cask with some oil that they put behind the opponent's goal, to attract the ball and to affect the goalkeeper." Cabaço vows, however, that in his time as a player, during the 1920s and 1930s, "there was no such thing," which is testimony to the social closure of football in this period.

The gradual arrival of suburban beliefs in downtown football, especially from the 1960s onward, was not met with stiff resistance on the part of the authorities and agents that regulated European football. On the contrary, the practice of resorting to the vovô was integrated, in a more or less informal way, in the teams' working processes, which signaled the autonomy of this field of activity within the framework of colonial state ideology, but also a proximity between the categories of knowledge and cognition on both sides of the fence. Armando Silva (b. 1930), an educated black man who worked as a public servant and who was also one of the AFA's directors,[38] remembers how Maurício, a player who moved from São José, the team from the mission of São José de Lhanguene, to Sporting de Lourenço Marques, promoted the vovô downtown: "When he was playing he would always joke: the vovô said we will win, the vovô said, the vovô said . . . and afterward the idea just spread." Armando reports that downtown teams also employed the vovô, not through the action of their directors, but on the athletes' own initiative. Abissínia Ali explains how the African players presented the problem to European managers: "We were careful and just said: Mr. So-and-So, we are like this, we work like this. Do you mind jumping over this smoke? It's nothing bad, just jumping. Just that." The players explained to the manager that cuxo-cuxo practices did not entail a lack of respect for his ability. "It isn't as if we don't accept or don't believe in the work that he does, but it's just to give him that extra bit of luck. If we win, the first one to be recognized is the manager. Then usually most of them accepted." The arguments were persuasive. He even stresses that "some managers who came from Portugal believed in it." In Ângelo's words, "Why shouldn't they believe in it?"

According to Armando, Severiano Correia, the manager of Ferrroviário who represented the modernity of tactical systems in Lourenço Marques football, when faced with vovô, "went along with it." This attitude aimed to protect the team's interests: "when the vovô begins to impose himself, the athlete ceases to play well because he becomes obsessed. Afterward, if he loses, he says he lost because he failed to do this or that. The best thing is to go along with it." Severiano Correia's tactical scheme worked better with players who were mentally fit. Seen in this light, the vovô contributed to the efficiency of tactical principles. Prevented from playing in the AFA championship, after the colonial administration forced its dissolution in 1959, suburban players took their beliefs to "the cement." Cruz recalls a match between Sporting and Indo-Português in which both managers, Botelho de Melo and Fernando Ribeiro, hired a vovô. "Fernando Ribeiro," continued Cruz, said, "I will pay for cuxo-cuxo but I'll pretend to not know about it, and cuxo-cuxo doesn't choose the team. I will pay but ignore it. I'm responsible for their physical preparation and for teaching them to play football. As a manager I will ignore it, although I know it exists, in all clubs."

Portuguese managers, whether or not they believed in the effectiveness of the vovô, still considered him to be an important element in the teams' management and motivational work. Many players from the metropolis had a number of superstitions that they adapted to the game. Some of them reproduced rituals typical of the Catholic tradition: the players blessed themselves, prayed, looked to the sky, and so forth. There were other superstitions with popular roots, based on beliefs the players had learned in the places they came from—many were from rural areas. Some players also made up their own superstitions: always wearing the same shirt, stepping onto the pitch with the right foot, kissing a ring. Considering the context of superstition that surrounded the downtown football game, suburban beliefs were not significantly different. Although the rituals were distinct, and the gestures and preparations of a different nature, the symbolic exchange was intelligible, for there was a common ground that enabled the sharing of beliefs. While there was a substantial degree of rejection ("those practices are not our own"), there was, simultaneously, an acceptance of the principles of its functionality. Metropolitan players did not adhere to these practices, which were still an "example of the black man's backward nature," but accepted them nonetheless. Ângelo explains this situation in straightforward terms: "Football unites people more than any other sport. Football unites many people, with various structures, customs and, usually, for us to be united, we need to respect each other's beliefs. If someone comes and says, man, we have to do this for this game, the others will go along with him, no one turns his back on him. Even in the city clubs." He concludes by stating that "these beliefs still live on today."

After his arrival downtown, the vovô crossed the Indian and Atlantic Oceans and landed in the metropolis, thanks to Lourenço Marques players who had moved to Lisbon's big clubs. Ângelo claimed that nowadays there are "some good healers in Portugal. Healers who came from here and from several other places in other countries and who now work in football in Portugal." The expressions gathered by Craveirinha in his glossary also traveled along with these beliefs. Matateu, Eusébio, Coluna, Hilário — great heroes of Portuguese football — used these local expressions among themselves, thus deceiving the metropolitan players: "the players who came from over here," says Ângelo, "when they played in the same team or in the national team, often used our dialect so that the opponents did not know what they were saying. That is a great advantage."

THE UNIVERSALITY OF THE VOVÔ: THE HUNGARIAN SORCERER

From the viewpoint of colonial ideology, the vovô's growing popularity downtown and afterward in the metropolis could be seen as an indigenization of European football, subject to an inverted assimilation. The indígena custom, a feature that distinguished the civilized from the uncivilized, adapted to European football with ease, coexisted alongside other beliefs and superstitions. As such, the vovô seemed to possess universal features that did not fit into the narrative of cultural incommensurability. His usefulness was felt a long way away from the suburbs of Lourenço Marques. Issufo Batata went even further: the vovô was an immanent element associated with the game's practice. This practice could not be explained without a reference to the vovô's language. The football game, regardless of the social and cultural space it was produced in, could be told through the vovô's narratives. The occult had a universal dimension and its influence explained a number of different incidents. Issufo tried to fill the gap between "African culture," filled with occult practices seen as obscurantist by the colonial power, and the world of other human beings, supposedly rational and ruled by different worldviews. To achieve this, he moved the field of analysis from the suburbs of Lourenço Marques to other places where football was also played. He chose an example that he knew and that came from the colonizer's universe. Issufo asserted that Benfica won the European Cup in 1961 and 1962 because the team benefited from the powers of a vovô. The person behind these practices was not an African healer, but the actual manager of the Lisbon team, the Hungarian Béla Guttmann.[39] Guttmann, a Jew and a renowned representative of the Magyar vanguard that transformed European football in the 1950s, was known as the *feiticeiro* (sorcerer, wizard). Issufo thought this title was not just due to his talent as a manager but also to his magic powers. Guttmann, the great manager, the great strategist, the man who mastered the game's rationalization principles, a master of tactics and systems, was, according to Issufo, a powerful sorcerer, someone with a deep knowledge of another realm, from where the game could be influenced at a different level from that of the performance itself. Everything that happened during the European Cup final in 1962, between Benfica and Real Madrid,[40] was proof of Guttmann's magical powers. Issufo provided an example: "Costa Pereira, Benfica's goalkeeper, at one point defended the ball, and the ball hit the post and, instead of going in, went straight to his hands." Guttmann knew what he was doing. "It was his doing," Issufo asserted. "These are things that you cannot write about, that you cannot prove." When Guttmann left the Lisbon club, he asserted that Benfica, without him, would never win another top competition in European football. Guttmann's "curse" remains and since then Benfica has lost eight European finals.

⁓

The Estado Novo's physical education theoreticians attempted to scientifically analyze the effect of religion on the athletes' motor system, how it induced emotions and stimuli and led the body to move in a certain way, creating moral and ideological meanings. A "Christian body" was thus idealized, a respectable body, adapted from the disciplined body that served as a metaphor for fascist society. In the suburbs of Lourenço Marques, the principle of belief behind the suburban players' bodily movement—far from being an ideomotor gesture driven by ideological and Christian devotion, translated into gymnastics' rectilinear movements or into the ideology of amateur fair play—was a magic libido of sorts, based on the dynamic traditions shared by a burgeoning community. Within the framework of colonial ideology, but also for those African elites that ascribed to football the role of a vehicle for the universalization of a respectable behavior that relied on abiding by the law, the expansion of the vovô seemed to suggest the prevalence of a "dangerous" indigenization enhanced by the relative racial overture of the late colonial period. Not circumscribed by the city's suburbs, the vovô, as the players' market grew, was integrated into the downtown market and even reached the metropole. These manifestations, however, implied much more than the prescription of a specific cultural model for interpreting the world. The vovô provided a grammar that sought to make sense of the rationales that underpinned the construction of life in the suburbs and answered the individuals' need to give an order to their practices. Thus they became a communitarian right. The vovô's knowledge also sought to subvert. These healers and sorcerers materialized in practices that reinforced the right of that community to create alternative accounts of the ways of the world. Once again, an ethos created under the conditions of urban development in the suburbs was turned into a life ethics. In the context of local football, the increasing pressure on performances driven by growing rivalries explained the development of the vovô's market, which was a local answer to the demand for efficiency. On the field of play, the vovô encouraged a local style of play, characterized by a forceful malice, devoid of the enchantment and guile that characterized the movements of the football game, where order was subverted by taking advantage of the fragility of the game's laws.

6 ⮒ Sweetness and Speed
Tactics as Disenchantment of the World

TACTICS AND THE BODY

THE signs that the process of sportization had arrived in the Lourenço Marques suburbs were not limited to the adoption of association football, its laws, and its regulations. The desire to take part in the wider surrounding society was expressed through the will to share opinions and experiences, to gain the right to play against teams representing other regions and countries, as well as through an aspiration for status and social mobility. The malicious economy that characterized the suburban game absorbed, in a more or less harmonious way, a series of external stimuli and propositions.

In the suburb, from early on, there was information available on other "ways of playing the game." From the cement city came news on football in the metropolis, on its major clubs and key players. The close ties with South Africa helped promote other interpreters and styles of play, which were employed by teams from neighboring areas in tournaments organized by the AFA. More sporadically and irregularly, there were also football news from more distant countries, details from international football's narratives, the knowledge of which guaranteed a valuable interactional capital and was a conspicuous sign of cosmopolitanism. This specific knowledge influenced the game in the suburbs of Lourenço Marques, changing the way it was played. In neighborhood matches, there were teams named after metropolitan, English, and Brazilian clubs; the moves of international stars, described in the newspaper and then spread by word of mouth, were reinterpreted. The transformation of the narrated events into bodily practice involved an effort of re-creation; using their imagination, local players were able to draw close to the skill of the best players in the world.

The relation between the prevalent interaction order in the suburb and these external influences was not a conflicting one. The adoption of the laws of association was a hinge for a connection with the outside world. An imaginative imitation, which underpinned the introduction of a number of different morphologies in the players' movements, did not threaten the local game's cunning principles: the malice employed to counter the rule, the pertinence of the motor repertoire that dominated this symbolic economy, as well as the appreciation and classification criteria shared by the players and public. Some external influences contributed, in some cases, to strengthening the intrinsic principles of the local style of play and the predominant dispositions in the athletes' motor habitus. Matine, for instance, talks about how "Italian toughness" was easily incorporated within "local intimidating tactics." At the time, he points out, "since television did not exist, we did not quite know how people played in other countries. There was always someone, however, who for one reason or another had visited these places and had spoken with someone or knew someone who had visited these places."

"One day someone said" that "the Italian team is tough as hell, they play well but are really tough and are quicker than the Portuguese." In Italy, people "play tough, they mark really close and use their bodies." Makeshift managers in neighborhood matches then started saying, "Our team must employ Italian toughness in the way it plays." Italian toughness quickly became a justification for the local game's impetuosity and even for breaking the game's official law. As people did not quite know "what Italian toughness was," Matine continues, "we often broke the rules: we were tough because that was Italian toughness and the biggest guy would lean on the other guy's body and say, "this is Italian toughness." And since it was "Italian toughness . . . it could not be a foul."

The Brazilian game's virtuosity, another relevant external influence, was easily incorporated into the local style of play. Accounts of their extraordinary footballing feats were confirmed when Brazilian clubs passed through Lourenço Marques in 1959 and 1960. The South Americans' performances live on in numerous narratives that are shared to this day. Hamido Nizamo compares the effect of these Brazilian tours to the impact made by the visit of a few South African teams to the suburb, where some "tricksters who played with the ball" stood out.[1] Brazilian football left a strong impression: "there were players who controlled the ball, stopped, and even sat on the ball. It was beautiful." The Brazilian game style was the complete affirmation, at an even more skillful and spectacular level, of local principles of appreciation. The Brazilian player's pause, as he sat on the ball, suggested the preparation of an illusionist act, filled with malice, or actually marked the execution of that action, a gesture that had a specific designation in the African suburbs: *hpfa*. The pause marked the trickster's victory, the supreme act of humiliation over his opponent. The Brazilians proved to be the masters of malice.

The symbolic exchange present in the local game was not as affected by the transmission of rudimentary principles for ordering the players on the pitch, such as tactical systems like the WM formation (see below). The course taken by the WM system, from when it was originally employed by Herbert Chapman's Arsenal team in industrial London in the early 1930s until it reached the suburbs of colonial Lourenço Marques, kept pace with the process of sportization. Saide Mogne claims that "at the time, the most notable football was England's. It was the universal model. In Portugal, much like everywhere else, the teams used this same model. It was the WM." The press helped popularize the positions of this tactical system, which were mentioned in match reports. According to Saide Mogne, in AFA matches teams employed the WM system, which was rather less likely to occur in neighborhood matches, where the fluctuating number of players rarely allowed it. Although at the AFA the WM served mainly as a model for distributing players across the pitch, it was a first level of the game pattern's organization. Mogne adds that meeting South African teams was crucial to this system's expansion. South African football, he says, since it was closer to the English game, developed more swiftly. The white South African teams that came to Lourenço Marques already employed the WM, which may have also been the case with African teams touring the suburbs. It is also likely, as mentioned by Armando Silva, that the system reached the suburbs through the influence of downtown football.

The employment of WM formations in AFA competitions took place, as reported by Mogne, by way of an "empirical process." The use of the WM and of other subsequent organizational systems was confirmed by these former players, who said that its rudimentary application was employed as a minimum ordering principle. The "tactical part," says Cruz, was virtually decided on the day of the game. The person whom everyone else saw as the most knowledgeable, "the one who had the best eyes," was the one who decided: "we will play like this, we will play like that." According to Cruz, in the 1940s the players were already selected "within that WM." Cruz explains its working logic:

the game system was different from nowadays; there wasn't any 4–2–4 or 3–2–5. We had the WM: three defenders, two midfielders, and five forwards. The three defenders had to cope with the five forwards, who would come toward them. In this kind of football, the defender had a lot more work to do. The midfielder was the guy who took care of the distribution to the forwards; he did little defending, very little.

The person responsible for the team's lineup, Ângelo says, would decide that "this guy will play as goalkeeper, right back, the other as left back, fullback and so on." The numbering of the shirts made the disposition of the WM on the pitch easier. Each number represented a position:

> the goalkeeper was no. 1 and the no. 12 was the substitute. The no. 2 was the right back, the no. 3 played as left back, the no. 5 as central halfback, then there was the no. 4, who was the right midfielder. The no. 6 was the left midfielder, the no. 7 the right winger, the no. 8 the right central halfback, the no. 9 the center forward, the no. 10 the left central halfback, and the no. 11 the left winger.

In neighborhood matches, as pointed out by Matine, this ordering principle was more precarious:

> What we knew was that when one team played another, it would be eleven against eleven. The group would choose, you're not very talented but you are strong, so you will be the right-back, you are left-handed so you will be the left back, you are both tall, so you'll play as fullbacks; we would say, if the other guys have a striker, you will mark him and the other will be free. Since at the time we played in a 4–2–4, we tried to order ourselves according to this pattern.

Hilário reports that the disposition of the eleven players in those suburban matches was behind a set of movements that he describes as "improvised." By allowing for improvisation, the players' ordering system was not at odds with the intrinsic principles of the local style of play. On the contrary, it became a useful mimicry, which did not conflict with the motor repertoire valued in the neighborhood; perhaps the latter would have suffered a certain degree of specialization, in line with each player's disposition and function, and a preliminary coupling between function and physical shape, which distinguished, at least partly, AFA competitions from the greater "freedom" allowed in neighborhood matches.

THE TACTICAL MENTALITY

However, tactical systems did not simply organize the game pattern's initial shape. The tactical model, besides indicating the athletes' positions, included a number of rules that conditioned their movement, principles that ordained individual action and, as such, the whole game dynamics. This latent second order of tactics wielded malicious powers. While the players' lineup on the field, according to more or less well-drawn letters that revealed the tactical model, may not have challenged the local moral economy of the game, the same was not the case with the mechanism that was intrinsic to this more inclusive role: a kind of second nature of the tactical scheme that resulted from the game's interaction order being aligned with the efficiency principles necessary to achieve victory. Employed under the supervision of a manager, this mechanism was the ground for a new kind of game, a revolution in the way the body's performance and behavior were conceived—in short, the establishment of a new motor habitus. The players could not move "freely" away from their original positions or manage their motor repertoire according to other principles of action. These positions became mere markers of a much more complex movement scheme. Their hypothetical effects on football in the suburbs of Lourenço Marques suggested a radical transformation in the economy of practices and symbolic exchanges that characterized the suburban spectacle.

When tactical schemes gradually reached the suburb, José Craveirinha was one of the first to regret their implications. Imported by metropolitan managers who arrived in Lourenço Marques and promoted by "some metropolitan sports newspapers that were passed hand to hand, they created, in the suburban footballer, the tactical mentality."[2] Tactics, according to the poet, gradually "destroyed the innate ability" of the African player to play football. The distinctive style of the neighborhoods of Lourenço Marques gave way to "tactics and more tactics. No. 4s in line, *ferrolhos* [lit., latches; holding midfielders], 4–2–4s, and other such things became popular and killed many good things in our players."[3] The African, having taken the European game and turned it into something that was his, was now hostage to "the tactical mentality." That mentality, a product of the "game's commercialization," homogenized the athletes' movements, suppressing gestures and their subtle meanings, eliminating the "freedom to create according to a natural and spontaneous intuition."[4] Tied to tactical schemes, the African players could not, in Craveirinha's view, show what they had brought anew to the game, how they had reformulated and recreated it. According to the poet, the tactical mentality penetrated the players' consciousness and transformed their body's' movements, it was a kind of modern sorcery, of European origin, which, much like the *práticas feiticistas* (witchcraft practices), limited the players' reflexes.[5]

Craveirinha felt that the imposition of an orthodoxy of movement introduced by tactical schemes was not simply a football matter but was tied to colonialism itself, to the destructive face of colonialism. The tactical mentality was not, however, a product of the ideological motor habitus proposed by the Portuguese Estado Novo, defined by the moralizing model that defended the regeneration of the body proposed by the regime's physical-education theoreticians. Moreover, it emerged in a context when football was headed, at different paces, toward professionalization, a tendency that the Portuguese Estado Novo saw as discrediting to the true values of sports, which were, above all, of an educational and moral nature. The tactical scheme did not have a direct ideological, moralizing, or pedagogic purpose; it was not promoted by the army, the church, or the school. And yet it disciplined bodies.

This drilling of the body did suggest, however, that a set of principles of action and social values demanded and imposed in Lourenço Marques by colonialism were forced upon the game: it subjected the player to a division of labor on the field, to a specialization of roles that conditioned the execution of his gestures and movements, which gave the player a different experience of movement in space as well as a different relation to time. Its implicit demands, by requiring the body's adhesion to a new norm, were similar to the demands required to deal with a set of mechanisms intrinsic to modern daily organization, namely those belonging to the economic organization of production, calculation, forecasting, and anticipation and to the rationalization of the gestures toward a predetermined purpose, as in a modern company.[6] Tactics became an attempt to reduce the game's unpredictability, by anticipating, forecasting, and measuring space and time. It was a response to the question posed by the result: what are the most efficient means of achieving a specific objective? Efficiency also presided over the basic objectives of the colonialist enterprise: exploration of resources, exploitation, and reproduction of the labor force. As demonstrated by the debates on colonial urban planning in Lourenço Marques, these objectives were pursued in many different ways; depending on its historical embeddedness, the materialization of an ideal type of economic system—determined, for instance, by the level of the rationalization of the working force—was uneven.

The direct association between the tactical scheme and the colonial enterprise, in their more predatory guises, has limitations. Linked with the emergence of specific social behaviors that were introduced within the context of colonial exploitation, the tactical system's origin was not the direct product of a doctrinarian intention or of an economic system. The rationalization of a formal language, as Max Weber described it in the case of modern music,[7] signaled the formation of a relatively autonomous field of relations, pervaded with specific practical orders and symbolic capitals, within which there were struggles over the "most accurate" definition of the notion of "practice itself." The search for a result stimulated the emergence of formulas aiming to define the most efficient ways to achieve victory. Football in the suburbs, over which the vovô intervened so as to influence the game by playing "beyond the lines," was on the receiving end of conceptions as to how the game might be decided more efficiently inside the lines. This pressure was felt in the suburbs of Lourenço Marques from the mid-1950s, when the "tactical issue" filled the newspaper pages. The persuasive powers of the tactical scheme, not unlike that of witchcraft practices, did not spring from a conscious belief, a fleeting fashion, or an ideological indoctrination but rather from the contextual and more or less deep significance of victory as a symbolic capital that benefited both players and public.

The history of the circulation of a tactical system such as WM testifies to the social constraints that surround the reception of a new outline for collective movement, enunciating contextual struggles and resistances not only on the part of the institutions but also the bodies now subject to a transformation in the their principles of motor action, homologous to wider practical senses. The tactical scheme demanded a modern worker, but one possessing specific resources, tailored to the conditions necessary for the construction of the spectacle. The football worker, fulfilling a function, sticking to a plan, a schedule, and whatever else was deemed essential to achieving the team's goals, still presented himself as an artist, performing before an audience.

THE CREATION OF AN EFFICIENT STYLE OF PLAY

After the offside rule was changed in 1925 by the International Board, for the benefit of the spectacle, players and coaches sought to adapt to the new conditions for the occupation of space that the new law imposed. In professionalized competitions, there was a search for the most rational actions, those that would enable them to achieve victory more effectively under the new system. The new system was created in England, the country where football's professionalization process was more advanced and national and regional competitions more developed. In the transition to the 1930s, Herbert Chapman put forward a new distribution of players that could more adequately respond to the change in the offside rule, and it established itself as an alternative to the then hegemonic "classic formation." Chapman's mode, which won Arsenal three league championships, became known by the two letters that depicted the players' positions on the field: WM. The letter M represented the defensive players' positions and W the disposition of the more offensive players. Chapman's success in the competitive English League led to an international debate on the advantages and disadvantages of the new system.

In 1935 the Portuguese manager and sports journalist Cândido de Oliveira[8] took part in a managing course organized by the Football Association in London.[9] On this journey he was able to do an internship with Chapman's Arsenal and to see some Scottish championship matches. Immediately after his return, he tried to share his experience and published the book *Football: Técnica e tática* (1935). In Portugal, besides the sports press's efforts and the circulation of a few handbooks, there were very few means to promote football's laws, theories, and methods. Despised by the physical-education theoreticians and by state institutions, the teaching of the sport to players and public came down to the work of enthusiastic players, doubling as self-taught scholars, almost exclusively through the newspapers.[10] It was up to these "educators," as noted by captain António Ribeiro dos Reis in the introduction to one of the first books on football to be published in Portugal—written in 1927, more than thirty years after the game's introduction in the country—to spread their knowledge of the game, particularly among the largely illiterate popular classes, who learned about the sport empirically, without being familiar with some of its elementary rules.[11]

To prove that "football is also an art and science,"[12] Ribeiro dos Reis described in his book the foundations for the division of labor on the playing field, often employing military metaphors, and the functions assigned to each footballer, according to their physical and psychological traits. Following the state of art of the time, the classic formation, an English invention constituted by one goalkeeper, two backs, three halfbacks, and five forwards, had resulted from a distillation of previous tactical models, which meant reducing the number of forward players, formerly nine or seven. Experience had dictated that the field should to be occupied in a more rational manner. Two schools ruled over football at the time: the English and the Scottish. The English game privileged the long pass and was grounded in the players' athleticism, in a style known as "kick and rush." The Scottish style, on the contrary, hinged on short passing and a more intricate pattern of play, with constant triangulation and circulation of the ball. Despite their national designations, the English and Scottish schools were exportable forms, two methods for the rationalization of the sport, based on two distinct motor repertoires.

Chapman's WM had taken the debate to a new level. The new tactical plan left an impression on Oliveira, spurring him to write his 1935 book. WM, a disposition that provided an adequate response to the problems raised by the offside rule, caused a revolution in the logic of collective movement. Through descriptive language and photographic material, resorting to abstract images, graphics, and diagrams, Oliveira constructed a dynamic representation of the game, disclosing the way in which the new tactic transformed the pattern of interdependencies. The WM proposed a different interaction order, requiring players to reformulate their gestures and incorporate new functions.

The abstract representation of the playing field and of players' movements suggested the creation of a tactical gaze, through the objectification of the players' concrete experience. The actual photographs, used to show how to correctly execute certain gestures and movements, enabled an analysis of the game's experience away from its concrete time and space frames. The mathematization of the game's substance led to a different pedagogy and a feasible control over the game's raw material. Athletes cover the stable geometry of the field's lines not arbitrarily but according to a specific tactical thought. Almost every single situation described by Oliveira, as in other didactic materials circulating throughout the world, involved a measuring of sorts: the shooting angle, the goalkeeper's position to block the shot, the place where the ball should be passed depending on distance, the speed of the ball, the opponent's physical frame. Everything that happened inside a football field could be measured in predetermined trajectories, lengths, heights, velocities, and predetermined movements. The abstraction of space, by putting immediate experience into perspective, enabled the construction of a new viewpoint on the game's language, influencing the players' experiences and the perception of the viewer. This symbolic construction of space and movement, comparable to formal breaks that took place in other fields of activity, was grounded in a rationalization geared to specific purposes. Although it did not present itself as an aesthetics as such, it constrained aesthetic possibilities. By devising the tactic that regulated the athletes' actions, the manager's task was similar, in some ways, to that of a choreographer. The choreography's "author" did not, however, have the chance to interpret it. A dancing choreography can be minutely prepared, but a football match, regardless of

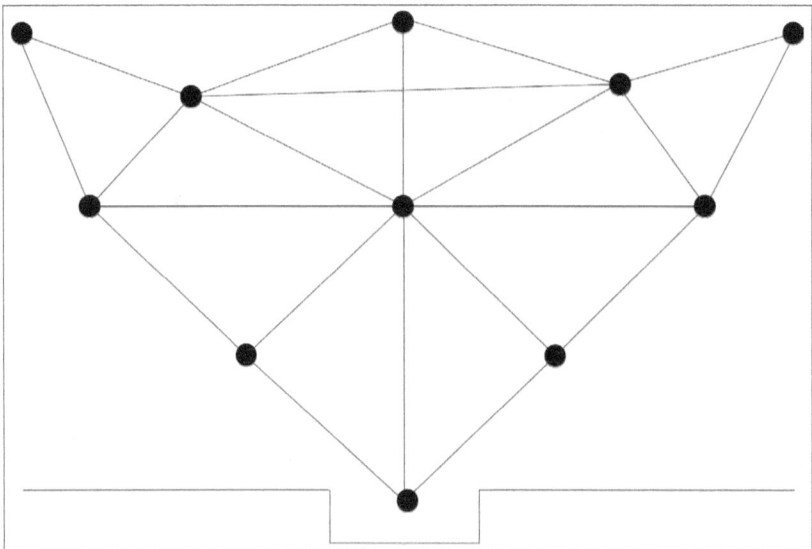

FIGURE 6.1. Dominant triangles in the short-pass game. Author: Ana Estevens. *Source:* Adapted from Cândido de Oliveira, *Football*, 15.

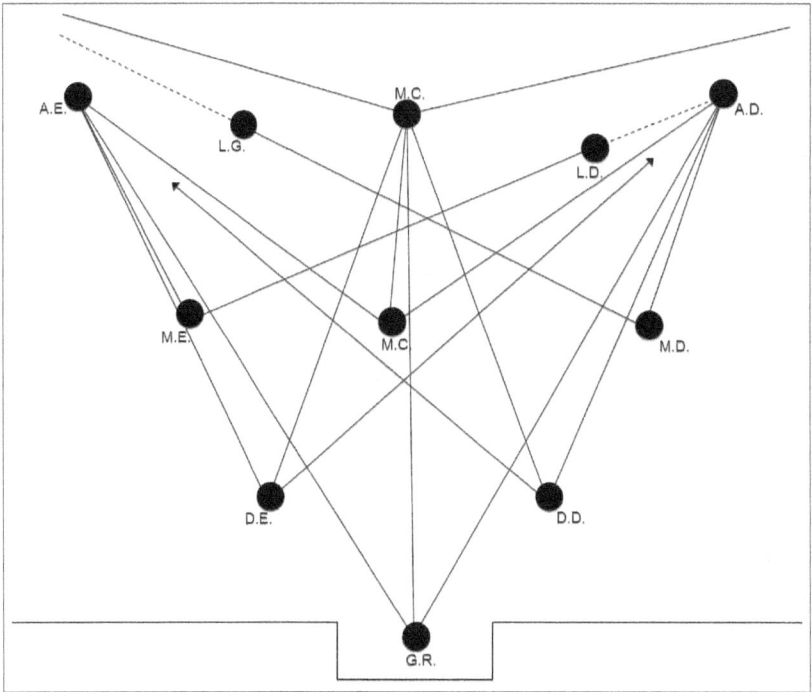

FIGURE 6.2. Dominant triangles in the long-pass game. Modern football's representation of space implied the creation of a kind of sheet music that players should interpret during their interactions in football's performative stage Author: Ana Estevens. *Source:* Adapted from Cândido de Oliveira, *Football*, 19.

how carefully rehearsed it may be, will always be highly unpredictable, based as it is on the interaction of two teams with opposing objectives. The game's rationalization process turned into a constant struggle to minimize its unpredictability. However, since it was not entirely reduced to this instrumental rationale, football's symbolic economy also hinged on the surprising and the extraordinary, capturing the public through its enchantment. It was this enchantment, grounded in the principles of appreciation that sustained the suburban game in Lourenço Marques and its dominant motor repertoire.

The absorption of rational principles of action was not limited to the assimilation and execution of certain gestures and movements. It was also necessary to carefully interpret how to move in space. The individual should assess his gesture collectively and be able to keep, at all times, a spatial notion of the team's organization and of his individual relation with that organization. To experience space in this way, it was necessary for the athlete to be able to see around him. The eyes, constantly strained by the game's dynamic, began to be seen as a component worthy of specialized training. Later, when the science of physical education became better articulated with football, sight was the target of a specific conceptualization.[13] The creation of a "practical experience of space" originates a perception that analyzes dynamics and movements. The trained eye, the "tactical eye," determines, throughout the match, each player's moving options, based on an intelligent anticipation of the action, which placed new demands on the individuals' motor habitus. This ability to "read space" requires an understanding, sustained by a "cultivated intuition," of the entire "process's sequence." The tactically trained eye almost becomes autonomous from the body movements. Training the intelligent eye, a "practical sense" driven by the imperative of efficiency, thus becomes the key to controlling the game's elements, namely its specific language: the individual gestures that, when integrated into a whole, facilitate logical collective movements. Tactical thought was a way to rationalize movement through an orchestration of creative individual wills.[14]

Many players in Portugal, as stated by Oliveira, learned to interpret space mobility empirically, through sheer practice. Experience made it possible to feel the body in a geometrized space—that is to say, it implied the development of a practical sense that was not dependent on the transmission of knowledge or on conscious awareness. The "experience of space" produced a kind of intelligence that did not necessarily imply a scholastic knowledge, grounded in reading and writing proficiency. To instruct the player's body was different from school literacy: "in football, you only need practical intelligence. . . . I have known players who were completely illiterate but who, despite this, when reading the game, through their technique, displayed their intelligence and even revealed a subtlety of mind that was uncommon in some educated people."[15]

Learning through the body, the basis of "practical intelligence," produced a specific type of perception that could not be translated orally or in writing, given its corporeal dimension. The recognition of this "intelligence" challenged the scholastic paradigm of "reading and writing" and artistic education. In the case of football, practical intelligence made demands on the athlete that surpassed the mechanical execution of gestures, as Craveirinha had recognized while interpreting the locally situated football created by Lourenço Marques's suburbs. As a singer integrated into a group of polyphonic voices,[16] the tactically intelligent player is aware that his own movement is part of a whole, an index of the degree of control over the game's language. Oliveira, after his internship in London with Arsenal, was convinced. Somewhat timidly, he suggested that the rationality of the WM did not impair the game's beauty. The Portuguese manager did not know whether Chapman's invention had presided over a deductive analysis on how to face the challenges posed by changes in the offside rules in a more efficient manner, or if the new scheme had rather been the product of observational experience. Regardless of whether it was empirically or deductively grounded, Cândido thought that its scientific nature was easily attested. The creation of conditions for the education of the body, only achievable via a certain degree of professionalization, became established as an indispensable part of the ability of the athlete's motor habitus to efficiently reproduce the practical sense demanded by the tactical scheme.

THE WM: THE FOUNDATIONS OF FOOTBALL'S RATIONALIZATION

Cândido de Oliveira became a dedicated champion of Chapman's WM in Portugal. He defended the system in the newspapers he wrote for and, above all, employed it in the teams he trained. In 1949 he published *WM: A evolução táctica no futebol* (WM: Football's tactical evolution),[17] where he argues that tactics were the modern game's rational basis, the evidence "that football was a sports game with a rational foundation, an intelligent game, and, may we add, a scientific one."[18] By challenging a hegemonic situation, the introduction of the WM was met with some resistance. Some of the critics considered that the tactical systems were not a basic element of football. According to them, a team's performance depended essentially on the players' technical and physical abilities. WM, by basing the game's dynamics on tactics, so the critics objected, imposed "the method's discipline and a subordination to a global plan that turned the player into a veritable automaton, devoid of self-will—and devoid of a soul!"[19] The relation between the game and its audience was regulated by the athlete's performative interpretation (as it still is, to a certain degree). To understand the tactical system's effectiveness and beauty demanded a much more educated perception. It was not immediately clear. Breaking with how the game was conceived and rationalized demanded a revolution in how it was perceived. The tactical outlook demanded that one move one's eyes away from the ball's magic, to focus on the logic of organization and movement. This shift in how the game was seen led to a different conceptualization, departing from one of the most important bases of the public's relation with the football spectacle: keeping your eyes on the ball.

To form a knowledgeable public also demanded a revolution in the eye, one that subverted how individuals had learned to enjoy a football match and its aesthetic principles. The need for a tactical outlook reconfigured the importance of superfluous gestures. These individual movements were, as far as the public was concerned, the soul of the game: "Individual play, showboating for the audience, personal accomplishment, a disordered match, subjected to instinct and emotional reactions, gave way, little by little, to a group match, team plans, tactical systems, methodical football based on preliminary studies by the manager and players. Individual action was thus harmonized with the team's group action."[20]

The clash between these two conceptions of the game can be discerned through the relation between two of the game's basic gestures: the dribble and the pass. The dribble, a movement that can have many shapes, is the prime instance of individual virtuosity, as seen in the Lourenço Marques suburban playing fields. A player able to execute a technical gesture that allows him to beat his opponent and keep possession of the ball was almost always the public's favorite. The dribble is an important part of the spectacle but, quite often, it is far from effective and does not contribute to collective movement. In such an instance, the team's tactical organization suffers. Executed in a small space, it does not allow, in the moment of its execution, for the perception of the team's movement. As such, football's modernization, and its concomitant labor specialization, aimed to discipline the dribble.[21] Its regular execution became a privilege of some players and this gesture was only executed at certain moments and in specific areas of the pitch. The pass, on the other hand, was the basis of tactics, the springboard to collective movement, the gesture defining the rhythm and choreography devised by the manager. The pass requires the player to possess a peripheral vision and be able to raise his head. Hence, the two schools that for a long time were the paradigms of competitive football, the English and Scottish, were respectively designated the long-pass and short-pass schools. The survival of dribbling, as a motor repertoire present in the game, rested on its adaptation to the intrinsic principles of passing. The relation between the dribble and the pass determined the morphology of the game pattern, the dynamic of its interaction order, and the team's style. Patterns of play characterized by the multiplication of dribbles were fundamentally different from patterns of play where this gesture was scarce. The fans' difficulty in understanding the reason why the players' individual freedom should be curtailed could not, from Oliveira's point of view, stand in the way of the game's rationalization. WM established itself on account of its efficiency.

The public would come to acknowledge the supremacy of tactics. Perhaps they could still celebrate its inner beauty in the same way that the competing athlete was happy to control some of his performative impulses without ceasing to be an able and more or less creative interpreter of the game, integrated in a collective logic. The game's tactical evolution had an educational effect on the spectator's outlook, even when they did not possess a thorough knowledge of the rational bases underpinning the performative changes. Individuality, for instance, came to be penalized when it harmed the team's objective; the change in the principles of classification resulted in an aesthetic devaluation. In this context, virtuosity lost its autonomy, which would prove ominous for some of the existing styles of play. However, the audience's aesthetic outlook is not automatically in line with the movements that emerged from modern tactical schemes. This generated some resistance and an obvious stylistic nostalgia.

Before the advent of WM, the classic formation distributed the players throughout the pitch. The offside rule dictated how the two defenders, whose positions were defined by the classic formation, should behave. If an opponent was ahead of one of these two men at the precise moment when his teammate passed him the ball, play had to be stopped. As such, the two defenders formed a diagonal and placed themselves so that the more advanced vertex was always stuck to the line of the five forward opposing players, seeking to place them in an offside position. When this defensive strategy was well executed, the line of five forwards had to move back in the field. Thus, following an actual rationalization moved by the need for efficiency, matches lost their spectacularity. Pushed far away from the goal line, the forward players were unable to score. When the law was changed, this defensive system lost its effectiveness and became riskier.

From then on, the forward players would not be in an illegal position if a teammate would pass the ball with just one defender ahead of them (and the goalkeeper). The players' distribution on the pitch was immediately changed, not on account of a theoretical viewpoint that created a new rationalization, but because players began to have a different experience of space. The proposal of a new disposition, better equipped to deal with this problem—Herbert Chapman's WM—emerged in the attempt to conceive of an offensive system. With the new disposition, it did not make sense to have five players placed side by side in attack as this would create a great deal of space behind the forward players. Hence, the inside forward players were moved back and the forward line became a W. The left and right wingers, closer to the side lines, and the center forward were still in line, but the inside forwards were closer to the midfield. With this distribution, the classic defense, with two players playing diagonally or in line, would be at a numerical disadvantage. Two defenders were not enough. The defense responded symmetrically to the changes made in attack. The central halfback moved to the middle of defense, into the position of the *stopper*, which demanded a strong and imposing player. The so-called *third-back game* was thus created. The midfield, placed further back on the field, would have two men closer to the center of the field, where an empty space had opened up in the period of the classic formation. This was how the M defensive system came to be.

In comparison with the classic formation, the WM system was more dynamic and the players' lines closer to each other. There was a need, however, to redefine the players' features—a different specialization. Oliveira explains these new roles: the central halfback, previously a cerebral player, became a normal defender whose main role was to neutralize the opponent's center forward; the right and left halfbacks, who were usually combative players, became creative players who had to have excellent ball control and the ability to organize the game and serve the forward players; the defenders started to play closer to the side lines; the center forward, previously a playmaker, became a shooter who needed to be physically strong; the inside forwards, originally combative shooters, were entrusted with dictating the attack and had to be able to expertly control the ball; the wingers, who had to be quick and know when to pass the ball to the three forward players closer to goal, had to combine speed with an ability to shoot.[22]

The game became a more intellectualized mechanism, centered on the magic square composed by the two halfbacks and the two inside forwards. This was the thinking center, formed by players with an acknowledged tactical intelligence. As the defensive M perfectly fit the attacking W, defensive markings became tougher and the forward players, used to having space in the previous system, had less time to execute their movements. According to Oliveira, this specific situation caused considerable problems for some players who found it difficult to adapt, which led to criticism of the WM.[23] Change, however, seemed inevitable. The space of stylistic possibles had shifted, providing a new frame for players' performances and for the demands imposed on their bodies.

THE WM'S CIRCULATION AND ITS ARRIVAL IN LOURENÇO MARQUES

Although Graham Chapman proved the efficiency of the WM in the early 1930s, the system did not cross the English Channel until 1936, during the Berlin Olympic Games.[24] In 1930s Lourenço Marques, Guilherme Cabaço remembers that managers were either "amateurs or former players" and quite often "newcomers," such as Gouveia Pinto, a manager "who never played football in his life." Out of "the love he had for his club," he "studied, read and owned many books on football, which he then applied with his players." The L. M. Athletic Club played an "English-style" game with "wider passes." Cabaço remembers the prevalent "'classic' ordering of the eleven players on the field." Cabaço's description suggests a not very dynamic game, with a weak interdependency, in which the forward players remained on attack and the defensive players stayed at the back: "whoever was up front was a forward. Only rarely did we go back, only if they asked for help. The backs and defenders should be able to take care of themselves. A guy came, he would kick a long ball, and then needed someone up front to keep the play going."

The Portuguese manager and journalist Severiano Correia became WM's promoter in Associação de Futebol de Lourenço Marques (Lourenço Marques Football Association). Severiano started managing Ferroviário in 1949, the same year Oliveira published, in the metropolis, *WM: A evolução táctica no futebol*, the book in which he explained the rationalizing power of the WM system.[25] Although he became the great advertiser and user of the system, it was not Correia who originally employed it in the "downtown championship" but rather António Borges Jacinto, a former Benfica player who had arrived at the capital of Mozambique in 1931, where he played for ten years for Ferroviário.[26] In 1944 he became technical director of all club levels and instituted the WM system. A year later, Ferroviário's directors, faced with the team's poor performances, asked him to return to the classic formation.[27] Borges Jacinto grudgingly complied with this request, since he believed, having studied Chapman's reasoning, in the WM's superiority. At that time, Ferroviário, at the forefront of football's organization in the city, had its players go through a rigorous training system: three weekly sessions, composed of theoretical and practical training, individual and group oriented, with a quarter to a half hour of gymnastics before training.[28] The players reluctantly accepted these methods. Used to the discipline and schedules of their own jobs, they saw football as a recreational exercise. Borges Jacinto argued for the importance of "theoretical trainings" as a means of training the footballer-worker, even if he knew that players did not enjoy lectures.[29] In his own words, they only "wanted the ball."

It is likely, however, that in 1937 the Scottish club Aberdeen, the first European team to play in the capital of Mozambique (hired on the occasion of a tour in South Africa), would have played in a WM formation. Tours in southern Africa, which began in 1897 when the English team the Corinthians visited South Africa, having returned once again in 1903, produced moments of urban effervescence and the occasion for sharing methods and performative techniques.[30] While there is no explicit reference to the WM among the reports on the match of 13 June 1937, the match's description, as well as previous accounts of the matches Aberdeen played in South Africa,[31] allow us to guess the employment of Chapman's system in the Scots' victory by 6–4 against the local-best eleven: "the tactics they presented were interesting and fruitful, with the centermidfielder staying back, offering a magnificent defense barrier and the wide midfielders playing as deep-lying forwards."[32]

Contact with Aberdeen's tactical scheme appears to have left no traces. It was only with Severiano Correia that the tactical components of the training were reinforced and that the WM became more definitively established. In 1951 the Ferroviário newspaper complimented Correia's work, which allowed for a "better adaptation of the 'pieces' to the WM system, by placing some players in their rightful positions." Correia was thus recognized not as the first person to employ the system but as the first to prove its efficiency, which was still not enough to shield him from numerous criticisms. Throughout his newspaper articles, Correia strove to redefine the game's state of the art.[33] Lourenço Marques's football fans, he said, were "people who had only seen football being played among ourselves, in small villages in our beloved continental Portugal, where the sport is a Sunday leisure activity."[34] Match reports, under Correia, showed how the bases for analyzing the game's movements had changed. The morphology of the "game time," marked by the chronological description of individual actions, gave way to an interpretation of movement in an articulated set of positions and functions, a grid created by the manager, who invented the team's style, much like a choreographer, a stage director, or a film director. The manager was the match's "author" and the player a "pawn" that should be "finely tuned, so that his movement could fulfill the goal of a collective formation."[35] In Correia's articles, the player was depersonalized, as in a modern labor structure, and was referred to by his position (halfback, right back) and by the movements he executed, which could usually be subject to some form of measurement: "triangulations," "diagonals."[36] The journalist's role was that of revealing the beauty of this mechanism to the public, the way in which this tactical work gained shape as a spectacle—in other words, of showing its aesthetic value. This value was grounded not only in the player's ability but through the assessment of the "manager's better or worse organization of the players in a game pattern that could be well or poorly conceived."[37]

It was through Severiano Correia's writings that Central European football conquests were scientifically and aesthetically narrated. In sub-Saharan Africa's eastern extremity, in an anticommunist political context, Hungary's victory at Wembley (6–3), in the famous 1953 match, was widely celebrated. *Guardian desportivo* crowned them, on the first page, "the new kings of football."[38] According to Correia, who was essentially interested in promoting the game's rational bases, Budapest, Prague, and Vienna had profited from tours by Scottish teams, whose football, "close to the ground, with short passes," now acquired a new dimension. It was a "geometrically drawn" style, "mathematical," and with a "scientific pattern" that made "improvisation less important."[39] The teams moved as "actual machines," the players submitting themselves to the manager's will, "completely relinquishing their individuality, with the certainty that this was the only way to achieve results."[40] The player who interpreted this scheme should fulfill his role and try to ignore the public's pleasure: "The player, no matter how much class he has, cannot exuberantly show that he wants to rejoice in the public's applauses. He must forget who he is in order to think, solely, about the role he is fulfilling as part of his team."[41] In Lourenço Marques, the superiority of Central European football was substantiated by a visit from Dynamo Prague.[42] For some time, the newspapers talked of "Czech masters" and their mastery of "every tactic and technique of modern football."[43]

Although logically superior, the tactical system was not always effective. Often, results and exhibitions did not please either the public or the media. The fallibility of the tactical system, its inability to control every unforeseen event in a match whose dynamics rested on successive interactions, endangered the work of the "manager as author." He was the first person accountable for the team's performance when things did not go as expected. In Lourenço Marques, Severiano Correia complained, the independence of the manager, a misunderstood artist of sorts,[44] was constantly challenged by the "social-moral nucleus, responsible not just for technical guidance but also for the establishment of the guiding principle of sports ideals."[45] Club directors, journalists, and the actual public, who did not understand the reasoning behind scientific football, felt free to share their opinions and to pass judgment. The game also belonged to them, as the suburban football's interaction order also depended on the local public's classification criteria, an element that acted upon collective performance and that was not stable, dependent as it was on local context.

The pressure to get results intensified the argument over the merits of the new tactical processes. In *Guardian desportivo*, António Marques, a journalist, wrote about the decadence of "old football."[46] At that time, when individual values "prevailed," the whole game could hinge on the inspired exhibition of a single player. The ball was not passed "between the various team players," the public marveled at "the so-called tricksters," who dribbled past "every opponent that came before them." The trickster's art was made easier by a "wide marking" that "gave a player enough room to, if he was a good '*dribleur*,' solve the problem by himself on behalf of his team." In Lourenço Marques there were, as everywhere else, "team players and tricksters." The future belonged to the first, the more sober players, the ones who avoided "showboating." The "modern" trickster displayed his abilities under a different set of conditions. This change indicated a Copernican revolution in their gestures and movements. The player who "dribbled often," the journalist added, did not possess "a clear passing vision." His eyes saw only the opponents directly facing him, which he dribbled past with greater or lesser ease. The modern player, on the other hand, even "before he received the ball," had already assessed the various options at his disposal.

The transformation of the players' motor repertoire did not depend on a simple adjustment to the tactical schemes; it required a change in the players' behavior. In a review of the 1951 season, the sports paper *Eco dos sports* remarked that

> athletes had to convince themselves that when they put a team's shirt they also accept great responsibilities and obligations that must be met. From that moment on, they are no longer their own selves but should be fully devoted to their club. They

should do nothing harmful to their health . . . they should get up early, at the break of dawn, walk, run, jump, and develop their "*souplesse.*"[47]

A few years later, *Guardian desportivo* posed the question, "Professionalism in local football?"[48] Sport had become a "business that, in order to be successful and profitable, required, much like any other business, capital investment." In Lourenço Marques there were indications, the journalist remarked, that "monetary prizes would be awarded for next season's results." The systematization of payments was another step in the professionalization process. The primary elements of this, "meals, transports, the promise of a job . . . travel compensations or paid expenses," had been a reality for a long time. The transformation of footballers into wage workers, as one would expect, increased their responsibility.

Tactical development and the chance for athletes to devote themselves to their sport as professionals were interdependent realities. The conditions necessary for players to absorb the tactical system's logic, adjusting their motor habitus to the need for of an efficient pattern of play and gradually wiping out "local footballs," however, was unevenly distributed. The same was true, indeed, of the conditions necessary for workers in the suburbs of Lourenço Marques to adjust themselves to a modern economic system.

TACTICS IN THE SUBURBS

In the suburbs of Lourenço Marques, the pressure on African teams to employ modern tactical processes, as shown by Craveirinha's objections, was insidiously felt. In 1951, *O brado africano* complained that suburban teams were "orchestras with well-known players but lacking a maestro."[49] It was required, then, that each team have a manager in charge, a person whose role was comparable to that of Phidias, the sculptor. The manager was the one who would mold African youth's "magnificent human clay": "only in this way can African association football reach the class it aspires to."[50] To reach a better performative level, a demand that came out of a comparison between different ways of playing, it needed to incorporate the basic principles of modernity, which indeed have already made their mark on a wide number of activities, from architecture and urbanism to music, cinema, or literature: "The team should be guided by the old theorem stating that the shortest path between two points is a straight line and ignore the tortuous paths filled by narrow streets and shortcuts."[51]

The tactical issue was at the center of an argument about football's future, a debate that was heightened by the press. "Downtown" managers, tours by metropolitan and foreign teams that passed through Lourenço

Marques, the greater circulation of football handbooks—all these had sparked a number of disputes on the benefits and disadvantages of various footballing systems.

"How did the game evolve?" Issufo asked and answered his own question: "Many were in South Africa and others in the city and they'd come here. And then, even in suburban football, [the WM]was the system. And when it changed to 4—2—4, suddenly it was the same all over the place. . . . Yes, but the 4—2—4 appeared when I was already a player. Otto Glória came here for some practice sessions. He came downtown to run a football manager's course. That was in 1956."

Hamido Nizamo read the handbook written by a metropolitan manager, Fernando Vaz, titled *Noções práticas de futebol* (Practical Football Concepts). Another handbook, written by the Spanish manager Pedro Escartin, was also becoming popular. *Cruzeiro*, a Brazilian magazine, often included images in which the mechanism of certain rehearsed movements was depicted. The metropolitan newspaper *A bola*, a target of José Craveirinha's criticism, was at the forefront of the tactical discussion and became the model for Severiano Correia's articles in *Diário de Lourenço Marques Guardian*. Although these publications had a limited circulation, the information they presented gradually spread. The success of Portuguese and international teams was increasingly associated with the talent of the manager, a figure that acquired a new and higher status.[52]

The challenge that tactical thought presented to suburban football was not solved, however, through a process of adherence or refusal. It was not a matter of imitating a gesture or a movement, or of using an international star's name, a shirt, or a cap. The tactical scheme demanded a reconversion of the athletes' motor repertoire, the refusal of a local grammar that had grown out of the interaction between players and public, and which had established itself as a repository of common values, a space that defined the frontiers of a style of play. The tactical system, in its apparent innocence, tested the suburban community, presenting a challenge to the conditions of production of the "local art." And yet, at the same time, these tactical schemes were claimed by the suburbs in the name of local football, growing rivalries, and the search for results. It was a formula with a proven record, used by the best teams in the world to win matches.

The improvement in each person's individual conduct—which the tactical model required, namely a specialization of the players' gestures and movements and of their overall perception of the game—demanded a number of conditions that suburban football could not provide. It was impossible, for example, for a player to become a professional. When

Dynamo Prague visited Lourenço Marques, making a strong impression, Saide Mogne witnessed the performance of a "veritable machine": "they insisted on a game play, five, ten, twenty times, and that play had to work." In Lourenço Marques, even in downtown football, where there was a more advanced system of rewards, the players, who had to work every day at their jobs, resisted the colonization of their leisure time and space by training, which was key to the fine-tuning of a team's dynamics. In these training sessions, there was a growing relevance given to physical preparation, to running, to repetitive movements, alongside the speeches in which managers put across their ideas as orders that had to be fulfilled. This preparation became increasingly similar to the processes the players had to face every day in their regular jobs. That is why the players "wanted the ball." The moment they touched the ball was when they started to enjoy the game. Many players in the downtown championship, like Fernando Lage, one of Desportivo de Lourenço Marques's stars, were unwilling to trade a well-paying job for an uncertain professional trajectory. In this context, it was difficult to fully implement the mechanism that led to the tactical scheme's assimilation. Tactics were only fully implemented when "they were embodied" and became a part of the athletes' motor habitus.

In suburban football this impossibility was even more conspicuous. The players, who also had jobs, besides having little time to train, lacked the material conditions to do so. Ângelo remembers that in AFA clubs there were virtually no training sessions: "A few clubs trained, those that owned a pitch would train, those that did not would train in their area." To train in their area meant to play on improvised pitches. The alternative was to gather the team in the club's head office, where they would "do gymnastics but not play football." The clubs without a pitch "usually trained in the head office's backyard. They would do gymnastics or something else so that when the weekend arrived they could play." Armando Silva says that AFA training sessions mostly took place on barren fields. The training session was composed almost entirely of practice matches: "The goals were put in place and we played." There was no supervision: "There were no technicians, no managers." As the famous Eusébio stated in an interview, "We are all coaches when we play in our neighborhood!."[53] Hamido Nizamo describes the precariousness of these training sessions, in which there was deficient "physical preparation" and the methods were far from advanced. When he played for Munhuanense Azar, the lack of proper conditions meant that you could not "ask for more." In the suburb, he recalls, "we did not train, we met." Sometimes, the people in charge of the club would make an appeal: "Man, go to bed earlier, we need you tomorrow. Don't go out partying." According to him, the clubs that did not own a pitch were often happy to have their players just run around on a barren field. Some were able to gather some money and rent Mahafil's or Beira-Mar's pitch for a short period. The clubs that owned a pitch could train better, although the players did not have much time to do so. António Cruz points out the difficulty of finding a slot for the training sessions because "every player had a job." "At five in the morning, everyone would wake up and go train. Little jogs, we would run round the pitch and we did some exercises." Other times, however, the dynamics of local sociability meant that, "at four or five in the morning," many players were coming out of "dance parties." The fields did not have artificial lighting, which prevented the players from training under decent conditions after work. "Only in the summer," Ângelo says, "from five p.m. to seven p.m., were we able to train a little bit, and at night we also trained in the dark."[54]

Mogne claims that "few people were able to put that into practice." The player's first thought, he says, went to his job; "he had to work." Almost all the white players managed to have good jobs, but those from the suburbs, except for a small minority, had neither the space nor the time to progress: "in 1948–49, you would finish the fourth grade and then stop, you couldn't go beyond that." Severiano Correia, he concludes, "wrote a lot about systems, made many comments, and assessed the players' technical skills; what shape they were in, the formation, how they should be, but, afterward, in practice, the colonial system did not give them many opportunities." Unlike the situation "downtown," the footballer's status in the suburbs was still defined in opposition to and not in agreement with the principles that defined a labor condition. Very few among them stood any chance of becoming professional players.

The universe of practices and meanings contained in the local style of play depended on the principles that generated a suburban habitus. To accept the "vovô's scheme" was to legitimize a community belief, an ordained right, that did not interfere with the players' tactical performance; to welcome the inspiration of a wide football narrative embedded in popular culture, by adopting great players' nicknames, by imitating their gestures and movements, christening informal groups after the names of great teams, all this made the local game more cosmopolitan and more connected with the wider world, but not necessarily different in terms of the interactional principles and symbolic exchange that it put into play; to accept the tactical scheme, however, was to challenge the relation established between performers and public in the suburbs of Lourenço Marques, from which a specific libido arose, one that dictated the performance and regulated the body's movement. In this sense, although there weren't relevant material rewards to encourage the performance, the athletes' action was neither "disinterested" nor complacent. Efficiency was thus locally defined, through a specific rationality in which the means were established in accordance with the ends of the actual economy of practices and symbolic exchanges intrinsic to the local style of play. This process was at odds with the rational behavior intrinsic to the tactical scheme, in which efficiency was defined by the final score and where the relation between means and ends adapted itself to this paramount value.

ANOTHER TYPE OF ASSOCIATION, ANOTHER COMMUNITY

The inability of tactical systems to penetrate into the suburb, despite Craveirinha's fears and the consumption trends that the suburb absorbed from the outside, was a sign of a structural impossibility. As the interaction order on the football pitch was close to the values negotiated by an evolving community, the tactical mentality seemed to be a projection of a new community, ruled by different practices and values that seemed not to have any rights to offer. Some suburban players, however, especially those who made the transition from AFA competitions to downtown teams, felt, in their bodies, the clash between these two conceptions of the game. These players remember downtown football as something serious that almost always demanded a great deal of work and matching rewards, at least for those who were used to the suburban system. Their opinions bring to the fore the contingencies of a period in which the meanings of gestures and movements that occur during a football match were being redefined, and in which their "practical sense" and motor habitus were being adjusted to a new interaction order. The experience of this transition not only reveals the more strictly bodily dimension of the process but also the two distinct ethical and aesthetic ways of experiencing the game.

Saide Mogne says that when the tactical system became too rigid, "there was no football in the WM." From the moment the game ceased to be a mere way of positioning the players on the field and became "a new mentality" that regulated all the players' gestures, association football disappeared. Mogne saw "association" as the game in which the performer could move according to the "course of events." Football was a game that allowed the athlete to have fun, to exhibit his individual ability and virility. Although the "course of events," as Mogne called it, depended on a specific balance of powers, on conventions that instigated malicious strategies, athletes felt reasonably free to execute their gestures. A motor habitus adjusted to a distinct symbolic exchange would feel ill-adapted to the course of events. The tactical scheme deprived the player of his freedom and curtailed the possibility of malicious movements. Football became a different game, filled with rules similar to those that defined "labor time": observance of the division of labor, specialization of roles, productivist pressure, acceptance of hierarchy, loss of autonomy. Respect for the "manager's guidance," as Ângelo puts it, was one of the great novelties of modern football.

With the advent of tactics, the players, in Ângelo's words, became "tied to the system." The tactical system tied the players up, limited their gestures, measured their steps, and penalized their fouls. Some of this system's features were similar to those of other "systems," to which, out of economic need, the individuals were also tied. The suburban game subjected the players to a set of principles that conditioned their movement, which also "tied them up" in a way. However, adherence to this style of play was not caused by economic need, nor was their performance entirely subject to imperatives of a productivist nature, in the utilitarian sense of the term. Elements such as the fear factor and the risk of, and the right to, face opponents with impetuous and enchanting gestures ruled supreme. The "tactical mentality," against which Craveirinha had voiced his opposition, was the application to a sports spectacle of some constituent principles of the colonial city's power, of the colonizer's power, albeit filtered by the specific language produced by a field of activity undergoing a process of specialization. As Mogne saw it, the tactical mentality tended to deprive the game of all its previous meanings. Matine explains: "When the manager tells me not to leave [my assigned defensive position] too often, this means that I will lose my initiative and cease to be creative. I become limited."

"In the AFA I was freer," Vicente insisted. "Downtown you had to cut down on the tricks and the juggling. I played with Guerreiro, a veteran, he played as a right [winger], with me to his left. He really knew his stuff, we used to beat Ferroviário, Desportivo, he had a really good tactical sense. Guerreiro would pass, first touch; he would find some space, [then] I pass it on to Guerreiro, he then plays it back to me. He sure knew what he was doing."

"In my day there were eleven on the pitch and we would just improvise, while downtown they had systems," Hilário said about the matches at Xipamanine. "For instance, it's like kids when they first enter the football academy and they want to dribble past everyone, and we tell them, 'Hey, football is a team sport, you dribble if and when you have to.' And they say, 'But if I don't dribble no one will notice me. If I don't use my tricks no one will notice me."

THE "DANCE" AS SYMBOLIC CAPITAL

The importance granted to improvisation within the context of the suburban interaction order enables various types of performative assessments. This was what allowed the players to establish themselves, as Ângelo recalled: "We lost but we gave them a dance." The dance of the defeated turned them into winners: the *baile dado* (lit., the given dance) was a sign of their efficiency, acknowledged by the local public. It extolled a malicious and illusionist motor repertoire. As an interaction repertoire, the "given dance" allowed for individual rhetorical accounts, filled with colorful descriptions of exceptional performances. This symbolic victory had enough strength to impose itself, under certain circumstances, over the power of the numbers that celebrated the winner. Mozambique's neighborhoods prided themselves on this.

Dance's victory, the proof of malice, was measured on the following day, when the gestures of the players who had played so well were remembered and became a part of the local memory, of the knowledge shared in social interaction by means of forms of rhetoric that either confirmed or challenged local values and practical senses. The players' and public's evaluation principles granted certain gestures an aesthetic autonomy and a particular meaning, giving them a prominent place within the narratives that surrounded the game. The only way for a dance to be given was if the players were allowed to dance. If they were tied to a rigid formation, that was impossible.

One of the gestures that was most criticized following the imposition of the tactical scheme was the trickster's movement, the dancer's move, celebrated by local improvisation. Tactics based on a more rational occupation of space eliminated the time needed for the virtuoso to execute his magic tricks. Before this imposition, in Ângelo's words, "there was more space, a player who was talented, who could dribble past two, three guys, who could feint, was accepted by the manager. That was how that player played and it was good for his own team and also for the spectator that goes to see a football game and enjoys that." Within the mechanism operating under the tactical conception, and devised with the end result in mind, the virtuoso's individualism, disconcerting and magical, was almost always inconsequential. This contradiction, visible to the trained eye, would also be punished by a public obsessed with victory. Battling within an increasingly dangerous space, the virtuoso saw his vocation to enchant and promote an aesthetic become increasingly difficult and go into decline. Its survival progressively depended on the contribution it made to the team's goals, framed and ruled by the discipline of the pass.

SWEETNESS AND SPEED:
THE DISENCHANTMENT OF THE WORLD

The suburban game, in Issufo's words, was defined by its *doçura* (sweetness). By sweetness, the former player meant the meanings produced by the gestures and movements of those who interpreted an improvisation executed to the rhythm of the local "association." What killed football's doçura, Issufo says, referring not just to the game played in the suburbs of Lourenço Marques, but to football in general, were the "tactical games." Tactical games "ruin everything." The game's tactics and the official law, he adds, killed the old association. Law and tactics leveled the players' gestures, conformed creativity to the precepts dictated by rules. All types of playing not confined by the system, within a specific historical context, had their sweetness. In the suburbs of Lourenço Marques, this sweetness reflected the principles of the malicious style of play, interpreted creatively through the virtuoso's action, intimidating tactics and the vovô's cunning. In those times there were situations, Issufo recalls, when "an outstanding player, composed" as he gazes at the opponent about to execute a violent gesture, "thinks: he's coming at me with everything he's got. And so he would stop and as the other guy got there he would just put the ball between his legs." And then there would be doçura, and malice was celebrated.

In opposition to this sweetness, which was often composed of leisurely gestures filled with meanings, there was *velocidade* (speed), a locomotor reflection of the modern tactical system's logic: "Football's sweetness," says Issufo, "vanishes with the use of speed. Everything is so fast." Speed altered the game's rhythms, withdrew the space and time needed for the enchantment produced by malice. Speed, however, possessed a different kind of malice, a destructive one. The tactical scheme, by reducing the time and space that players had to execute their gestures, forced them to move more quickly, to have a practical perception and a peripheral vision of the game that allowed them to anticipate the action that followed. The lack of speed conditioned the player's productivity, a value that gradually became as important as efficiency. Anticipation, predictability, and calculation were demands of the modern game, values framed by a specific utilitarian rational conduct. Being an art of time and of space, football changed as these coordinates changed, and its universe of stylistic possibilities shifted.

The need for speed, a value that conditioned productivity, was a basic element in the labor relations imposed by colonialism. The production of a series of stereotypes about the African, among which were his supposed laziness, was rooted in the violent process that surrounded the integration of the colonized populations in relations of production that required a constant speed and productivity, where the clock and the whistle ruled. The colonial process demanded a different rhythm. The demand for an individual behavior geared toward productivity, in which speed was paramount, had a crushing effect on former ways of living. The tactical mentality, by forcing the player to reconfigure every principle of his motor habitus, broke the enchantment produced by the suburban game once and for all. Simultaneously, by proposing a new economy of gestures, it eliminated the validation of the rights intrinsic to the use of the local motor repertoire. The tactical scheme represented, to some extent, the acceptance of a new worldview.

THE GREAT MOZAMBICAN INTERPRETERS AND THE CONSEQUENCES OF PROFESSIONALIZATION

Many suburban players moved from local to downtown pitches out of economic necessity, when the transfer market became more active. In doing so, they abandoned the local game's prevalent doçura, although some continued to play in the suburb, in neighborhood matches, and in AFA competitions. Following the success of players such as Matateu, Vicente, and Coluna in the metropolis, the suburban market became attractive. Football's transformation into a popular spectacle, with a wide media impact, heightened the gulf between the stronger teams (already undergoing a process of professionalization) and the weaker ones. This hierarchization, which was also acknowledged by the suburban public, meant that African teams were considered less important than downtown teams and even less so than the metropolitan clubs. The great clubs were no longer just the center of relations of proximity and encounters in the neighborhoods, they were no longer just structures that organized various activities (see chapter 7). They increasingly became symbols of a mediatized popular culture, of a group of supporters who, much like Benedict Anderson observed when he wrote about national imagery, did not need to know each other in the here and now in order to know that they belonged to a community of supporters.[55] All they had to do was to read the newspaper.

Among the major beneficiaries of this ongoing process of professionalization were the Mozambican players hired by metropolitan teams.[56] Professionalization, besides bringing financial compensation, forced them to accept modern footballing values, daily training, and tactical schemes, all of which regulated their gestures and movements.[57] This adjustment was driven by both their will and need but demanded a great deal of self-discipline, as Matine points out: "The move from the suburbs of Lourenço Marques to the metropole was like climbing a mountain. Because the athlete needs to prove himself. . . . He was the best in his neighborhood, or one of the best, and now when he gets downtown he needs to be the best again so they'll notice him and take him out of there."

Hilário offers a more compelling explanation:

> The guys in the suburbs were disciplined. And then there is the question of need. What need is that? Survival. You want to move up, you work harder; you want to eat, you want money, you want to buy a car. The big problem with football players these days is that they have a lot of money. They're not humble enough and that makes life difficult for their coaches. An individual who lived in the suburbs and didn't have enough of this, that, or the other and all of a sudden comes over here, gets a nice house, a nice car, nice food, a nice wage, travels around a lot, plays in front of fifty thousand people, forty thousand people, and doesn't have the structure to deal with it. There are plenty of players who came and just couldn't handle it. Then you start being harassed, solicited for this or that. You need someone to be by your side, but back then there . . . were no agents or anything of the sort. You'd get here and either you were humble and things didn't go to your head or you were up against it.

The demands of sports professionalism would, however, go much further. So that their bodies could satisfy the club's demands, with the precision required by efficiency, the rationalization of their gestures and movements had to begin in their daily lives. In football, modern labor's rationalization logic was felt with particular intensity. The production of a more effective motor habitus hinged on the creation of a socializing bubble. The players did not simply cease to be their own selves during matches or training sessions. Alberto da Costa Pereira, the Mozambican goalkeeper signed by Benfica in 1954, talked to *Guardian desportivo* about his adaptation, as well as that of his colleagues Coluna and Naldo, to the Portuguese capital club.[58] Costa Pereira remarked that an entire month of training in Lourenço Marques corresponded to a week of training in Lisbon: "Naldo has already put on four kilos and even appeared taller, because over here 'they mean business.'" The training was so serious that Benfica's manager, the Brazilian Otto Glória, created what they referred to as the Solar (Mansion): "a training center of sorts where bachelor players lived and where they would be joined by the married players on Fridays." Costa Pereira complained that in Lisbon one could not "casually go from a place such as Lourenço Marques's Scala theatre to the Polana Hotel or from the Continental Café to a cinema." In the same edition, *Guardian desportivo* published the Benfica's *Regulamento geral da secção de futebol* (General Regulations for the Football Section).⁵⁹ The document established a series of norms regulating a player's life, his schedules, his activities, and his options. For instance, it was

> expressively forbidden to go to places that have an intrinsically pernicious environment—discos, gambling establishments, etc.—which considerably reduce the moral and physical cleanliness so crucial to a sports activity. These establishments generate in the player an erroneous notion of an easy and comfortable life and corrupt his sense of duty; to take part in gambling and to indulge in any kind of excess; the abusive use of alcoholic drinks and smoking, which go against the minimum conditions required to produce an ideal physical performance.⁶⁰

Players should also be at home by eleven at night, except in cases of force majeure, which had to be specified. The regulations demanded a rigid hierarchical subservience and forbade discussions and conflicts within the group. It was within this grid, which did not just control their gestures and movements on the pitch but also their own lives, that men such as Coluna or Eusébio became major interpreters of the football game around the world.⁶¹

One of the moments where this competence was more widely appreciated was perhaps the ruthless defensive performance of Vicente in the 1966 World Cup, in the match between Portugal and Brazil. Mogne describes with relish how Vicente neutralized Pelé's art:

> Vicente was kind of slow, but he knew how to mark opponents, and he was able to mark Pelé without breaking a sweat. He was a midfielder that played in that holding system. You see, he was a midfielder and Pelé a left-wing midfielder. In that system he played in, he would just cling to him. Wherever Pelé was, he was there too. If Pelé tracked back to defend deep, he tagged along. Two players here, two players there. The game didn't allow for any display of skills because there was no room for that, players were tied up in pairs.

Players from the suburbs of Lourenço Marques did not just adapt the game of football, creating their own versions of it; they also revealed their ability to interpret modern "languages," such as the one demanded by tactical reading. Even though the language of modern football is based on principles that severely restrain the body, one needs to consider the possibility that it also enables formal, creative, and inventive manipulation. The motor habitus shaped by tactical logic, limiting the players' motor repertoire, was able to reshape the performative framework. In different periods and stages, distinct conceptions of individual and collective movement drew the contours of a space of stylistic possibles, tailored to the athletes' performative potential, while simultaneously disciplining their bodies. Even in the most professionalized contexts, this space of stylistic possibles was subject to assessments that exceeded the utilitarian calculus of the result, introducing aesthetic autonomies—various languages, as in other artistic fields—also relevant as symbolic capital used in the interactions among supporters. Where the process of professionalization was less felt, the performance was open to heterodox reconfigurations of movement, more dependent on the public classification criteria and less so on the language produced by a specific field of activity undergoing a process of autonomization.

In the precarious Lourenço Marques suburbs, the game of football, an instance of social integration, emerged as a space with a relative autonomy from tactical impositions. Still a long way from having a professional sports experience, African players, like most of the suburban population, organized their lives according to "tortuous paths," filled with "narrow streets and shortcuts" similar to those that characterized the urban structure they lived in. This collective condition was uniquely expressed in football's dominant moral economy. In the local spectacle, dribbling and intimidating gestures, considered violent by a sensibility educated within a different economy of practices, prevailed. This ingrained practical sense (a sense of one's place, to use Erving Goffman's expression), founded on the interactional risk that was the condition for the production of "sweetness," had an affective dimension, expressing the features from which a local structure of feeling emerged. In the interaction order organized by tactics, the pass signaled the growth of interdependencies among individuals, a more complex specialization and division of labor, and an individual internalization of principles of action and worldviews. Symbolic exchange was subordinated to the search for a result, thus triggering an adjustment of players' motor repertoire to the expectations of a host of agents, from managers to the public. Progressively,

FIGURE 6.3. Eusébio shooting before the friendly match between Ajax and Benfica (2–1), Amsterdam, Ajax Stadium, 9 May 1965. Author: Jac. de Nijs (ANEFO). GahetNA (Nationaal Archief NL). *Source:* Wikimedia.

the association between the tactical scheme and the achievement of victory, whereby a near causal chain was established between one and the other, conditioned the proliferation of game patterns and defined the foundations from which football styles could develop, under the injunction that aesthetics should be at the service of efficiency.

7 ⤻ Football Narratives and Social Networks in Late Colonial Mozambique

IN the suburbs of Lourenço Marques, besides the neighborhood matches themselves, regular competitions organized by the AFA and its clubs also involved a public recruited in the suburbs. Gestures, performances, and sports heroes now integrated a specific chronology, narrated in multiple accounts that circulated through contacts and interactions. The suburbs, however, did not just reproduce the narrative they had locally created. The fast dissemination of an urban popular culture projected other narratives toward the periphery of Lourenço Marques, in particular those that arrived from "downtown" football or from the metropolitan competitions. All these narratives could coexist, but they did not have the same opportunities for dissemination. The way in which football narratives were shared in Lourenço Marques, especially after the 1940s, was closely linked to the distinct features of the urbanization process in the capital of Mozambique. Directly tied to the development of a specialized, relatively autonomous, and mediatized field of sports practices and consumptions, these narratives were molded by political and economic transformations. More important, their length depended on the way in which they were vehicles for expectations and aspirations. It was also on the grounds of a universal football idiom that many suburban inhabitants began to look beyond their closest living spaces. Football offered the means for suburban men to take part in a specific public space that had wider contours than those of the civic public space of the colonial city. This led to a particular process of exchange in urban colonial Lourenço Marques, one that should not be read as the linear result of political openness. While it is true that the development of an urban popular culture can make clear that the city center and the peripheries were not airtight territories, and that there were exchanges, fluxes, and passages, one nonetheless needs to weigh the actual substance of a political causality in these transformations. This chapter will argue that these transformations in the late colonial period have to be understood not only through a political lens, but by means of a more subtle analysis of the role popular culture played in the process of urban consolidation, allowing for the construction of wide social networks.

FOOTBALL AND CULTURAL DECADENCE

In 1953, José Manuel, former secretary of the Associação Africana (African Association), former president of the Centro Associativo dos Negros da Colónia de Moçambique (Associative Center for the Black Men of the Colony of Mozambique) and president of the suburban club São José de Lhanguene, wrote a series of six articles in *O brado africano* titled "A mocidade e o futebol" (Youth and Football). The author advocated an "all-out war against the game." He claimed that football thwarted African evolution and drained "thought from the brain."[1] This assessment semed to prove the failure of the emancipation project grounded in the activity of sports associations. José Manuel, highlighting the existential dramas of an African petite bourgeoisie, created an image to illustrate the contamination mechanism that was intrinsic to the disease of football:

> The ball rolls and enters the homes, manages to insinuate itself into family talks at the dinner table, and becomes common currency among father, mother, sons and daughters, relatives, and even the servants. There are family scuffles because affinities are divided between different clubs and their respective colors. Those evenings filled with tales, reading aloud, reciting verses, tales, and poetic dreams have come to an end. . . . Still not satisfied, the ball . . . keeps on rising and seduces people with serious responsibilities, victoriously bringing them to its rectangles, turning them into its vassals. . . . And the ball continues to bounce, from the European countries of its birth to Africa. And here it is among us, turning and bouncing among us, just when we were on the threshold of civilization.[2]

Football betrayed those who raised "the intellectual worth of the black man to great heights," proving that "besides strong muscles, his body also harbors an attribute with which God, besides matter, endowed the human being, without distinction between colors of the epidermis—the Mind."[3] Football was a disease, an alienation. Young men wasted "their intellectual energies ... devoting them entirely to studying and getting to know football matters."[4] Football, the author added, was also responsible for "a considerable percentage decline in production, due to constant interruptions in work to listen to and reply to others who are talking about football matters at that precise moment, a decrease that when added up at the end of each year amounts to inestimable losses to the companies."[5]

As serious as this last feature, especially to a Catholic such as José Manuel, was the direct competition between football and church around the occupation of Sundays. "God's temples" were "sadly empty and the priest had to preach to a meager group of faithful, mostly female."[6]

THE FOOTBALL DISEASE AS SOCIAL CONTACT

In Lourenço Marques, the "football disease," exacerbated by the development of competitions and growing rivalries, spread by means of three dominant football narratives, sources for the accumulation of football information of many city inhabitants. How that information was distributed depended on the individuals' position and trajectory within the system of local social relations, characterized by a changing colonial situation that affected the process of urbanization and the dissemination of an urban popular culture.

One narrative was based on suburban football's worldview, especially in the competitions organized by the AFA, its institutionalized version. Regular competitions allowed for the development of local bonds, with a family, regional, or religious foundation. Football affinities also contributed to the formation of strong neighborhood identities, which often overlapped with other forms of social identification. However, football fandom, which favored strong social bonds—what Max Gluckman calls "multiplex" relationships—also led to the creation of new ties among the city's inhabitants. Despite the apparent fragility of these new bonds, they had a structural significance. One has to acknowledge the effects of "the strength of weak ties."[7] Football also proved that the development of networks based on such ties could imply conflictual relations,[8] reproduced through increasingly wider interdependency networks. These conflicting relations were a key condition for the existence of a malicious and creative rhetoric. The many stories about the great local football interpreters (including the vovôs), the shared ethics and aesthetic classifications, the creation of a sense of place, demonstrate that the suburb was more than the sum of its parts, it was a community in the making, contrasted with the universe of the cement city, from which it was separated by force.

A second narrative, based on the downtown competitions, namely the AFLM championship, came into existence through the dynamism of the settler community. Football's expansion downtown, promoted by the media, followed the growth of other urban leisure activities. In this case as well, the football narrative embodied the representation of a community built by the settlers and their offspring in a foreign land. Strongly identitarian and inclusive, yet grounded in competitions that excluded the participation of most of the city's population, this narrative contained significant internal divisions, by separating influent clubs, led by established elites, from a more scattered and poorer sports associativism, often grounded in regional relations.

The settlers who arrived in Lourenço Marques and other Mozambican cities reasserted the strength of a third narrative, present in the territory from early on. This third narrative, the "metropolitan" one, was nurtured by the newspapers and the radio, both in Mozambique and in the metropolis, and by the umbilical ties between many AFLM clubs and the main metropolitan clubs. The knowledge created by this narrative, inscribed in the metropolitan popular culture, made the settlers' social integration easier, namely that of the men, helping them gain access to institutional leisure networks. The filial relation between the "downtown narrative" and the "metropolitan narrative" moved through tense and at times ambiguous terrain, namely whenever an opposition between a settler identity and a metropolitan identity emerged. The football narrative, as did other sports in certain instances, sometimes was the vehicle for a more deep-seated resentment.[9]

The worldview presented by the downtown and metropolitan football narratives in Lourenço Marques was not limited, however, to the cement city. Suburban supporters, especially those physically, socially, and culturally located in the borderlands between the suburb and the European city, had access to the narratives that came from the center of the colony's capital. The stock of knowledge of some suburban inhabitants included, from early on, information about the three great football narratives. This triple identification, originally limited to a number of individuals who lived in the vicinity of the cement city, gradually spread as time went on. The morphology of the different social networks that sustained these three narratives evolved in different ways. The most significant aspect of this evolution was the growth of the network of people who carried the downtown and metropolitan narratives to the suburbs. This became particularly important from the 1950s onward and there was a clear expansion during the 1960s. The dissemination of football narratives through urban networks makes it possible to analyze football's role as a repertoire of interaction, a constituent of "communities of practices," in the specific urbanization process of Lourenço Marques.

THE PIONEERS AND THE REPRESENTATIONAL EFFECT

During the 1920s, *O brado africano*, in its Portuguese pages, reported only on AFLM championship events, in which only a small number of nonwhite athletes played. Some members of the local petite bourgeoisie passionately followed sports organized by the colonizer. The downtown narrative's presence in the suburbs, although tenuous during these first decades, depended a great deal on these elements of contact. Armando Silva can count on the fingers of his hands the number of players who moved, in these first few decades of football in Lourenço Marques, from the AFA to the AFLM: Guilherme de Haan, Barata, Jorge Américo, Mário Coluna, and not many more. All these players were mestiços. In 1.º de Maio, an impoverished club located on the border with the suburbs, the doors were opened for some black men, such as Matateu. Footballers, Armando says, came from the suburbs to play in 1.º de Maio's team and, after the match, would catch a transport back to the caniço so they could also perform on Xipamanine's pitch. Many good AFA athletes, he points out, could not prove their worth in the AFLM championship, as they were prevented from doing so by the existing racial barrier. The presence of these players in downtown football created an expectation in the suburbs. These were athletes who had grown up on Xipamanine's pitch, local performers who still lived in the suburbs and played in neighborhood matches and in AFA matches. Their talent caught the attention of the downtown clubs, proving that suburban football could compete on equal terms with AFLM football. They represented the suburbs in cement city football. As a consequence of this representation, there was greater attention paid by suburban inhabitants to the AFLM narrative, which to some extent became a source of local pride. When in 1952 the mestiço teams Vasco da Gama and Atlético de Lourenço Marques were included in the AFLM, a move intended to pacify the educated and assimilated elites, this inclusion definitely relocated the club-based identification of many mestiço supporters from the suburbs to downtown.

Issufo remembers hearing about Benfica "since he was very young, since his childhood." This knowledge was definitely spread when the Lisbon club came to Lourenço Marques, in 1950, for the inauguration of Desportivo's new pitch. Saide Mogne was able to see one of the matches Benfica played there. He entered the pitch carrying the boots of a defender

FIGURE 7.1. S. L. Benfica football team, before the Ajax-Benfica match, Amsterdam, Ajax Stadium, 9 May 1965. On the left is Mário Coluna; on the far right, Eusébio; the goalkeeper is the Mozambican Costa Pereira. Author: Jac. de Nijs (ANEFO). GahetNA (Nationaal Archief NL). *Source:* Wikimedia.

and his idol at the time, Félix [Assunção Antunes]. During Benfica's visit to Lourenço Marques, to inaugurate Desportivo's new stadium, there were many rituals and ceremonies.[10] The team arrived on 28 July and was received by the governor general.[11] A few days later they visited the city's suburbs, where they were welcomed by an AFA delegation. The Benfica players and directors watched a parade and a match between two local teams on Xipamanine's pitch. In this ceremony, which was watched by a large public, there were speeches by representatives from the main African associations. Francisco de Haan talked on behalf of *O brado africano* and the Associação Africana. Enoque Libombo talked on behalf of the Centro Africano dos Negros de Moçambique (African Center for Mozambique's Black Men).[12] Some days later, Vasco da Gama organized a reception for the Lisbon team.[13]

Benfica's popularity, which grew with this tour, became even greater when the club signed Mozambican players such as Naldo, Costa Pereira, and Coluna. Issufo adds that Mário Coluna "had many fans over here and when he arrived in Lisbon he caused a frenzy." Before this "Benfica's visit had livened things up. In Benfica, we saw great players such as Rogério, Francisco Ferreira, and José Águas. This heightened the impact even more, when Coluna and all those others went there." Issufo then describes the transmutation process: "The supporters over here were already [club] supporters over there." "When Juca, Mário Wilson, Matateu, and Coluna went there," says Hilário, people became even more interested. And then Sporting, Benfica, Marítimo, Ajax, and Académica came over here. We started looking around for information about everything. We discussed, we followed the matches. There were those who supported Benfica, those who supported Sporting and everyone argued. We always followed [football], and [since then] more and more so."

The signing of Mozambican players by metropolitan clubs had its decisive moment in 1949, when two young men—a settlers' son named Júlio Cernadas Pereira, known as Juca, and a mestiço Mozambican named Mário Wilson—traveled by ship from Lourenço Marques to Lisbon. The biggest leap, however, was that of Matateu. Born Sebastião Lucas da Fonseca and raised in the poor neighborhood of Alto Maé, he started playing football in the AFA championship, for the team João Albasini. In 1947 he moved to 1.º de Maio, securing a job as a locksmith in building construction. When in 1951 he came to Lisbon to play for Belenenses, a club to which 1.º de Maio was affiliated, Matateu signed a contract guaranteeing him a monthly income.[14] By then he was coveted by several clubs in the metropolis. After Matateu, his brother Vicente, together with Coluna, Hilário, and Eusébio also moved to Lisbon. Thanks to their talents, these players quickly became increasingly recognizable symbols of a metropolitan popular culture.

Although he remembers that during his childhood people already "discussed" it, in school and later at work, the metropolitan narrative only "became more important when the players started going to the metropolis." The impact of suburban football's worldview was a powerful one. Matine says that "he wanted to be like Travassos, like Coluna. I had references, so those were my idols. I saw it in the newspapers." Within the context of the established power relations under Portuguese colonialism, the transition of African football players to metropolitan clubs was extraordinary, only possible due to metropolitan football's semiprofessionalized status. The popularity of metropolitan clubs in the suburbs, Mogne says, was firmly established "from the moment our players started going over there. Matateu's transfer to Belenenses, in 1951, was, according to Ângelo da Silva, the defining moment that "turned us on to football. When the players started moving to Portugal and began to succeed in Portugal, we became really interested in Portuguese football." When these suburban players "became idols, many people started to like the clubs these players had joined." António Cruz confirms the nature of the identification process: "We started to look to all those people, Matateu and the like. After Mozambican players started to establish themselves over there, we did not discuss that player who moved over there and went unnoticed, we discussed the player who had an impact. Every Mozambican player, with a few exceptions, had immediate success in Portugal." "It was a source of pride," Vicente recalls. "Because . . . we came, we saw, and we conquered. In the time of the Julinhos, in Benfica, with all the ace players, Travassos, all those famous players, Jesus Correia, Arsénio, Pipi, these were all famous players and we got in there among them, Barrigana, Hernâni."

Mogne regretted, however, that other great suburban players never had the chance to leave: "At the time, before people like Coluna, we had players who were equally gifted but who, should they arrive in Portugal, would not stay there, they would move on to play in other countries. But as this trip was an impossibility, there was no interest. When Benfica arrived over here, they started to notice that Mozambique has some good players."

TRIPLE TIES

Hamido Nizamo, in defining the structure of club-based preferences in the neighborhood where he grew up, talks about the existence of a triple tie: "a guy supported a neighborhood club, in the area belonging to Mahafil or Beira-Mar, or whatever it was. He supported a so-called downtown club. He supported Beira-Mar, Mahafil, Ferroviário, or Sporting. And then he supported Benfica or Belenenses." The triple tie led to the growth of this specific stock of knowledge and reconfigured local identifications. The same person, confirms Hilário, supported a suburban club, a downtown club, and a metropolitan club: "We talked about everything." Matine supported João Albasini, Desportivo, and Benfica. Some, he says, even supported a Brazilian club: "I heard a guy saying he supported Botafogo, another saying he supported Fluminense, clubs we had never seen, whose colors we didn't know, but we had heard about them."

Identifications with downtown and metropolitan clubs were not organized along the same lines that defined suburban networks. Downtown and metropolitan football narratives helped to create a mediated relation with other scales of urban life, thus widening sociabilities beyond a narrow parochial scale. This form of participation in city life and in the "affairs of the world," as football was a universal language, occurred predominantly in the suburban neighborhoods. As a ground of shared knowledge, downtown and metropolitan narratives, by breaking away from the narrowness of local belonging, strengthened the opportunities, which were already offered by the suburban narrative, for the creation of routines and social encounters in the suburbs. Clearly, the football "disease" favored daily interactions. Matine points out that the football disease "always existed, it exists anywhere football is played. When the diseased leaves his neighborhood, he is already carrying the disease. This person ceases to be a normal person and becomes diseased. For his club, for his neighborhood, fanaticism trumps everything." The "diseased wants to know everything, devours anything associated with that club," and his goal, according to Matine, is to "master his area, namely his neighborhood, he tries to be the master of the club he loves." To master this knowledge became a necessary condition to "master his area," his social space of encounters, within the neighborhood's daily life. For Matine, information about Matateu's exhibitions in Belenenses or those of Coluna in Benfica became the basis of daily rituals in the public space, where arguments were held and discussions were fostered.

Matine was one of many diseased by and for Benfica:

> I did not miss a single report featuring Benfica. My dad had a little radio, always tuned to Emissora Nacional, the metropolitan national radio. It was three o'clock over here, five over there. We had finished everything, I had played in the morning in my neighborhood, had played on Saturday, and on Sunday I would listen to my club play. We lived the match as if we were there, watching it live. That disease still exists today. I knew every single Benfica player, the entire team, managers and all that. I was fortunate enough to receive the club newspaper. There was a Portuguese man over there, who owned a photography company and subscribed to Benfica's newspaper. After reading it, he passed it on to me. Even if it was last week's, I wanted to know everything that was going on at my club. There was that disease. Even today, I keep every single sports newspaper and send them to my brother in Maputo—*O jogo*, *A bola*, and *Record*—and he passes them on to the guys who are in *Notícias*'s sports section, so that they know what's going on.

"Downtown" and metropolitan narratives offered an operative interaction repertoire, on a scale that was beyond the reach of the suburban narrative. It is not easy to assess to what degree the downtown and metropolitan narratives spread in the suburbs. It is likely that they developed through the suburban narrative's dominant social network, gathered in the frontier between the cement city and the reed city, in the more urbanized areas of the Munhuana, Xipamanine, and Chamanculo neighborhoods.[15]

This repertoire was less present, then, in the furthest outskirts, where a more recent population still reproduced the ways of living proper to a rural context. Football's disease spread through increasingly wider social networks, and this transmission did not take place merely within the scope of proximity relations. In this contamination process, the media had a crucial role, projecting the process of dissemination of football narratives beyond the interactional "here and now."

THE MEDIA

Mass media created the conditions that allowed football to turn into one of the mainstays of an emerging popular culture. The growing amount of space devoted to sports in the media went hand in hand with a general increase in news on the various types of urban entertainment, a mark of the diversification of local leisure activities.[16] Between 1935 and 1945 the number of Mozambican publications did not exceed eighteen per year. In 1945 there were only three newspapers with a circulation of more than 1,900 copies. In 1940 there were 4,401 radio receivers in Mozambique, of which 2,254 were in Lourenço Marques. Ten years later, that number had doubled; there were 8,670 receivers in Mozambique and 4,493 in the capital. That same year the number of publications in the colony reached twenty, of which five had a circulation exceeding 1,900 copies. There were three daily newspapers. This continuous growth underwent an even more striking evolution during the following decade. In 1960 there were thirty-three publications in Mozambique, of which fourteen had a circulation exceeding 1,900 copies, 36,927 radio receivers, of which 19,347 were in Lourenço Marques. Five years later, the number of receivers had reached 52,906 in Mozambique and 26,557 in the capital,[17] and there were thirty-eight publications, of which sixteen were daily, with a total circulation of over 18 million copies. Data from the 1970s attest to the importance of Lourenço Marques within the total number of periodical publications published in Mozambique: thirty-one of the thirty-eight publications were produced in the capital. The annual circulation had reached 27,839,000 copies and at the time there were 125,748 receivers, 55,002 of which in Lourenço Marques. Three years later, the number of receivers reached 176,562, of which 71,629 were in the capital.

The media growth reinforced the conditions that enabled the expansion of sporting identifications. In this context, however, the three dominant football narratives in Lourenço Marques were not treated equally. The constant absence, in the city's media, of information about the social, economic, and cultural life of the suburban population also extended to sports practices. Football in Lourenço Marques, if we look only at the newspaper coverage, boiled down to reports of matches played downtown and in the metropolis. *O brado africano* was a lone crusader in the attempt to disseminate the suburban sport, with particular emphasis, at least until the mid-1950s, on AFA competitions. In its pages all three narratives were given a stage, a telltale sign of the social standing of their readership. In 1933, *O brado africano* had one of its first news items about metropolitan competitions, when it reported that Belenenses had won the Portuguese championship by beating Sporting Lisbon.[18] In the mid-1940s news about metropolitan sports was still scarce, as can be seen by the limited space given to the inauguration of the Estádio Nacional, in 1944.[19] The news about the match between Portugal and Spain in 1945 had greater prominence, although the article about this meeting was originally published in the *Lourenço Marques Guardian*.[20] At the time, the newspaper was busy following the AFA competitions, as well as the evolution of African competitions outside the capital, especially in Inhambane. Following Benfica's visit in 1950, *O brado africano* began to cover the downtown championship more closely, a tendency that was reinforced when Vasco da Gama and Atlético moved to the AFLM. Toward the end of the 1950s, before AFA's dissolution, downtown and metropolitan narratives were already major features in the pages of *O brado africano*.

In other city newspapers, aimed at the settler readership, there was an increase, especially from the 1950s onward, in metropolitan football coverage. As the local and metropolitan championships did not take place simultaneously, for a large portion of the year news from Lisbon dominated the newspaper's pages. *O brado africano*, although later than other newspapers, followed the "metropolonization" trend in the sports news, a process that reflects the changes in the morphology of its market and in the preferences of its readership. The circulation of metropolitan sports newspapers grew over the same period. In 1953, the stationer's and bookshop Minerva Central advertised that it sold *O norte desportivo*, *A bola*, *O mundo desportivo*, and the Brazilian *Esporte ilustrado*.[21] Saide Mogne points out that the newspaper *A Bola* circulated "from family to family," adding that "if someone got hold of the newspaper, he would not read it, he would study it." António Cruz also read *A bola* and, as he was a Benfica member, received the club's newspaper through the mail. The presence of Portuguese newspapers, as Cruz recalls, enabled people to gain a specialized knowledge, so they began to know "who the players were on Benfica's and Sporting's teams. People knew everything." Those able to read would then spread the information.

THE INTEGRATION AND SUBALTERNIZATION OF A MEDIA NARRATIVE

Abissínia Ali went to the sports section of *Diário de Lourenço Marques Guardian* in 1954 and presented its editor, the journalist and football manager Severiano Correia, with an "absurd question: Mr. Severiano Correia, how much would I pay for advertisements with commentaries on AFA matches?" He answered, "You're welcome to it, in fact we're the ones that will pay. You start tomorrow." Abissínia Ali's work was inspired by the work of local journalists such as Severiano Correia and the style of *A bola*, a newspaper to which he subscribed. *Notícias de Lourenço Marques*, which was also trying to tap into this particular market niche, hired the journalist Jorge Levi to follow AFA competitions. In the mid-1950s the two main daily newspapers in Lourenço Marques started publishing regular news items about AFA competitions. In the newspapers, but also on the radio, the rising number of ads aimed at the African consumer showed that there were important business opportunities beyond the limits of the cement city.

The *Guardian*'s sports section, Abissínia Ali points out, prioritized the coverage of the downtown and metropolitan championships. Contradictory interpretations emerged from the presence of the suburban narrative in the cement city newspapers. On the one hand, it was a sign of integration: a competition previously confined to the suburban space and to the coverage of *O brado africano* had been included in the newspapers that represented the colonial power's worldview, usually delimited by the coverage of local and metropolitan political and economic affairs, the life of European society, their leisure activities, their football. A part of suburban life had now become a mediated reality. On the other hand, although it was included in the newspaper, the news about AFA competitions occupied secondary status. The inclusion of African football in news about urban life, uniting what was separated, produced a hierarchy. The institutionalization of this inequality became a reality when, following the AFA's dissolution by government decree, some of its clubs had no other choice than to take part in the AFLM's third division. This integration served both to unite and to subordinate. The media would foster this hierarchy, although *O brado africano*, especially through the action of the journalist Guerra Manuel in the 1960s, made an effort to dignify the third-division championship. When, following the end of the indigenato, some of the best African players moved to AFLM clubs, the downtown narrative definitely imposed itself in the suburbs. Guerra Manuel, who also played in the AFA, for Inhambanense, remembers how, through his professional activity as a journalist, he came to realize that "the end of the AFA weakened African football." The prevalent divisions between local clubs, present in the neighborhood identities, in regional or religious interest groups, did not help, according to the former *O brado* journalist, "to consolidate the unity" that would be necessary to counter the negative effects of that sort of social integration. The suburban narrative was largely sustained by bonds based on rivalry. Football helped build a community of practices, a "community in itself," consolidated through a particular experience of the city. It did not, however, serve as a ground for a mobilizing political unity in the suburbs, even though the conditions for such unity to grow had expanded, a fact attested by the government's misgivings about the dissemination of a nationalist discourse and the formation of a class consciousness among the dominated population.

The integration of nonwhites in "downtown" and metropolitan football narratives gave the suburbs a more salient iconographic presence in the cement city newspapers. The rare photographs of black individuals often rehashed a "tribalized" representation, at odds with the urban lifestyle of most suburban inhabitants. In sports pages the only black men whose image occasionally appeared were the great stars of American boxing, such as Joe Louis or Sugar Ray Robinson.[22] On 21 January 1953, Mário Coluna, a football player and track athlete, was pictured winning the eight-hundred-meter race at a meet between Desportivo de Lourenço Marques and a team representing Durban.[23] From this photograph, taken from a great distance, it was not immediately obvious that he was not white. In 1954, following the Lourenço Marques team's 4–2 victory over Northern Transvaal, the same Coluna was entitled to a passport-type photograph, something unheard of in this publication.[24] Some months later, a photograph of the player Vicente, a black Mozambican, not a mestiço like Coluna, was also published.[25] In 1954, Coluna's and Matateu's success in metropolitan football, which led to them being called up for the Portuguese national team, earned them a place on the newspaper's front page.[26]

The iconographic existence of the African sportsman was one of the most important consequences of athletic success. Their increasingly higher media profile had proven decisive for the change in their social condition. Only during the 1960s did sports news start to include pictures of nonwhite players more regularly. This iconographic representation, however, was justified by the service these athletes did on behalf of colonial sports institutions, usually the city's football teams, the team of *naturais* (homeborn), Lourenço Marques's football team or metropolitan teams, among these the Portuguese national team. The iconography would be adapted to the regime's propaganda. While those whose portraits figured in newspaper were few and far between, they were given due prominence.

RADIO NARRATIVES

The role of print media in football's dissemination and in the establishment of a hierarchy between the various narratives was not as decisive, however, as the role of radio. By popularizing a form of verbal communication, radio was able, with greater ease, to overcome the barrier erected by the culture of writing.[27] The experience of the Spain-Portugal broadcast in 1934 inaugurated a new form of collective listening, which opened up a new relation between supporters and their teams: the matches were listened to near the entrance to *Notícias*'s head office, where loudspeakers reproduced the sound sent by a Marconi radio. During the 1950s the sudden popularity of battery-powered transistor radios, as Armando Silva says, revolutionized Mozambique. Radio's growing popularity also benefited from the local interest in following metropolitan sports. At the beginning of the 1950s, Telefunken advertised its new car radios by appealing to settlers' football ties: "listen to metropolitan football in your car, the best universal car radio."[28] In the suburbs, ownership of a radio, almost always through installments, contributed to a person's local status. On Sundays people began to visit public places such as cafés, canteens, and bars, which now entered into direct competition with religious services. Football reports were originally followed through Emissora Nacional. Finding "the 13 meters," the wavelength for the metropolitan radio broadcasts, became a Sunday obsession: "Everyone who wanted a radio," says Mogne, "had to know if it could tune in to Emissora Nacional." It was not just any radio, assures Ângelo, "that could receive it. The set had to be able to work on 'shortwave' to tune in the 13-meter mark on Sundays. There were, Mogne recalls, "a few battery-powered radios and others that operated on AA batteries. Some people made antennas to have better broadcast reception." António Cruz describes a similar situation: "On Sundays it was awful. Those old radios, with their interference, were not like today's, which can be tuned in with greater ease. It was a disease."

Ângelo admits that his passion for Benfica was fostered by the football reports he heard "since he was a kid." He remembers Artur Agostinho, Emissora Nacional's announcer, who became the voice of Portuguese football in Africa, a man who, in Lourenço Marques, "was incredibly famous." On Sundays, Ângelo says, "we all grabbed a radio, those battery-powered radios, with a car battery, because in the old days there were no AA batteries. We either used an electrical or a battery-powered radio to listen to Portuguese football." On the streets, at home, Hamido Nizamo notes, everyone "had his ears glued to the radio." When Benfica became European champion, in 1961, Nizamo and his friends were "constantly" passing by the door of a restaurant that was broadcasting the report, and "everyone was glued to the radio. It was crazy. Once the game ended, there were great celebrations everywhere, in the suburbs, downtown, everywhere." Hilário confirms that, "all over the place, if you had a AA battery–powered radio, a group of people would gather around you to listen and to have some drinks." Issufo remembers the gatherings in canteens, where people listened to the reports. People went from Munhuana to Alto Maé, where there were many commercial establishments with radios. Summing up, Issufo says that "a disease of affinity with metropolitan clubs has spread somewhat," through Emissora Nacional: "you could hardly hear the report, on the 13-meter mark, 19 and 25 meters, then the AA battery-powered radio appeared and you could get it. The reports were heard through the voices of Amadeu José de Freitas and other announcers such as Artur Agostinho." Radio, as Issufo notes, led to an exponential growth in the daily discussions about the game: "People argued about football a lot." Before becoming a central figure in the reports broadcasted from the metropolis, Mário Coluna listened to reports on matches with players who had gone to Lisbon before him: "there were always radios around to listen to Benfica, Sporting, and Belenenses reports, to hear about Matateu, Mário Wilson."

In 1958, the Rádio Clube de Moçambique (RCM) broke Emissora Nacional's monopoly on reports in Lourenço Marques and started doing reports on the local matches. In 1966, the RCM opened an office in Lisbon and, after some pressure from the local market, also started to broadcast metropolitan matches. João de Sousa, the RCM's announcer in the 1960s, assures that when a metropolitan match took place at the same time as a local one, the metropolitan match was the one transmitted. This choice, he states, was justified on commercial grounds—it was the match more people wanted to hear. The announcer insisted that he did not mean just white people: "while it is true that people were interested because there was a great rivalry in the local championship, it is no less true that the rivalry between Benfica, Sporting, and Porto was also absorbed by people over here." During the 1957–58 season, the RCM inaugurated a new channel broadcasting exclusively in the local "dialect." (The colonial administration, since 1952, had considered the possibility of broadcasting in the local language.)[29] In 1955, the RCM inaugurated a traditional local music program. Halfway through 1957, it started broadcasting every

Sunday in the Ronga language. One of the sponsors of these broadcasts was the local Philips representative, who was interested in selling radio receivers to the African population.[30] When the Ronga channel started, there were some tentative reports of AFA matches. When, in the following year, the AFA was dissolved, the channel started including reports on third-division matches, into which African clubs had been absorbed, but also of first-division matches. These were transmitted simultaneously, on both channels, one in Portuguese and the other in Ronga. João de Sousa justified the option to broadcast in the native language due to its commercial viability. If until 1961 the broadcaster did not have a "clear political orientation" and it mostly offered entertainment programs,[31] the outset of the colonial war, in 1964, changed the situation. Under the influence of Serviços de Acção Psicossocial (Psychosocial Action Services), the radio became a more effective instrument of propaganda.[32]

The AFA area, says João de Sousa, had an "extremely important segment of the population, especially in the city of Maputo. We realized that to report on an area in the periphery, outside the cement city, could bring in more listeners to the radio and have a commercial dimension, because this is also an area under a considerable commercial influence." The Rádio Clube de Moçambique's directors realized that radio transistors were spreading quickly: "Any grocer's, any shop we visited at the time had an AA battery–powered receiver." If someone "walked into a bar or a canteen, there was always a radio." Some supporters who knew the players through radio reports, the announcer says, would go to the stadium with their transistor radios, to identify the bodies and faces of those players they knew but did not recognize: "people heard about João, Joaquim or José but did not know who they were. I realized that people heard about a guy but did not know what he looked like and when they took the radio to the field they could put that name to a face."

The radio inaugurated a new relation between the game and its supporters. More than newspapers, it contributed to a growth in the production and reproduction of the networks based on this common knowledge. It was particularly active, however, in the promotion of the "downtown" and metropolitan narratives. As such, it was instrumental in the creation of a new hierarchy of sports heroes and a new club identification. Radios were the objects that marked the suburban encounter, in various gatherings, including discussions in cafés, bars, or canteens. At a certain point, on both sides of the circunvalação road, despite segregation, individuals gathered to celebrate common heroes, to identify with the same clubs, to imagine the athletes' movements through the oral report of someone who was there, at the pitch, seeing everything that went on. While being in two separate spaces, individuals gathered similar information, creating the possibility of a bond anchored in a shared representation.

Football created in Mozambique a quite unique instrument for imagining communities whose frontiers were wider than the colonial political, social, and economic communities themselves. Under certain circumstances, the three narratives were based on conflicting visions, while in others these visions coalesced. The faculty of the imagination was linked with the desires and expectations of diverse populations and social strata and with the way in which they projected, within certain limits and possibilities, their future. The suburban narrative could legitimate identitarian worldviews but could also reify the birth of an interconnected urban community, built on the margins, and in response to, the colonizer's power. Suburban supporters, as they followed "downtown" and metropolitan narratives, projected themselves onto a wider universe, in which they desired to take part, by keeping up with the achievements of the most talented African players, citizens of the world. For the settlers, the metropolitan narrative allowed for the celebration of an affective bond with their homeland; often, however, identification with the "downtown clubs" was a ground for claiming rights for the settler community, marginalized by the policies emanating from the imperial center.

URBAN TRANSFORMATIONS

Political and economic changes had an impact on the conditions for sports practice, but also on the relation between those narratives and urban popular culture. The possibilities for the dissemination of this specific knowledge across wider and more complex social networks resulted from the emergence of a set of urban conditions. Despite the persistence of social and racial segregation, the development of the local economic system brought about greater worker mobility; an increase in the density of interactions among diverse segments of the population, namely as a result of an increment in the social division of labor; the expansion of transport and communication networks; the creation of new interest groups; the local community's loss of autonomy; and, to a much lesser degree and mostly under coercion, the development of bureaucratic institutions, which came to replace the former personal-support networks.[33]

From the 1950s onward, the investment of metropolitan capital in the economic life of Lourenço Marques went hand in hand with a demographic boom. A city that historically had relied on the neighboring regions of South Africa now gained a greater degree of autonomy.[34] In

1968 the number of migrant workers among the African population of Lourenço Marques amounted to no more than 15 or 16 percent.[35] Most Africans coming from the countryside wanted to settle in the city. The evolution of the social division of labor made the hiring of the suburban labor force a pressing need, both for less-qualified workers and for trades that required specific technical skills. The integration of more individuals into the local labor market increased mobility within the city.[36]

According to Matavela,

> When the armed struggle broke out in Mozambique a lot of things began to change, and black folks started being integrated into society a little bit more. From 1966 in particular, but in fact ever since the armed struggle broke out in Mozambique, there was a change—in political life and in the world of sports. People had to come into the city to go to work. In the period of armed struggle, a lot of factories started to appear, like Sabrina, in the '60s. The Matola area was a factory area. In the 1970s Av. do Brasil, nowadays Av. das Forças Populares [de Libertação de Moçambique], was built, and then factories started to appear alongside it. When I came over here [to the metropole] for the compulsory military service, in 1971, I bought a shirt and when I checked the label, I saw it had been made in Mozambique. It was made in a place just across from the zoo in Maputo, the Koala factory where the best coats in Mozambique were manufactured.

Despite its many inadequacies, the urban transport network expanded, during the 1950s and 1960s: bus and coach services were increased.[37] In 1945, bus routes mostly covered the connections between downtown and the residential area of Polana, with only one bus route reaching the suburban border, in Alto Maé neighborhood. In 1955 there were already a few bus routes that went beyond the circunvalação road and entering Avenida de Angola and Rua dos Irmãos Roby, local axes of commercial and labor relations.[38] These transformations revealed the tension between, on the one hand, the continuities that went hand in hand with the persistence of a discriminatory and racially endogamous system, a precarious labor market, and a vigilant state and, on the other hand, the dynamics of economic growth fostered by state initiative as well as private capital, in a context in which Portuguese space was opening itself up to foreign markets. While in 1950 the city had 4.1 percent of the industrial establishments in the territory, in 1973 this number had gone up to 36.8 percent.[39] A substantial portion of these establishments were devoted to food production, but other industries were also clearly on the rise: metal, paper, textiles, chemical, timber, transport equipment, and office supplies. Lourenço Marques also had an oil refinery. Industries that required more space and a larger labor force would cluster in peripheral zones, such as Matola and Machava, but also near the various axes that crossed the suburbs.[40]

SPATIAL DYNAMICS AND SOCIAL MOBILITY

The interdependencies between the settler and suburban populations, a consequence of labor mobility, did not put an end to the prevalent spatial stratification and the hostility felt toward both the suburban dwellers that crossed over to the "downtown" area and toward those who lived there, such as servants, porters, watchmen. The interactional conventions imposed on suburban inhabitants when they traveled to the cement city discouraged any desire of spatial mobility. The expectations of residential mobility among the populations of all Lourenço Marques's neighborhoods in 1970, surveyed by Maria Clara Mendes, revealed that a dividing line between the two parts of the city persisted. Few suburban inhabitants hoped to live in the European city and almost none wished to move in the opposite direction. The hopes of residential mobility were circumscribed to the suburban space. The more urbanized neighborhoods, near the border with the cement city—Munhuana, Chamanculo, Lagoas, and Xipamanine—were those where people most wanted to live, particularly the populations that lived in the more peripheral neighborhoods. On the European side, the prevailing desire was to move to the neighborhoods of the colonial haute bourgeoisie, Polana and Sommerschield.[41]

The principles presiding over the cement city's dominant interaction order were still hostile to the suburban inhabitant. The unstable conventions created by the suburban neighborhoods' inhabitants, their localized routines and social encounters, still provided them with greater assurance than the "social contract" the colonizer's daily life had to offer, a life defined by practical and symbolic exchanges that subdued and demeaned them. Ângelo Gomes da Silva refers to this when he talks about the suburban player's dilemma when faced with the possibility of playing football downtown: "There was also the person's courage factor, having to leave that place to travel downtown. How will I be received on the other side?"

In spite of this adversity, economic need led the suburban inhabitants to move in the direction of the cement city and also toward the new industrial areas of Matola and Machava. Within the context of the suburban labor market, football talent played a unique role as a mediator in the employment process. This phenomenon was hardly new and had long benefited the newly arrived young settlers. With a greater intensity after the demise of the AFA, in 1959, and even more so after the end of indigenato, suburban players integrated these forms of recruitment that signaled a preprofessionalization of football as well as the impact that the success of pioneering suburban players would have in the downtown and metropolitan clubs. While giving a tour of Clube Ferroviário's trophy room with some pride—where the impressive Salazar Cup, won by the club in 1951, holds a prominent place—Ângelo confirmed that the players that started moving downtown, toward the end of the 1950s, were basically looking for jobs. The club's directors looked for the best players in the AFA pitches The inclusion of these athletes in "downtown clubs," besides offering them a job, often in rather favorable conditions, gave them status: that of characters in a more cosmopolitan football narrative disseminated by urban popular culture.

The poet and writer Luís Polanah, in an article for O brado africano, where he tried to assess the degree of integration of "the nonwhite in areas dominated by the European element," emphasized the "specific case of football."[42] Sport, through "its projection on the public sphere, through its moral magnification and great emotional strength, does offer compensation to the reduced number of its beneficiaries" when compared with the integration of other fields, such as "religious juntas" and "public and private jobs." Sport had the capacity to shatter the "social, religious, and racial barriers that divided men from the same community," although it could only "effectively shelter . . . a small number of protégés." These protégés, having become public figures, changed their social status: "A black man playing for Sporting isn't an ordinary black man; he has ceased to be a 'mamparra.'"[43] The black man, the mulatto, the Indian, they would lose this blemish once they started playing for this or that sports club."[44] Polanah concluded that sport, in its integrative role, "surpasses everything else," and one could not but "accept it as the quickest and smoothest way to promote interaction between races without raising too many problems."

"Downtown football" also offered other benefits. Issufo Batata mentions the importance of being part of a football club in trying to achieve assimilado status. He gave the example of mixed-race players whose European fathers did not recognize them or register them: "Mixed-race children who were here and had not been registered by their fathers were not able to play; they had to show their documents. The club could easily register a man through court or some other means, even if he had an indígena mother, because a mixed-race person had that right. The clubs controlled this." The interests surrounding the football world managed to hold their sway. By overcoming, by means of their influence, existing legal barriers, they had a hand, albeit indirectly, in extending citizenship rights.

In the Ferroviário junior-team photograph, at the end of the 1950s, an image unearthed by Ângelo in the club's headquarters, there was only one black man. Matine recalls that from the 1960s onward neighborhood players were integrated into downtown clubs and "employed to learn a trade." Many players from the Xipamanine neighborhood, where Matine grew up, went to Central, Ferroviário, Alto-Maé. Matine and his friends chose Clube Central, which played in AFLM's second division. The club, he remembers, gave them "transport fare," although the players saved it and went on foot, "because the money was needed for breakfast; because there was no bread, we lived in dire straits": "he gave us that money, we walked anyway and then at one o'clock in the morning we would buy some bread and take it home. We got home and maybe there was dinner, maybe not. Bread for breakfast was already assured." When he was registered as a junior in the club, Matine was able to get a job:

> at the time, I had finished my primary-school education and was already in high school when Mr. António, Central's section leader, came to me and asked me what I did. I answered that my father had died, there was only my mother and a bunch of brothers and that my life didn't seem to be going anywhere, because I did not have any means of survival. He then told me to go to the city hall and learn a trade. I learned the trade of surveyor of measures in petrol stations, and of agrarian measures and taximeters. I went there and learned all that. There were others who were placed elsewhere and trained as mechanics. After a year, a year and a half, two years, we started to get some money from the places we were placed at. We became part of the staff. I remember that I got four hundred escudos a month. I could use this money to feed my family. One of Central's directors had a factory called Companhia Industrial da Matola, which produced various types of pasta and cookies. At the end of the month he gave me a *rancho:* ten kilograms of sugar, ten kilograms of rice, two soap bars, milk, butter, cookies, and some money for my mother. If I got four hundred [escudos] I would give three hundred to my mother and keep one hundred. That was to protect myself; if my brothers asked me for something, they wouldn't lack anything. This was how I got by. I grew as a

man and as a respected football player because I truly had the chance for it, and I worked for it.

There were numerous cases like Matine's during the 1960s. The clubs had connections to various business interests and sent the suburban players to these jobs, as Matine recalls:

> those who worked in the railway played for Ferroviário, those who worked in public construction played for Desportivo, in 1.º de Maio people worked in transport, those who played for Malhangalene maybe worked in a butcher's, those of Indo-Português, where *monhés* [a pejorative term for Indians] played, also had their things, clothes shops.... They got those jobs for their athletes. Some punched holes in tickets as transport inspectors, others sold gas in gas stations. Everything was connected.

Vicente recalls,

> When I joined 1.º de Maio I got a job. The club was owned by the public works. Desportivo was part of Smae (which was owned by Paulino dos Santos Gil); Ferroviário belonged to the Railway.... Players in Sporting would work for the police force. When I played for 1.º de Maio I got a job in public works. I had nothing to do really; I'd be sent as a driver to some place or other, but in fact I had nothing to do; then I went to work at the grinding station, close to Abubakar [a grocer], but I'd go there, see what the others were doing, but did nothing. It was a job, but only so they could say I had one.

Many people, according to Matine, learned a trade by way of football. In a context where they were "socially marginalized, we were able to achieve something through football." Football allowed access to some places that, Matine says, were barred to Africans, even if they had some education:

> We did not have the option of turning up in certain areas, even if we were students. Our parents advised us: carry on with your studies and the like.... In my generation with the fourth grade or with the fifth or sixth grade we already had problems, we had problems in the high schools. Why? Because guys with a bit of a mind of their own were persecuted and we realized that this was happening. And now where will I go? I'll look to football, or something in sports. Sports helped a lot of families. Clubs were run by people who came from Portugal, or by their children.

They knew how to run football and they offered some help; the better ones had some assistance. The clubs were able to solve people's problems. The alternative was to go find a job directly.

The ones who benefited most from the opportunities offered by football clubs ended up being the ones, as we shall see later, who already had some resources, namely educational ones. There were numerous obstacles on the road from neighborhood matches to the downtown championship; to overcome them, football talent was not enough.

FOOTBALL CITIZENSHIP

Economic necessity led many suburban inhabitants to enter the dangerous interactional field of daily life in the cement city, where colonial power, coercive and paternalistic, defined social interactions. For the suburban inhabitants these situations were risky and dangerous, and to challenge this colonial malice was virtually unthinkable. It was in this context that the knowledge gathered by some suburban inhabitants about sports competitions became an interactional resource and a regulator of this symbolic violence. Faced with the impossibility of avoiding all contacts in the cement city, there was a need to create new routines that could make everyday life safer. Mastering a sports narrative that went beyond the physical and social boundaries of discrimination and that was intertwined with urban popular culture was crucial; knowledge of facts and events gave some individuals a valuable resource for social participation in a specific public space.

On some occasions the actual settlers were the ones introducing football as an interactional device. Ângelo Gomes Silva remembers that suburban workers, in their jobs, talked with "colleagues who had come from the metropolis and who supported their own clubs. The black men and mestiços had to be known, had to fit in." The metropolitan Portuguese would ask, "So, which club do you support? I have no club. You don't, then you have to support [Portugal's] Sporting. . . . So you are a man, how come you don't support a club?" Choosing a club was a matter of honor. Many of these suburban people "who had never listened to radio reports, also started favoring clubs in this way." In other cases, identification with a club had already been established in school and was constantly reproduced in daily interactions: "There were heated discussions between supporters of different clubs. We had many Portuguese people over here. All the Portuguese had a club they supported." The definition of a club identity gave these suburban inhabitants the chance to "be known," to borrow

Ângelo's phrase. Identification was akin to a social promotion. Black and mestiço supporters now shared a characteristic with the settler population, a rare circumstance in colonial Lourenço Marques. Football knowledge also encouraged a certain male complicity, which defined fairly regulated networks of cooperation and conflict. In short, to be a Benfica or a Sporting supporter granted individuals a specific interactional citizenship in this urban space.

When Hilário, after being signed by Sporting, went to work for the Companhia das Águas (Water Company), most of his teammates had arrived from the metropolis not long before. Their conversations were based on football, almost always metropolitan football, as a common denominator as well as an icebreaker, making it possible to strike up a conversation. Matine, who went through a similar experience, remembers conversations about football during work breaks:

> People talked more about metropolitan football than our own. We started to get all kinds of information about football. As I read Benfica's newspaper, I knew more about the club than some guys who were there. I devoured that newspaper to know more about Benfica, about every sport. If I saw a magazine with things about Sporting I would also grab it and would not pass it to anyone before finishing it.

The diversification of social relations between the various groups who lived in the city, a consequence of the growing labor mobility, invested football with the role of contact language. A vehicle of representation of the local community, through the players who shone on downtown pitches, in the metropolis, and all across Europe, football was a gateway to city life, an effective resource not only in the local context but beyond the frontiers of discrimination. This resource established itself as an interactional right, a means for individuals who had little or no interactional rights to voice their opinions, to argue and even to disagree, without offending the structures of domination present in the daily interaction order.

WHAT HAPPENED TO THE SUBURBAN NARRATIVE?

The propagation of the narrative sustained by the suburban game was severely limited. The dissolution of the AFA was a powerful blow to the institutional organization of suburban football. The African clubs' transition to the AFLM's third division institutionalized a hierarchy already fixed by the media discourse. In the third division, matches were held on the downtown clubs' pitches, during leisure hours, almost always early in the morning. Having been uprooted, the competition broke its bonds with the suburban community, with its own space, its references, and rituals.[45] In June 1959, the year when the new competition started, a game between Azar and Sport Nacional Africano was called off because of the latter's nonattendance. The game had been scheduled for 6:45 a.m. on one of the downtown fields.[46] The following year, in an interview with *Diário de Lourenço Marques Guardian*, entitled "Descontentamento nos clubes desde a filiação na AFLM" (Dissatisfaction in clubs since their filiation in the AFLM), an associate of the African club Gazense protested:

> In the old days we had our competitions, our championships, and things happened with great regularity. Then, on account of the new regulation, we joined the AFLM. We were happy because we would have access to new means and become official, so to speak. I mean, it did not make sense for us to have a separate association. However, the last year passed and we still did not get our championship. This year the same is happening. We now have an organized competition: Infante D. Henrique's Cup, but there are many problems. Our players have to be inspected, but they go to inspection once, twice, three times, and often more and are told to return the following day. The competition has already begun and while in some clubs all eleven players have been inspected, in others only six or seven.[47]

The "interest," says Mogne, had gone. In AFA times, "when Thursday arrived, we were already thinking about the Sunday game. That's the truth. You wouldn't leave your house. You'd do your training preparation at home; no one fooled around." Ângelo acknowledges that the inclusion of AFA clubs in the AFLM, a long-standing claim, ended up breaking the suburban dynamics. The interchanges with South Africa almost ground to a halt. In the AFLM, the African clubs had to abide by the metropolitan legislation, which included a number of obligations. The bureaucratic rule over football was very damaging: "They needed a permit from here, another from over there," Hamido Nizamo notes. Suburban inhabitants were also hurt by the obligation for athletes to have minimum schooling. This measure, implemented in the metropolis in 1956, following a prior attempt to introduce it in 1944, by the then recently created Direcção Geral de Educação Física, Saúde, e Desporto Escolar (General Office of Physical Education, Health and School Sports), undermined football associations, which recruited a considerable number of their athletes among working-class groups. Without minimum schooling, the players could not compete. This classist policy was adapted in its own specific way in the colonial territories. The incredibly low literacy rates meant that the law was only gradually enforced. Even so, for many suburban players it became impossible to play in city competitions. As Ângelo notes, "if they didn't have the fourth grade they couldn't be registered; it wasn't worth it. I had to present my fourth-grade diploma." The consequence, he says, is that "some great players never even left the suburbs." While for some this measure became an incentive for going to school, for many families, pressured by economic need, investment in school only delayed the entry into the labor market. The social mobility opened up by football talent ended up benefiting the individuals with more resources. Many of those who had access to the AFA's communitarian football, which was not subject to these bureaucratic shackles and rigid mechanisms of social selection, were excluded from the city's official football world. In a few cases, when the player had an undeniable talent, and even if he did not meet the bureaucratic criteria, the schooling demands were not so rigid.

Outside the communitarian space that sustained them, and without a competition of their own, AFA clubs withered. The main basis for the construction of a stock of knowledge based on local football went into decline. This circumstance made it easier for the AFLM and metropolitan narratives to become the dominant ones. Those who for a long time fought for Africans' integration into the AFLM championship and who rejoiced in 1959 when they received this piece of news, quickly realized that another subtler form of discrimination had been erected. Still in 1959, José Craveirinha had already remarked that the AFA's integration into the AFLM was positive but that "the initial intention was only partly achieved." The AFLM included African clubs but "kept them apart from the other clubs."[48] A few years later, in 1963, Guerra Manuel, journalist for *O brado africano*, underlined the devaluation of the second and third divisions, noting that there were no pitches to train on, that competitions were deficient and that the public was also missing:[49] "These facts are in blatant contrast with the idea we had in mind when these clubs were included in this very association, following the AFA's dissolution. At the time, we thought the clubs could only benefit from such a measure, but given the current conditions we should be allowed to say that the competitions organized by the AFA easily beat those of the local associação (AFLM).[50]

In 1963, with a fifteen-day interval, two African clubs, Grupo Desportivo Nova Aliança and Grupo Desportivo Chamanculo, formerly Sport Nacional Africano,[51] wrote, respectively, to the governor general and to the CPEF's president, showing great concern over the financial viability of both clubs. Samo Matafene, on behalf of Chamanculo, stated that in "football competitions organized by the AFLM there is no revenue for third-division teams, not even subsidies by the government or by the local city hall." And they added that while "the Associação de Futebol Africana was active, its teams always received their share, which they needed to deal with debts and fines." The club, facing a serious financial crisis, asked for a CPEF subsidy.[52] Nova Aliança's letter was identical. That club added that, with the start of the season imminent, there was no money to buy balls, boots, equipment, and medication, or even for the players' registration.[53]

Some months before the outbreak of the colonial war in Mozambique and a year before he was arrested by the Portuguese authorities, José Craveirinha wrote an article about the situation of African clubs.[54] At the time, in his view, the situation seemed irreversible. According to the poet, who seemed to believe in the virtues of some existing social integration measures, the role these clubs played had come to an end, considering that the conditions that justified their "sociosporting programme" had ceased to exist:

> Once the doors of Lourenço Marques's big teams had been thrown wide open, the outcome was that the suburban supporters became increasingly interested in the football movement of the so-called downtown clubs. There was a strong reason for such a change. Individuals from the most humble social milieus had become famous and had improved their living conditions. The downtown clubs began to attract those who wanted to achieve some glory and enjoy better bread as well as, for that matter, did those who, because of close affinities or other factors, saw their frustrated rosy dreams finally come true. This was an El Dorado within their reach, which could not be wasted. And that was not all. Downtown clubs were also the easier launch pad for a flight to Lisbon, Oporto, or some other metropolitan city. And that was a tempting prize. Having reached this stage, there was a mass defection due to this natural option. No one refuses a place in the sun. A target of various means of persuasion, suburban youth invaded Sporting, Desportivo, Ferroviário, etc., as opposed to their traditional Beira-Mar, João Albasini, Inhambanense, Azar, Mahafil, etc. And these clubs, which were once so powerful, at present face serious difficulties in sending eleven players onto the pitch, properly equipped and on time. Is this a passing crisis? Unfortunately, no. These clubs' crisis is the effect of an irreversible social evolution. These clubs are doomed.

> Within the context of Lourenço Marques's sports, these clubs have fulfilled their destiny, in their own time. There is no place for them now. Being part of a segment, as soon as this segment ends they cease to have a ground for their existence and this will simply mean their death. They are a thing of the past. Time is unforgiving; this is the price we have to pay for progress.

People should, he continues,

> learn to get used to new values; to integrate themselves into new cycles of evolution and progress; to love the symbols associated with their own time. I have a friend from the old football days, Vicente, who was a great player for GD Beira-Mar and one of its greatest fans. Well, every time I hear him discuss football, he speaks of Desportivo from over here and Benfica from over there. This is inevitable. He is caught in the gears of his time.

Craveirinha would soon lose his belief in the gears of his time. And yet for him, back then, football seemed to be in the vanguard of a process of change.

THE NEW STATUS OF NEIGHBORHOOD MATCHES

Focusing on the changes in the sporting identifications of suburban supporters, Craveirinha's article did not discuss the impact this process had in the game's practice in the suburbs, a subject that had aroused his curiosity in the mid-1950s. The progressive hegemony of the downtown and metropolitan narratives in the suburbs as well as the subsequent subordination of the suburban narrative, did not put an end to the features that defined the local game. The suburbs continued to produce a localized adaptation of the European game, in which players' gestures and movements had locally shared meanings. The increase in social contacts within the city, the intensification of exchanges, propelled by the growth of economic interdependencies, the greater circulation of workers, money, and goods, did not eliminate the structural division between the cement city and the suburbs. The greater number of exchanges lived alongside a prevailing spatial and social stratification. The unstable social contract remained a source of rights and conditions for a minimum existential security. In neighborhood matches, the game's symbolic economy remained an expression of the vicissitudes of the urban process of adaptation. When the AFA ended, says Matine, "we became involved in neighborhood football and even took advantage of Mahafil's pitch to play there." Betting emerged once again as a central element of these matches: "And why did we play?," asks Matine, "because the bet at the time was a hundred paus per team." When the neighborhood matches involved higher bets, the best players were enlisted, even if they came from other neighborhoods: "when those from Chamanculo neighborhood had a game they thought was hard or with a high bet of a hundred and fifty paus, they would have one or two players from another neighborhood. For instance, they got Eusébio from Mafalala, Matine from Xipamanine, and vice versa; sometimes Xipamanine would play against Eusébio's team and I would get Abel, who also played for Porto or Zeca or Messias." Many players who had been hired by downtown teams also came every weekend to play in these suburban neighborhood matches: "suppose we play downtown on Sundays, so the training session ends on Friday and everything is organized for us to play on Sunday... so around three o'clock or so that would be the end of it, but we immediately went to Xipamanine, where we play on Saturday, morning and afternoon, and Sunday mornings as well, and afterward we would go play football downtown."

Returning to the suburb brought the old neighborhood association back to life, and with it there returned its subtle meanings, rivalries, the rules of a particular symbolic exchange. Free from the tactical mentality imposed downtown, the suburban player's bodies readapted to the local appreciation framework. The space needed for the exercise of the faculty of malice, the guiding principle for managing movement, and of intimidating gestures and virtuoso skills, key elements in the suburban player's motor repertoire, expanded once again. The local moral economy, based on a consistently situated practice, survived the fall of the AFA and the withering of its clubs. After all, the malice of the suburban game had been born in neighborhood matches. And that's where it remained.

The proliferation of neighborhood matches and new clubs organized more or less informally proved so dynamic that the colonial administration became worried. In 1965, the same year PIDE (Polícia Internacional de Defesa do Estado [International and State Defense Police]) closed the Centro Associativo dos Negros de Moçambique,[55] the DSAC asked the governor of the district of Lourenço Marques about the "operating conditions of Associação Académica de Chamanculo and the Futebol Clube de Chamanculo and if they had submitted any statutory project there."[56] The district governor, Augusto Vaz Spencer, answered, transcribing the information he received from the Administração do Concelho de Lourenço Marques (Lourenço Marques Council Administration).[57] The groups mentioned were not legally registered and did not have internal regulations. As for the Associação Académica de Chamanculo, it was not an association, as it pompously calls itself, but merely a group of boys who like football and get together in whatever time they have free from professional or educational obligations, at their homes, to arrange football matches with other such groups. Their present leader, who calls himself the president, is Rafael Natal, who works as a driver in the Hunt Leuchars [and Hepburn] company in Matola, and the former leader was the parish administrator, Frederico.

He then added: "There are maybe ten other groups in this same area in similar conditions and they have all recently used the city hall pitch in Xipamanine for their matches, paying a registration fee of MZE 100. Whoever wins keeps all the money and uses it to get equipment or food from the nearest canteen." Regarding Futebol Clube de Chamanculo, the case was "similar to the first one, and the leader was its founder, the *cantineiro* (canteen owner) Bazílio Fontoura Fernandes, a Futebol Clube do Porto supporter, which is why he chose white and blue as the group's colors and originally paid for their shirts. The group is composed exclusively of canteen customers (Botequim Chamanculo) between the ages of fourteen and twenty-five." The author advises that Associação Distrital de Futebol de Lourenço Marques (Lourenço Marques Football Association) should be informed about the existence of these groups, so they can be integrated in the AFLM's third division. Among the groups that participated in these matches, there were, according to the same document, Barcelona de Xipamanine, União Xipamanine, Morrumbene de Chamanculo, Desportivo de Chamanculo, Brasileiros da Mafalala, and Águias Negras da Mafalala.

Abissínia Ali was one of the founders of one of these neighborhood clubs: CUF da Mafalala. CUF (Companhia União Fabril) was one of the great Portuguese economic groups,[58] with a head office in Barreiro's industrial area, on the south bank of Lisbon's Tagus River. CUF sponsored some metropolitan football clubs, namely Barreirense and CUF, which gained some prominence during the 1960s and 1970s. CUF da Mafalala was inspired by the club organized by the industrial company. The promoters behind this new suburban club sent a letter to Barreiro to inform the company of their initiative and to ask for some sports equipment. The metropolitan team agreed to help them. The members of CUF da Mafalala became members of the club. When the team won an athletics trophy, they asked a roller-skate hockey team who traveled to the metropolis to hand it over in Barreiro. According to Issufo, it should still be in the

Portuguese club's showcase, a club that is presently named Grupo Desportivo Fabril do Barreiro: "They sent a dozen shirts and we, to thank them, asked them to become our associates. We sent photographs and became members of CUF." At the Machava's stadium inauguration, which was then called Salazar Stadium, CUF da Mafalala paraded with the Portuguese club's banner.

José Craveirinha, Abissínia Ali recalls, did not like the club's name: "Who owns CUF de Mafalala? he asked us. We own it, we answered. Then couldn't you think of a name other than CUF? Tell me why you named it CUF? We haven't any money to buy shirts and we thought that by naming it CUF we could at least get some shirts from Portugal. No, this was wrong." The poet then proposed an alternative: "You could have named it Clube Tsumbula de Mafalala. You could have come to me and I would have given you the shirts." *Tsumbula* means cassava: the Mafalala Cassava Club. Choosing the name of one of the most characteristic foods in the African diet was meant to raise local consciousness, in stark contrast with the reference to a club that represented a company with numerous interests in the colonial world and responsible for the insertion of the African in the production logics that colonialism had brought along with it. For the young founders of CUF da Mafalala, however, *cassava* was not good capital to brandish around in neighborhood matches filled with teams with international names, symbols of a particular local cosmopolitanism.

After the AFA's dissolution, local football became even more protected from the "dangers" of tactical imposition. This suburban style continued to produce its stories, its heroes, and its game plays, celebrating the players' malicious strategies and the logic of their symbolic economy, and collectively rejoicing in the meanings produced by athletes' gestures. This knowledge, increasingly more circumscribed by proximity relations and overlooked by media narratives, held limited interactional resources. Daniel Matavela, establishing a distinction between the matches played in the neighborhoods and the official downtown matches, said that "in the suburbs, every weekend . . . there were matches with direct bets. Downtown, there were championships." The nonexistence of an institutionalized competition that would award a trophy to the winner and simultaneously to its supporters, broke the mechanism of representation or reduced it to occasional moments, shared among small informal groups and friendship networks. The bet, as stated before, served as a means to motivate the performers. The trophy, on the other hand, was shared by a larger collective and announced to the community through the press. The

FIGURE 7.2. Eusébio (*right*) and Flora (*center*), leaving the Netherlands with the Benfica team, Schiphol Airport, 6 April 1972. A few years after leaving the suburbs of Lourenço Marques, Eusébio was the epitome of a meteoric trajectory of social mobility. Author: Punt. ANEFO. GahetNA (Nationaal Archief NL). *Source:* Wikimedia.

vibrant sports movement, which had been erected during the 1920s and 1930s, had lost one of its crucial dimensions. In the 1960s, the trophies that were celebrated in the suburbs were those won by Desportivo, Ferroviário, or, more lastingly, by Benfica, Sporting, FC Porto, and Belenenses. The suburban game, as a local practice, became progressively dissociated from its expression as part of a mediated urban popular culture, dominated by the downtown and metropolitan narratives. As social-contact idioms these narratives were more effectively adjusted to the phenomenology of everyday encounters generated by the increase in social and spatial mobility in Lourenço Marques; at the same time, their reference universes were better suited to handle the existing expectations of mobility and social participation.

SOCIAL NETWORKS IN THE COLONIAL CITY

The ties created through interactions based on a knowledge embedded in diverse social identities offered a unique laboratory for the study of the role of social networks in individuals' adaptation to the urban environment.[59] The morphology of social networks, their dimension, their reachability, density, and durability allow us to examine the bonds between individuals, but also the resistances and barriers to the creation of relations with other groups and individuals.[60] What does the process of development of an urban popular culture based on football narratives tell us about the late colonial period in Lourenço Marques? How can the morphologies of social networks based on this shared knowledge help us interpret the colonial process?

Composed of daily rituals and performative rhetoric, football networks reified preexistent identities, confined and dense, both in the suburban and in the cement city. Club identification created a symbolic bond that reinforced religious, ethnic, class, and neighborhood communities. But football also created bonds between people from different backgrounds, both in the suburbs and in the cement city. These ties, instigated by competition, were weaker when compared with the multiplex nature of previous ones, but they nonetheless helped create a settler identity in the city center and a suburban identity in the periphery. In the suburbs this bonding function was the consequence of the relations propelled by the AFA league's competitions, a hallmark for the building of a local collective imagination. In a similar way, the downtown league reinforced the settlers' identity, despite the differences between elite teams and second-rate teams, between settlers' old teams, and new regionally bound clubs. However, cohesion among settlers also depended on their affiliations with metropolitan teams, whose competitions were continuously followed by the local media. Moreover, the most famous metropolitan clubs had local branches throughout the territory, which reinforced these ties in the context of face-to-face interactions. The integrative function of football competitions would reach its most exceptional outcome when it created the possibility of a community that integrated both the suburban population and the white population of the city center. It is in this framework that we can think about the functions of "weak culture" in the establishment of social networks based on weak links.[61] Like most relations revolving around football, this was not a harmonious community, as it was traversed by identitarian tensions, conflicts, and debates about personal preferences and ethic and aesthetic judgments that are disputed in daily performances. This performative dynamic is a crucial dimension of the social embeddedness of these networks of popular culture, as it allows individuals to have resources for social participation.

The knowledge gathered within a popular-culture idiom opened up the possibility of a more equal interaction, within a colonial context where interactions between suburban inhabitants and settlers were defined by a radical inequality. A string of interconnected causes, in which the presence of a tiny but very successful group of African football pioneers in downtown and metropolitan football narratives was paramount, made this community of popular culture consumers possible and was thus able to challenge some of the secular divisions instigated by colonial racism and labor exploitation. The interactional resources accumulated by the individuals of the suburbs were a consequence of their exposure to the city's culture: of the institutionalization of associations, spaces of sociability and leisure; of all the information about football that came from local relations, from across the South African border, and from the rest of the world. By becoming fluent in this social idiom, they created an ontological proximity with the settler. At the same time, these bodies, alphabetized in the urban space, put pressure, on a small scale, on the social organization. This acquired social capital—translated into information but also into the possibility of offering stances and public opinions in interactional settings that were traditionally violent and humiliating for the suburban dweller—was not granted to them by a colonial system that did little to promote the generalization of any skill—most of all educative—though the period of timid overture of late colonialism may have made it more effective.

In a period when colonial power was forced to demonstrate that Portuguese colonialism was exceptional and not racist, it is crucial to bear in mind the importance of a political causality behind the strategy

FIGURE 7.3. Children playing in Chamanculo, 2010. In many ways, the conditions for young kids playing football in the Lourenço Marques suburbs have not changed considerably. Photo by Nuno Domingos.

of winning hearts and minds, on the international front but also in the colonial terrain, where wars and unrest occupied and spurred the apparatus of information and propaganda. However, to fully interpret the role that football played in the process of urbanization in Lourenço Marques one has to take into account the specific interactional characteristics of the mediums of popular culture, such as the local football narratives, which spring from the activities of relatively autonomous fields of social relations. Urban individuals and groups, mainly through masculine acquaintance networks, followed football competitions searching for entertainment but also for ways to reinforce and create social relations through which they could connect with society. This investment, this social libido, so embedded in the urban fabric, cannot be reduced to the official narrative of political reason, disputed by the champions of lusotropicalism, contemporary colonial nostalgics, as well as those who, through a reductive critical perspective, denounce sports as an alienating force, a means to recolonize consciousness.

8 ∽ Embodied History

THE bodies of Lourenço Marques footballers, inscribed into a colonial situation that severely constrained them, not only expressed the conditions of their situation creatively but opened onto interpretations of history with which they interacted and which they indeed challenged. The analysis of the wide network of mediations and interdependencies that overdetermined the athlete's but also the supporter's bodily knowledge of the game of football allows us to delve into the lived experience of populations with little access to means of expression and scant opportunities to record their practices, strategies, and worldviews during colonial occupation. The study of the dynamics and tensions at play in a football match thus offered a way into a history of processes made flesh, an embodied history,[1] a ground of practices, representations, interests, and strategies, that often remain hidden, repressed by readings of the colonialism that integrate the social processes into economic, political, national, ideological, or imperial narratives. Ultimately, the economy of symbolic practices and exchanges that governed the local football game also enabled an enquiry into the development, within the suburbs of Lourenço Marques, of a tacit social contract, with its own singular conventions, legitimated and disputed by the members of a community that was being formed under harsh conditions.

At least since the first years of the twentieth century, football entered the everyday life of the inhabitants of Lourenço Marques. In the cement city it followed the development of local leisure practices; at first limited to a colonial elite dominated by the British, the game gradually reached other social groups. For male settlers it represented an important means of social integration and of occupation of public space. More dependent on the dynamics of the sport's associations than on the initiative of the state, the development of a field of sports practices and consumptions reproduced the major social and racial divisions imposed by colonialism.

Played in the impoverished neighborhoods of the periphery, football later became institutionalized, influenced by the associative dynamic of neighboring South Africa. In the suburbs, the social networks grounded in the game's more or less formalized practice and consumption contributed to an unstable process of social integration. They did so in conjunction with other networks of organized interests, such as the ones that configured systems of traditional and ethnic power, religious institutions, commercial activities, as well as the relations strengthened by the work of labor and leisure associations. The colonial state sought to oversee and use these centers of social life, namely those of a religious nature. For political control purposes, this indirect rule proved largely successful, albeit through a regime of surveillance, intimidation, and persecution. The failure of the official project that aimed to educate a body shaped by the ideology of the Estado Novo coexisted with the exercise of political control through relations of complicity with associative leaders as much as through the permanent institutional vigilance, namely in the suburban area. However, regardless of its degree of political action, these networks of associations contributed to the formation of urban individuals, adapted to the stringencies of the city, resourceful, developing interests and aspirations for which modern patterns of existence served as a frame of reference.

In the late colonial period, economic developmentalists considered this logic of urban integration as framed by the indigenato system to be rather deficient; they demanded a more effective intervention from the state. The presence of the state would perfect the control over this growing population and, simultaneously, make it more productive, as the modernizing economic interests—for whom the suburb was an abscess to be drained, a dysfunctional imbalance—called for. For decades this abscess had fed the colonial system developed by the Portuguese. The colonial system based its rule on the illegalization of the suburban space and its populations, who were controlled and watched, excluded from citizenship rights, constituting a disposable labor force, unskilled and reproducible at a low cost. Strongly represented in the domestic services of a servile nature, this working force was subjected to labor relations dominated by paternalism and violence, wider principles regulating the encounters between the colonized and the colonizers. Restricted to the suburbs by an urban policy of racial separation, African workers were forced to survive by their own means.

For the colonial modernizers, however, many of which were experts working for the state and large private companies that reproduced the economic and political agendas of international institutions, this suburban "self-management" was no longer functional. What mattered in this late colonial period was to stabilize the African labor force—the old indígenas now converted into "economically fragile" individuals—and form a respectable, predictable, and productive working class. Though the discussion about the intervention of the state in this peripheral space was old and in spite of a few initiatives put forth since the 1960s, in a wartime context where the conquest of hearts and minds was decisive, the state was unable to bring "order" to the suburbs, or to build streets, new neighborhoods, and housing, to supply sewers, water, electricity, and transportation, to implement new labor policies and social-security schemes, nor was it sufficiently effective to stabilize a labor force that was still dependent on extended family networks and economic links to the hinterland.

Appropriated by the inhabitants of the suburbs, the language of modern football revealed some of the characteristics of the suburban habitus that emerged from this indirect model of social integration and its particular social contract. A consequence of a strategic adjustment to the urban conditions of existence, these bodily dispositions reveal some of the features that defined the predominant model of social domination in the capital of colonial Mozambique. They also disclose how, conditioned by this model, suburban populations were able to negotiate unstable norms of coexistence: how they moved about, how they deciphered the space around them, how they defined everyday interaction, how they defended themselves, how they sought to overcome or sidestep the order that hindered them. The local style of play thus offered a symbolic mediation of broader interpretations and classifications, therefore becoming a means of acknowledging the effectiveness and legitimacy of daily conducts. On the football pitch, an existential ethos shaped by the urban condition under colonial rule was transformed into a specific representation of a set of ethical principles. While absorbing moralities and practical knowledge, the performance defined a space of stylistic possibles, which was constantly reproduced and changed by the individual and collective movements of the athletes on the pitch. The more highly valued movements in the athletes' motor repertoire were the basic cells of an economy of symbolic exchanges that consecrated specific ways of doing and of perceiving the world. Appreciation for these gestures took place within a particular interactional environment, marked by the fragile standing of the law of the game, which cleared the path for a decentralization of legitimate violence and for the predominance of fear as a factor that conditioned and molded the performance.

Malice was the fundamental property of this style of play. While permeating football's language, malice gave a distinct morphology to the game, as the bodies that sustained the performance, both on and off the pitch, brought their dispositions and mental structures onto the pitch. Collectively celebrated in the course of the performances, malice was considered a rightful element of cunning individual strategies that the poet José Craveirinha celebrated as creative and transformative. Transmuted in a sportive gesture, malice motivated the intimidation strategies of the players, granting them the right to defend and protect themselves, even when that defense led to the subversion of the law of football. The juggling gestures, the extraordinary dribbles that demonstrated the possibility of challenging an interaction order that exposed the players to the bigger risks, were grounded in malice. Though conflicting with official association rules, yet keeping them as the basic condition of the performance, the suburban game assumed its own morality. The arguments and the verbal and gestural rhetoric used by the players and the audience to express views and opinions about the statute of the gesture—"if it was fair," "if it was beautiful," "if it was tolerable"—were no less malicious. These were the foundations for the formation of a local public space where, through the shared language of a modern game, the conditions for the construction of a common social territory were negotiated. By exalting malice, the suburbs celebrated a daily management capital, necessary to face the unstable and precarious performative existence, subject to multiple risks and insecurities, that characterized life in the suburbs. The motor habitus of the players exhibit the dispositions of a general suburban habitus.

This malicious body distinguished itself from that imagined by a suburban petite bourgeoisie that, in the leadership of clubs and associations from the periphery, ascribed the game a civilizing function. Gathering around the Grémio Africano de Lourenço Marques, this elite had a plan to educate through sport, projecting its aspirational, legalist, respectable logic onto the game. Instead of becoming an educational space located in the suburbs, the football pitch started celebrating the ability of the individual to face unpredictable interactions, maliciously protecting himself from a decentralized violence and the proliferation of conflict relations.

Outside the suburbs, in the interaction order of the cement city, this cunning was invested in a performance of strategic subordination.

The few players from the suburbs who headed to the downtown and metropolitan teams, from the 1950s onward, adopted the role of the "good boy," of the respectable and dedicated worker. But unlike what happened in other activities, the suburban arrived in this specific labor market with acquired skills, stimulated by the intense competition in the periphery. Some of these athletes, who overcame the barrier of racial separation, benefiting from the semiprofessionalization in local football and especially in the metropolis, felt in their bodies the shock produced by the submission to the rules of modern football, the social division of labor, and the process of specialization that characterized the tactical schemes. In their words, they became "tied to a system," a situation that contrasted with the sweet freedom they admitted feeling in the suburban matches. Some of the values intrinsic to colonial modernization were reproduced through the logic of tactical schemes, models of the ordering of individual gestures and collective movements, induced by calculations, predetermination, speed, the rationalization of the means to reach a precise aim. By moving closer to the suburbs, not through the actions of the state, the modern company, or the missionary effort, but rather through the networks of popular culture and as a result of the process of sportization, tactics clashed with the conditions of the suburban social contract and the moral economy of the local game. However, tactics were an unintended, albeit inevitable, consequence of the game's expansion and success.

In the suburbs, players and teams preferred to resort to traditional forms of knowledge, like vovô, used in the name of success and stimulated by local rivalries. Healers and sorcerers were performers in this game and main characters of the local football narratives, celebrated for their undeniable power. The explanation they offered for the outcome of matches was intelligible for suburban residents, as were the solutions they offered to deal with the numerous existential questions that were faced by a population experiencing a radical change in their ways of life. Some of the players who traveled to Lisbon brought with them some of these practices, as well as the words listed in Craveirinha's football glossary. But it was also the way they mastered modern football and its tactics that allowed Mozambican players like Matateu, Coluna, Vicente, Hilário, or Eusébio to acquire the skills that made them creative interpreters of the game's language.

The success of the pioneers, explained by the unique historical encounter between the professionalization of football and the political opening of so-called late colonialism, created in the suburbs a renewed and vigorous interest in the narratives of the football played downtown and in the metropolis, followed with passion on the radio and in newspapers. For local supporters, these competitions connected them to a wider world. In the same period, suburban clubs started declining. This situation, a result of the extinction of the African Football Association, in 1959, was also due to the symbolic subalternization of the suburban narrative, made all the worse by a very uneven media coverage. However, downtown and metropolitan clubs were also rewarding as platforms of social mobility for some inhabitants of the suburbs, investing them with an added social value. In the suburbs, the institutionalization of the game offered a means of reproduction of social identities but also the possibility for the creation of bonds between its residents. While football, in subtle ways, reinforced identities in the cement city and in the suburbs, it was also the basis for a greater contact among urban individuals. This contact took place through the social sharing of both techniques and a specific knowledge, nurtured in the late colonial period by an increase in interactions within the urban space, but also by means of the media. This social use of the game allows one to escape an interpretative alternative that would explain football's function of integration during this period as a direct outcome of a political action, of a humanist and reformist nature in some cases, and merely instrumental in others.

By being converted into a social idiom that allowed for an expressive participation in daily life, football was used in the suburban neighborhoods but also beyond their borders, where the identification of an African with downtown and metropolitan clubs was a valuable capital to mitigate an ingrained hostile interaction order, namely in the workplace. Football narratives, used as a common language from which it was possible to establish social relations traversed by rhetoric, opinions, and interpretations offered the conditions for the exercise of a specific urban citizenship. By manipulating the matches' narratives, the public revealed specific criteria in the classification of performances, filled with judgments and opinions, ethical and aesthetic discourses, which opened up a space for the confirmation of values, legitimated ways of acting and dominant worldviews, as well as for the exposure of contradictions, conflicts, and constant negotiations. In the small-scale society of the football pitch there was an explicit incorporation of practical principles and worldviews, classifications, arguments, and aesthetic and ethic judgments. In the suburbs of Lourenço Marques, the dynamics and tensions present in the game's language, which had little room to gain autonomy from the surrounding social context, created a bodily representation of the urban condition, including the negotiations and contradictions among conflicting views of that experience.

Before the independence of Mozambique, in June 1975, the bodies of the football players of the capital's suburbs continued, in their neighborhoods, to reproduce a malicious style of play. Produced in the longue durée, malice signaled the permanence of the concrete bases of a system of domination but also revealed the strategies developed to meet its challenges. At the same time, these urban bodies, limited in their geographical and social mobility, demanded a different relation with the world. The language of football provided them with the resources to participate in this wider universe of relations.

Notes

TERMS IN THE NOTES

Acta (minute)
Artigo (article)
caixa (box)
decreto (decree)
diploma legislativo (piece of legislation)
lei (law)
livro (book)
parecer (report)
portaria (edict)
portaria provincial (provincial edict)
processo (process)
regulamento da AFA (AFA regulations)
secção (section)

FOREWORD

1. Thomas Hylland Eriksen, *Small Places, Large Issues: An Introduction to Social and Cultural Anthropology* (London: Pluto Press, 1995).

CHAPTER 1: FOOTBALL AND THE NARRATION OF A COLONIAL SITUATION

1. José João Craveirinha was born in Lourenço Marques in 1922. A renowned poet and reporter, he worked for various periodical publications, namely *O brado africano, Itinerário, Notícias, Mensagem, Notícias do bloqueio,* and *Caliban.* He was an employee of Lourenço Marques's Imprensa Nacional and played football for several Lourenço Marques clubs. He was imprisoned by the Portuguese political police (PIDE) for five years. Following Mozambique's independence, he became a member of Frelimo (one of the liberation movements that fought the war against Portuguese colonialism and that came into power after the Portuguese had left) and presided over the Associação Africana. He received the most important Portuguese literary award, the Camões Prize, in 1991. He is one of the most distinguished poets in the Portuguese language and among the greatest African writers. His first work, *Xibugo,* was written in 1964.

2. José Craveirinha, "Terminologia Ronga no futebol, em conjugação oportuna e sua interpretação," *O brado africano,* 12/2/1955, 8. Ronga is a southeastern Bantu language dominant in the south of Mozambique.

3. The newspaper *O brado africano* was founded in 1918 as part of the local policy of the GALM, whose actions and influence I will analyze in great depth.

4. Craveirinha, "O negro, o desporto e o feiticismo," *O brado africano*, 22/1/55: 8. Craveirinha had been in contact with the works of American cultural anthropologists, such as Margaret Mead and Melville Herskovits, whom might be an important inspiration.

5. Craveirinha, "Terminologia Ronga," 8. Football was used as a vector in the analysis of "the African's ability," a testament to his natural skills, but also to his capacity to adopt and reinvent the European game. By praising the African football player, the poet was able to avoid the seemingly inevitable trap of discussing the "Mozambican's evolution" on the basis of criteria of "modernity" imposed by the Portuguese colonial assimilation system: a scholastic, nationalist, and Catholic education; the Westernization of his ways of being, acting, dressing, and eating; a solid work ethic; the rejection of old custom and traditions. Inspired by Senghor, he considered suburban football, like other local activities, an example of exchange: Mozambicans should neither "let go of an indígena culture, nor reject the European ways." As he denounced in one of his numerous polemics against members of Lourenço Marques's mestiço and black petite bourgeoisie—which looked toward the "European standard" as a behavioral benchmark—a snobbish attitude that despised local traditions would destroy any aspiration to cultural miscegenation. *O brado africano*, 6/11/55, 6.

6. *O brado africano*, 22/1/55, 8.

7. Georges Balandier, "La situation coloniale: Approche théorique," *Cahiers internationaux de sociologie* 11 (1951): 44–79.

8. Eric Dunning, "The Figurational Dynamics of Modern Sport," *Sportwissenschaft* 9, no. 4 (1979): 358–59.

9. Norbert Elias and Eric Dunning, "Folk Football in Medieval and Early Modern Britain," in *The Sociology of Sport: A Selection of Readings*, ed. Dunning (London: Frank Cass, 1971), 116–32.

10. Based on Bourdieu's theory, but from a critical perspective, George Steinmetz defines the colonial state as a semiautonomous field of power characterized by specific struggles. Steinmetz, "Le champ de l'état colonial: Le cas des colonies allemandes (Afrique du Sud-Ouest, Qingdao, Samoa)," *Actes de la recherche en sciences sociales* 1–2, no. 171 (2008): 122–43.

11. Several different authors have developed important criticisms of the uses of these notions. Regarding the notions of rule and model, see Pierre Bourdieu, *Outline of a Theory of Practice* (Cambridge: Cambridge University Press, 1977); regarding the concept of identity, see Rogers Brubaker and Frederick Cooper, "Identity," in Cooper, *Colonialism in Question: Theory, Knowledge, History* (Berkeley: University of California Press, 2005): 59–90; regarding the concept of culture, see Adam Kuper, *Culture: The Anthropologists' Account* (Cambridge, MA: Harvard University Press, 2000); Kate Crehan, *Gramsci, Culture, and Anthropology* (Berkeley: University of California Press, 2002).

12. The assumption of a national or imperial agencialism, anchored in the reification of historical subjects—"English colonialism carried out," the "Empire set out," "Portuguese colonialism was"—turns historical narratives into means of acquitting or condemning these national collective subjects. Something similar happens with the logic of adjectivization, which boils down to a political formula, with a distinct political slant (as in the case of the Portuguese empire in Africa, Hammond's "noneconomic colonialism," Filho's "colonialism of the weak," and Anderson's "ultracolonialism"). All this simplifies complex processes in which domination is not exclusive to the institutional apparatuses but rather extends to the lenses through which individuals are perceived, foreclosing the analysis of wider dynamics, essential to the understanding of actions and interests of individuals and groups and their meaning-production contexts. R. J. Hammond, *Portugal and Africa, 1815–1910: A Study in Uneconomic Imperialism* (Stanford: Stanford University Press, 1966); Wilson Trajano Filho, "A constituição de um olhar fragilizado: Notas sobre o colonialismo português em África," in A *persistência da história: Passado e comtemporaneidade em África*, ed. Clara Carvalho and João de Pina-Cabral (Lisbon: ICS, 2004), 21–59; Perry Anderson, *Portugal e o fim do ultracolonialismo* (Lisbon: Civilização, 1966).

13. In the more sophisticated versions of this externalism, the style of play is seen to reflect the logic of an economic system (capitalism), a political system (communism), or a specific domination mechanism, as in the notion of a cultural bond applied to the colonial project, or of cultural exchange, analyzed, for example, by concepts such as "creolization." Ulf Hannerz, *Transnational Connections: Culture, People, Places* (London: Routledge, 1996), 64–80.

14. The division between the African and the European is one of the most powerful ways of classifying the human groups who took part in the colonial encounter. The problems with this classification are well known, as it is unraveled by various historical processes that produce other frequently overlapping classifications: indígena, black, Mozambican, etc. Depending on the specific context, I will try to use the term that best describes, at any given moment, the group to which the noun refers.

15. The term Peter Berger and Thomas Luckmann use to refer to the knowledge gathered by individuals and then shared in the course of social interactions. Berger and Luckmann, *The Social Construction of Reality* (New York: Anchor, 1967), 41.

16. Catherine Coquery-Vidrovitch, "The Process of Urbanization in African (From the Origins to the Beginning of Independence), *African Studies Review* 34, no. 1 (April 1991): 1–98.

17. On the colonial process in Mozambique, see Leroy Vail and Landeg White, *Capitalism and Colonialism in Mozambique. A Study of Quelimane District* (London: Heinemann, 1980); Allen Isaacman and Barbara Issacman, *Mozambique. From Colonialism to Revolution, 1900–1982* (Boulder: Westview, 1983); Joana Pereira Leite, "La formation de l'économie coloniale au Mozambique: Pacte colonial et industrialization: Du colonialisme portugais

aux réseaux informels de sujétion marchande, 1930–74 (PhD diss., École des Hautes Études en Science Sociales, Paris, 1989); Malyn Newitt, *A History of Mozambique* (Bloomington: Indiana University Press, 1995); Jeanne Marie Penvenne, *African Workers and Colonial Racism: Mozambican Strategies and Struggles in Lourenço Marques, 1877–1962* (London: James Currey, 1995); David Hedges, ed., *História de Moçambique*, 2 vols. (Maputo: Livraria Universitária de Maputo, 1999); Valdemir Zamparoni, "Entre Narros e Mulungos: Colonialismo e paisagem social em Lourenço Marques, c. 1890–c. 1940 (PhD diss., Faculdade Letras e Ciências Humanas da Universidade de São Paulo, 1998); Bridget O'Laughlin, "Proletarianisation, Agency and Changing Rural Livelihoods: Forced Labour and Resistance in Colonial Mozambique," *Journal of Southern African Studies* 28, no. 3 (2002): 511–30; Harry G. West, *Kupilikula: Governance and the Invisible Realm in Mozambique* (Chicago: University of Chicago Press, 2005); Penvenne, *Women, Migration and the Cashew Economy in Southern Mozambique: 1945–1975* (Rochester: James Currey, 2015).

18. This variety became one of the axes of the development of colonial and postcolonial urban studies in Africa and a reason for conducting comparative research that focuses on multiple aspects, from the type of production structure to ethnic composition. Despite focusing on the functionalist question of adaptation and urban social stability, researchers working on Rhodes Livingstone Institute, founded in northern Rhodesia in 1937 under the banner of the British Colonial Office, sought methodological and theoretical solutions for a set of new problems brought about by the process of colonial urbanization. On Africa colonial urbanization, see the classic studies by A. L. Epstein, "Urban Communities in Africa," in *Closed Systems and Open Minds: The Limits of Naïvety in Social Anthropology*, ed. Max Gluckman (Chicago: Aldine, 1967); Anthony D. King, *Colonial Urban Development: Culture, Social Power and Environment* (London: Routledge and Kegan Paul, 1976); Frederick Cooper, ed. *Struggle for the City: Migrant Labor, Capital, and the State in Urban Africa* (Beverly Hills: Sage, 1983); J. C. Mitchell, *Cities, Society, and Social Perception: A Central African Perspective* (Oxford: Clarendon Press, 1987); Coquery-Vidrovitch, "Process of Urbanization"; Bill Freund, *The African City: A History* (Cambridge: Cambridge University Press, 2007).

19. Coquery-Vidrovitch, "Process of Urbanization," 49.

20. Michael Mann, *The Sources of Social Power*, 4 vols. (Cambridge: Cambridge University Press, 1986–2013), vol. 2.

21. The colonial ideological discourse on the Portuguese imperial exception was soon denounced by Marvin Harris in 1958, after a stay in Lourenço Marques between 1956 and 1957. Harris, *Portugal's African "Wards": A First-Hand Report On Labor and Education in Moçambique* (New York: American Committee on Africa, 1958). R. J. Hammond, in a much-disputed work, made the case for the noneconomic nature of Portuguese colonialism. Hammond, *Portugal and Africa, 1815–1910: A Study in Uneconomic Imperialism* (Stanford: Stanford University Press, 1966). Subsequently, several works have avoided

the trap of circumscribing colonialism within its national context and have integrated the Portuguese case within the structural features of colonialism, namely its economic premises. Outstanding among these are the pioneering works of Valentim Alexandre, *Origens do colonialismo português moderno* (Lisbon: Sá da Costa. 1979); Vail and White, *Capitalism and Colonialism*; Isaacman and Isaacman, *Mozambique*; Gervase Clarence-Smith, *The Third Portuguese Empire (1825–1975): A Study in Economic Imperialism* (Manchester: Manchester University Press, 1985), Leite, *Formation de l'économie*.

22. Leite, *Formation de l'économie*, 56–71. While the south of Mozambique was deeply influenced by the economy of labor migration, in the country's central regions there reigned a plantation system of copra, sugar, and tea led by international companies. Vail and White, *Capitalism and Colonialism*; Isaacman and Isaacman, *Mozambique*. Up north, the forced cultures of cotton, strongly promoted by Estado Novo protectionism policies, violently shaped the local societies. Carlos Fortuna, *O fio da meada: O algodão de Moçambique, Portugal e a economia mundo, 1860–1960* (Porto: Afrontamento, 1993); Anne Pitcher, *Politics in the Portuguese Empire: The State, Industry and Cotton, 1926–1974* (Oxford: Clarendon Press, 1993); Allen Isaacman, *Cotton Is the Mother of Poverty: Peasants, Work, and Rural Struggle in Colonial Mozambique, 1938–1961* (Portsmouth, NH: Heinemann, 1997).

23. Marvin Harris, "Labour Emigration among the Moçambique Thonga: Cultural and Political Factors," *Africa: Journal of the International African Institute* 29, no. 1 (January 1959): 50–66; Harris, "Emigration among the Moçambique Thonga: A Reply to Sr. Rita-Ferreira," *Africa: Journal of the International African Institute* 30, no. 3 (July 1960): 243–45.

24. Adelino Torres, *O império português entre o real e o imaginário* (Lisbon: Escher, 1991), 58–59.

25. José Capela, *O movimento operário em Lourenço Marques, 1898–1927* (Porto: Afrontamento, 1984), 9.

26. Patrick Harries, *Work, Culture, and Identity: Migrant Laborers in Mozambique and South Africa, c. 1860–1910* (Portsmouth, NH: Heinemann, 1993), 198; Hedges, *História de Moçambique*, 2:5–6.

27. After the 1926 military coup that ended the First Republic, Portugal had a military dictatorship that led, in 1933, with the approval of a new constitution, to the creation of the Estado Novo under Salazar's leadership.

28. Terence Ranger, "Pugilism and Pathology: African Boxing and the Black Urban Experience in Southern Rhodesia," in *Sport in Africa, Essays in Social History*, ed. W. J. Baker and J. A. Mangan (New York: Africana Publishing, 1987), 196–213.

29. Harold Perkin, "Teaching the Nations How to Play: Sport and Society in the British Empire and Commonwealth," epilogue to *The Cultural Bond: Sport, Empire, Society*, ed. J. A. Mangan (London: Frank Cass, 1992), 216; Roger Hutchinson, *Empire Games: The British Invention of Twentieth-Century Sport* (Edinburgh: Mainstream Publishing, 1996), 178–79.

30. *O brado africano*, 22/1/55, 8.

31. Eugen Weber, "Gymnastics and Sports in *Fin-de-Siècle* France: Opium of the Classes?" *American Historical Review* 76, no. 1 (February 1971): 70–98; Allen Guttmann, *Games and Empires: Modern Sports and Cultural Imperialism* (New York: Columbia University Press, 1994); Gertrud Pfister, "'Cultural Confrontations': German *Turnen*, Swedish Gymnastics and English Sport: European Diversity in Physical Activities from a Historical Perspective," *Culture, Sport, Society* 6, no. 1 (Spring 2003): 61–91.

32. E. A. Azambuja Martins, *Acção educativa sôbre as populações indígenas de Moçambique, consequente de instrução militar do soldado indígena* (Lisbon: I Congresso da História da Expansão Portuguesa no Mundo, 1938): 16–17.

33. Emerging as a dynamic sphere of research and of conceptual analysis, cultural analysis became the focus of investigations in colonial and postcolonial Africa. Karin Barber, "Popular Arts in Africa." *African Studies Review* 30, no. 3 (September 1987): 1–78; Barber, ed., *Readings in African Popular Culture* (Bloomington: International African Institute / Indiana University Press, 1997); Ulf Hannerz, "The World of Creolization," in Barber, *African Popular Culture*, 12–17; Johannes Fabian, *Moments of Freedom: Anthropology and Popular Culture* (Charlottesville: University Press of Virginia, 1998); Stephanie Newell and Onookome Okome. *Popular Culture in Africa: The Episteme of the Everyday* (London: Routledge, 2013). On the colonial popular culture of Angola's capital, see Marissa J. Moorman, *Intonations: A Social History of Music and Nation in Luanda, Angola, from 1945 to Recent Times* (Athens: Ohio University Press, 2008). Recently, historian António Sopa published an important book on the history of popular music in colonial Lourenço Marques. Sopa, *A alegria é uma coisa rara: Subsídio para a história da música popular urbana em Lourenço Marques (1920–1975)* (Maputo: Marimbique, 2013).

34. Phyllis M. Martin, *Leisure and Society in Colonial Brazzaville* (Cambridge: Cambridge University Press, 1995); Laura Fair, *Pastimes and Politics, Culture, Community, and Identity in Post-abolition Urban Zanzibar, 1890–1945* (Athens: Ohio University Press, 2001); Peter Alegi, *Laduma! Soccer, Politics and Society in South Africa* (Natal: University of KwaZulu-Natal Press, 2004). Bea Vidacs, *Visions of a Better World: Football in the Cameroonian Social Imagination* (Berlin: LIT Verlag, 2010).

35. Bea Vidacs, "Through the Prism of Sports: Why Should Africanists Study Sports?" *Afrika Spectrum* 41, no. 3 (2006): 331–49.

36. Some authors have revealed continuities between modern sports practices and African traditions of physical activity. However, the context in which modern sports emerge has structural specificities, as Elias has shown, which imply a clear break between these two historical realities. John Blacking, "Games and Sport in Pre-colonial African Societies," in Baker and Mangan, *Sport in Africa*, 3–22. In his classic *Usos e costumes dos Bantu*, Henri Junod describes some of the "traditional" games and leisure activities of adult Africans in the south of Mozambique. This included "drinking beer," "the favourite pastime of men in southern Africa." Junod, *Usos e Costumes dos Bantu* (Campinas: Instituto de Filosofia e Ciências Humanas, Universidade Estadual de

Campinas, 2009 [1912–13]), 281. However, the most popular game was *ncuva* (a board game played on the floor), which the missionary describes in great detail (285–87). Junod also lists a number of children's games (90–94). He makes references to hunting and fishing, "the great indigenous sports" (287), although he made the point that these activities were "also work, naturally" (278). José Craveirinha also mentioned the existence of a traditional field of sports practices in Mozambique. In a newspaper article he made reference to traditional sports like *homa* (or *homana*), *mugaíço*, *xibakela*, *fenete*, and *n'kati*. Craveirinha, *O folclore moçambicano e as suas tendências* (Maputo: Alcance Editores, 2008), 277–80. Modern urban sports, fundamentally, exist outside of working hours, within the frame of the emergence of leisure activities. Be that as it may, the recognition of these breaks should not preclude research on the transference of principles of classification and appreciation of physical activities, on frames of sociability, on the employment of forms of traditional knowledge, in short, of the various exchanges between traditional and modern sports.

37. On the dynamics of popular culture in Africa, see David Coplan, "The African Musician and the Development of the Johannesburg Entertainment Industry, 1900–1960," *Journal of Southern African Studies* 5, no. 2 (April 1979): 135–64; Coplan, *In Township Tonight! South Africa's Black City Music and Theatre* (New York: Longman, 1985).

38. See Alegi, *Laduma!*, 56–57. In 1956 anthropologist Clyde Mitchell used a traditional dance form, the *kalela*, as a performative observatory from which he examined the process of urban adaptation in the Copperbelt. Mitchell, *The Kalela Dance: Aspects of Social Relationships among Urban Africans in Northern Rhodesia* (Manchester: Manchester University Press, 1956). Almost twenty years after *Kalela*, Terence Ranger used a dance, *mbeni*, a forerunner of kalela, as a means to examine the political history of eastern Africa in the longue durée. Ranger, *Dance and Society in Eastern Africa, 1890–1970: The Beni Ngoma* (London: Heinemann, 1975. Although it falls outside the definition of sports practice, Clifford Geertz's classic work on cock fighting in Bali is a situated case study from which a whole symbolic order is investigated. Geertz, "Deep Play: Notes on the Balinese Cockfight," in *The Interpretation of Cultures: Selected Essays* (New York: Basic Books, 1973), 412–53.

39. In the conceptual tradition of E. P. Thompson and James Scott. Thompson, "The Moral Economy of The English Crowd in the Eighteenth Century," *Past and Present* 50, no. 1 (1971): 76–136; Scott, *Weapons of the Weak Everyday Forms of Peasant Resistance* (New Haven: Yale University Press, 1985); Scott, *Domination and the Arts of Resistance: Hidden Transcripts* (New Haven: Yale University Press, 1990).

40. Individuals accumulate this information, turned into a specific social stock of knowledge, understood as a specific store of information. For Berger and Luckmann, this reservoir of social knowledge was comparable to a store of diverse sets of knowledges but also of "typificatory schemes" that allow individuals to deal with daily routine. Berger and Luckmann, *Social Construction*, 43.

41. It is possible to establish logical correlations between this clustering effect and the emergence of other instruments for reading the world that responded to practical purposes, such as the "social idiom" (faculty) that the anthropologist John Peel attributed to monotheistic religions, in the context of the growth of large-scale African cities under colonial rule. J. D.Y. Peel, "Social and Cultural Change," *The Cambridge History of Africa*, 8:142–91 (ch. 4) (Cambridge: Cambridge University Press: 1984), 154. The effect is similar to that described by Thomas Eriksen in *Common Denominators*. He describes his concept as "the principle of the lowest common denominator in a social interaction between members of different ethnic groups. Briefly put, the dictum implies that similarities and shared horizons, or platforms for discourse and interaction, are actively sought in everyday practices as well as in politics." Eriksen, *Common Denominators: Ethnicity, Nation-Building and Compromise in Mauritius* (Oxford: Berg, 1998), 18. In these contexts, the creation of a class consciousness was a response, in various guises, to problems generated by new living conditions, creating bonds between individuals.

42. Links between social positions and certain leisure practices and social and cultural consumptions had been established by classical research studies. Thorstein Veblen, *The Theory of the Leisure Class: An Economic Study in the Evolution of Institutions* (New York: Macmillan, 1899); Mary Douglas with Baron C. Isherwood, *The World of Goods: Towards an Anthropological Approach to Consumption* (London: Penguin, 1978); Pierre Bourdieu, *Distinction: A Social Critique of the Judgement of Taste*, trans. Richard Nice (London: Routledge, 1998),

43. This narrative texture is not here taken as a sequence of determined events, from which a fixed chronology emerges, or as a closed history, sealed by tradition or official approval.

44. Nuno Domingos and Rahul Kumar, "A grande narrativa futebolística," in *Estudos de sociologia da leitura em Portugal no século XX*, ed. Diogo Ramada Curto (Lisbon: Fundação Calouste Gulbenkian), 575–638. The formal faculties of sports narratives are comparable, in particular ways that are worth spelling out on another occasion, to other narratives produced within the frame of urban popular cultures. Think, for example, of cinematic or television narratives, or of those that feature in entertainment and lifestyle magazines.

45. Erving Goffman, *The Presentation of Self in Everyday Life* (Harmondsworth: Penguin, 1971).

46. The production of a pleasing excitement through sports performances, as mentioned by Elias, gained a new scale, not bound by the duration of the match but rather spilling out into other interactional times and spaces. Norbert Elias and Eric Dunning, *The Quest for Excitement: Sport and Leisure in the Civilizing Process* (Oxford: Blackwell, 1986).

47. Conceived as an "interaction material." Erving Goffman, "The Interaction Order," American Sociological Association, 1982 presidential address, *American Sociological Review* 48, no. 1 (February 1983):11.

48. Transformed into an interaction repertoire, the knowledge of the game sustains the existence of "verbal communities" that are also, more generically, communities of practices. Tzvetan Todorov, *Mikhail Bakhtin: The Dialogical Principle* (Minneapolis: University of Minnesota Press, 1984), 48.

49. Bea Vidacs uses the expression "visions of a better world" to designate the possibilities football confers to social participation and imagination. Vidacs, *Visions of a Better World.*

50. On the relevance of sport as an identitary tool, see Jeremy MacClancy, ed., *Sport, Identity and Ethnicity* (Oxford: Berg, 1996); Mike Cronin and David Mayall, *Sporting Nationalisms: Identity, Ethnicity, Immigration, and Assimilation* (London: Frank Cass, 1998); Gary Armstrong and Richard Giulianotti, eds., *Football Cultures and Identities* (London: Macmillan, 1999); J. A. Mangan and Andrew Ritchie, eds., *Ethnicity, Sport, Identity. Struggles for Status* (London: Frank Cass, 2004). On football and conflict, see Gary Armstrong and Richard Giulianotti, eds., *Fear and Loathing in World Football* (Oxford: Berg. 2001).

51. Max Gluckman, *Custom and Conflict in Africa* (Oxford: Blackwell, 1955); Gluckman, *Essays on the Ritual of Social Relations* (Manchester: Manchester University Press, 1962).

52. Lewis Coser, The *Functions of Social Conflict* (Glencoe, IL: Free Press, 1964). Thus, the ability to sustain relations of conflict while avoiding a breach fosters the specific role of sports as a means of producing excitement. Elias and Dunning, *Quest for Excitement.*

53. Mark Granovetter, "The Strength of Weak Ties," *American Journal of Sociology* 78, no. 6 (May 1973): 1360–80.

54. Recently Jennifer Schultz and Ronald L. Breiger developed a theoretical relation between popular culture and the "strength of weak ties" that Granovetter had conceptualized in 1973. Paramount for their conceptualization was Bonnie Erickson, "Culture, Class and connections, *American Journal of Sociology*, 102, no. 1 (1996): 217–51; C. K Ansell, "Symbolic Networks: The Realignment of the French Working Class, 1887–1894," *American Journal of Sociology* 103, no.2 (1997): 359–90. In some situations, these uses took place in the context of what Goffman calls "contact rituals." Schultz and Breiger, "The Strength of Weak Culture," *Poetics* 38, no. 6 (2010): 610–24. If we think of ceremonials as narrative-like enactments, more or less extensive and more or less insulated from mundane routines, then we can contrast these complex performances with "contact rituals, namely, perfunctory, brief expressions occurring incidental to everyday action—in passing as it were—the most frequent case involving but two individuals." Goffman, "Interaction Order," 10.

55. The representational function implies that the management of this knowledge, grounded on specific practical conditions, is emotionally structured, serving a platform of feelings. This manifestation of an existence draws us close to the concept of "structure of feeling," coined by Raymond Williams, referring to the feeling of a particular community. Williams, *The Long Revolution* (Harmondsworth: Pelican, 1965), 63–64. In *Marxism and Literature,* his

use of the term "practical consciousness" favors a dynamic and less parochial description. This feeling was manifested, then, through a practical consciousness, which remained inarticulated or unconscious. Williams, *Marxism and Literature* (Oxford: Oxford University Press, 1977), 130–31.

56. With an effect similar to that of "fashion," as described by Georg Simmel. Simmel, "Fashion," *International Quarterly* 10, no. 1 (October 1904): 130–55, reprinted in *American Journal of Sociology* 62, no. 6 (May 1957): 541–58.

57. Norbert Elias and Eric Dunning, "Dynamics of Group Sports with Special Reference to Football," in *Quest for Excitement: Sport and Leisure in the Civilizing Process* (Oxford: Blackwell, 1986), 51–52.

58. Norbert Elias, "The Genesis of Sport as a Sociological Problem," in Dunning, *Sociology of Sport*, 88–115, 92.

59. The International Board was founded in 1886 by the football associations of England, Scotland, Wales, and Ireland. FIFA was founded in 1904 in Paris.

60. Elias and Dunning, "Folk Football."

61. Eric Dunning, "Figurational Dynamics," 341–59, 354–55. As questioned by Elias, when comparing the games' sportization—which implies its regulation—and the industrialization process, "can one discover in the recent development of the structure and organisation of those leisure activities which we call 'sport,' trends which are as unique as those in the structure and organization of work which we refer to when we speak of the process of industrialization?" Elias, "Genesis of Sport," 92, 95.

62. Given the way in which competitive football adopted modern rationales of labor specialization and organization, in training but also during matches, some authors have suggested its contiguity with the development of the capitalist mode of production. It is true that the game's rationalization implied the adoption of principles proper to the modern economic calculus. However, this process of rationalization does not hinge solely on external factors—as if it was a simple projection of a system of factory production. Seeing the game only as a consequence of an instrumental rationality tends to eliminate the possibilities of creative adoption, of subversion, as well as the analysis of the diversity of localized practices, which were greatly dependent on specific historical, social, and cultural features that influence the dissemination and development of modern football. In his work on the rational foundations of modern music published in 1921, Max Weber, on the basis of a formal analysis of a distinctive object, described a process of formal absorption of structural features, namely those that characterized an ideal-type of modern capitalism. The modern rationalization of musical form, based on the possibility of measuring sounds and on the development of a notation system, allowed for a control over language through anticipation and calculus. Max Weber, *Os fundamentos racionais e sociológicos da música* (São Paulo: Editora da Universidade de São Paulo, 1995 [1921]), 53–55, 26–27. In the case of the organization of the musical field explored by Weber, the development of a singular language was closely tied to the formation of a field of production

with a high degree of autonomy, where the agents' investment was carried out in relation to criteria of appreciation and assessment imposed by the field itself, general speaking a set of institutions that provide teaching, research, and dissemination of knowledge, consecrated through peer relations and a specialized audience. Given the conditions for the formation of a field of sports activities, the chances of there emerging patterns of play independent from a modern calculus motivated by the search for victory were scarce. It would be difficult, therefore, to witness something like football's version of dodecaphony or serialism. On Weber's notion of rationality, see Rogers Brubaker, *The Limits of Rationality: An Essay on the Social and Moral Thought of Max Weber* (London: Allen and Unwin, 1984).

63. For instance, the aesthetics produced by efficiency may not correspond with the fans' aesthetic expectations. The game's fruition also hinged on its spectacular and performative dimension, and supporters often did not identify with the game-pattern rationale—that is to say, they did not establish a direct link between a certain rationalization of players' gestures and the achievement of results. In his monograph Christian Bromberger clearly demonstrates how the enjoyment of a football match also involved other kinds of evaluations. Bromberger, *Le match de football: Ethnologie d'une passion partisane à Marseille, Naples et Turin* (Paris: Maison des Sciences de l'Homme, 1995).

64. As defined by Bourdieu, "social agents are endowed with *habitus*, inscribed in their bodies by past experiences. These systems of schemes of perception, appreciation and action enable them to perform acts of practical knowledge, based on the identification and recognition of conditional conventional stimuli to which they are predisposed to react; and, without any explicit definition of ends or rational calculation of means, to generate appropriate and endlessly renewed strategies, but within the limits of the structural constraints of which they are the product and which define them." Pierre Bourdieu, *Pascalian Meditations*, trans. Richard Nice (Stanford: Stanford University Press, 2000), 138. The habitus can be seen less as an automatic mechanism of social reproduction and more a creator of strategies ("a system of dispositions to be and to do is a potentiality, a desire to be which, in a certain way, seeks to create the conditions of its fulfilment," 150) and also a source of performative innovation.

65. As designated by Arlei Sander Damo, "Senso de jogo," *Esporte e sociedade* 1, no. 1 (November 2005–February 2006): 9–10. See also, Damo, *Do dom à profissão: A formação de futebolistas no Brasil e na França* (São Paulo: HUCITEC, 2007).

66. Bourdieu, *Distinction*, 169.

67. In this context, the interacting bodies are a reservoir of knowledge and rules that are confirmed in performances, daily encounters, bodily automatisms, and bodily memory. Connerton, *How Societies*, 1–5. As Schieffelin notes, performance doesn't merely confirm previous knowledge, but also introduces formal innovations. Edward L. Schieffelin, "Performance and the Cultural

Construction of Reality," *American Ethnologist* 12, no. 4 (November 1985): 707–24, 720.

68. Bourdieu, *Distinction*, 474. Some researchers developed concepts that sought to situate and dynamize the more generic formulation of habitus, such as that of bodily praxis, put forward by the anthropologist Michael Jackson or that of practical schemata with which Loïc Wacquant studied the movements of Chicago boxers. The anthropologist José Sérgio Leite Lopes suggested the term "bodily habitus" in his historic anthropology of the Brazilian football playing style. The expression bodily practices, in turn, sustains Paul Connerton's analysis (1989) of the mechanisms of social memory in the context of institutional and ceremonial relations. Jackson, "Knowledge of the Body," *Man*, n.s., 18, no. 2 (June 1983): 327–45, 328; Wacquant, *Body and Soul: Notebooks of an Apprentice Boxer*, Oxford, Oxford University Press, 2004), 104; Leite Lopes, "Sucesses and Contradictions in 'Multiracial' Brazilian Football," in *Entering the Field: New Perspectives on World Football*, ed. Gary Armstrong and Richard Giulianotti, 53–86 (Oxford: Berg, 1997), 74; Connerton, *How Societies Remember* (Cambridge: Cambridge University Press), 1989.

69. According to Erving Goffman, who celebrated the concept, "the workings of the interaction order can easily be viewed as the consequences of systems of enabling conventions, in the sense of the ground rules for a game, the provisions of a traffic code or the rules of syntax of a language." Goffman, "Interaction Order, 5." Goffman adds to this definition: "Emotion, mood, cognition, bodily orientation, and muscular effort are intrinsically involved, introducing an inevitable psychobiological element. Ease and uneasiness, unselfconsciousness and wariness are central" (3). The use of the concept of interaction order suggests an interpretation within a more circumscribed and situated scale, authorizing comparisons between football's practical and symbolic performances and the organized logic of everyday social situations such as those taking place in the suburb of Lourenço Marques. The interaction order, as a historically situated social form, does not possess a specific autonomy, even if it determines its own behavioral scale—the patterns that Elias and Dunning designate as "game-pattern." "In order to play a game, people group themselves in specific ways. As the game runs its course, they continually regroup themselves in a manner similar to the ways in which groups of dancers regroup themselves in the course of a dance. The initial configuration from which the players start changes into other configurations of players in a continuous movement. It is to this continuous movement of the configuration of players to which we refer when we use the term 'game-pattern.'" Elias and Dunning, "Dynamics of Group Sports," 389.

70. Bourdieu, *Distinction*, 208–24. In the context of a situated performance the interaction order plays as a conceptual role analogous to the concept of field. As such, in the interaction order, by adapting Karl Marx's known formulation, individuals create history under specific conditions, those that can be decoded, negotiated, or subverted by their habitus. Marx, *The Eighteenth Brumaire of Louis Bonaparte* (London: Allen and Unwin, 1926 [1852]).

71. "The ways in which from society to society [people] know how to use their bodies." Marcel Mauss, *Sociologie et anthropologie* (Paris: Presses Universitaires de France, 1989), 97.

72. Penvenne, *Women, Migration*.

73. Inês Brasão, *Dons e disciplinas do corpo feminino: Os discursos sobre o corpo na história do Estado Novo* (Lisbon: ONGCCCIDM, 1999); António Gomes Ferreira, "O ensino da educação física em Portugal durante o Estado Novo," *Perspectiva* 22, special issue (July–December 2004): 212–16.

74. António Leal de Oliveira, "Bases para a Organização da Educação Física Escolar." *I Congresso da União Nacional: Discursos, teses e comunicações*, 8 vols. (Lisbon: União Nacional, 1935), 7:312.

75. Diários da Assembleia Nacional (National Assembly Reports), session 39, of the Assembleia Nacional, 25/2/1939.

76. Penvenne, *Women, Migration*, 126–27.

77. It is crucial to acknowledge from the start that to assume the existence of a suburban habitus tends to typify a social experience that in fact was rather heterogeneous. The fact that this football world was mostly composed of men obviously needs to be taken into account. Suburban experiences were manifest in the way different groups, with distinct lifestyles and life projects, would engage in negotiations and conflicts for the definition of values and principles of action. These differences, which also found an expression in the game of football, translate distinct visions, linked with the position held by individuals and groups within the "suburban society," as well as their specific relation with the world of the colonizer. Be that as it may, and while taking this diversity into account, it is arguable that the colonial system engendered a set of conditions that enable us to interpret the suburb as a universe with traits of its own—like a Weberian ideal type, whose contours are defined, despite their internal variation, against the background of the inequalities inscribed in the existing social organization.

CHAPTER 2: A COLONIAL SPORT'S FIELD

1. Alexandre Lobato was the official historian of Lourenço Marques during the Estado Novo. Despite the heroic and nationalistic tone of his accounts, which reinforce the basic traits of the Portuguese civilizing mission, Lobato left some relevant works, both on the foundation of the Portuguese Lourenço Marques and on the social history of the modern city. Lobato, *História da fundação de Lourenço Marques* (Lisbon: Edições da Revista Lusitânia, 1948); Lobato, *História do presidio de Lourenço Marques*, 2 vols. (Lisbon: Estudos Moçambicanos, 1949–60); Lobato, *Lourenço Marques, Xilunguíne: Biografia da cidade* (Lisbon: Agência-Geral do Ultramar, 1970).

2. José Capela, *O movimento operário em Lourenço Marques, 1898–1927* (Porto, Afrontamento, 1984), 12.

3. Valdemir Zamparoni, "Entre Narros e Mulungos: Colonialismo e paisagem social em Lourenço Marques, c. 1890–c. 1940" (PhD diss., Faculdade Letras e Ciências Humanas da Universidade de São Paulo, 1998), 321.

4. Frederick Cooper, *Struggle for the City: Migrant Labor, Capital, and the State in Urban Africa* (Berkeley: Sage, 1983), 26.

5. António Rita-Ferreira, *Os Africanos de Lourenço Marques*, Memórias do Instituto de Investigação Científica de Moçambique / Instituto de Investigação Científica de Moçambique, vol. 9, series C (1967–68): 183.

6. Zamparoni, "Entre Narros e Mulungos," 308.

7. Maria Clara Mendes, *Variação especial da densidade de população urbana em Lourenço Marques* (Lisbon: Centro de Estudos Geográficos da Universidade de Lisboa, 1976), 34.

8. Amâncio de Alpoim Guedes, "The Caniços of Mozambique," in *Shelter in Africa*, ed. Paul Oliver (New York: Praeger, 1971), 200.

9. Rita-Ferreira, *Os Africanos*, 9:165.

10. Ibid.

11. Ibid., 9:168–69.

12. James Duffy, *Portuguese Africa* (Cambridge, MA: Harvard University Press, 1959).

13. The institution of passbooks by the labor regulations of 1914 (Decree no. 951, 14/10/14) was followed by a 1917 ordinance that required individuals to seek authorization prior to any change of from 1918 forward a penalty of correctional labor was applied to those who were caught in Lourenço Marques without a permit: women and children could enter only if they held a work contract (Edict no. 908, 21/9/18); the first identification regulation, which would result in the creation of an identity card for individuals over fourteen was passed in 1919 (Decreto do Alto Comissário 312, 4/12/22).

14. Penvenne, *African Workers*, 4; Zamparoni, "Entre Narros e Mulungos," 93–108.

15. In 1926 the former high commissioner of Mozambique, the Republican Brito Camacho, demonstrated his discontent at the morphology of the Lourenço Marques's labor market: "There is an enormous waste of labour power ... many thousands of blacks are employed as servants, the younger ones [*os moleques*], and those employed in load services are also in the thousands, each one carrying 25kgs on their backs The black man should be employed only in those jobs where whites cannot be used, or where their work cannot be done by machines or beasts ... the white man, as a worker, is inferior to the black man ... but to make beds, to clean the furniture, to set the table or wait at the table, to help the ladies get dressed or entertain the children, it does not seem licit to pull men away from the fields and workshops for activities that would be better suited for white or black women. As for load services. ... Why did Man invent cars and Our Lord create donkeys?" Camacho, *Moçambique: Problemas coloniais* (Lisbon: Livraria Guimarães, 1926), 203–4.

16. In 1869 a decree extended Portuguese citizenship to all the African population. In 1878 a new law permitted any individual to choose his professional occupation. Zamparoni, "Entre Narros e Mulungos," 30–35.

17. Isabel Castro Henriques, "A sociedade colonial em África: Ideologias, hierarquias, quotidianos," in *História da expansão portuguesa*, ed. Francisco

Bethencourt and Kirti Chaudhuri, 5 vols. (Lisbon: Círculo de Leitores, 1999), 5:230.

18. Zamparoni, "Entre Narros e Mulungos," 467.

19. *Regime Provisório para a Concessão de Terrenos do Estado na Província de Moçambique,* decreto (decree) 09/07/1909.

20. According to this law, individuals of the black race and their descendants who had entirely abandoned the uses and customs of that race, who spoke, read, and wrote the Portuguese language, who adopted monogamy, who had a job compatible with the European civilization or who had earned money, through licit means, for themselves and their families' food, housing, and clothes, would be considered assimilados. Portaria provincial (provincial edict) no. 317, 13/1/1917. At this time 80 percent of the metropolitan population would not meet these terms. A. Rocha, *Associativismo e nativismo*, 238n122.

21. Diploma legislativo (legislative diploma) 36. 12/11/1927.

22. In 1955, in a total population of 764,362 individuals, 117,405 were considered "civilized," a number that included 4,554 blacks. *Anuário estatístico de Moçambique* (Lourenço Marques: Repartição Técnica de Estatística, 1958), 20.

23. Miguel Bandeira Jerónimo, *Livros brancos, almas negras: A "missão civilizadora" do colonialismo português (c. 1870–1930)* (Lisbon: Imprensa de Ciências Sociais, 2010), 170–75.

24. Zamparoni, "Entre Narros e Mulungos," 250–360.

25. Valdemir Zamparoni, in his PhD thesis on the colonial era in Lourenço Marques between 1890 and 1940 (1998), designated this group as "pequena-burguesia filha da terra" (home-born petite bourgeoisie). Zamparoni, "Entre Narros e Mulungos." In his view, which clashed with those of Jill Dias ("Questão de identidade"), Jeanne Marie Penvenne (*African Workers*), and Ilídio Rocha (*Imprensa de Moçambique*), the term *elite* doesn't accurately define the position of this group within the context of a new power structure characterized by the emergence of class relations that redefined the social location of the group. Zamparoni, 386–93. This view is pertinent. The term *elite* can obscure the logical structure of hegemonic relations, which is better revealed by the concept of class. However, within a context of racialization of the social structure, as was the case in Lourenço Marques, the term *elite* is not without its merits. Although the colonial process is responsible for the creation of a new class structure, where all groups were related, its racialized nature suggests the existence of a double social structure. The effect of this double structure resembled a caste system, as described by Bourdieu for the Algerian colonial situation: "It is, in point of fact, composed by two distinct, juxtaposed 'communities' which have not unified to form a larger group. Membership in each of these communities is determined by birth. . . . But while each caste has its own system of graded social positions, and each individual is permitted to climb the rungs of the social ladder of his caste, it is practically impossible to cross the abyss that separates the two ladders. Caste spirit stifles class consciousness, a fact that is clearly demonstrated by the attitude of the European

lower classes." Bourdieu, *The Algerians* (Boston: Beacon Press, 1962), 132–34. If, as Zamparoni argues, this African elite in Lourenço Marques was, within the class structure, a petite bourgeoisie; in its role as intermediary between the colonial power and the local populations it constituted a local elite. This reality is obvious in an analysis of the context of certain manifestations of the social status. For instance, in reference to the construction of houses in the caniço, the architect Pancho Guedes notes, "Great status is attached to the better houses and many Africans who could afford to move into a house or apartment in the city prefer to remain in the caniço and enjoy their high social standing and influence." Guedes, *Caniços*, 207. Throughout the present work, the expression *African elite* mainly refers to the status that a particular group enjoys among the suburban population. This is useful in an analysis of a social space such as the suburb, where the relations were partly dependent on local forms of organization and hierarchization. On a few occasions, however, when it is important to understand the position of this local elite within the wider context of colonialism, I shall use the expression *petite bourgeoisie*. Jill Dias, "Uma questão de identidade: Respostas intelectuais às transformações económicas no seio da elite crioula da Angola portuguesa entre 1870 e 1930," *Revista internacional de estudos africanos* 1 (January–June 1984): 61–94; Penvenne, *African Workers*; Rocha, *Associativismo e nativismo*. On this petite bourgeoisie, see Rocha, *Associativismo e nativismo*.

26. On this colonial petite bourgeoisie, see Valdemir Zamparoni, "Entre Narros e Mulungos"; Jeanne Marie Penvenne, "João dos Santos Albasini (1876–1922): The Contradictions of Polities and Identity in Colonial Mozambique," *Journal of African History* 37, no. 3 (1996): 419–64; Rocha, *Associativismo e nativismo*; David Hedges, ed., *História de Moçambique*, 2 vols. (Maputo: Livraria Universitária de Maputo, 1999).

27. Olga Neves, "Em defesa da causa africana—Intervenção do Grémio Africano na sociedade de Lourenço Marques, 1908–1938" (PhD diss., Universidade Nova de Lisboa, 1989); Rocha, *Associativismo e nativismo*, 191.

28. Rocha, *Associativismo e nativismo*.

29. Bridget O'Laughlin, "Class and the Customary: The Ambiguous Legacy of the Indigenato in Mozambique," *African Affairs* 99, no. 394 (2000): 5–43.

30. In 1925 the Ross Report denounced the persistence of forced-labor regimes in Portuguese colonial territories.

31. Penvenne, *African Workers*.

32. Decreto 27 552, 5/3/1937, applied to the Portuguese colonies the basic laws that supported the metropolitan corporative regime.

33. Patrick Harries, "Christianity in Black and White: The Establishment of Protestant Churches in the South of Mozambique," *Lusotopie* (1998): 317.

34. Teresa Cruz e Silva, *Igrejas protestantes e consciência política no sul de Moçambique: O caso da Missão Suíça (1930–1974)* (Maputo: Promédia, 2001). In 1898, during the South African war, the return of more than sixty thousand Mozambican workers was crucial to the growth of Protestant churches in the south of Mozambique. Harries, "Christianity," 330.

35. Marvin Harris, *Portugal's African "Wards": A First-Hand Report on Labor and Education in Moçambique* (New York: American Committee on Africa, 1958); Valentim Alexandre, *Origens do colonialismo português moderno* (Lisbon: Sá da Costa, 1979); Cláudia Castelo, *O modo português de estar no mundo: O luso-tropicalismo e a ideologia colonial portuguesa (1933–1961)* (Porto: Afrontamento, 2001). Lusotropicalism makes the case for a particular disposition of the Portuguese to mix with other "races." This quality would have differentiated Portuguese colonialism from other colonial experiences. In the 1950s, when Portugal began to receive international complaints about its colonial rule, the Estado Novo revived Freyre's theory to justify the continuation of the empire Gilberto Freyre, *O mundo que o português criou* (Lisbon: Livros do Brasil. 1951); Gilberto Freyre, *Integração portuguesa nos trópicos* (Lisbon: Junta de Investigações do Ultramar, 1958); Freyre, *O luso e o trópico* (Lisbon: Comissão Executiva das Comemorações do Quinto Centenário do Infante D. Henrique, 1961).

36. Yves Leonard, "O império colonial salazarista," In Bethencourt and Chaudhuri, *História da expansão*, 5:48.

37. Organized, respectively, by decretos no. 5565 (12/6/44) and no. 7798 (2/4/49).

38. The first of these plans (1953–58) privileged investments in infrastructure, mostly in transport and communications. Hedges, *História de Moçambique*, 2:167. Within the second plan (1959–64), 19 percent of the investment was allocated to social policies, mainly in education, health, and culture. Ibid. In the 1950s industrial production increased as well as the number of employees in all sectors of activity. Ibid., 171–72. Inland trade managed to raise its industrial consumption quota: 28 percent in 1942, 40 percent in 1955, and 46 percent in 1960. Ibid., 171. In 1961 the creation of a Portuguese Economic Area, which included the overseas territories, was planned (by decreto 44016, 8/11/1961).

39. Gervase Clarence-Smith, *The Third Portuguese Empire (1825–1975): A Study in Economic Imperialism* (Manchester: Manchester University Press, 1985).

40. Adelino Torres, "Pacto colonial e industrialização de Angola (anos 60–70)," *Análise social* 19, nos. 77–78–79, (1983): 1101–19.

41. Joana Pereira Leite, "La formation de l'économie coloniale au Mozambique: Pacte colonial et industrialisation: Du colonialisme portugais aux réseaux informels de sujétion marchande, 1930–74" (PhD diss., École des Hautes Études en Sciences Sociales, Paris, 1989), 726.

42. Rita-Ferreira, *Os Africanos*, 225.

43. In 1968 only 21 percent of the individuals interviewed by Rita-Ferreira had been born in the city. Ibid., 226.

44. Brigitte Lacharte, *Enjeaux urbains au Mozambique, de Lourenco Marques a Maputo* (Paris: Karthala, 2000), 51.

45. In 1898 foreigners represented 34 percent of Lourenço Marques's population; 21 percent were English and 9 percent had Indian origins.

46. In a match played in 1923, between a team of Portuguese and a team of Englishmen, "there were plenty of refreshments, cakes, tea and other drinks, as well as chairs and covered stands." *Lourenço Marques Guardian*, 23/6/23, 5. The British consul as well as the head of English business affairs was invited to attend. Some special matches, which almost invariably featured English teams, usually the Athletic Club, were played for charity causes. In those events, the Lourenço Marques high society showed itself, the civil governor would be present, dance balls were organized, and bands were invited to play.

47. Hunting as a survival activity by the local population was in stark contrast with its recreational, but also commercial, appropriation by the colonizers. John M. Mackenzie, *The Empire of Nature: Hunting, Conservation and British Imperialism* (Manchester: Manchester University Press, 1988). Edward I. Steinhart, *Black Poachers, White Hunters: A Social History of Hunting in Colonial Kenya* (Athens: Ohio University Press, 2006).

48. The interests of this ruling class were represented in the government council and in influential institutions such as the Câmara do Comércio (Chamber of Commerce), and the Associação de Proprietários (Owners' Association), both created in 1905, and also in the Associação de Fomento Agrícola (Association for Agricultural Development) and the Associação dos Lojistas (Shopkeepers Association).

49. Ismael Mário Jorge was an influential man who contributed to the development of sport in Lourenço Marques. He was a military captain, a teacher, the leader of the local scouts' organization, president of the Salvation Army, and also belonged to the board of the Football Association of Lourenço Marques.

50. Ismael Mário Jorge, "L'éducation physique et le sport," in *Portugal, Colonie de Moçambique* (Paris: Exposition Coloniale Internationale, 1931), 8.

51. In 1905, Sport Clube Português; in 1910, Grupo Lusitano; in 1912, Grupo Desportivo Francisco. There is also reference to clubs such as Adamastor and Club Sportivo de Lourenço Marques. *O Africano*, 29/11/1961.

52. On the dynamics of the city's everyday life during this period, Alexandre Lobato offers an interesting account, from the settlers' perspective. Lobato, *Lourenço Marques, Xilunguíne: Biografia da cidade* (Lisbon: Agência-Geral do Ultramar, 1970). This narrative could be profitably read alongside José dos Santos Rufino's famous photographic albums on Lourenço Marques. José dos Santos Rufino, *Álbuns fotográficos e descritivos da colónia de Moçambique*, 10 vols. (Hamburg: Broschek and Co., 1929).

53. *Anuário de Lourenço Marques*, 1916.

54. João Sousa Morais, *Maputo: Património da estrutura e forma urbana topologia do lugar* (Lisbon: Livros Horizonte, 2001), 101.

55. This concession, taken by Oscar Sommerschield, Allen Wack, and the Eastern and South African Telegraph Company, was finished in 1950.

56. Morais, *Maputo*, 110.

57. Ibid.

58. Ibid., 130.

59. Hedges, *História de Moçambique*, 2:263–65; Valdemir Zamparoni, "Monhés, Baneanes, Chinas e Afro-maometanos: Colonialismo e racismo em Lourenço Marques, Moçambique, 1890–1940," *Lusotopie* (2000): 191–222. Between 1835 and 1845, a significant Indian community, constituted by Hindus and Muslims from Damão and Diu and Catholics from Goa, was established in Lourenço Marques. Ibid.

60. Today, Avenida 25 de Setembro. Before 1910 it was named Avenida D. Carlos I; and, between 1910 and the independence, Avenida da República.

61. The club was founded on May 1, 1917, by Luís Gomes Jardim, Artur Joaquim Maia, Manuel Vitorino, José Ferreira, and Artur Cruz, anarchist railway workers. Capela, *Movimento operário*, 227–28.

62. The International Football Association Board (IFAB) is the universal body that determines the laws of the game of association football.

63. Zamparoni, "Entre Narros e Mulungos," 247–362.

64. Zamparoni, "Monhés, baneanes."

65. Gilberto Teles, Armando Nunes, and Júlio Belo were members of the Commercial Association of Mozambique.

66. In 1934, Desportivo's president was Frank Martins, a prominent doctor, the General Assembly's president was Adriano Maia, president of the proprietors' association; in 1935 heading the General Assembly was the capitalist Paulino dos Santos Gil. In 1940 its vice president was Carlos Gouveia Pinto, member of the Chamber of Commerce.

67. Bernardette Deville-Danthu, *Le sport en noir et blanc: Du sport colonial au sport africain dans les anciens territoires français d'Afrique occidentale (1920–1965)* (Paris: L'Harmattan, 1997), 52. For further examples, see Phyllis M. Martin, *Leisure and Society in Colonial Brazzaville* (Cambridge: Cambridge University Press, 1995), 118; Peter Alegi, *Laduma! Soccer, Politics and Society in South Africa* (Natal: University of KwaZulu-Natal Press, 2004).

68. The percentage of English members in sports associations in Mozambique decreased from 13 percent in 1930 to 2 percent in 1958. According to the 1935 *Anuário*, the English were 4.2 percent of the total members of sports associations in Lourenço Marques, 3.2 percent in 1945, and 1.8 percent in 1955. These percentages are based on the numbers given by the section Desportos e Educação Física of the *Anuário estatístico de Mozambique* (Mozambique's Statistical Yearbook), 1926–73.

69. Rocha, *Associativismo e nacionalismo*, 144–54.

70. In one of the rare works on the theme, Daniel Melo stressed the importance of regional identification within the process of urban adaptation in Portuguese colonial settings. Regional associations in the colonies benefited from the metropolitan associative movement during the transition to the twentieth century. In Lourenço Marques the following were founded: Clube Transmontano (1912), Grémio dos Lisboetas (1935), Casa das Beiras (1938), Casa do Porto (1947), Casa do Algarve (1953), Casa dos Poveiros (1953), Casa do Alentejo (1954), Casa do Minho (1956). Daniel Melo, "Longe da vista perto do coração: O associativismo regionalista no império português," *Comunicação*

ao VIII Congresso Luso-Afro-Brasileiro de Ciências Sociais, 16–18 de Setembro de 2004, 3.

71. Benfica's first delegation in Lourenço Marques might have been a club named Sport Lisboa that played during the 1920s. In that same period other teams were active that would soon disappear: the Delagoa Bay Football Club, Grupo Lusitano, Clube Império, Clube Victoria, and Sport Club Viriato de Lourenço Marques (1925).

72. Sporting's delegations were created in Beira (1931), Mozambique (1932), Quelimane (1933), Gaza (1934), Nampula (1948), Guijá (1949), Mucucune (1959), Massinga (1962), Pucucune (1962). Grupo Desportivo de Lourenço Marques, Benfica's delegation, opened branches in Mozambique (1931) and Quelimane (1931). Under the name of Benfica, new branches were created in Nampula (1954), Machava (1955), Lourenço Marques (1955), Chimoio (1957), Guruè (1961).

73. The major railway strikes occurred in 1917, 1920, and 1925–26. Capela, *Movimento operário*, 166–90.

74. John Hargreaves, *Sport, Power, and Culture* (Cambridge: Polity Press, 1986).

75. John Nauright, *Sports, Cultures and Identities in South Africa* (London: Leicester University Press, 1997), 110; Cecile Badenhorst and Charles Mather, "Tribal Recreation and Recreating Tribalism: Culture, Leisure and Social Control on South Africa's Gold Mines, 1940–1950," *Journal of Southern African Studies* 23, no. 3 (September 1997): 473–89; Alegi, *Laduma!* For the Copperbelt, see P. Martin, *Leisure and Society*. In South Africa, in the suburban *townships* of Johannesburg such as Sophiatown or Alexandra, in large-scale industrial contexts, such as the mines of Witwatersrand, football served as a moralization of leisure time. The good players were able to get better working conditions. Nauright, *Sports, Cultures*, 110. In the 1950s the state sought to counter the effects of a "black urbanization" through a policy of retribalization of "African popular culture," an initiative that had previously been carried out by the mining industry employers. Badenhorst and Mather, "Tribal Recreation," 481. Within the sports universe, this policy was reflected in the promotion of traditional practices such as stick-fighting, *amalaita* contests, and organized "tribal dancing." Nauright, *Sports, Cultures*, 116.

76. There were other football clubs linked to the railway expansion in Mozambique, such as the Trans-Zambezia Railway Recreation Club (1930), which became Clube Ferroviário de Inhaminga in 1953, and the Grémio Desportivo Ferroviário do Lumbo (1931). In 1947 was instituted the Sturrock Cup, which opposed Mozambican and South African railway teams. In 1940 the AFLM organized a corporative league. Anuário de Lourenço Marques, 1943. Before the Second World War several football clubs were created in connection with public services, such as Clube dos Correios e Telégrafos, Clube da Câmara Municipal, Clube da Polícia Civil, Clube da Repartição da Fazenda, and Clube das Obras Públicas. Anuário de Lourenço Marques, 1941. After the

war the number of clubs linked to public and private companies increased. Some of these clubs, such as Grupo Desportivo da Companhia de Seguros Nauticus (1948), Clube Recreativo e Desportivo da Companhia dos Algodões de Mozambique (1950), Grupo Desportivo Obras Públicas de Inhambane (1951), Clube Recreativo dos Empregados da Companhia do Boror (1951), Clube dos Empregados da Sena Sugar Estates de Marromeu (1970), Grupo Desportivo da Fagor (1972), and Grupo Desportivo dos Empregados do Banco Pinto e Sotto Mayor (1972) had their statutes approved in 1972 but most of them did not officialize their activities.

77. In 1930, *O brado africano* announced on its front page the arrival of Mr. Catolino Brandão, goalkeeper of the Portuguese team Vilanovense, who would play for Ferroviário. *O brado africano*, 26/4/1930, 1.

78. Hedges, *História de Moçambique*, 2:165.

79. Malyn Newitt, *A History of Mozambique* (Bloomington: Indiana University Press, 1995), 467.

80. The club was founded by two commercial workers, Luís Fonseca and Manuel Antunes, from the Central neighborhood. Arquivo Histórico de Moçambique (AHM), DSAC, section A, Administração, Agremiações regionais de recreio, defesa, desporto e estudo. Associações Desportivas, Recreativas e Culturais, caixa 31, processo 27/173, 1.º de Maio).

81. Lourenço Marques's expansion created new residential neighborhoods and the development of an industrial belt concentrated in the areas of Matola and Machava. In these areas new football clubs were established: Clube Desportivo da Matola (1961); Clube Desportivo do Bairro do Fomento, based in Matola (1966); Clube Recreativo os Bairristas de Mavalane, based in the Bairro do Aeroporto (1967); Clube Recreativo, Desportivo e Cultural do Bairro do Jardim (1969); Clube Recreativo, Desportivo e Cultural do Bairro Choupal (1971); Clube do Bairro Silva Cunha, Council of Matola, Clube Desportivo e Recreativo "Os Ferrageiros," Clube Desportivo Real Sociedade de Mozambique, and Grupo Desportivo e Recreativo da Catembe (1972).

82. Dane Kennedy, *Islands of White: Settler Society and Culture in Kenya and Southern Rhodesia, 1890–1939* (Durham: Duke University Press, 1987).

83. After its creation, *Eco dos sports* became one of the active voices within the sports community against the lack of state intervention. In 1949 the editor of *Eco dos sports*, Cerqueira Afonso, wrote in the first page of his journal a missive to the governor general demanding the state provide a structure that could coordinate local sport and invest in new facilities. *Eco dos sports*, 20/12/1949, 1.

84. Benedict Anderson, *Imagined Communities: Reflections on the Origin and Spread of Nationalism* (London: Verso, 1993).

85. The editor of *Eco dos sports*, Cerqueira Afonso, mentioned this prospect in 1942. In 1953, *Guardian desportivo*'s journalists Carlos Dinis and Severiano Correia began a journey through the territory to measure the possible interest in organizing a competition to determine Mozambique's champion. *Guardian desportivo*, 18/11/53, 1.

86. Aberdeen (1937), Newcastle (1952), Dundee United (1953), Djurgardens, with Stanley Matthews (1955), Dinamo de Praga (1956), Ajax (1958), Portuguesa de Santos (1959), Ferroviário de Araraquara (1960).

87. Académica de Coimbra (1939, 1951), Marítimo (1950), Benfica (1950, 1962), Atlético (1951) Sporting (1954), FC Porto (1958), Belenenses (1960). In 1968, Portugal played Brazil in Salazar's Stadium inaugural ceremony.

88. Within this context, the split between Benfica and its delegation in Lourenço Marques—Desportivo—was politically significant. Desportivo refused to change its black-and-white shirts for the red shirts of Benfica: "our clubs, even if they are metropolitan clubs' delegations, should be respected." The reporter for the *Lourenço Marques Guardian* finished his piece by challenging metropolitan clubs: "This is our way, in Mozambique." *Lourenço Marques Guardian*, 20/1/56, 7.

89. Journalist F. Paula was, during the 1950s, one of the most critical voices in the press. See, for instance, "O ultramar e as relações desportivas com a metrópole," *Lourenço Marques Guardian*, 3/4/55, 11.

90. On 10 April 1958, Deputy Sarmento Rodrigues, overseas minister between 1950 and 1955 and future governor of Mozambique, defended, in the National Assembly, the participation of overseas teams in the national leagues. This request was repeated various times in the National Assembly by other members of Parliament, such as Jorge Jardim in 1956. Diários da Assembleia Nacional, sess. 136, 5–6 April 1956.

91. *O brado africano*, 23/3/34, 2.

92. J. A. Mangan, ed., *The Cultural Bond: Sport, Empire, Society* (London: Frank Cass, 1992), 3–4.

93. C. L. R. James's youth in British Trinidad was an expression of this scholastic sportive inculcation. Recalling his sportive education at Queen's Royal College in 1911 he describes cricket's role as a main educator: "rapidly we learned to obey the umpire's decision without question, however irrational it was. We learned to play with the team, which meant subordinating your personal inclinations, and even interests, to the good of the whole." Roger Hutchinson, *Empire Games: The British Invention of Twentieth-Century Sport* (Edinburgh: Mainstream Publishing, 1996), 165.

94. Bernard S. Cohn, *Colonialism and Its Forms of Knowledge: The British in India* (Princeton: Princeton University Press, 1996); Jean Comaroff and John Comaroff, *Christianity, Colonialism, and Consciousness in South Africa*, vol. 1 of *Of Revelation and Revolution* (Chicago: University of Chicago Press, 1991), 313.

95. The opportunities given by the football game were highlighted, in 1934, in a letter written by a reader from Inhambane and sent to *O brado africano*. Titled "O Futebol e o desemprego" (Football and unemployment), the letter acknowledged that "football is also a profession, a diploma through which some unemployed footballers managed to get a job in various places, public or private. Long live football, which is offering a solution to the great unemployment problem. Today, if you are a footballer, you can easily get a

job, so long as there is someone interested in football in the place where you want to work or someone close to the different groups." *O brado africano*, 9/4/34, 4.

96. *O brado africano*, 12/3/38, 3.

97. The *escudo moçambicano* (Mozambican escudo) was the currency in Mozambique.

98. *O brado africano*, 9/8/41, 3.

99. As had already been recognized by *O brado africano* on 28/7/34, 2.

100. Beira-Mar's integration, Jack argued, was a way of honoring the assimilation process. During his time at the paper, Jack denounced racist practices among the clubes da baixa. *O brado africano*, 10/7/43, 5.

101. *O brado africano*, 18/9/43, 5; 24/7/43, 5.

102. In May 1954, after criticizing the existence of two football associations in Lourenço Marques, the paper listed the players who moved from the AFA to the AFLM and then to the metropolis: Amoreira, Jorge Nicolau, Monteiro, Matateu, Joseph Wilson, Coluna, Justino; the players who moved directly from the AFA to the metropolis: Mário Wilson, Albasini, Adalberto, Naldo; and the players who moved from the AFA and were playing in the AFLM at that time: Merali, Barata, Amerali, Justino, J. Albasini. *O brado africano*, 29/5/54, 3.

103. In 1949 only white athletes were involved in the match between the Lourenço Marques team and South Transvaal. *O brado africano*, 15/10/49, 5. In 1955, before a match in South Africa, 1.º de Maio left its nonwhite players at home. *O brado africano*, 8/10/55, 6.

104. In 1955, *O brado africano* challenged the SNI to organize a match between the AFLM's team and a team of African players. *O brado africano*, 15/10/1955, 6.

105. North American athletes' exhibitions during the Berlin Olympics in 1936 were celebrated by *O brado africano*. The newspaper took the opportunity to make some considerations on the "quality of the race." Black athletes had shown "incontestable muscular superiority." *O brado africano*, 12/9/36, 5.

106. While carrying his cultural guerrilla campaign against colonial essentialism José Craveirinha didn't escape this kind of reductionism, justifying the proficiency and ingenuity of the African player by resorting to essentialist criteria, which crystallized an African racial identity. The black player's predisposition to adopt football, he emphasized, "could be attributed not merely to the virtues of resistance and elasticity with which nature gifted the vast contingent of black races, but also to a strange and unusual power of assimilation and improvisation, through which the instinctive sense, not as blunt as that of Western man's, is revealed exuberantly in the Westernized African. The black man experiences—and with what fervor!—any given sport by surrendering himself to a sensory vibration that is very rare in other racial groups." *O brado africano*, 22/1/55, 8.

107. See article 7.

108. Article 20 (no. 3) affords the colonial administration the right of supervision and approval of the statutes of diverse types of associations. This prerogative was confirmed by *Carta orgânica do império colonial português* (art. 37).

109. Article 20 (no. 3) affords the colonial administration the right of supervision and approval of the statutes of diverse types of associations. This prerogative was confirmed by *Carta orgânica do império colonial português* (art. 37). According to the RAU's article 560 the administrative corporations included private associations with public-utility status and nonprofit associations. Religious associations were framed by a different legislation. Private associations would be extinguished if the existence of any activity against the public interest was proven (art. 563).These prerogatives were confirmed by the *Carta orgânica do império colonial português*, approved in 1933 (art. 37, no. 5).

110. That also had a section for Agremiações Regionais de Recreio, Defesa, Desporto e Estudo (Regional leisure, defense, sports, and study organizations).

111. Torre do Tombo, Fundo dos Serviços de Centralização e Coordenação da Informação de Moçambique (SCCIM).

112. Diploma legislativo 238 de 17 de Maio de 1930, Boletim Oficial de Moçambique, no. 20. The curriculum of *escola de habilitação de professores indígenas* (indígena training school) (normal education) allocated, across the two years of the course, 111 hours to the discipline of physical education. Portaria [edict] 1044, 18/1/30, Boletim Oficial de Moçambique, no. 3. The regulations of this course described physical education as "Swedish gymnastic exercises in primary elementary teaching, marching, head, trunk, arm, and leg exercises. School games. Theoretical notions on physical education." Portaria 1106, 26/4/30, Boletim Oficial de Moçambique, no. 17.

113. In 1938 the curriculum that resulted from the Educational reformation of Carneiro Pacheco was applied to the colonies (Portaria 3. 312, 7/2/38. On the Estado Novo's educational project, see António Nóvoa, "A Educação Nacional," in *Nova história de Portugal*, ed. Joel Serrão and A. H. De Oliveira Marques; "Portugal e o Estado Novo," vol. 12 (1930–1960), ed. Fernando Rosas (Lisbon: Presença, 1999), 455–519.

114. Luís Miguel Carvalho, "Explorando as transferências educacionais nas primeiras décadas do século XX," *Análise social* 40, no. 176 (2005): 499–518.

115. Jorge Crespo, "História da educação física em Portugal: Os antecedentes da criação do INEF," *Ludens* 2, no. 1 (1977): 45–52; Crespo, "A educação física em Portugal: Génese da formação de professores," *Boletim da SPEF*, no. 1 (1991): 11–19; António Gomes Ferreira, "O ensino da educação física em Portugal durante o Estado Novo," *Perspectiva* 22, special issue (July–December 2004): 197–224.

116. Some of these models became hegemonic, as was the case with the German *Turnen* and Swedish gymnastics—the Ling method. Eugen Weber, *Gymnastics and Sports* in *Fin-de-Siècle* France: Opium of the Classes?" *American Historical Review* 76, no. 1 (February 1971): 70–98; Allen Guttmann,

Games and Empires: Modern Sports and Cultural Imperialism (New York: Columbia University Press, 1994); Gertrud Pfister, "'Cultural Confrontations': German *Turnen*, Swedish Gymnastics and English Sport: European Diversity in Physical Activities from a Historical Perspective," *Culture, Sport, Society* 6, no. 1 (Spring 2003): 61–91.

117. The sports manipulation strategies employed by the Portuguese policy in its colonial sphere, reliant on the teaching of physical education, were similar, in their overall premises, to the francophone model. Deville-Danthu, *Sport en noir et blanc*. It is essential to consider that although it is possible to define a general model, there were considerable differences in its application in each territory.

118. One year before the Mocidade Portuguesa, the Estado Novo created, in 1935, the Fundação Nacional para a Alegria no Trabalho (FNAT, National Foundation for Joy in Work). Inspired by its German and Italian counterparts, the Italian Opera Nazionale Dopolavoro (1925) and the German Kraft durch Freude (1933), it was the official body responsible for managing leisure time and organizing physical exercises for the Portuguese workers.

119. Such as l'École Supérieure d'Éducation Physique de Joinville-le-Pont, the University of Ghent's Higher Institute of Physical Education, and Stockholm's Royal Central Gymnastic Institute.

120. Daniel Melo, *Salazarismo e cultura popular (1933–1958)* (Lisbon: Imprensa de Ciências Sociais, 2001).

121. Celestino Marques Pereira was one of the most important physical education theorists in Portugal. He had his PhD at the Free University of Brussels, and a teacher at the MP and at the INEF. He was a student at the Escola de Educação Física do Exército and in 1934 he was awarded a scholarship by the Instituto para a Alta Cultura, which allowed him to study at the Instituto Real Central de Ginástica de Estocolmo. From his experience in Sweden and Denmark, he wrote a report, published in 1939, that became one of the axes of the physical education reform promoted by the Estado Novo, namely the creation of a specialized institute, such as the INEF. Celestino Marques Pereira, *A educação física na Suécia e na Dinamarca: Contribuições para o seu estudo em Portugal* (Lisbon: Ministério da Educação, Instituto para a Alta Cultura, 1939).

122. In 1932, decreto 21 034, 18/3/32, that created, near the Ministério da Instrução Pública (Ministry of Public Instruction), the Direcção dos Serviços de Educação Física (Head Office of Physical Education), considered sports games the "antithesis of all education" and a means to "physical deformation" and "moral perversion." The high-school physical education regulation, approved in 1932, by decreto 21 110 (16/4/1932), forbade "Anglo-Saxon sports and athletic games, and all competitions in general, namely football matches, as their educational role are null and their dangers obvious." These arguments were deeply influenced by French books on the subject. For instance, physical education teacher Lt. Artur Rebelo de Almeida, based *O futebol tornado perigo social* (Football as a social danger; 1928) on Georges Hébert (*Le sport*

contre l'éducation physique), Phillippe Tissié (*L'éducation physique de la race*), and Herbert Spencer, A *educação intelectual, moral e física* (from its French translation). Rebelo de Almeida, *O futebol tornado perigo social* (Lisbon: Tipografia de o Sport, 1928).

123. Unlike the cases of Spain and Italy's regimes, an in-depth study of football's role in the Portuguese Estado Novo, especially as a mechanism for social regulation, has yet to be made. However, it is widely known that football's pedagogic, medical, and scientific usefulness was always rejected by the group of specialists responsible for the implementation of the official physical-education model of practices in Portugal. On Spain, see Teresa Gonzalez Aja, "Spanish Sports Policy in Republican and Fascist Spain," in *Sport and International Politics: The Impact of Fascism and Communism on Sport*, ed. Pierre Arnaud and Jim Riordan (London: E. and F. N. Spon, 1998), 97–113. On fascist Italy, see Simon Martin, *Football and Fascism: The National Game under Mussolini* (Oxford: Berg, 2004); Angela Teja, "Italian Sport and International Relations under Fascism," in Arnaud and Riordan, *Sport and International Politics*, 147–70. A decisive recent contribution to the theme is Rahul Kumar, "A pureza perdida do desporto: Futebol no Estado Novo" (PhD diss., Faculdade de Ciências Sociais e Humanas, Universidade Nova de Lisboa, 2014).

124. Kumar, "Pureza perdida," 209–311.

125. António Leal de Oliveira, "Bases para a organização da educação física escolar," *I Congresso da União Nacional: Discursos, teses e comunicações*, 8 vols. (Lisbon: União Nacional, 1935), 7:299.

126. Ibid.

127. António Leal de Oliveira, "A pessoa e a sua educação física," *Boletim do INEF*, no. 2 (1940): 131.

128. The importance of a Latin inheritance in the context of this model of physical practices was stressed repeatedly in articles in the INEF's bulletin. For example, Viana, M. Gonçalves, "Os problemas da selecção, orientação, preparação e treino do desportista, considerados à luz da pedagogia," *Boletim do INEF*, nos. 1–2 (1955): 29–53. In fact, both Leal de Oliveira and Marques Pereira studied in Catholic universities in Belgium, and their worldview was influenced by the Catholic sports movement based mostly in Spain, Italy, France, and Belgium. On the Belgian Catholic gymnastics movement, see Jan Tolleneer, "The Belgian Catholic Gymnastic Movement in Its International Context, 1908–1940," in Arnaud and Riordan, *Sport and International Politics*.

129. António Leal de Oliveira, "Generalidades sôbre o as attitudes e movimento do corpo humano em educação física," *Boletim do INEF*, no. 3 (1941): 275–76.

130. Ibid., 282.

131. Ibid., 284.

132. Ibid.

133. Ibid., 285.

134. Ibid., 283.
135. António Leal de Oliveira, "Os movimentos," *Boletim do INEF*, no. 4 (1941): 382. On the influence of Ling's method in the Portuguese educational system, see Rui Gomes, "Poder e saber sobre o corpo—a educação física no Estado Novo (1936–1945)," *Boletim da Sociedade Portuguesa de Educação Física*, no. 2–3 (1991): 109–36; Carvalho, "Explorando as transferências." See also Carneiro Pacheco, in Manuel Rocha, "Notável discurso de sua ex.ª o senhor ministro da educação discurso," *Boletim do INEF*, no. 3 (1941): 257–58.
136. Ibid.
137. Manuel Deniz, "'La musique a besoin d'une dictature': Musique et politique dans les premières années de l'État Nouveau (1926–1945)" (PhD diss., Paris: Université de Paris VIII, 2005).
138. Leal de Oliveira, "Os movimentos," 395.
139. Ibid., 398.
140. Ibid., 400.
141. Inês Brasão, *Dons e disciplinas do corpo feminino: os discursos sobre o corpo na história do Estado Novo* (Lisbon: ONGCCCIDM, 1999); Ferreira, "Ensino da educação física," 212–16.
142. Mesquita Guimarães, "Biotipologia e orientação do desporto," *Boletim do INEF*, no. 2 (1941): 144–54. Guimarães, physician and teacher at the INEF, stated in 1941 that professional guidance should be supervised by the science of anthropotechnic, a means of channeling individuals to the profession most appropriate for their biotype. Based on the works of the Italian School, he emphasized the need to classify bodies in terms of their physical and psychic features. Ibid., 144.
143. António Leal de Oliveira, "Construção e conservação dos gimnásios e do respectivo material didáctico," *Boletim do INEF*, no. 1 (1942): 22–55
144. As defined by Erving Goffman in *Asylums: Essays on the Social Situation of Mental Patients and Other Inmates* (Harmondsworth: Penguin, 1968).
145. Nobre Guedes, "O desporto particular: Forma interventiva do estado," *Boletim do INEF*, nos. 3–4 (1947): 17–18.
146. António Faria de Vasconcelos, *O que é que deve ser a educação física, conferência no Ginásio Club Portuguez* (Lisbon: Papelaria Mais, 1928), 7.
147. António Leal de Oliveira, "A lição de gimnástica educativa—1.ª lição de ginástica para o ensino primário," *Boletim do INEF*, no. 2 (1940): 176–77.
148. Ibid.
149. In the specific context of the British public school system, the use of sports games as an educational instrument led to the isolation of the games' practice areas from the surrounding society: the public school became a modern social technology that socialized and normalized upper-class children. Hargreaves, *Sport, Power*.
150. Celestino Marques Pereira, "A função da ginástica perante o desporto como meio de formação física na juventude," *Boletim do INEF*, nos. 1, 2 (1947): 16–17. Marques Pereira developed several studies where he strove to adapt sports practice to the orthodoxy of Swedish gymnastics, and even though

his analysis became increasingly technical, it remained a motor representation of an ideological conception of the world. See Marques Pereira, "Função da ginástica."

151. Ibid., 18. These shortcomings could be overcome, in Marques Pereira's opinion, through physical education's harmonious and progressive action on the locomotive system (17). Marques Pereira, "A Função da ginástica," 22–23. The *Inspector geral dos desportos* (General Inspector of Sports), Salazar Carreira, agreed that competitive sports should be subordinated to gymnastics. The DGEFDSE regulation compelled sports clubs to hire a gym teacher. Ling's method, so Salazar Carreira argued, "develops in sportsmen a complex of virtues and habits that are of the utmost social importance: from discipline to cohesion, from self-reliance to a knowledge of their own resources." Salazar Carreira, "A influência social da Ginástica de Ling," *Boletim do INEF*, nos. 1–2 (1947): 73. Marques Pereira's goal was to achieve a prior control of sports movements, as well as to regulate the entire psychophysiological process preceding the gesture. To achieve this, he argued that psychophysiological techniques should be employed, namely the principles of conditioned reflex applying the model of orthodox gymnastics to competitive sports. Marques Pereira, "Sur la justification psyco-physiologique de la valeur éducative des compétitions sportives de la jeunesse," *Boletim do INEF*, nos. 1–2 (1950): 83–105.

152. Decreto 31 908, the application of which in Mozambique was regulated by portaria 10 122 (24/6/42).

153. Decreto 32 234, 31/8/42.

154. This mission was coordinated by the Marques Pereira brothers, sons of Gen. Alberto Feliciano Marques Pereira, a top colonial public servant. Alberto Marques Pereira was a physical education teacher at Mocidade Portuguesa, FNAT, the Escola Colonial, and the Instituto Superior de Ciências Sociais e Políticas Ultramarinas.

155. Decreto 32 946, of 3/8/43. "Actas do Conselho Legislativo," in *Boletim oficial de Moçambique*, acta 2, 10/4/57, p. 14.

156. Artigo 29, artigo 31; diploma-legislativo 1670. This attempt to impose a gymnastics-based model on clubs that essentially promoted football was carried out in Angola, but not in Mozambique. In 1959 the Angolan CPEF published a *Manual de preparação física no futebol* (Manual of Physical Preparation in Football) in which the game was conceived of as a space within which gymnastic preparation could be developed (Conselho Provincial de Educação Física da Província de Angola, 1959).

157. In the assessment written by Celestino Marques Pereira, he pointed out that colonial competitions served as a stimulus for youths' education and for the formation of their character, as had occurred with the "French, Belgian, Anglo-Saxon, and Boer youth of our neighboring overseas territories." Actas da Câmara Corporativa, 72, VI Legislatura, 1956, 20/1, parecer 34/VI.

158. The Corporative Chamber was a specialized council, divided by areas of knowledge, responsible for the appreciation of laws that were presented to

the National Assembly, the name given to Parliament during the Estado Novo.

159. Actas da Câmara Corporativa [Corporative Chamber Minutes] N.° 72, VI Legislatura, 1956, 20/1, parecer 34/VI.

160. In 1957 the Conselho Legislativo de Mozambique (Mozambique Legislative Council) passed a law that created an instrument for the execution of the sports policies contained in the law of 1956. See diploma 1670, 4/5/57. Mozambique was the first Portuguese overseas territory to execute lei (law) 2083. See art. 101.

161. "Actas do Conselho Legislativo," in *Boletim oficial de Mozambique*, acta 2, 10/4/57, 19–20.

162. "Legislação e Doutrina," in *Boletim da DGEFDSE*, vols. 1, 2 (1948): 419.

163. Lourenço Marques had 63.5 percent of the all members of sports associations in 1960, and 56 percent in 1964. These percentages are based on data from the *Anuário estatístico de Moçambique* (1959–64).

164. "The continuous action of these struggles could give the 'indígena' the wrong conception of watching fights between whites and 'indígenas,' something that will inevitably lead to confrontations between players and the public." AHM, Direcção dos Serviços de Administração Civil—Secção A—Administração Civil, Agremiações regionais de recreio, defesa, desporto e estudo. Associações Desportivas, Recreativas e Culturais 1934–1971, caixa 14, processo 27/191, Assunto: Grupo Desportivo Vasco da Gama—1934–52.

165. A report by the Administração do Concelho on 4/8/52 called for a complete renovation of the "indígena sport," which was in "true chaos." The proposed creation of an Associação do Desporto Indígena (Indigenous Sports Association) would control local competitions but also allow the "assimilados" to join the AFLM recently created second division. AHM, Administração do Concelho de Lourenço Marques—Administração Agremiações regionais de recreio, defesa, desporto e estudo, 1941–1951, caixa 4, Informação sobre a crise da AFA, 4/8/52.

166. *O brado africano*, after criticizing the existence of two football associations in Lourenço Marques, listed the players who moved from the AFA to the AFLM and then to the metropolis: Amoreira, Jorge Nicolau, Monteiro, Matateu, Joseph Wilson, Coluna, Justino; the players who moved directly from the AFA to the metropolis: Mário Wilson, Albasini, Adalberto, Naldo; the players who moved from the AFA and were playing at that time in the AFLM: Merali, Barata, Amerali, Justino, J. Albasini. *O brado africano*, 29/5/54, 3.

167. Moreover, this demonstrated that, when compared with the black population, the leisure activities of the mestiços were closer to those of the settler population.

168. "Actas do Conselho Legislativo," in *Boletim ficial de Mozambique*, acta 8, 30/4/57, 58.

169. The Conselho Provincial de Educação Física (Provincial Council on Physical Education) requested the Repartição de Instrução Pública's opinion.

The Repartição wrote to the governor general, who asked the SNI's to give the solution. AHM, Direcção dos Serviços dos Negócios Indígenas—secção A—Administração Agremiações regionais de recreio, defesa, desporto e estudo. Associações Desportivas, Recreativas e Culturais, caixa 4, Grupo Desportivo Carreira de Tiro solicita autorização para inscrever jogadores indígenas.

170. The CPEF redirected the issue to the Repartição de Instrução Pública (Public Instruction Department). The latter, in turn, wrote to the governor general. The clerk at the governor general's office, Juvenal de Carvalho, redirected the issue to Negócios Índigenas (Indígena Affairs) and then to the Conselho Provincial de Educação Física (Provincial Council on Physical Education). AHM, Direcção dos Serviços dos Negócios Indígenas—secção A—Administração Agremiações regionais de recreio, defesa, desporto e estudo, Associações Desportivas, Recreativas e Culturais, caixa 4, Grupo Desportivo Carreira de Tiro solicita autorização para inscrever jogadores indígenas.

171. Ibid.

172. Peter Alegi reports that in 1958, under threat of expulsion by FIFA, the leaders of the South African white football association (FASA) tried to promote the integration of other South African football associations, namely the ones composed of blacks. Alegi, "Football and Apartheid Society: the South African Soccer League, 1960–1966," in Armstrong and Giulianotti, *Football in Africa*, 111–14. Although there is no evidence that FIFA's pressure was linked to the process that resulted in the end of the AFA, it is possible to conceive that this was taken into account by the Portuguese Football Federation and by the local Mozambican authorities.

173. As one reads the minutes of the CPEF meeting that took place on March 25, 1960, it was the government that supported AFLM's third division: "It was decided to request the AFLM to start its third-division championship. The expenses should be accounted separately. Any deficit should be paid by the CPEF." ACPEFM, Actas das Reuniões do Conselho Provincial de Educação Física de Moçambique, livro 2, 25/3/1960.

174. DSAC issued a document requesting the elimination from the associations' statutes of words that could express racial discrimination. AHM, DSAC, secção A, Administração, Agremiações regionais de recreio, defesa, desporto e estudo. Associações Desportivas, Recreativas e Culturais, caixa 22, processo 27 1.ª—Corporações administrativas, sua organização, fundação, informação de Afonso Ivens Ferraz de Freitas, administrador de primeira classe, 14/11/59).

175. In 1955, within a population of 5,764,362 individuals, only 117,405 were considered civilized, including only 4,554 black Africans. *Anuário de Moçambique, Lourenço Marques*, 1958, 20.

176. In 1951, the MP had fifteen centers and 2,703 members in the Sul do Save section, seven centers and 5,749 members in the Manica and Sofala section, two centers and 1,888 members in the Zambezia section, and two centres and 514 members in the Niassa section. Only two centers, the ones included in the Liceu Salazar (Salazar High School) and the Escola Técnica (Technical School) had their own facilities. Most of the schools did not have

the facilities to host the MP's activities. Some MP centres only had one local supervisor and one or two school teachers. AHM, Governo Geral, caixa, 348, Mocidade Portuguesa, Elementos para o relatório do Governador Geral, Informação do Comissariado da Mocidade Portuguesa de Moçambique, António da Rosa Pinto ao Chefe de Gabinete do Governo Geral.

177. There were not enough gym teachers in the local schools. The Liceu Salazar had only one, who could not teach the majority of high school students. In Sá da Bandeira's Technical School, which served more that a hundred students, there was no gymnastics teacher at all. AHM, Governo Geral, caixa 508, 1949–58, Comissariado Colonial da Mocidade Portuguesa, processo S-11, MP Organização, pessoal, material, etc., Informação a sua excelência o governador-geral em 10/3/49, Mocidade Portuguesa.

178. In 1951, the MP's director informed the governor general that the lack of equipment did not allow for the completion of gym classes. AHM, Governo Geral, caixa 508, 1949–58, Comissariado Colonial da Mocidade Portuguesa, processo S-11, MP Organização, pessoal, material, etc. Mocidade Portuguesa, Informação do Comando da Mocidade Portuguesa ao Governador Geral, 23/19/51. In the following year there was a new complaint: there weren't enough uniforms to supply the MP students. AHM, Governo Geral, caixa 508, 1949–1958, processo S-11, MP Organização, pessoal, material, etc. Mocidade Portuguesa, Milícia, relatório das actividades no ano lectivo de 1951–1952 por Hermes Araújo de Oliveira, comandante da Milícia, a 18/8/52. Instituted by art. 37 of decreto 38 980, 8/11/52. The center would be organized in 1953 by portaria 9 868 de 2/5/1953. In 1952, the creation of the Centro de Medicina Desportiva (Sports Medicine Center), which had powers of coordination and supervision over clubs and associations, aimed to increase state control over local activity.

179. The state's donations to sports clubs and associations, however, increased in the 1950s. In Lourenço Marques state contribution reached 4.1 percent of club revenues in 1943, 3.8 in 1948, 13.0 in 1951, 9.8 in 1953, 10.8 in 1955, and 10.4 in 1958. *Anuário estatístico de Moçambique*, 1943–58.

180. The funding of sports activities by Totobola was approved through diploma legislativo 2600, 16/6/1965.

181. 50 percent of Totobola's profit was channeled to the CPEF. Until 1966 the CPEF's budget came from the general budget of Mozambique and from the Fundo de Expansão Desportiva (Sports Expansion Fund). Between 1957 and 1971, the Fundo de Expansão Desportiva contributed a little over 7 percent of CPEF's budget (MZE 2,910,970 from a total of MZE 40,713,640). Feio, *Plano de trabalhos*, 67. Totobola's profit, contributing only from 1966, amounted, within the same period of time, to 60 percent of the total CPEF budget (MZE 24,555,712), whereas state direct investment reached only 32.5 percent (MZE 13,246,958). Ibid., 67. The state's direct investment was strengthened in 1969, after the creation of the Fundo de Fomento Gimnodesportivo (by decree 49 339, 30/10/1969), though 80 percent of its receipts actually came from Totobola. Ibid., 8.

182. Between 1966 and 1971 the amount of money from the state's budget destined for the CPEF dropped abruptly: 38 percent in 1966, 20.5 in 1967, 10.5 in 1968, 3 in 1969, and 5 in 1970 and 1971. Ibid.

183. It was not possible to locate, in the ACPEFM, all the CPEF's official report books. There are some periods missing, such as the ones between 1957 and 1958, February 1967 to July 1968, and all the books after October 1970.

184. As stated by Salazar Carreia, Inspector-Geral dos Desportos (Sports General Inspector), *Lourenço Marques Guardian*, 30/8/55, 7.

185. Decreto 30 279, 22/6/53.

186. Lei 2004, 30/5/1960.

187. As stated in the legislation: "Sports' professionalization is a social fact, though from the point of view of 'pure sport' it is a deviation from or, more precisely, a corruption of the high principles that govern sports' activity. However, there is nothing that could turn professionalization in itself into something socially negative. Sports and professionalization . . . are two distinct realities and thus they should be approached differently." Lei 2004, 30/5/1960.

188. Portaria 19809 of the Direcção-Geral do Ensino, 15/4/63.

189. In the 1960s the colonial government regularly gave subsidies to local associations, including some of the suburban clubs. AHM, Governo do Distrito de Lourenço Marques—Administração Assistência e beneficência Públicas, 1964–1968, caixa 51, pasta 1965, A/6, Informação Interna, 7/4/65.

190. The number of transfers was written in the official reports' books of the CPEF's direction meetings. ACPEFM, Actas das reuniões do Conselho Provincial de Educação Física de Moçambique.

191. The implementation of article 22 of decree to 40 964 (1956) in the Portuguese colonial territories was, because of local authorities' demands, constantly delayed. In 1967 the overseas minister Silva Cunha finally extended this norm to all the colonies, with the exception of Macau, by portaria 21.323 4/6/1964.

192. The reform of the Instituto Nacional de Educação Física (National Institute for Physical Education), in 1957, marked the consecration in Portugal of a more technically inclined thought on sports, in which the premilitary component lost its central place. See José Esteves, *O desporto e as estruturas sociais* (Lisbon: Prelo, 1967); António Gomes Ferreira, "O ensino da educação física em Portugal durante o Estado Novo," *Perspectiva* 22, special issue (July–December 2004): 208.

193. The INEF's new curriculum, after the 1957 reform, replaced the military, ideological, and religious rhetoric with a more technical discourse. Decreto 41 447, 17/12/57.

194. Noronha Feio, *Plano de Trabalhos* (Lourenço Marques: Fundo de Fomento Desportivo, 1972), 18, emphasis in original.

195. The institutional structure that prepared this plan included the Escola de Instrutores de Educação Física de Lourenço Marques (Physical Education Instructors School of Lourenço Marques), the Gabinete de Engenharia

e Arquitectura Desportiva (Sports Engineering and Architecture Office), the Centro de Documentação e Informação (Documentation and Information Centre), and the Gabinete de Estudos e Programação Técnico-Pedagógico (Office of Studies and Techno-Pedagogic Programming). Feio, *Plano de trabalhos*.

196. Marcos Cardão, *Fado tropical: O luso-tropicalismo na cultura de massas (1960–1974)* (Lisbon: Unipop, 2015). In the Portuguese case, it would be crucial to carry out a study along the lines of John McKenzie's, on the relation between imperial propaganda and public space in England. MacKenzie, *Propaganda and Empire: The Manipulation of British Public Opinion, 1880–1960* (Manchester: Manchester University Press, 1984). In Portugal, João Nuno Coelho's study on football tried to explore some of the terms of this relation. Coelho, *A equipa de todos nós: Nacionalismo, futebol e media* (Porto: Afrontamento, 2002).

197. Eusébio only won the Champions Cup in 1962.

198. In 1960 the minister of education promoted a national sports award ("medalha de mérito desportivo") enabling the nationalization and politicization of sports victories.

199. Marcos Cardão, "Um significante instrumental: Eusébio e a banalização lusotropicalismo na década de 1960," in *Esporte, cultura, nação, estado: Brasil e Portugal*, ed. Victor Andrade de Melo, Fabio de Faria Peres, Maurício Drumond (Rio de Janeiro: 7Letras: 2014), 172–88.

200. Augusto Nascimento, Marcelo Bittencourt, Victor Andrade de Melo, eds., *Mais do que um jogo: O esporte e o continente africanos* (Rio de Janeiro: Apicuri, 2010), 211–42; Nascimento, Bittencourt, Nuno Domingos, and Melo, eds., *Esporte e lazer na África: Novos olhares* (Rio de Janeiro: 7 Letras, 2013); Melo, *Jogos de identidade: O esporte em Cabo Verde* (Rio de Janeiro: Apicuri/CNP, 2011); Nascimento, *Esporte e vez de política no São Tomé e Princípe* (Rio de Janeiro: 7 Letras, 2013).

201. Marcos Cardão, "Peregrinações exemplares: As embaixadas patrióticas dos clubes metropolitanos ao 'ultramar português,'" in *Esporte e lazer*, ed. Nascimento, Bittencourt, Domingos, and Melo.

202. João Nuno Coelho analyzed the evolution of sports media discourse on the Portuguese national team, focusing on the role of media as an instrument of "banal nationalism." See Michael Billig, *Banal Nationalism* (London: Sage, 1995). The submission of players' gestures and movements to a national style of play, which reflected itself in popular imagery, became an instrument of national construction. Coelho, *Equipa de todos nós*.

203. This article was especially written for the first edition of the Mozambican sports newspaper *A equipa*, 15/12/66, 1.

204. Freyre applied his general theory to football's specific case. Inspired by Ruth Benedict's *Patterns of Culture* (1933), he made a distinction between the European Apollonian players, rational and formal, and the Brazilian Dionysian players, who played an impulsive, individualistic, and emotional football. See Freyre's preface to Mário Filho's *O negro no futebol brasileiro* (Rio de Janeiro: Mauad, 2003 [1947]).

205. Coelho, *Equipa de todos nós*; Ana Santos, *Heróis desportivos: Estudo de caso sobre Eusébio: De corpo a ícone da nação* (Lisbon: Instituto do Desporto de Portugal, 2004); José Neves, "O eterno fado dos últimos 30 metros, nacionalismo e corpo," in A *época do Futebol: O jogo visto pelas Ciências Sociais*, ed. José Neves and Nuno Domingos (Lisbon: Assírio e Alvim, 2004).

206. *A bola*, 5/5/1962.

CHAPTER 3: FOOTBALL AND THE MORAL ECONOMY OF THE LOURENÇO MARQUES SUBURBS

1. Alexandre Lobato, *Lourenço Marques, Xilunguíne: Biografia da cidade* (Lisbon: Agência-Geral do Ultramar, 1970).

2. José de Oliveira Boléo, *Monografia de Moçambique* (Lisbon: Agência-geral do Ultramar, 1971), 161–62.

3. Besides *Actualidades de Moçambique* [Mozambican Newsreels] (1955–74), several films showed the capital of Mozambique: *Lourenço Marques* (Felipe de Solms, 1950), *Férias em Lourenço Marques* (Miguel Spiguel, 1960), *Aspectos de uma capital: Lourenço Marques* (Carlos Marques/Filipe Solms, 1952), *África* (João dos Santos Ferreira, 1964).

4. Published in English in the same year was Eusébio da Silva Ferreira, *My Name Is Eusébio* (London: Routledge and Kegan Paul, 1967).

5. António Rita-Ferreira, *Os Africanos de Lourenço Marques*, Memórias do Instituto de Investigação Científica de Moçambique / Instituto de Investigação Científica de Moçambique, vol. 9, series C (1967–68), 192–95.

6. Between 1964 and 1968, 206 housing units were lost as a result of fires in uninsured buildings. Ibid., 197.

7. Ibid., 270.

8. Ibid.

9. Ibid., 275.

10. Ibid., 271. As an underlying cause for the phenomena of delinquency, the author highlighted the perverse effects of certain books and films, particularly westerns and "cop-and-robber" films, whose morality was surprisingly in line with the indígena worldview.

11. Ibid., 273.

12. Rita-Ferreira, *Africanos de Lourenço Marques*, 428.

13. Ibid., 429. A 1959 inquiry had identified a widespread shortage of calories among this population, particularly among women and children, whose diet did not include the necessary quantities of calcium, iron, phosphorus, or vitamins A, B, and C. Ibid., 430. The high incidence of liver tumors in the suburbs was grounds for the formation, in 1956, of a Brigada de Tumores Malignos (Malignant Tumor Brigade). The study group identified a fungus that contaminated the food and propagated in unsanitary environments, afflicting individuals with vitamin-poor diets more sharply. Ibid., 431–32.

14. Rita-Ferreira quoted an inquiry from the Assistência Pública (Public Welfare Office) among 109 family units in the Xavane neighborhood. Ibid., 423.

15. Ibid., 424.

16. Ibid., 433.

17. As suggested by various works published at the time, especially *Estudo sobre o absentismo e a instabilidade da mão-de-obra africana*, 3 vols. (Lisbon: Junta de Investigações do Ultramar, 1959–60).

18. Rita-Ferreira, *Africanos de Lourenço Marques*, 353.

19. These data confirmed the findings of previous studies. In the survey conducted in the Bairro da Munhuana in 1964, the salaries of the inhabitants that were interviewed were exclusively spent on basic needs, namely food and housing; residential spaces did not have the most basic hygiene conditions. *Inquérito habitacional realizado no bairro da Munhuana* (Lisbon: Junta de Investigações do Ultramar, Estudos de Ciências Políticas e Sociais, Centro de Estudos de Serviço Social e de Desenvolvimento Comunitário, 1964), 48. Of all males interviewed, 48.6 percent were skilled industry workers (46).

20. Rita-Ferreira, *Africanos de Lourenço Marques*, 314.

21. As late as 1973 the official magazine of the Mozambique Industrial Association reported, "Out of the manufacturing industry's labor force, which at this point is estimated at 110,000 active individuals, only about 25 percent are qualified workers. In the course of the last six years, the total of the industrial labor force has risen steadily at a rate of 8 percent per year, a rise, however, that is very different in the two major segments of the staff—the unskilled and the qualified." According to the same source, unskilled labor had risen at an annual rate of 6 percent, and the qualified at 20 percent. Given this scenario, the author raised the question, "At this pace, where will one be able to gather qualified labor force?" "Formação profissional," *Indústria de Moçambique*, no. 3 (1973): 67.

22. As summed up by Rita-Ferreira: "Knowing that they will only be tolerated by the monetary economy while they are able to sell their work, they still see the tribe, their family and agricultural work, as safe harbors they can turn to in case they're rejected by employers." Rita-Ferreira, *Africanos de Lourenço Marques*, 339.

23. Ibid., 232. Rita-Ferreira's work singles out the 1959 meeting of the Conselho Científico para o Sul do Saara (Scientific Council for Sub-Saharan Africa) as the first step toward a more systematic approach to thinking about the urban question in the Portuguese context.

24. Ibid., 358–59.

25. Ibid., 468.

26. Ibid., 385. A 1964 research led by António Rita-Ferreira had already highlighted the displacement of "thousands of youngsters of rural origins" into the urban centers, searching for "jobs as servants, foremen, clerks." The "existence of this ever-growing group of disgruntled outcasts" was deemed "potentially dangerous." It was estimated that this contingent amounted to 3.5 percent of the population. *Promoção social em Moçambique*, Centro de Estudos de Serviço Social e de Desenvolvimento Comunitário, junto do Instituto Superior de Ciências Sociais e Política Ultramarina. Estudos de Ciências Políticas e Sociais, N.º 71 (Lisbon: Junta de Investigações do Ultramar, 1964), 19.

27. Ibid., 22.
28. Rita-Ferreira, *Africanos de Lourenço Marques*, 237.
29. Ibid.
30. Ibid., 235–36.
31. When in 1962 the housing tax (*imposto domiciliário*) replaced the indígena tax, it was up to local authorities to register and identify the suburban inhabitants, which they did quite inefficiently, given that the actual population was substantially larger than that registered. In 1968, there were 34,380 residents registered in Munhuana. The local estimated population reached 140,000. Ibid., 159; diplomas legislativos 2815 and 2186, 30/12/61; portaria 5659, 20/1/62.
32. Portaria 21724, 25/1/69.
33. Rita-Ferreira, *Africanos de Lourenço Marques*, 162–63.
34. Ibid., 159.
35. Torre do Tombo (TT). Fundo dos Serviços de Centralização e Coordenação de Informações de Moçambique, Centro de Documentação. Estudos e informações gerais confidenciais sobre Moçambique, Questionários estudo da situação, Lourenço Marques, PT-TT SCCIM/A/1/8.
36. In 1968 there were only 35,000 suburban inhabitants registered whereas 165,000 were considered to "fluctuating." Rita-Ferreira, *Africanos de Lourenço Marques*, 295.
37. The administrators were often financially rewarded for giving their consent. Amâncio de Alpoim Guedes, "The Caniços of Mozambique," in *Shelter in Africa*, ed. Paul Oliver (New York: Praeger, 1971), 206.
38. On the corporative question in Portugal, see Philippe C. Schmitter, *Portugal: Do Autoritarismo à Democracia* (Lisbon: Imprensa de Ciências Sociais, 1999).
39. Diploma legislativo 1595, 28/4/56.
40. Rita-Ferreira, *Africanos de Lourenço Marques*, 388.
41. The 1930s inaugurated urban studies in Africa, which became more common in the following decade. Daryl Forde, the author of the bibliographic review, identifies Orde Browne's *The African Labourer* (Oxford University Press, International African Institute, 1933) and the volume on the Copperbelt edited by J. Merle Davies, *Modern Industry and the African* (Macmillan, 1933), as the first to address in a more systematic fashion the urban question in Africa. Forde, ed., *Social Implications of Industrialization and Urbanization in Africa South of the Sahara* (London: International African Institute, 1956), 12.
42. Such as the Comissão de Cooperação Técnica em África ao Sul do Saara (CCTA; Commision for Technical Cooperation in Sub-Saharan Africa); the Conferência Interafricana de Trabalho Rural (Inter-African Conference on Rural Work), which met for the first time in Lourenço Marques in 1953; the Economic Commission for Africa, created by the United Nations Economic and Social Council in 1959; the International Labour Organization; the International Institute of Differing Civilizations (INCIDI); the International African Institute. The situation in the colonial world, in a postwar

scenario where North American hegemony gained ground, was still thought to be within the frame of large-scale international organizations concerned with the international regulation of markets and the labor world—the IMF, the World Bank, the Organization for Economic Cooperation and Development, the International Labour Organization. However, colonial policies were also influenced by the knowledge exchanged in international forums, such as the Inter-African Labour Conference and in the Inter-African Labour Institute, which served as an inspiration for Portuguese institutions, such as the Comissão de Estudos de Planos de Fomento (Research Commission for Development Plans) and the Comissão de Planeamento Regional do Sul (Southern Regional Planning Commission).

43. Colonial agrarian reforms, articulated with policies for "rural welfare," fostered an agricultural modernization that would introduce new African farmers into the circuits of a capitalist economy and simultaneously halt the exodus into the cities, thus attenuating the growing urban unemployment and subemployment. "Social promotion" handled the populations's integration, proposing new structures, such as rural administrative councils (regedorias). Created by decretos 43 896 and 43 897, 6/9/1961.

44. The number of industrial establishments in Mozambique rose from twenty-five in 1950 to five hundred in 1970. Maria Clara Mendes, *Maputo antes da independência: Geografia de uma cidade colonial* (Lisbon: Centro de Estudos Geográficos das Universidade de Lisboa, 1979), 249.

45. Silva Cunha was overseas minister between 1965 and 1973. His doctoral thesis ("O sistema português de política indígena: Subsídios para o seu estudo," 1953) was an important mark in the reform of Portuguese colonial policies. Adriano Moreira became the executor of a new way of conceiving of the Portuguese colonial science, already noticeable in the texts for *Revista do Gabinete de Estudos Ultramarinos*, edited from 1951 by the Centro Universitário de Lisboa da Mocidade Portuguesa (Lisbon University Centre for Portuguese Youth). Two years earlier, this same center inaugurated another publication, *Revista do Gabinete de Estudos Corporativos*. In the two journals, despite their different scopes, there was a clear impetus to transform the methods of the political and social management in the national territories, in line with a more developmentalist approach. Moreira also left his mark on the *Revista de estudos ultramarinos*, particularly after 1959, when he became its director. The publication, founded in 1948 as *Revista de estudos coloniais*, was published by the Escola Superior Colonial (Colonial Technical College). In 1963 it would change its name to *Revista de estudos políticos e sociais* and fell under the responsibility of the then Instituto Superior de Ciências Sociais e Política Ultramarina (Higher Institute for Social Sciences and Overseas Policies). In 1941, Caetano—at the time the Comissário Nacional da Mocidade Portuguesa (Portuguese Youth National Commissioner), before taking on, in 1944, the Ministério das Colónias (Ministry of the Colonies), had already expressed to the Conselho do Império Colonial (Colonial Empire Council) the urgency of categorizing the new indígena clusters resulting from contact with

the colonial system. According to Silva Cunha, Caetano's intervention was one of the first warning shots on the need to frame a segment of "semiassimilados" that had been gathering on the peripheries of African cities. Joaquim da Silva Cunha, "O enquadramento social dos indígenas destribalizados," *Revista do Gabinete de Estudos Corporativos*, nos. 5–6 (January–June, 1952): 26–27. In 1952, Silva Cunha bemoaned the absence of Portuguese legislation to deal with the "detribalization" issue. Ibid., 12–13. The "evolved" indígena, who remained categorized by the state as a "traditional" individual, under the authority of traditional institutions, was caught within an urban and labor condition that demanded "social categorization," one that could operate as a way to handle the social challenges resulting from urban life and the transformation of labor conditions. Silva Cunha wrote several books on the dangers of the black worker's proletarianization and on the relation between "detribalization" and the emergence of subversive associative movements. Silva Cunha, *Movimentos associativos na África portuguesa* (Lisbon: Ministério do Ultramar, Junta de Investigações do Ultramar, 1956); Silva Cunha, *Aspectos dos movimentos associativos na África negra (Angola)*, 2 vols. (Lisbon: Junta de Investigações do Ultramar, 1959), vol. 2. In the 1950s, work in institutions such as the Centro de Estudos Políticos e Sociais (Center for Political and Social Studies), founded in 1956 and run by Adriano Moreira, sought to fill some of these social gaps. In 1960, Adriano Moreira stressed that the priority of social-action policies should be the cities and border areas, which were more exposed to social instability. Adriano Moreira, "Problemas sociais no ultramar," *Estudos ultramarinos* 10, no. 4 (1960): 8. The "detribalized" masses reached two hundred thousand in Luanda and one hundred thousand in the suburbs of Lourenço Marques. "Clusters such as Musseques and Xipamanine," demanded "intense social action" (12).

46. In 1956, Forde's *Social Implications of Industrialization*, which resulted from the conference on urban questions in Africa (organized by UNESCO and the International African Institute two years earlier in Abidjan) made no reference, in the comprehensive list of indexed works, to any study on the Portuguese colonies. Five years later, in the *Boletim do Instituto de Investigação Científica de Moçambique* (Bulletin of the Scientific Research Institute of Mozambique), Pegado e Silva, who held a degree in Altos Estudos Ultramarinos (Overseas Higher Studies) and was a member of the Institute, published a study on the research in urban sociology in sub-Saharan Africa, where he confirmed the backwardness of the Portuguese colonial situation. J. R. Pegado, "Panorama das investigações efectuadas, até 1961, sobre sociologia urbana em África ao sul do Saara," *Boletim do Instituto de Investigação Científica de Moçambique* 2, no. 2 (1961): 391–97. Pioneering studies in South Africa are singled out. Ellen Helman and Mónica Hunter, linked with the University of Witwatersrand and the African International Institute, have been the pioneers in this field, in 1945 and 1935. In Angola, up to that point, four surveys had been conducted, all of them in Luanda. Pegado made reference to the works of Castilho Soares, Maria da Conceição Tavares Lourenço e Silva, Ilídio do

Amaral and the priest Bettencourt. On Lourenço Marques there were no studies, except for the academic research of the South African sociologist Hilary Flegg. Flegg, "Age Structure in Urban Africans in Lourenço Marques" (PhD diss., University of the Witwatersrand, 1961). When A. L. Epstein did a state of the art on urban studies in 1967 he did not include any reference to Portugal. Epstein, "Urban Communities in Africa," in *Closed Systems and Open Minds: The Limits of Naïvety in Social Anthropology*, ed. Max Gluckman (Chicago: Aldine, 1967).

47. The Centro de Estudos Políticos e Sociais organized several missions and working groups, such as the Missão de Estudo da Atracção das Grandes Cidades e do Bem-Estar-Rural (Mission for the Study of the Attraction of Major Cities and Rural Well-Being), the Missão para o Estudo dos Movimentos Associativos Africanos (Mission for the Study of African Associative Movements), the Sector de Estudo das Questões Internacionais do Trabalho (Department of Studies on International Labour Issues), the Sector de Estudos Económicos do Ultramar Português (Department of Economic Studies on the Portuguese Overseas Territories), the Sector de Estudos dos Problemas das Terras (Department of Studies on Land Issues), and the Sector de Estudos da Mão-de-obra (Department of Studies on Workforce Issues) in the field of internal affairs. The Missão para o Estudo da Atracção das Grandes Cidades e do Bem-Estar Rural, which addressed social stability in large urban clusters subject to the effects of a market economy as well as the poorly controlled and potentially dangerous circulation of ideas and forms of association, was headed by Sampaio d'Orey and would be shut down in 1959. On the Portuguese colonial social science, see Alfredo Margarido, "Le colonialisme portugais et l'anthropologie," in *Anthropologie et imperialism*, ed. Jean Copans (Paris: Maspero, 1975); Donato Gallo, *O saber português: Antropologia e colonialismo* (Lisbon: Editores Reunidos, 1988); Rui Mateus Pereira, "Introdução à reedição de Os Maconde de Moçambiques," in *Os macondes de Moçambique*, ed. Jorge Dias, vol. 1, *Aspectos históricos e económicos* (Lisbon: Comissão Nacional para as Comemorações dos Descobrimentos Portugueses, Instituto de Investigação Científica Tropical, 1998), xxv; Pereira, "Conhecer para dominar: O desenvolvimento do conhecimento antropológico na política colonial portuguesa em Moçambique, 1926–1959 (PhD diss., Universidade Nova de Lisboa, FCSH), 24–30; Harry G. West, "Invertendo a Bossa do Camelo: Jorge Dias, a sua mulher, o seu intérprete e eu," in *Portugal não é um país pequeno: Contar o império na pós-colonidade*, ed. Manuela Ribeiro Sanches (Lisbon: Cotovia, 2006), 141–92; Frederico Ágoas, "Estado, universidade e ciências sociais: A introdução da sociologia na Escola Superior Colonial (1952–1972)," in *O império colonial em questão* (Lisbon: Ed. 70, 2012), 317–48. The Junta de Investigações do Ultramar (Overseas Research Board) gathered together several research institutes, missions, institutes, and brigades.

48. Rita-Ferreira, *Africanos de Lourenço Marques*, 177.

49. Ibid., 180. In the debate with Marvin Harris at the *Journal of the International African Institute* on Mozambican emigration and labor policy,

Rita-Ferreira employed a similar culturalist argument to justify populational displacements. António Rita-Ferreira, "Labour Emigration among the Moçambique Thonga: Comments on a study by Marvin Harris," *Africa: Journal of the International African Institute* 30, no. 2 (April 1960): 141–52.

50. According to Penvenne, the number of domestic servants grew from 9,500 in 1940 to 20,000 in 1960. It was common for the middle class to have three servants. Jeanne Marie Penvenne, *African Workers and Colonial Racism: Mozambican Strategies and Struggles in Lourenço Marques, 1877–1962* (London: James Currey, 1995), 142–43.

51. Led by the mayor, Guilherme Azevedo, and by Augusto da Lima Vida, president of the Câmara do Comércio (Chamber of Commerce)

52. The journalist and founder of Grémio Africano de Lourenço Marques and of the newspapers *O africano* and *O brado africano*, João Albasini, analyzed this commission's report in *O brado africano* In Durban, in the four compounds located near their workplaces, there lived six thousand indígenas, who slept in bunk beds placed in rooms that accommodated thirty to seventy individuals. The most "evolved" possessed their own quarters. There were bathrooms, showers, and toilets. Workers paid for their accommodation as well as for food, which was dispensed in eating houses. Women had their own quarters. It was the municipality's responsibility to oversee the eating houses, food and beverages (e.g., offering low-alcohol beer), as well as the hiring processes and salaries. João Albasini agreed with this rationalization of work; he only lamented that the South African solution for controlling alcohol intake had been rejected by the commission. *O brado africano*, 13/5/16, 1.

53. Valdemir Zamparoni, "Entre Narros e Mulungos: Colonialismo e paisagem social em Lourenço Marques, c. 1890–c. 1940" (PhD diss., Faculdade Letras e Ciências Humanas da Universidade de São Paulo, 1998), 318. In 1936 the *delegado de saúde da região* (regional health delegate) pointed out that the renting of these houses had proved a failure, perhaps, he suggested, because it was expensive. *O brado africano* suggested that the problem was the lack of a backyard, a key element in the everyday of the indígenas recently arrived from the countryside. At that point, the construction of a new indígena neighborhood had already been announced. The *Brado africano* journalist considered it an example of the imposition of a Transvaalian segregation model. *O brado africano*, 22/2/1936, 1.

54. *O brado africano*, 4/6/21, 1.

55. Decreto no. 312, 4/12/22.

56. With the exception of state employees, domestic servants, commercial and office workers, foremen, and individuals who had completed primary education. Rita-Ferreira, *Os Africanos de Lourenço Marques*, 198.

57. Ibid.

58. Zamparoni, "Entre Narros e Mulungos," 320.

59. Portaria 332, 5/6/26.

60. Decreto 616, 16/11/38.

61. Diploma legislativo [Legislative Diploma] 616, 16/11/38.

62. The neighborhood only had 362 houses, 240 of which had only one bedroom. *O brado africano* 20/7/40. The Chefe da Repartição Técnica de Obras Públicas de Lourenço Marques (Lourenço Marques Head of Public Works, Technical Division) made several visits to Johannesburg during the neighborhood's planning stage, AHM, DSAC, Administração, caixa 134, Bairro Indígena. AHM, DSAC, Administração, Fundo Administração Civil. Assuntos Municipais e dos seus organismos autónomos. Câmara Municipal de Lourenço Marques—1937–1938, caixa 134, Bairro Indígena, Carta da Secção Provincial da Administração Civil da Província do Sul do Save sobre a dissolução da Comissão para a Construção de Pousadas e Bairros Indígenas, 30/12/40.

63. Approved, respectively, by portarias 4950, 19/12/42; 5565, 12/5/44. According to these regulations and the Estatuto dos Indígenas (Indígenas Statute) of 1954, it was a criminal offense for healthy young people over eighteen not to sell their work. Unemployment was considered a crime. As a penalty for these infractions, the state condemned transgressors to periods of forced labor.

64. Penvenne, *African Workers*, 137.

65. Ibid., 142. In 1949 the new servants' regulation attenuated some of the existing restrictions on mobility. Portaria 7798, 2/4/49.

66. Portaria 6490, 15/6/46. The Lei Orgânica do Ultramar (Overseas Organic Law) of 1953 and the new indígena statute of 1954 allowed indígenas access to property as long as they opted for common law and a municipal judge granted them this option. However, in practice, multiple bureaucratic complications obstructed this possibility.

67. Created in 1944, the office changed its name to Gabinete de Urbanização do Ultramar (Office for Overseas Urbanization) in 1951. It was extinguished in 1957, when its services were transferred to the Direcção dos Serviços de Urbanismo e Habitação (Urbanization and Housing Services Directorate) of the Ministério do Ultramar (Overseas Ministry).

68. João de Sousa Morais, *Maputo: Património da estrutura e forma urbana topologia do lugar* (Lisbon: Livros Horizonte, 2001), 161.

69. João António de Aguiar, *L'habitation dans les pays tropicaux* (Lisbon: Federation internationale de l'Habitation et de l'urbanisme [XX° Congrès], 1952).

70. Ibid., 23.

71. *Notícias*, 26/8/61.

72. Ibid.

73. Decretos n.°s 44 309 e 44 310 de 27/4/62, Lourenço Marques, Imprensa Nacional de Moçambique, 1962.

74. According to article 3 of the code, "unskilled manual workers in activities linked with agricultural exploration and produce collection or those activities that make such exploration possible."

75. From 1966 onward, domestic-service workers were framed by their own set of regulations, an attempt to regulate an activity that relied heavily on informal relations. Regulamento dos empregados domésticos, diploma legislativo n.° 2702, 30/5/66.

76. António Rita-Ferreira, "Estudo sobre a evolução, em Moçambique, da mão-de-obra e das remunerações, no sector privado, de 1950 a 1970," *Indústria de Moçambique* 6, no. 5 (1973): 139. An editorial in *Indústria de Moçambique* considered the Código do Trabalho (Labor Code) "a progressive legal instrument, and one that is malleable enough to cover labor force policies adapted to the times and to sociological realities, and even to be called on to address aspects that lie beyond the framework of legal relations that it was meant to encompass," but thought the 1959 law was outdated, given the "swift evolution of sociological labour relations." The l diploma legislativo n.º 57/71 changed some of these dispositions. Ibid., 127. This, however, failed to solve the problem: what was needed was a "regime so wide and malleable that it may cover the diversity and dynamism of the underlying sociological reality, with no hiatuses at company level."

77. Decreto 44 111, 21/12/61.
78. "Economia e educação," *Indústria de Moçambique*, no. 5 (1972): 127.
79. Pancho Guedes, "A cidade doente," *A tribuna*, 9/6/73, 6–7.
80. Ibid.
81. Torre do Tombo (TT), Fundo dos Serviços de Centralização e Coordenação de Informações de Moçambique, Centro de Documentação, Processos de Informação sobre Política Social, 1960–1972. O Problema Habitacional nos bairros suburbanos, Bairros suburbanos de Moçambique. Estudo elaborado por elementos do Grupo Central de Trabalhos. PT-TT SCCIM/A/6/7. Among the members of this group were the Associação Africana (African Association), the Centro Associativos dos Negros de Moçambique (Associative Centre for Mozambican Blacks), the newspaper *A tribuna*, Rádio Clube de Moçambique, and individuals such as Domingos Arouca, president of the Centro Associativo dos Negros and later arrested, in 1965, when the center was closed. Ibid., 3.
82. "Estudo elaborado por elementos do Grupo Central de Trabalhos," PT-TT SCCIM/A/6/7, 21.
83. Ibid., 54
84. This study sought to interpret the differences between the various suburban populations, separating the "economically fragile" (earning over MZE 1,800 per year) from the "sub-economically fragile" (MZE 1,800). "O Problema Habitacional dos Economicamente Débeis, Estudo elaborado por elementos do Grupo Central de Trabalhos," PT-TT SCCIM/A/6/7, 34.
85. Ibid., 25.
86. Ibid., 26.
87. Ibid., 23.
88. Ibid., 22.
89. Ibid., 31. On the land policies in Mozambique, see Bárbara Direito, "Land and Colonialism in Mozambique: Policies and Practice in Inhambane, c. 1900–c.1940," *Journal of Southern African Studies* 39, no. 2 (2013): 353–69.
90. Ibid., 23.
91. Rita-Ferreira, *Africanos de Lourenço Marques*, 434.

92. Morais, *Maputo*, 173. In 1963 the architect Pancho Guedes published an urban manifesto in the newspaper *A tribuna*, in which he criticized the official urban politics (or lack thereof) for the suburbs. He proposed a general intervention plan for the caniço. His main objective was to create the conditions that would unite a city that was continuing to grow divided. *A tribuna*, 9/6/63, 7.

93. This new architectural practice was synthesized in Mário de Oliveira's, *Problemas essenciais do urbanismo do ultramar* (Lisbon: Agência-Geral do Ultramar, 1962). In the 1950s urbanism became a tool for social insertion policies. Within a context of indígena-labor regulation, colonial urban planning aimed to create the conditions necessary for people from different origins to live together. This policy was supported by the creation of the Junta de Povoamento (Settlement Board), decreto 43 895, 6/9/1961.

94. Rita-Ferreira, *Africanos de Lourenço Marques*, 203. The III Plano de Fomento (Development Plan) stated that Lourenço Marques would need thirty-five thousand extra housing units, even though only sixty-seven hundred units were projected, in land yet to be expropriated. Ibid., 205.

95. Mendes, *Maputo*, 419.

96. Decreto 48 860, 22/2/69.

97. On 29 November. Mário Azevedo, *O plano director de urbanização de Lourenço Marques* (Lourenço Marques: Separata do Boletim no. 7 da Câmara Municipal de Lourenço Marques, 1969).

98. Morais, *Maputo*, 172. The architect José Bruschy headed the Gabinete de Urbanização de Lourenço Marques (Lourenço Marques Urban Planning Cabinet), a position he held between 1967 and 1973.

99. As the plan phrased it, "the set of housing clusters, of a spontaneous or undisciplined nature, with precarious materials, or according to traditional building methods, transposed from *indígena* rural and communitarian life onto the urban context which they are trying to integrate." Azevedo, *Plano director*, 19.

100. Carried out by a task force of technicians from the metropolis, led by the sociologist José Carlos Bizarro Mercier Marques, a graduate of the Instituto Superior de Ciências Sociais e Políticas Ultramarinas (Higher Institute for Overseas Social and Political Sciences), and member of the Gabinete de Urbanização e Habitação de Lourenço Marques (Lourenço Marques Urban Planning and Housing Cabinet), AHM, pasta U/9a—Obras Públicas e Transportes, Gabinete de Urbanização, 1969–73, Informação ao Governador Geral do Director do Gabinete de Urbanização, Rogério da Cunha e Sá, 17/12/69.

101. Rita-Ferreira, for example, rejected the process of expropriation of the suburb for the construction of houses by the state, defending instead that official entities should construct basic infrastructures, leaving the rest in the hands of the inhabitants' initiative. António Rita-Ferreira, "O problema habitacional dos Africanos de Lourenço Marques," *Indústria de Moçambique* 3, no. 5 (May 1970): 176–78.

102. One of the aspects of this plan was the construction of various sports facilities in the «reed», such as swimming tanks and outdoor gyms, which fell within the scope of the action of Noronha Feio as head of the Conselho Provincial de Educação Física (Physical Education Provincial Council; ACPEFM), folder 414-C, Actas das Reuniões do Gabinete de Urbanização de Lourenço Marques.

103. Rita-Ferreira, *Africanos de Lourenço Marques*, 191.

104. Diploma legislativo 2023, 5/11/61.

105. Rita-Ferreira, *Africanos de Lourenço Marques*, 244.

106. Ibid., 365.

107. Ibid., 347.

108. Ibid., 346.

109. Of the 6,418 Africans employed in the administration, 4,596 (71.6 percent) occupied the two lowest professional categories, 5,446 (84.9 percent) were to be found among the three least qualified, and 5,872 (91.5 percent) among the four least qualified. There were no Africans among the higher categories and very few in the intermediary ones. Ibid., 343.

110. Jeanne Marie Penvenne, "'Here Everyone Walked with Fear': The Mozambican Labor System and the Workers of Lourenco Marques, 1945–1962," in Cooper, *Struggle for the City*, 157–58.

111. These activities broke the colonial state's law. According to a 1927 law, to engage in commerce with the same rights as a European, Africans had to speak Portuguese, abandon indígena customs, and be trained in a commercial or industrial profession. Diploma 36, 12/11/27. Finally, they had to hold the status of assimilado. This legal disposition was in force until the end of the indigenato; subsequently, the marginalization of the African small retailer was preserved through bureaucracy and taxes. Rita-Ferreira, *Africanos de Lourenço Marques*, 365.

112. Penvenne, "'Here Everyone Walked,'" 142–44; Rita-Ferreira, *Africanos de Lourenço Marques*, 361, 131–66.

113. Penvenne, "'Here Everyone Walked,'" 142–43.

114. Ibid., 156.

115. Penvenne, *African Workers*, 143; Penvenne, *Women, Migration and the Cashew Economy in Southern Mozambique: 1945–1975* (Rochester: James Currey, 2015), 95.

116. James C. Scott, *Domination and the Arts of Resistance: Hidden Transcripts* (New Haven: Yale University Press, 1990), 2–17.

117. Ibid., 45–68.

118. On the development of networks of prostitution both in the suburbs and in the cement city, see Zamparoni, "Entre Narros e Mulungos," 350–63.

119. José Capela, *Vinho para o preto* (Porto: Afrontamento, 1973); M. Goretti Matias, "A questão do álcool e a exportação de vinho para o ultramar: O debate de 1902," in *O douro contemporâneo*, ed. Gaspar Martins Pereira and Paula Montes Leal (Porto: Grupo de Estudos de História da Viticultura Duriense, 2006), 233–46.

120. *O brado africano*, 5/2/55, 1.
121. Guedes, "Caniços of Mozambique," 206.
122. Referring to the daily roles played by performative activities in the Johannesburg's suburbs, David Coplan comments, "The concert parties, dances, and shebeens not only provided the kind of communal diversion which made life more bearable; they also created expressive cultural images which served as repositories for emerging social value systems." Coplan,"The African Musician and the Development of the Johannesburg Entertainment Industry, 1900–1960," *Journal of Southern African Studies* 5, no. 2 (April 1979): 141.
123. In 1926, both in the newspaper's Portuguese and Ronga sections, several articles made reference to these suburban matches. See *O brado africano*, 12/6/26, 1, and 3/7/26, 3.
124. *O africano*, 28/10/1911, 9.
125. *O africano*, 1/3/1912, 3. There was a local beer, associated with the producers of Castle Beer, that was called Esperanto. Following a different line of inquiry, the Durban newspaper *Llange lase Natal* ran several articles in 1907 and 1908 on the formation of a Club Esperanto in Durban, promoted by the reverend William Cullen Wilcox of the American Zulu mission, created in 1835. Wilcox, who had close ties with John Dube, the founder of the African National Congress in 1912, did his first missionary work in Mozambique (Inhambane), where he served between 1881 and 1896. Simangaliso Kumalo, "Meeting the Cowboy Turned Renegade Missionary: William Cullen Wilcox," *Studia historiae ecclesiastica* 39, suppl. (August 2013): 337–52.
126. *O brado africano*,19/7/1919, 2.
127. *O brado africano*,14/1/1920, 3.
128. The presence of Catholic missions in the region was a reaction to the Protestant's presence and actions. Until 1882, Catholic missionary work was directed only to Europeans, Goans, and "assimilados." David Hedges, ed., *História de Moçambique*, 2 vols. (Maputo: Livraria Universitária de Maputo, 1999), 2:15. Catholic Missions of African and Timor statutes, approved in 13/10/26, by decreto 12 485 did not mention any initiative related to physical education or sport (art. 21). In 1929 the government protected the Catholic missions' activities and imposed Portuguese as the idiom of religious rituals and education by diplomas legislativos 167 and 168, 3/8/29. The Missionary Statute of 1941 reified the main missionary principles: nationalization and moralization of the indígenas and their acquisition of working habits.
129. E. A. Azambuja Martins, *Acção educativa sôbre as populações indígenas de Moçambique, consequente de instrução militar do soldado indígena* (Lisbon: I Congresso da História da Expansão Portuguesa no Mundo, 1938), 16–17.
130. S. José Mission was founded in 1892. The mission increased its activity during the 1920s and 1930s. Its head, D. António Barroso, described, in that very year, in a letter sent to the minister of the navy and overseas, the guiding principles of its missionary work: "The major goal of this mission is to civilize the blacks in the district, and particularly those in the city, through agriculture and shopwork, where professional training is offered to indígenas, thus establishing

in that region a Portuguese and Catholic influence to counter the English and Protestant influence that has been gaining ground." *Relatório da Missão de S. José de Lhanguene* 1942, 5. Facing many difficulties at first, this mission expanded its activity from the 1920s and 1930s, when it built several schools workshops. In 1942 the mission had under its jurisdiction a vast area around Lourenço Marques. Ibid. From 1927 the mission published the newspaper *O evangelho*.

131. Bernard Cohn, *Colonialism and Its Forms of Knowledge: The British in India* (Princeton: Princeton University Press, 1996).

132. Mendes, *Maputo*, 64.

133. Patrick Harries, *Work, Culture, and Identity: Migrant Laborers in Mozambique and South Africa, c. 1860–1910* (Portsmouth, NH: Heinemann, 1993), 99–103.

134. John Nauright, *Sports, Cultures and Identities in South Africa* (London: Leicester University Press, 1997), 102–4, Peter Alegi, *Laduma! Soccer, Politics and Society in South Africa* (Natal: University of KwaZulu-Natal Press, 2004), 15–18. The first black sports association in South Africa, the South African Coloured Rugby Football Board, was created in 1897. In Rhodesia, the game was passed on by miners who worked in Transvaal. Richard Giulianotti, "Between Colonialism, Independence and Globalization: Football in Zimbabwe," in Armstrong and Giulianotti, *Football in Africa*, 82.

135. Football matches organized near the Swiss mission in Lourenço Marques were a component of some Mozambican players' childhoods, such as Mário Coluna or Vicente Lucas. Renato Caldeira, *Coluna, o monstro sagrado* (Maputo: Edisport, 2003), 20. Missions were an important focus point of football's dissemination in Africa. Hans Hognestad and Arvid Tollisen, "Playing against Deprivation: Football and Development in Nairobi, Kenya," in Armstrong and Giulianotti, *Football in Africa*, 220; Wiebe Boer, "A Story of Heroes, of Epics: The Rise of Football in Nigeria," in Armstrong and Giulianotti, *Football in Africa*, 66; Laura Fair, "Ngoma Reverberations: Swahili Music Culture and the Making of Football Aesthetics in Early Twentieth-Century Zanzibar," in Armstrong and Giulianotti, *Football in Africa*, 103–13.

136. Literally "kill the beast," which means eating a light meal to "kill the hunger."

137. Literally "sticks." One pau equaled one escudo.

138. Gary Armstrong, "The Migration of the Black Panther: An Interview with Eusébio of Mozambique and Portugal," in Armstrong and Giulianotti, *Football in Africa*, 253–54.

139. On the music scene in Lourenço Marques, see António Sopa, *A alegria é uma coisa rara: Subsídios para a história da música popular urbana em Lourenço Marques (1920–1975)* (Maputo: Marimbique, 2014).

140. There were historical links between the Comoro Islands and the north of Mozambique, based on the slave trade and other trade routes. Edward Alpers, "A Complex Relationship: Mozambique and the Comoro Islands in the Nineteenth and Twentieth Centuries," *Cahiers d'études africaines* 41, no. 161 (2001): 75.

141. The first Muslim school in Lourenço Marques, the Escola Mahometana Madrassá Islamia, was founded in 1903.

142. Valdemir Zamparoni, "Monhés, baneanes, chinas e Afro-maometanos: Colonialismo e racismo em Lourenço Marques, Moçambique, 1890–1940," *Lusotopie* (2000): 214–15. Descendants from Indian and Arab traders whose presence in southern Mozambique had been felt since the end of the nineteenth century, these Muslims came from different backgrounds: the offspring of an Indian father and a black mother; the offspring of an Indian father and mestiço mother, or blacks who had converted to Islam. Raúl Bernardo Honwana, *Memórias* (Porto: Edições ASA, 1989), 72.

143. See Lorenzo Macagno, *Outros muçulmanos: Islão e narrativas coloniais* (Lisbon: Imprensa de Ciências Sociais, 2006), 144.

144. Zamparoni, "Monhés, baneanes," 214.

145. Ibid., 214–15.

146. ACPEFM, Processo do Grupo Desportivo Beira-Mar (no. 177), "Discurso proferido no Acto de Apresentação dos nossos trabalhos em 29 de Março de 1970." I did not find any other reference to Tigre Gulama. If instead of "Gulama" the word was "Gulamo" there is a range of possible Muslim connections. Gulamo was a relatively common name. In the same period, in the Macua territory, for instance, a Muslim khalifa was called Muhamade Amade Gulamo. Alpers, "Complex Relationship," 86.

147. Patrick Harries, "Christianity in Black and White: The Establishment of Protestant Churches in Southern Mozambique," *Lusotopie* (1998), 195. Valdemir Zamparoni introduced the name Primrose in a different context. In 1922 the city of Beira's police arrested two Mozambican miners who had just returned from Cape Town. They were both members of the Universal Negro Improvement Association and African Communities (Imperial) League, led by Marcus Garvey, and attended its headquarters in Cape Town's Primrose Street. There were several Mozambican miners in this association. Zamparoni, "Entre Narros e Mulungos," 166–68.

148. The first records of African football matches show the existence of a club named New King, latter converted to Novo Rei, its Portuguese equivalent.

149. ACPEFM, Processo do Grupo Desportivo Beira-Mar (n.° 177) "Discurso proferido no Acto de Apresentação dos nossos trabalhos em 29 de Março de 1970."

150. On João Albasini, see Penvenne, "João dos Santos Albasini."

151. *O africano*, 22/10/1922, 3.

152. Zamparoni, "Entre Narros e Mulungos," 507.

153. Aurélio Rocha, *Associativismo e nativismo em Moçambique: Contribuição para o estudo das origens do nacionalismo moçambicano (1900–1940)* (Maputo: Promédia, 2002), 225. This church, which had more than eighty missions in the region, was connected to the movement of independent churches in South Africa. Harries, "Christianity," 332. The messianic churches were established in the south of Mozambique during the first two decades of the twentieth century. Rocha, *Associativismo e nativismo*, 72–73.

154. During an interview given to the sports newspaper A *equipa*, the club's president, Inácio Tomé Magaia, reported that the expression *azar* (bad luck) in the club's name came from a traditional song that said "the bad luck that bad luck has." Originally this "bad luck" was related to the unfortunate destruction of a new game ball from Lisbon under a local truck. Though the club's direction wanted to suppress the expression, the supporters fought for its permanence. A *equipa*, 1/67, 8.

155. Among its founders were important members of GALM, such as Eugénio da Silva Júnior, a typographer, responsible for O *brado africano*'s Ronga section; Francisco de Haan, a former railway employee; and Francisco Benfica, also a typographer.

156. O *brado africano*, 3/1/31, 1–2.

157. O *brado africano*, 10/1/31, 2.

158. In 1931, AFA's board of directors included leading members of GALM, such as its president, Miguel da Mata, and Gabriel Malta, its vice president. Other GALM members, such as Francisco Dias Morgado and António dos Santos Ceita, were responsible for a technical commission that dealt with sporting affairs.

159. O *brado africano*, 3/1/31, 1–2.

160. Pereira was also Vasco da Gama's president. The meeting that signaled the statutes' approval was attended by Francisco Xavier Oliveira (Munhuanense Azar), Simões da Costa Correia (Nova Aliança), Jorge Rodolfo Poitevin (Atlético Mahometano), Chopes Manecas (Sport Nacional Africano), Joaquim Domingos (Atlético Luso-Africano), Luís Inhambisse (Grupo Desportivo Beirense), António Pascoal (Alto Mar Nhafoco) António dos Santos Ceita (Beira-Mar), Taybot Parsotam Tricamo (Mahafil Isslamo), Samson Augusto Simões (São José), and Victor Tavares (João Albasini).

161. São José was constituted by educated blacks, under the supervision of the Catholic Church. Various GALM members were educated at the mission, the only one that celebrated São Benedito, a black saint cherished by the pan-African movement. Rocha, *Associativismo e nativismo*, 327n63.

162. Lourenço Marques's urban black population reached 28,300 individuals in 1930, including 14,950 from the province of Lourenço Marques, 2,872 from Inhambane, 617 from Quelimane, 627 from Mozambique, 417 from Manica and Sofala, and 416 from Tete. Rocha, *Associativismo e nativismo*, 114.

163. Torre do Tombo (TT), Fundo dos Serviços de Centralização e Coordenação de Informações de Moçambique, Centro de Documentação, Processos de Informação sobre Associações Recreativas e Culturais. Associações onde predominam elementos de cor, Informações recebidas sobre a Associação Afro-Mahometana de Lourenço Marques, PT-TT SCCIM/A/3/3, no. 41.

164. O *brado africano*, 2/3/35, 1.

165. Zamparoni, "Entre Narros e Mulungos," 436; Hedges, *História de Moçambique*, 2:61; Rocha, *Associativismo e nativismo*, 37. DSAC's files show the enduring links between Instituto Negrófilo and GALM and the colonial administration. AHM, DSAC, secção A, Administração, Agremiações regionais de recreio, defesa, desporto e estudo, Associações Desportivas, Recreativas

e Culturais, caixa 3, processo 27/38 Associação Africana da Província de Moçambique—1916–1971, and caixa 12, processo 27/70—Centro Associativo dos Negros da Província de Moçambique). In 1937 the imposition of the Corporative Law on the colonies attributed official exclusivity to terms such as Grémio or Institute. Therefore, the Instituto Negrófilo became the Centro Associativo dos Negros de Moçambique (Associative Center of the Mozambican Black) and GALM became the Associação Africana de Lourenço Marques (Lourenço Marques African Association).

166. Zamparoni argues that what lay behind the less rigid conception of assimilation presented in the 1927 law, when compared with the 1917 edict, was precisely the aim to create a class of assimilated blacks that would lead to a schism within the African associative movement. Zamparoni, "Entre Narros e Mulungos," 476–77.

167. The African associative movement in Lourenço Marques was not able to answer a variety of problems felt by African workers. Still, GALM was connected to the only African labor association in the city, the União dos Trabalhadores Africanos (African Workers' Union), founded in 1911. This project would soon come to an end. Rocha, *Associativismo e nativismo*, 193. Lourenço Marques's class-based organizations, which were numerous during the first two decades of the century, were directed exclusively at European workers. José Capela, *O movimento operário em Lourenço Marques, 1898–1927* (Porto: Afrontamento, 1984), 37.

168. AHM, DSAC, secção A, administração, Administração Civil, Agremiações regionais de recreio, defesa, desporto e estudo. Associações Desportivas, Recreativas e Culturais 1934–1971, caixa 16, processo 27/97—Grupo Desportivo Beirense, 1936–1950, Informação da DSAC, 29/4/1940.

169. As were the cases of Grémio Educativo de Moçambique (21/11/1937), the Grémio Luso-Africano de Tete, and the Grupo Desportivo Nova-Aliança de Lourenço Marques. 1937. AHM, DSAC, secção A, Administração, Agremiações regionais de recreio, defesa, desporto e estudo. Associações Desportivas, Recreativas e Culturais, caixa 16.

170. AHM, DSAC, secção A, administração, Administração Civil, Agremiações regionais de recreio, defesa, desporto e estudo, Associações Desportivas, Recreativas e Culturais 1934–71, caixa 16, processo 27/97—Grupo Desportivo Beirense, 1936–50, Carta do Governador da Província, em 7 de Setembro de 1940, à DSAC transcrevendo uma nota do Administrador do Concelho de Lourenço Marques.

171. The hypothetical connections to Protestant churches led the colonial administration to investigate several African associations, such as the Grémio Educativo de Moçambique, the Grémio Luso-Africano de Tete, and the Clube Desportivo Nova Aliança de Lourenço Marques. AHM, DSAC, secção A, administração, Administração Civil, Agremiações regionais de recreio, defesa, desporto e estudo, Associações Desportivas, Recreativas e Culturais, caixa 16, União dos Negros Lusitanos. Aprovação dos Estatutos em 1936–37.

172. Beirense's and Gazense's cases were, however, exceptions. Individual processes organized by the DSAC and Serviço dos Negócios Indígenas

(Native Affairs Service) on African clubs did not include, in most cases, more than one copy of their statutes and a list of their directing bodies.

173. AHM, DSNI, secção A, administração, Administração Civil, Agremiações regionais de recreio, defesa, desporto e estudo, Associações Desportivas, Recreativas e Culturais, caixa 2, Processo Associação Africana de Inhambane, Carta do Chefe da Repartição Central dos Negócios Indígenas, A. Montanha ao Secretário-Geral dos Negócios Indígenas, 12/10/49.

174. *O brado africano*, 20/7/35, 2.

175. *O brado africano*, 16/5/36, 3.

176. *O brado africano*, 18/6/32, 1.

177. José Manuel's speech, on behalf of the Centro dos Negros de Moçambique (Center for Mozambican Blacks) was, on that occasion, profoundly servile. *O brado africano*, 24/6/39, 1.

178. James Scott uses the term "rituals of subordination" to define one of the mechanisms that confirm, within what he calls the "public transcript," relations of social domination. Scott, *Domination and the Arts*, 66.

179. *O brado africano*, 19/3/39, 1.

180. The preponderance of local notables in the sports movement's leadership, people whose notability was bolstered by colonialism, reproduces the institutionalization pattern of black sports in South Africa. Nauright, *Sports, Cultures*, 55. Nauright argues for the importance of this "class" during the development of black sport in South Africa, from the end of the nineteenth century. Sport was a means of integration for an African "petite bourgeoisie," educated by the missions. Part of the South African black political elite grew up under the moral discipline infused by British sport. Since the beginning of the twentieth century segregation policies led Africans to organize their own clubs and competitions. In 1898 the Orange Free State Bantu Soccer Club was founded in 1930, followed by the Orange Free State Bantu Soccer Association, and the South African Bantu Soccer Association (which in 1933 had delegations in Transvaal, the Orange Free State, Natal, and the Northern Cape) and, in 1932, the JAFA (Johannesburg African Football Association). Ibid., 104–7.

181. José Magode, *Pouvoir et réseaux sociaux au Mozambique, Appartenances, interactivité du social et du politique (1933–1994)* (Paris: Éditions Connaissances et Savoirs, 2005), 119. These individuals, axes of social networks, were designated, as Ulf Hannerz puts it, by different expressions: "the evolues, the assimilados, the brown sahibs, the Afro-saxons." Hannerz, *Transnational Connections: Culture, People, Places* (London: Routledge 1996), 72.

182. *Relatório do governador geral de Moçambique (1945)* 1940–31/12/43, General José Tristão da Cunha, 2 vols. (Lisbon: Divisão de Publicações e Bibliotecas, Agência Geral das Colónias 1945), 2:317.

183. Ibid., 316.

184. The concept "community of readers" was proposed by Janice Radway, *Reading the Romance: Women, Patriarchy, and Popular Literature* (Chapel Hill: University of North Carolina Press, 1984).

185. *O brado africano*, 6/5/33, 2.

186. P. Martin, *Leisure and Society*, 118.

187. As were the cases of Grupo Desportivo João Albasini, Beira-Mar, and Sport Nacional Africano.

188. *O brado africano*, 10/7/43, 5.

189. The *uputo* mentioned by Vicente is a traditional beer made from fermented corn. The name is probably a derivative from *wuptusu*. Eduardo Medeiros, *Bebidas Moçambicanas de fabrico caseiro* (Maputo: Arquivo Histórico de Moçambique, 1988).

190. Penvenne, "'Here Everyone Walked,'" 123.

191. António Rita-Ferreira, "A oscilação do trabalhador africano entre o meio rural e o meio urbano," *Indústria de Moçambique* 2, no. 3 (1969): 98.

192. António Rita-Ferreira, "Distribuição ocupacional da população africana de Lourenço Marques," *Indústria de Moçambique* 2, no. 6 (1969): 200.

193. Ibid.

194. AHM, DSAC, secção A, administração, Administração Civil, Agremiações regionais de recreio, defesa, desporto e estudo, Associações Desportivas, Recreativas e Culturais 1934–71, caixa 16, processo 27/97—Grupo Desportivo Beirense, 1936–50, Carta do Governador da Província, em 7 de Setembro de 1940, à DSAC transcrevendo uma nota do Administrador do Concelho de Lourenço Marques.

195. Information given by the club's president to the sports newspaper *A equipa*, 29/12/66, 1.

196. In the beginning of the season, as Saide Mogne describes it, players chose their clubs during the so-called preparation tournaments: "I went to the pitch and registered with one club and played. The next Sunday I would register with another club, and so on, until I chose the best one." On one occasion, Mogne changed clubs because that was the wish of his fiancé's family, who lived in a different neighborhood than his.

197. In 1939 the first official match between the teams representing the Munhana and Chamanculo districts was announced. *O brado africano*, 22/4/39, 3.

198. Zamparoni, "Entre Narros e Mulungos," 505–20; Sopa, *A alegria*. During the first decades of the century the most luxurious parties were the dance balls given by the Athletic Club. GALM, Atlético, and Vasco da Gama's gatherings featured jazz bands. These balls and concerts included jazz music, polkas, "rondas," Cape Verde's "mornas," and Mozambican "marrabenta." Rocha, *Associativismo e nativismo*, 326n58.

199. Rocha, *Associativismo e nativismo*, 326n58.

200. Zamparoni, "Entre Narros e Mulungos," 332–64.

201. *O brado africano*, 6/5/33, 2.

202. On 12/7/1930, *O brado africano* announced the first match between Lourenço Marques and Johannesburg.

203. In 1934 the Nova Aliança went to Johannesburg to play against the Bantu Men's Social Centre, one of the oldest black clubs in South Africa. *O brado africano*, 29/9/34, 2. The Bantu was founded in 1924 by Ray Philips, a missionary. Alegi, *Laduma*, 42.

204. The All-Blacks was a mining club that belonged to the Witwatersrand District Native Football Association. Alegi, *Laduma*, 40.

205. Benedict Anderson, *Imagined Communities: Reflections on the Origin and Spread of Nationalism* (London: Verso, 1991).

206. In 1936 the All-Blacks Football Club from Johannesburg beat the AFA team 8–3. Several articles in *O brado africano* voiced general dissatisfaction regarding the players' selection.

207. Beira-Mar was the first African club to leave Lourenço Marques, playing at Inhambane.

208. Referring to black South African suburbs, Alegi uses the phrase "cultural autonomy." Alegi, *Laduma*, 54–55.

209. *O brado africano*, 30/3/35, 2.

210. Mendes, *Maputo*.

CHAPTER 4: A SUBURBAN STYLE OF PLAY

1. António Rita-Ferreira, *Os Africanos de Lourenço Marques*, Memórias do Instituto de Investigação Científica de Moçambique / Instituto de Investigação Científica de Moçambique, vol. 9, series C (1967–68), 417.

2. Contrary to the aspirations of the organizers of the cricket match that Gary Kildea and Jerry Leach filmed in the Trobriand Islands, in the context of the institutionalization of football in the black suburbs of Lourenço Marques, it was not a case of reinventing a sports practice as a way of promoting a nationalist political agenda of a culturalist nature, to counter a sports practice promoted by the colonizer. Kildea and Leach, *Trobriand Cricket: An Indigenous Response to Colonialism* (Royal Anthropological Institute, 1974), DVD.

3. One of the most original adaptations was based on the principle that a certain number of corners were equivalent to a goal. AHM, DSAC, secção A—Administração Civil, Agremiações regionais de recreio, defesa, desporto e estudo. Associações Desportivas, Recreativas e Culturais, caixa 14, processo 27/115, Assunto Grupo Desportivo Beira Mar 1934–71, Regulamento da AFA (AFA regulations), 1935.

4. Approved by portaria 2:283, 1/8/1934.

5. In the words of Norbert Elias and Eric Dunning, "without agreement among the players on their adherence to a unified set of rules, the game would not be a game but a 'free-for-all.'" Elias and Dunning, "Dynamics of Group Sports with Special Reference to Football," *British Journal of Sociology* 17, no. 4 (1966): 389.

6. The importance of the law was further acknowledged in the statutes of the AFA governing bodies, in the rules that framed discussions within its board meetings, as well as in the disciplinary principles presiding over its general assemblies.

7. Jack Goody, *The Logic of Writing and the Organization of Society: Studies in Literacy, Family, Culture and the State* (Cambridge: Cambridge University Press, 1986).

8. According to the AFA statutes, the referees would be examined by a theoretical and a practical test on the Portuguese Football Federation's rules. The AFA's technical council could issue internal regulations, offer explanations and elaborate reports, examine referees, confer diplomas and oversee player registration.

9. August 10, 1935, *O brado africano* announced that Francisco de Haan would give a lecture on the authority of the referee. On September 14, 1935, the same newspaper advertised a lecture by António Maria Pereira, the then AFA president, on the offside rule. *O brado africano*, 14/9/35, 3.

10. AHM, DSAC, caixa 14, processo 27/115, Assunto Grupo Desportivo Beira Mar 1934–1971, Regulamento da AFA.

11. The AFA regulation, which dictated the structure, duration, and classification of the competition, was also set out to deal with numerous other situations, such as the need to repeat a match (e.g., due to lack of light on the pitch or poor weather conditions) or complaints regarding technical issues (which would be reviewed by the technical council). Teams that were late to a match had only a fifteen-minute tolerance, after which they would forfeit the match. Any team that left the pitch before the end of the game would lose its share of the match's profits. The regulation established sanctions for players who were not duly registered, or any conduct outside the rules of the game (from a simple reprimand to expulsion). It also organized the distribution of expenses and profits among the teams. Ibid.

12. Five percent of the income would go to a fund set up to help with regular match expenses: police force, doormen, and other expenses connected with personnel, taxes, advertisement, and healthcare. Ibid.

13. *Eco dos sports*, 21/6/38, 4. Matsinhe was president of Sport Nacional Africano.

14. *Eco dos sports*, 21/6/38, 4.

15. *Lourenço Marques Guardian*, 11/9/23, 3.

16. *Lourenço Marques Guardian*, 11/9/23, 4.

17. *Lourenço Marques Guardian*, 5/8/1924, 3.

18. *Relatório do governador geral*, 320–21.

19. *O brado africano*, 6/12/1930, 5.

20. May 2, 1931, *O brado africano* (p. 3) criticized the use of "violence" in the match between Vasco da Gama and João Albasini. In the same AFA tournament, the Beirense team, in their very first outing, used "violent plays." *O brado africano*, 27/6/33, 1.

21. *O brado africano*, 21/9/35, 1.

22. *O brado africano*, 15/8/36, 5.

23. *O brado africano*, 29/8/36, 6.

24. *O brado africano*, 31/10/36, 5.

25. *O brado africano*, 17/10/36, 5.

26. *O brado africano*, 4/9/37, 6. Already on the previous weekend, the AFA competition was "chock-full of accidents." *O brado africano*, 30/8/37, 3.

27. *O brado africano*, 11/9/37, 3.

28. *O brado africano*, 11/12/37, 3.
29. *O brado africano*, 16/4/38, 4.
30. *O brado africano*, 18/6/38, 4.
31. *O brado africano*, 2/7/38, 4.
32. *O brado africano*, 3/10/42, 4.
33. *O brado africano*, 11/12/43, 7.
34. *O brado africano*, 17/3/45, 5.
35. *O brado africano*, 17/3/45, 5.
36. *O brado africano*, 17/9/49, 5.
37. *O brado africano*, 19/11/49, 5.
38. *Guardian desportivo*, 15/4/53, 6–7.

39. The most fervent among Italian football supporters are usually referred to in Italian as Tifosi. The origin of this word is *typhus*, a contagious disease that spreads in impoverished and insalubrious environments. High fever and delirium are among its most common symptoms.

40. In much the same way as certain historians, criticized by E. P. Thompson, had depicted preindustrial "crowds" and "mobs." Thompson, "The Moral Economy of The English Crowd in the Eighteenth Century," *Past and Present* 50, no. 1 (1971): 76–136.

41. *O brado africano*, 18/4/36, 2. Cantine was also a teacher at Sá da Bandeira, a school for indigenous people, and for a short period was also the director of *O brado africano*. Valdemir Zamparoni, "Entre Narros e Mulungos: Colonialismo e paisagem social em Lourenço Marques, c. 1890–c. 1940" (PhD diss., Faculdade Letras e Ciências Humanas da Universidade de São Paulo, 1998), 152.

42. *O brado africano*, 18/4/36, 2.
43. *O brado africano*, 18/4/36, 2.

44. *O brado africano*, 18/4/36, 2. The wordplay in the passage is lost in translation: "discutimos sobre a bola, reunimos para a bola, organizamos soirées dançantes para o desenvolvimento da bola, enterros de muito dinheiro na preparação de campos para a bola. Bolas."

45. *O brado africano*, 18/4/36, 2.

46. *O brado africano*, 18/4/36, 2. Cantine's criticism of a community built around "football, dance, and booze" was replicated in other newspaper articles that championed the respectability of labor and education against the unruly pleasures of the body. See, for instance, Augusto Conrado, "A nossa falsa posição," *O brado africano*, 2/12/39, 3.

47. *O brado africano*, 7/1/50, 4.

48. In 1953, José Manuel, a black assimilated Catholic, whose case will be further addressed in subsequent chapters, recommended gymnastics as an antidote to football: "Sports practice at the mercy of a ball is not in the least beneficial to men. Gymnastics, on the contrary, brings benefits to our health, the perfection of physical improvement for both young and old." *O brado africano*, 3/10/53, 2.

49. *O brado africano*, 19/4/58, 1.

50. The Associação Africana's gymnastic team's expedition to Lisbon, where it took part in a tournament at Ginásio Clube Português, was widely celebrated by *O brado africano* (9/3/63, 1). This trip was possible only because the team received a state subsidy.

51. *O brado africano*, 10/1/59, 7.

52. *O brado africano*, 21/10/57, 7.

53. *O brado africano*, 21/10/57, 7.

54. This seems to be the case with African boxing in Southern Rhodesia, as described by Terence Ranger. The use of sport as a means of social control stopped short of including boxing, a source of public disturbance and the basis for the formation of urban groups that colonial cadres framed under the label "urban tribalism." Ranger, "Pugilism and Pathology: African Boxing and the Black Urban Experience in Southern Rhodesia," in Baker and Mangan, *Sport in Africa*, 204.

55. *O brado africano*, 12/2/1955, 8.

56. *O brado africano*, 6/11/54, 6.

57. Jeanne Marie Penvenne, *African Workers and Colonial Racism: Mozambican Strategies and Struggles in Lourenço Marques, 1877–1962* (London: James Currey, 1995), 126.

58. *Tymba* appears in Padre António Lourenço Farinha's dictionary, meaning precisely "to tie up." Farinha, *Elementos de gramática landina (shironga)* (Lourenço Marques: Imprensa Nacional, 1917), 195.

59. These terms are found in the dictionary of Torre do Valle. *Beketela* is defined as "to tidy up, to place with care; to order; distribute; to store or place in order" (54). *Pandya* is equated with "to crack" (132), and *tymbela* with "to tie up" and "to prepare food with" (167). Torre do Valle, *Diccionarios shironga-portuguez e portuguez-shironga* (Lourenço Marques: Imprensa Nacional, 1906). A decade earlier, Henri Junod also defined *beketela* as tidying up and arranging in order (68). Junod, *Grammaire ronga* (Lausanne: Georges Bridel, 1896). Rodrigo de Sá Nogueira adds nothing to the meaning of *beketela*. To the definition of *pandya* he adds "to gash" and "to tear" (397). Nogueira, *Dicionário ronga-portugues* (Lisbon: Junta de Investigações do Ultramar, 1960). In 1936, James Maclaren, referred to *phandla* as "hurt or strike or dazzle the eye" (130). Maclaren, *A concise xhosa-english dictionary* (London: Longmans, Green, 1936).

60. *O brado africano* called them mestiços. *O brado africano*, 23/10/37, 4.

61. Some former players stated that *Conholar* was the local verb for the art of dribbling.

62. To some extent it is possible to conceive of this "parallel law" as a hidden transcript, as defined by James Scott—a law whose logic remains attached to the game's official rule, which in this case is a kind of public transcript. James C. Scott, *Domination and the Arts of Resistance: Hidden Transcripts* (New Haven: Yale University Press, 1990), 88.

63. *O brado africano*, 12/2/1955, 8. The term *wupfetela* derives from a cooking technique and may also mean, according to Torre do Vale

(*Shironga-portuguez*, 171), "to blow the flame out," or, in Nogueira's description, "ripen to blow" and "to fan the flame." Nogueira, *Dicionário ronga*, 540. According to Nogueira, the word *wupfa* had a similar meaning: "to ripen, to be ripe." Nogueira offers the following example: "They are incomplete beings, they have yet to ripen, they were loathed by the heavens." Ibid., 540.

64. Eduardo Archetti, *Masculinities: Football, Polo and the Tango in Argentina* (Oxford: Berg, 1999). José Sérgio Leite Lopes, "Sucesses and Contradictions in 'Multiracial' Brazilian Football," Armstrong and Giulianotti, *Entering the Field*, 53–86. The gestures and movements of the game can be related with other bodily traditions. For example, Archetti makes a connection between football movements and tango in Argentina. "The bodily images produced in tango were transferred to Argentinian football. I have shown that the individual style of great players was based on the 'dribble.' Many of my informants also made the association between tango figures—the *cortes* and *quebradas*—and the great dribblers in Argentinian football." Archetti, "Playing Football and Dancing Tango: Embodying Argentina in Movement, Style and Identity," in *Sport, Dance and Embodied Identities*, ed. Noel Dyck and Archetti (Oxford: Berg, 2003), 228.

65. On Garrincha, see José Sergio Leite Lopes and Sylvain Maresca, "La disparition de 'la joie du peuple,'" *Actes de la recherche en sciences sociales* 79, no. 1 (1989): 21–36. Ruy Castro, *Garrincha: The Triumph and Tragedy of Brazil's Forgotten Footballing Hero*, translated by Andrew Downie (London: Yellow Jersey Press, 2004).

66. According to Nogueira, *Pseti*, meant "to be poor, to be indigent." Nogueira, *Dicionário ronga*, 416.

67. Craveirinha did not include this expression, possibly because its meaning is more universal.

68. Bullfights had been organized in Lourenço Marques at least since the beginning of the century.

69. By analyzing the systems of the French Grandes Écoles, Pierre Bourdieu articulates the transformation of the social ethos of a group into an ethics of life. The conversion of an ethos into a life ethic was carried out by "transmuting the objectively systematic principles of a shared habitus, nearly universalized within the confines of a group, into an intentionally coherent system of explicit norms with claims to universality." Bourdieu, *The State Nobility: Elite Schools in the Field of Power*, trans. Lauretta C. Clough (Oxford: Polity, 1996 [1989]), 44.

70. José Craveirinha, *O brado africano*, 22/1/55, 8.

71. James Scott refers to the "trickster" as a figure, typical of peasant societies, that wins not by using his strength but rather through cunning: "Only by knowing the habits of his enemies, by deceiving them, by taking advantage of their greed, size, gullibility, or haste does he manage to escape their clutches and win victories." Scott, *Domination and the Arts*, 162. This figure, as the author points out, embodies the typical dilemmas of subordinate groups: "the more common folk hero of subordinate groups—blacks included—has

historically been the trickster figure, who manages to outwit his adversary and escape unscathed." Ibid., 41.

72. Bourdieu's term when referring to the governing principles of practical experience, shaped in a context where the latter was defined by a set of diverse and often conflicting conventions. Bourdieu, *The Algerians*, translated by Alan C. M. Ross (Boston: Beacon Press, 1962).

73. Scott, *Domination and the Arts*, 45–69.

74. As Harries claims, regarding the labor resistance strategies within the context of South African mines, the individual manipulation of the existing order through the effect of "tricksterism" is mostly a cautious and defensive move: "Tricksterism is a strategy of defence, not attack. It does not reflect an assertive or aggressive group consciousness but rather a cautious and defensive attitude." Patrick Harries, *Work, Culture, and Identity: Migrant Laborers in Mozambique and South Africa, c. 1860–1910* (Portsmouth, NH: Heinemann, 1993), 98.

CHAPTER 5: WITCHCRAFT PRACTICES IN FOOTBALL'S SYMBOLIC ECONOMY

1. In the BDLP dictionaries of both Réunion Island and the Democratic Republic of Congo, malice was linked to witchcraft. See *Base de données lexicographiques panfrancophone* (Réunion, Congo-Brazzaville: BDLP, 2001).

2. Fréchaut Neto, "O 'Cuxo-Cuxo' e as perplexidades da ignorância," *O brado africano*, 6/8/1966, 1.

3. Rui Mateus Pereira, "A 'Missão etognósica de Moçambique': A codificação dos 'usos e costumes indígenas' no direito colonial português: Notas de Investigação," *Cadernos de estudos africanos* 1 (2001): 125–77.

4. Neto, "Cuxo-Cuxo,'" *O brado africano*, 6/8/1966, 1.

5. Fréchaut Neto might be a pseudonym. I would not be a surprised if this text had been written by José Craveirinha.

6. According to Luís Polanah, the *cuscuxo*, as he pronounced it, is the "onomatopoeic expression that mimics the sounds of the divinatory little bones as they are shaken between the hands by the Uá bula (fortune-teller) during a consultation." Luís Polanah, *O Nhamussoro e as outras funções mágico-religiosas* (Coimbra: Instituto de Antropologia, Universidade de Coimbra, 1987), 141n10.

7. Fréchaut Neto, "'Cuxo-Cuxo,'" 6/8/1966, 1.

8. Luís Polanah, quoting the Portuguese lieutenant Simões Alberto, who received the information from a doctor at the health services in Gorongosa, describes the "cuscucheiro" as "both a sorcerer and a healer who treats his patients using magic arts, throwing stones, shells and sticks as if they were darts; he also makes special prayers and uses his medicines around the patients' arms, legs and abdomen, and so on." Polanah, *O Nhamussoro e as outras funções mágico-religiosas* (Coimbra: Instituto de Antropologia, Universidade de Coimbra, 1987), 69. Within his work on the subject Polanah doesn't grant scientific relevance to this description.

9. Neto, "'Cuxo-Cuxo,'" 13/8/66, 5.

10. Ibid.
11. Ibid.
12. Ibid.
13. Ibid., 27/8/66, 3.
14. Ibid., 3/9/66, 5.
15. Ibid., 17/9/65, 1, 5.
16. Ibid.
17. *O brado africano*, 22/1/55, 8.
18. *O brado africano*, 22/1/55, 8.
19. N. A. Scotch, "Magic, Sorcery, and Football among the Urban Zulu: A Case of Reinterpretation under Acculturation," *Journal of Conflict Resolution* 5, no. 1, The Anthropology of Conflict (March 1961): 70–74. There aren't many academic works focusing on the uses of these traditional beliefs within football matches. Scotch, who interprets the phenomenon by drawing inspiration from Max Gluckman's work, was one of the first to consider the subject as an autonomous research topic.
20. This formulation was included in the Estatuto dos Indígenas Portugueses das Províncias de Angola e Moçambique (Statute of the Portuguese Indígenas of the Provinces of Angola and Mozambique), decreto 39 666, 1954, art. 56.
21. Fr. S. Santandrea describes the "vuvu," as "the spirits of the dead." *Vodun* is the African word for spirit (West Africa). Santandrea, "Evil and Witchcraft among the Ndogo Group of Tribes," *Africa: Journal of the International African Institute* 11, no. 4 (October 1938): 459–81.
22. Anne Leseth, "The Use of Juju in Football: Sports and Witchcraft in Tanzania," in Armstrong and Giulianotti, *Entering the Field*, 172.
23. Ibid.
24. The term "juju" is common in the Yoruba language and is usually related to West African traditions.
25. A. Pires Prata, *Dicionário Macua-Português* (Lisbon: Instituto de Investigação Científica Tropical, 1990), 85.
26. Nogueira, *Dicionário Ronga-Português*.
27. According to the Ronga dictionary there are no words that begin with *j*. Nogueira, *Ronga-português*. Although it appears that the words *vuvu* and *juju* do not belong to the predominant languages in the south of Mozambique, the *Dictionary of African-American Slang* claims that *juju* has a Bantu origin and means both "danger" and "fetish against harm." http://www.randomhouse.com/wotd/index.pperl?date=20010510.
28. Stories involving individuals with other characteristics are rare.
29. This multiplicity of tasks was initially discussed by Henri Junod's pioneer study (1912–13) and later mentioned by Luís Polanah, *O Nhamassouro*.
30. This option can imply a simplification of this practice as it does not take into account all its internal differences.
31. West, *Kupilikula*, 19.
33. António Rita-Ferreira mentions that when traditional courts tried a case of black magic, the defendant was the client and never the practitioner,

who was presumed innocent of any wrongdoing. Rita-Ferreira, *Os Africanos de Lourenço Marques*, Memórias do Instituto de Investigação Científica de Moçambique / Instituto de Investigação Científica de Moçambique, vol. 9, series C (1967–68): 446.

34. As famously described by E. P. Thompson, "Time, Work-Discipline, and Industrial Capitalism," *Past and Present*, no. 38 (December 1967): 56–97.

35. As I insisted in asking Mogne if all the watches had really stopped, he said that the watch of one of the directors had stopped working: "He decided that we had time to return and then we lost the game. We did not even enter the pitch."

36. Eric Hobsbawm, *Primitive Rebels: Studies in Archaic Forms of Social Movement in the 19th and 20th Centuries* (New York: Norton, 1959); Hobsbawm, *Bandits* (London: Abacus, 2003 [1969]. On social banditry in the rural Mozambican context, see Allen Isaacman, "Social Banditry in Zimbabwe (Rhodesia) and Mozambique, 1894–1907: An Expression of Early Peasant Protest," *Journal of South African Studies* 4, no. 1 (1977): 1–30.

37. Pereira, "Missão etognósica."

38. Armando managed to get a job at the Ferroviário club as a typist.

39. On Béla Guttmann, see the biography by Detlev Claussen, *Béla Guttmann: Uma história mundial do futebol* (Lisbon: Paquiderme, 2015 [2006]).

40. The second European Cup won by Benfica, in 1962, after a victory (5–3) over the Spanish team.

CHAPTER 6: SWEETNESS AND SPEED

1. Peter Alegi, in the course of analyzing the development of football in Johannesburg, detailed the features of the Marabi football, a street football filled with dribbles and improvisation that was locally appreciated and that served as an inspiration to the style of play of some clubs. Peter Alegi, *Laduma! Soccer, Politics and Society in South Africa* (Natal: University of KwaZulu-Natal Press, 2004), 56–57.

2. *Notícias da tarde*, 11/4/59, 6.

3. Ibid.

4. Ibid.

5. *O brado africano*, 22/1/55, 8.

6. Penvenne refers to the emergence of a modern work ethic among the female cashew factory workers in Lourenço Marques. Penvenne, *Women, Migration and the Cashew Economy in Southern Mozambique: 1945–1975* (Rochester: James Currey, 2015), 102.

7. Max Weber, *Os fundamentos racionais e sociológicos da música* (São Paulo: Editora da Universidade de São Paulo, 1995 [1921]).

8. Cândido de Oliveira played for Casa Pia and Benfica. He became famous as a manager and a journalist. He was one of the most important promoters of the game in Portugal. On Cândido de Oliveira, see Homero Serpa, *Cândido de Oliveira: Uma biografia* (Lisbon: Caminho, 2000).

9. Cândido de Oliveira describes what happened in this course in a report sent to the Football Association Portuguese Federation in 1936. Cândido de

Oliveira, *Relatório da minha viagem a Inglaterra ao serviço do Football Nacional* (Lisbon: Federação Portuguesa de Futebol, 1936).

10. On the history of the sport's press in Portugal, see Francisco Pinheiro, *História da imprensa desportiva em Portugal* (Porto: Afrontamento, 2011).

11. António Ribeiro dos Reis, *Foot-Ball* (Lisbon: Livraria Popular de Francisco Franco, 1927), 6. On Ribeiro dos Reis, see Astregildo Silva, *Ribeiro dos Reis: Biografia* (Lisbon: Caminho, 2004).

12. Ribeiro dos Reis, *Foot-Ball*, 7.

13. The eyes' significance within collective sports practices was recognized in 1966, three decades after Cândido de Oliveira's book, by Friedrich Mahlo, a physical-education theoretician. Mahlo would later call this "associative thought." Mahlo, *O acto táctico no jogo* (Lisbon: Compendium, 1987 [1966]), 111–22.

14. Ibid.

15. Cândido de Oliveira, *Football: Técnica e tática* (Lisbon: Edição de Autor, 1935), 135.

16. There are interesting similarities between this process and the description of modern musical polyphony proposed by Max Weber, in which several voices, with their own rights, are harmonically interconnected. The progression of each voice affects all the others and, as such, the overall sound logic. M. Weber, *Fundamentos racionais*, 9–10.

17. Cândido de Oliveira, *WM: A evolução táctica no futebol* (Lisbon: published by the author, 1949). This book resulted from a lesson given by Cândido de Oliveira in a course organized in 1948 by the Royal Spanish Football Federation.

18. Ibid., 13.

19. Ibid., 14.

20. Ibid., 177.

21. Elias and Dunning show how the act of dribbling was repressed in English football toward the end of the nineteenth century: "Team co-operation became accentuated at the expense of opportunities for the individual to shine competitively within the team. Thus, the balance between individual and team interests changed. Individual dribbling receded and passing the ball from one member of a team to another came to the fore. It is possible to analyse the reasons for this change with considerable stringency. An increase in the number of teams, the establishment of floral competitions, increased competitive rivalry among teams, and the beginning of playing for a paying public were among them." Elias and Dunning, "Dynamics of Group Sports with Special Reference to Football," *British Journal of Sociology* 17, no. 4 (1966): 399.

22. Oliveira, *WM*, 61.

23. Ibid., 68–69.

24. Ibid., 71. In Portugal, the WM was used for the first time in 1937 by Ribeiro dos Reis, on an experimental basis, when he managed Benfica (72). The system established itself in Portugal during the 1938–39 football season and revealed an enormous defensive efficiency (72). The classic formation

continued to be used in some countries, such as Austria and Spain. Meanwhile, the first variations and adaptations of the WM system emerged. These were attempts to make it more efficient and tailor it to each given context. WM's usefulness in Portugal was first demonstrated by the Belenenses' Argentinean coach, Alexandre Scopelli (72–73).

25. Severiano Correia knew Cândido de Oliveira from the newspaper *A bola*, where they both had worked in the same period.

26. According to an article by the journalist João C. Reis in Clube Ferroviário's newspaper, *O ferroviário*, June–July 1946, 9. This was confirmed latter by Severiano Correia. *Diário de Lourenço Marques Guardian*, 23/6/54.

27. *O ferroviário*, nos. 7–8, 1946, 3–4.

28. Ibid.

29. *O ferroviário*, no. 3 (September 1945), 10.

30. The *Lourenço Marques Guardian* compiled a record of European clubs' tours in South Africa. After the Corinthians, the English national team went there in 1910 and 1930. Aberdeen did their first tour there in 1927, followed, in 1931 and 1934, by Motherwell. In 1935, the Combines Service Football Team and, in 1936, the Viena Athletic Club also had tours in the country. *Lourenço Marques Guardian*, 12/6/37, 3.

31. *Lourenço Marques Guardian*, 3/6/37, 3.

32. *Lourenço Marques Guardian*, 15/6/37, 4.

33. In July 1953 the *Diário de Lourenço Marques Guardian*'s sports supplement announced that Severiano Correia would be their next editor-in-chief.

34. *Guardian desportivo*, 19/8/53, 6–7.

35. *Guardian desportivo*, 26/8/53, 1.

36. *Guardian desportivo*, 16/3/55, 11.

37. *Guardian desportivo*, 26/8/53, 1.

38. *Guardian desportivo*, 2/12/53, 1.

39. *Guardian desportivo*, 2/12/53, 9.

40. *Guardian desportivo*, 2/12/53, 9.

41. *Guardian desportivo*, 20/10/54, 1.

42. According to the *Diário de Lourenço Marques Guardian* (1/10/55, 5), later on it was considered the best team to ever have played in South Africa.

43. *Lourenço Marques Guardian*, 6/10/55, 10.

44. *Guardian desportivo*, 23/12/53, 1.

45. *Guardian desportivo*, 17/2/54, 1.

46. *Guardian desportivo*, 5/8/53, 7.

47. *O eco dos sports*, 15/3/52, 9.

48. *Guardian desportivo*, 3/3/54, 1.

49. *O brado africano*, 26/4/51, 4.

50. *O brado africano*, 26/4/51, 4.

51. *O brado africano*, 26/4/51, 4.

52. Some local coaches, Ângelo argues, tried to imitate their style: "We had coaches who called themselves Otto Glória or [José Maria] Pedroto. They began to wear a small hat during practice, just like Pedroto." Glória, the

Brazilian coach who led the Portuguese national team during the 1966 World Cup, taught a course in Lourenço Marques in 1958. He promoted the 4-2-4 system consecrated by the Brazilian national team during Sweden's World Cup that same year.

53. Gary Armstrong, "The Migration of the Black Panther: An Interview with Eusébio of Mozambique and Portugal," in Armstrong and Giulianotti, *Football in Africa*, 257.

54. The fact that they owned a training pitch contributed to Beira-Mar and Mahafil's successful careers.

55. Benedict Anderson, *Imagined Communities: Reflections on the Origin and Spread of Nationalism* (London: Verso, 1991).

56. *Diário de Lourenço Marques Guardian*, 2/3/55, 7.

57. On the migration of colonial African players to Portugal, see Todd Cleveland, "Following the Ball: African Soccer Players, Labor Strategies and Emigration across the Portuguese Colonial Empire, 1949–1975," *Cadernos de estudos africanos* 26 (2013): 1–19.

58. *Guardian desportivo*, 8/9/54, 3.

59. *Guardian desportivo*, 8/9/54, 6.

60. *Guardian desportivo*, 8/9/54, 6.

61. The recognition of suburban African players' technical and tactical expertise is a crucial interpretative element, one that enables us to avoid the error of considering their qualities as the result of natural gifts. African players intelligently master modern football's dynamic. Alfredo Margarido, when deconstructing the supposedly "positive" natural qualities of the black man celebrated by Sartre in *Black Orpheus* (for instance, his sense of rhythm), insists precisely on the African's ability to adapt, recreate, and manipulate new techniques. Margarido, *Negritude e humanismo* (Lisbon: Casa dos Estudantes do Império, 1964). As David Kirk notes, criticizing some Foucauldian approaches, the body that has learned a specific embodied language is also a creative machine, capable of its own creations, precisely because it has learned a structure that serves as a basis for its performance. Kirk, "Foucault and the Limits of Corporeal Regulation: The Emergence, Consolidation and Decline of School Medical Inspection and Physical Training in Australia, 1909–30," *International Journal of the History of Sport* 13, no. 2 (1996): 114–31.

CHAPTER 7: FOOTBALL NARRATIVES AND SOCIAL NETWORKS IN LATE COLONIAL MOZAMBIQUE

1. *O brado africano*, 8/8/53, 2.
2. *O brado africano*, 8/8/53, 2.
3. *O brado africano*, 8/8/53, 2.
4. *O brado africano*, 15/8/53, 2.
5. *O brado africano*, 3/10/53, 2.
6. *O brado africano*, 3/10/53, 2.
7. Mark Granovetter, "The Strength of Weak Ties," *American Journal of Sociology* 78, no. 6 (1973): 1360–80.

8. Lewis Coser, *The Functions of Social Conflict* (Glencoe, IL: Free Press, 1964).

9. The end of the link between Desportivo de Lourenço Marques and Benfica, in 1954, triggered by Benfica's demand that Desportivo play in red shirts, not the traditional black and white, is an example of the tensions that traversed these processes.

10. Desportivo's stadium was named after Paulinho dos Santos Gil, one of the most important local businessmen. On Santos Gil, see Valdemir Zamparoni, "Entre Narros e Mulungos: Colonialismo e paisagem social em Lourenço Marques, c. 1890–c. 1940" (PhD diss., Faculdade Letras e Ciências Humanas da Universidade de São Paulo, 1998), 151.

11. *O brado africano*, 29/7/50, 1.

12. *O brado africano*, 12/8/50, 5.

13. More than five hundred people gathered in an atmosphere described as "elegant" by the *O brado africano* reporter. *O brado africano*, 12/8/50: 5.

14. João Nuno Coelho, *Portugal, a equipa de todos nós: Nacionalismo, futebol e media* (Porto: Afrontamento, 2002), 397.

15. The Lourenço Marques neighborhoods where less than 10 percent of people worked in agriculture were all located in the cement city, with the exception of the suburban neighborhoods of Chamanculo, Munhuana, Lagoas, Tlhabane, Xipamanine, Aeroporto, and Kock. In Sommerschield, Chinhambanine, Jardim, Choupal, Infuelene, and most of Benfica between 10 and 42 percent of the population worked in agriculture. Maria Clara Mendes, *Maputo antes da independência: Geografia de uma cidade colonial* (Lisbon: Centro de Estudos Geográficos da Universidade de Lisboa, 1979), 64.

16. On 11 November 1952, *Guardian desportivo* reentered the publishing market, this time along with a cinema newspaper, *O cinéfilo*, which focused predominantly on the Hollywood star system.

17. In this year, for the first time, a statistical category was created that measured weekly sports broadcasts.

18. *O brado africano*, 8/7/33, 1.

19. *O brado africano*, 17/6/44, 5.

20. *O brado africano*, 17/3/45, 5.

21. *Diário de Lourenço Marques Guardian*, 4/3/53, 10.

22. Louis and Robinson were portrayed in the *Guardian desportivo e cinéfilo*, on 10/12/52 and 31/12/52, respectively.

23. *Guardian desportivo e cinéfilo*, 21/1/53, 6.

24. *Guardian desportivo e cinéfilo*, 19/5/54, 6–7.

25. *Guardian desportivo e cinéfilo*, 23/6/54, 6–7.

26. *Guardian desportivo e cinéfilo*, 13/10/54, 1.

27. The relevance of radio broadcasts in Africa is extensively addressed in Richard Fardon and Graham Furniss, eds., *African Broadcast Cultures: Radio in Transition* (Oxford: James Currey, 2000).

28. *Guardian desportivo*, 3/11/52, 7.

29. Ernesto Barbosa, *A radiodifusão em Moçambique: O caso do Rádio Clube de Moçambique, 1932–1974* (Maputo: Promédia: 2000), 87.

30. Ibid., 88.

31. Ibid., 68.

32. Ibid., 91–92. Still in 1962, os Serviços de Acção Psicossocial created a musical program called *A voz de Moçambique* (Voice of Mozambique), essentially a light entertainment.

33. In this sense, these conditions expressed the emergence of a constellation of elements, more or less manifest depending on the overall African context, as well as that of colonial Lourenço Marques, that characterize social networks in urban metropolitan spaces. Barry Wellman, ed., *Networks in the Global Village: Life in Contemporary Communities* (Boulder: Westview, 1999), 6.

34. Maria Clara Mendes, *Variação especial da densidade de população urbana em Lourenço Marques* (Lisbon: Centro de Estudos Geográficos da Universidade de Lisboa, 1976), 34–36; Joana Pereira Leite, "La formation de l'économie coloniale au Mozambique: Pacte colonial et industrialisation: Du colonialisme portugais aux réseaux informels de sujétion marchande, 1930–74" (PhD diss., École dês Hautes Études en Sciences Sociales, Paris, 1989).

35. António Rita-Ferreira, *Os Africanos de Lourenço Marques*, Memórias do Instituto de Investigação Científica de Moçambique / Instituto de Investigação Científica de Moçambique, vol. 9, series C (1967–68), 337.

36. Penvenne gives a fair account of this process in her recent study of the women workers of the Lourenço Marques cashew factories. Penvenne, *Women, Migration*, 191, 192.

37. Mendes, *Maputo*, 426–29.

38. Ibid., 431–32.

39. Mendes, *Maputo*, 247.

40. Ibid.

41. Mendes, *Maputo*, 409–11.

42. *O brado africano*, 12/7/58, 1.

43. *Mamparra* is a depreciative Afrikaans term for a poor black Mozambican miner. For a more detailed explanation see Zamparoni, "Entre Narros e Mulungos," 142, 150.

44. This recalls the statement by the Brazilian player Robson, recorded by Mário Filho in his classic book: "I was black once, and I know what that's like." Filho, *O negro no futebol brasileiro* (Rio de Janeiro: Mauad, 2003 [1947]), 308.

45. The Mozambican process differs from what occurred in neighboring South Africa, where an increasingly greater racial segregation led to a more dynamic sports associativism, something that allowed for the institution of an alternative football narrative, which became hegemonic after the end of the apartheid regime. Today, the most important South African football clubs are the ones that played in black competitions under the apartheid regime. John Nauright, *Sports, Cultures, and Identities in South Africa* (London: Leicester University Press, 1997); Peter Alegi, *Laduma! Soccer, Politics and Society in South Africa* (Natal: University of KwaZulu-Natal Press, 2004).

46. *O brado africano*, 20/6/59, 6.
47. *Lourenço Marques Guardian*, 21/6/60, 8.
48. *Notícias da tarde*, 12/9/59, 6.
49. Regarding this process, *O brado africano*'s sports journalist Guerra Manuel asked: "The other thing that we don't understand is why the third-division champion can't play in the second division." *O brado africano*, 18/11/7, 6.
50. *O brado africano*, 2/3/1963, 3.
51. Sport Nacional Africano (African National Sport) had to change its name because of its connotations.
52. ACPEFM, Processo: Grupo Desportivo Chamanculo, Carta do Grupo Desportivo Chamanculo ao Presidente do CPEF, 16/4/63.
53. ACPEFM, Processo: Grupo Desportivo Nova Aliança, Carta do Grupo Desportivo Nova Aliança ao Governador geral de Moçambique em 1/5/63.
54. José Craveirinha, "Clubes suburbanos o que foram e o que são" (Suburban Clubs, how they were and how they are now), *Voz de Moçambique*, 13/6/1964, 4.
55. Its leader, Domingos Arouca, a former director of *O brado africano*, was arrested and would only be released seven years later. On Arouca's trial, see Francisco Salgado Zenha, *A prisão do Doutor Domingos Arouca* (Porto: Afrontamento, 1972). On the political life of Domingos Arouca, see Carolina Peixoto and Maria Paula Meneses, "Domingos Arouca: Um percurso de militância nacionalista em Moçambique," *Topoi: Revista de História* 14, no. 26 (2013): 86–104.
56. AHM, DSAC, secção A, Administração, Agremiações regionais de recreio, defesa, desporto e estudo. Associações Desportivas, Recreativas e Culturais, caixa 22, Grupo Desportivo Chamanculo, Carta da DSAC ao Governador do Distrito de Lourenço Marques, 13/12/65.
57. AHM, DSAC, secção A, Administração, Agremiações regionais de recreio, defesa, desporto e estudo. Associações Desportivas, Recreativas e Culturais, caixa 22, Grupo Desportivo Chamanculo, Carta do Governador do Distrito de Lourenço Marques à DSAC, 17/2/66.
58. The Companhia União Fabril was founded by Alfredo da Silva in 1898 and would later be owned by the Mello family. The CUF operated across various economic sectors, from agro-industry to finance, insurance, and banking; chemical, metalworking, and textile industries; and shipbuilding. At the time of the April 1974 revolution, it was the largest Portuguese industrial and financial group. An important facet of its entrepeneurial activity was located in the colonies. A significant portion of the CUF group investments was also in the colonial space. In Guinea-Bissau, since 1921 (after the company had acquired Sociedade António da Silva Gouveia), they produced oilseeds, exporting peanuts and cashews. In the 1950s the group controlled 30 to 40 percent of the import-export trade in Guinea. As recorded by Gervase Clarence-Smith, in Angola the group operated through the Companhia do Congo Português, Comfabril, the Império insurance company, and Banco Standart

Totta (which also operated in Mozambique) and had a share in the Sociedade Portuguesa de Lapidação de Diamantes [Portuguese Society for the Lapping of Diamonds]. In São Tomé the bank had invested in a group of plantations and owned the Companhia da Ilha do Príncipe. The manufacture and trade of bags to Angola and Mozambique, where it owned factories, generated significant profits for the company. In Mozambique it had a stake in Tabaqueira (Philip Morris's affiliate in Portugal) and in textile factories in Pungué and Cicomo, and it managed a cashew-peeling factory in Nacala, called Socaju. Gervase Clarence-Smith, *The Third Portuguese, 1825–1975: A Study in Economic Imperialism* (Manchester: Manchester University Press, 1985).

59. Others sought to capture this reality through methodologies such as research on "social situations," after Max Gluckman's classic "Analysis of a Social Situation in Modern Zululand," *Bantu Studies* 14, no. 1 (1940): 1–30.

60. Displaying a keen interest in interdisciplinarity, these authors reclaimed the heritage of studies such as that of John Barnes on Norwegian fishing communities or of Elizabeth Bott on family networks. In the African context, Philip Mayer's study on the urban adaptation of populations coming from rural spaces also defined the research agenda. Barnes, "Class and Committees in a Norwegian Island Parish," *Human Relations* 7 (1954): 39–58; Bott, *Family and Social Network* (London: Tavistock, 1957); Mayer, *Townsmen or Tribesmen: Conservatism and the Process of Urbanization in a South African City* (Cape Town: Oxford University Press, 1961). On the uses of the concept of social network in African contexts, see Clyde Mitchell, *Social Networks in Urban Situations: Analyses of Personal Relationships in Central African Towns* (Manchester: Manchester University Press, 1969); Ulf Hannerz, "Thinking with Networks," in *Exploring the City: Inquiries toward an Urban Anthropology* (New York: Columbia University Press, 1980), 163–201.

61. Jennifer Schultz and Ronald L. Breiger, "The Strength of Weak Culture," *Poetics* 38, no. 6 (2010): 610–24.

CHAPTER 8: EMBODIED HISTORY

1. Pierre Bourdieu, "Le mort saisit le vif [Les relations entre l'histoire réifiée et l'histoire incorporée]," *Actes de la recherche en sciences sociales* 32–33 (1980): 2–4.

Bibliography

ARCHIVES

Mozambique

Arquivo do Conselho Provincial de Educação Física de Moçambique (ACPEFM) (held at the Ministério da Juventude e Desportos de Moçambique)
Arquivo Histórico de Moçambique (AHM)
Administração do Concelho de Lourenço Marques
Direcção dos Serviços de Administração Civil
Direcção dos Serviços dos Negócios Indígenas
Governo do Distrito de Lourenço Marques
Governo-Geral

Portugal

Arquivo Histórico Ultramarino (AHU)
Direcção Geral de Educação
Torre do Tombo (TT)
Fundo dos Serviços de Centralização e Coordenação de Informações de Moçambique, Centro de Documentação

PERIODICALS

Anuário de ensino de Moçambique (1935–73)
Anuário de Lourenço Marques/Anuários de Moçambique (1913–69)
Anuário de Moçambique, planeado e coordenado por Sousa Ribeiro (1908)
Anuário estatístico de Moçambique (1926–73)
A bola (1945–74)
Boletim da Direcção Geral de Educação Física Desporto e Saúde Escolar (1944–63)
Boletim da Sociedade de Geografia (1923–74)
Boletim oficial da Província de Moçambique (1915–26)
Boletim oficial da Colónia de Moçambique (1927–75)
O brado africano (1918–74)
Diário das sessões da Assembleia Nacional (1926–74)
O eco dos sports (1938–1956)
A equipa de Lourenço Marques (1966–67)

Estudos coloniais, revista da Escola Superior Colonial (1948–54)
Estudos ultramarinos (1955–62)
O ferroviário, boletim mensal do Clube Ferroviário (1945–1955)
Guardian desportivo/Guardian desportivo e cinéfilo (1951–55)
Jornal da Mocidade Portuguesa de Moçambique (1947–53)
The Lourenço Marques Guardian/Diário de Lourenço Marques Guardian (1920–74)
Notícias da tarde (1952–69)
Notícias de Lourenço Marques (1926–74)
A tribuna (1962–70)

INTERVIEWS

Armando Silva, 24/5/2006, Maputo.
Guerra Manuel, 13/6/2006, Maputo.
António Cruz, 25/2/2006, Maputo.
João de Sousa, 31/5/2006, Maputo.
Mário Wilson, 28/4/2005, Lisbon.
Saide Mogne, 15/4/2006 and 18/04/2006, Maputo.
Ângelo Gomes da Silva, 25/04/2006, Maputo.
Hamido Nizamo, 02/05/2006, Maputo.
Issufo bin Haji, 22/5/2006, Maputo.
Abissínia Ali, 02/06/2006, Maputo.
Guilherme Cabaço, 06/06/2006, Maputo.
Mário Coluna, 04/07/2006, Maputo.
Hilário da Conceição 11/12/2007, Lisbon.
Augusto Matine, 13/12/2007, Lisbon.
Daniel Matavela, 28/5/2008, Lisbon.
Vicente Lucas, 4/9/2008, Lisbon.

REFERENCES

Ágoas, Frederico. "Estado, universidade e ciências sociais: A introdução da sociologia na Escola Superior Colonial (1952–72). In *O império colonial em questão*, edited by Miguel Bandeira Jerónimo, 317–48. Lisbon: Ed. 70, 2012.

Aguiar, João António de. *L'habitation dans les pays tropicaux*. Lisbon: Federation Internationale de l'habitation et de l'urbanisme (XX° Congrès), 1952.

Aja, Teresa Gonzalez. "Spanish Sports Policy in Republican and Fascist Spain." In Arnaud and Riordan, *Sport and International Politics*, 97–113.

Alegi, Peter. "Football and Apartheid Society: The South African Soccer League, 1960–1966." In Armstrong and Giulianotti, *Football in Africa*, 114–34.

———. *Laduma! Soccer, Politics and Society in South Africa*. Natal: University of KwaZulu-Natal Press, 2004.

Alexander, Jeffrey. *La réduction: Critique de Bourdieu*. Paris: Cerf, 2000.

Alexandre, Valentim. *Origens do colonialismo português moderno*. Lisbon: Sá da Costa, 1979.

Almeida, A. Rebelo. *O futebol tornado perigo social*. Lisbon: Tipografia de o Sport, 1928.
Alpers, Edward. "A Complex Relationship: Mozambique and the Comoro Islands in the Nineteenth and Twentieth Centuries." *Cahiers d'études africaines* 41, no. 161 (2001): 73–95.
Anderson, Benedict. *Imagined Communities: Reflections on the Origin and Spread of Nationalism*. London: Verso, 1991.
Anderson, Perry. *Portugal e o fim do ultracolonialismo*. Lisbon: Civilização, 1966.
Ansell, C. K. "Symbolic Networks: The Realignment of the French Working Class, 1887–1894." *American Journal of Sociology* 103 (1997): 359–90.
Appadurai, Arjun. "Playing with Modernity: The Decolonization of Indian Cricket." In *Consuming Modernity: Public Culture in a South Asian World*, edited by Carol A. Breckenridge, 23–48. Minneapolis: University of Minnesota Press, 1995.
Archetti, Eduardo. "'And Give Joy to My Heart': Ideology and Emotions in the Argentinian Cult of Maradona." In Armstrong and Giulianotti, *Entering the Field*, 31–51.
———. *Masculinities: Football, Polo and the Tango in Argentina*. Oxford: Berg, 1999.
———. "Playing Football and Dancing Tango: Embodying Argentina in Movement, Style and Identity." In Dyck and Archetti, *Sport, Dance*, 217–29.
Armstrong, Gary. "The Migration of the Black Panther: An Interview with Eusébio of Mozambique and Portugal." In Armstrong and Giulianotti, *Football in Africa*, 247–68.
Armstrong, Gary, and Richard Giulianotti, eds. *Entering the Field, New Perspectives on World Football*. Oxford: Berg, 1997.
———, eds. *Fear and Loathing in World Football*. Oxford: Berg, 2001.
———, eds. *Football Cultures and Identities*. London: Macmillan, 1999.
———, eds. *Football in Africa: Conflict, Conciliation, and Community*. Houndmills: Palgrave Macmillan, 2004.
Arnaud, Pierre, and Jim Riordan, eds. *Sport and International Politics: The Impact of Fascism and Communism on Sport*, edited by Pierre Arnaud and James *Riordan*, 97–113. London: E. and F. N. Spon, 1998.
———. *Sport et relations internationales (1900–1941): Les démocraties face au fascisme et au nazisme*. Paris: L'Harmattan, 1998.
Asad, Talal. "From the History of Colonial Anthropology to the Anthropology of Western Hegemony." Afterword to *Colonial Situations: Essays on the Contextualization of Ethnographic Knowledge*. History of Anthropology, vol. 7, edited by George W. Stocking Jr. Madison: University of Wisconsin Press, 1993.
Azevedo, Mário. *O plano director de urbanização de Lourenço Marques*. Lourenço Marques: Separata do Boletim no. 7 da Câmara Municipal de Lourenço Marques, 1969.
Badenhorst, Cecile, and Charles Mather. "Tribal Recreation and Recreating Tribalism: Culture, Leisure and Social Control on South Africa's Gold

Mines, 1940–1950." *Journal of Southern African Studies* 23, no. 3 (September 1997): 473–89.
Baker, William L., and J. A. Mangan, eds. *Sport in Africa: Essays in Social History.* New York: Africana Publishing, 1987.
Balandier, Georges. "La situation coloniale: Approche théorique." *Cahiers internationaux de sociologie* 11 (1951): 44–79.
Bandeira Jerónimo, Miguel. *Livros brancos, almas negras: A "missão civilizadora" do colonialismo português* (c. 1870–1930). Lisbon: Imprensa de Ciências Sociais, 2010.
Barber, Karin, "Popular Arts in Africa." *African Studies Review* 30, no. 3 (September 1987): 1–78.
———, ed. *Readings in African Popular Culture.* Bloomington: International African Institute/Indiana University Press, 1997.
Barbosa, Ernesto. *A radiodifusão em Moçambique: O caso do Rádio Clube de Moçambique, 1932–1974.* Maputo: Promédia, 2000.
Barnes, John. "Class and Committees in a Norwegian Island Parish." *Human Relations* 7 (1954): 39–58.
Becker, Howard. *Art Worlds.* Berkeley: University of California Press, 1982.
Berger, Peter, and Thomas Luckmann. *The Social Construction of Reality.* New York: Anchor, 1967.
Bethencourt, Francisco, and Kirti Chaudhuri, eds. *História da expansão portuguesa.* 5 vols. Lisbon: Círculo de Leitores, 1999.
Billig, Michael. *Banal Nationalism.* London: Sage, 1995.
Blacking, John. "Games and Sport in Pre-Colonial African Societies." In Baker and Mangan, *Sport in Africa,* 3–22.
Boer, Wiebe. "A Story of Heroes, of Epics: The Rise of Football in Nigeria." In Armstrong and Giulianotti, *Football in Africa,* 59–79.
Boléo, José de Oliveira. *Monografia de Moçambique.* Lisbon: Agência Geral do Ultramar, 1971.
Bott, Elizabeth. *Family and Social Network.* London: Tavistock: 1957.
Bourdieu, Pierre. *The Algerians.* Translated by Alan C. M. Ross. Beacon Press: Boston, 1962.
———. *Distinction: A Social Critique of the Judgement of Taste.* Translated by Richard Nice. London: Routledge, 1998 [1979].
———. *Language and Symbolic Power.* Translated by Gino Raymond and Matthew Adamson. Cambridge: Polity Press, 1991.
———. "Le mort saisit le vif [Les relations entre l'histoire réifiée et l'histoire incorporée]," *Actes de la recherche en sciences sociales* 32, 23–33 (1980): 2–4.
———. *Outline of a Theory of Practice.* Translated by Richard Nice. Cambridge: Cambridge University Press, 1977.
———. *Pascalian Meditations.* Translated by Richard Nice. Stanford: Stanford University Press, 2000.
———. *The Rules of Art: Genesis and Structure of the Literary Field.* Translated by Susan Emanuel. Stanford: Stanford University Press, 1996.

——. *The State Nobility: Elite Schools in the Field of Power*. Translated by Lauretta C. Clough. Oxford: Polity, 1996 [1989].
Brasão, Inês. *Dons e disciplinas do corpo feminino: Os discursos sobre o corpo na história do Estado Novo*. Lisbon: ONGCCCIDM, 1999.
Brohm, Jean-Marie. *Sport: A Prison of Measured Time: Essays*. Translated by Ian Frasier. London: Ink Links, 1978.
Bromberger, Christian. *Le match de football: Ethnologie d'une passion partisane à Marseille, Naples et Turin*. Paris: Maison des Sciences de l'Homme, 1995.
Brubaker, Rogers. *The Limits of Rationality: An Essay on the Social and Moral Thought of Max Weber*. London: Allen and Unwin, 1984.
Cahen, Michel. "Salazarisme, fascisme et colonialisme: Problèmes d'interprétation en sciences sociales, ou le sébastianisme de l'éxception." Centro de Estudos sobre África, Ásia, e América Latina, *Documentos de trabalho*, no. 47. Lisbon: CesA, 1997.
Caillois, Roger. *Man and the Sacred*. Glencoe, IL: Free Press of Glencoe, 1959 [1939]).
Caldeira, Renato. *Coluna, monstro sagrado*. Maputo: Edisport, 2003.
Camacho, Brito. *Moçambique: Problemas coloniais*. Lisbon: Livraria Guimarães, 1926.
Capela, José. *O movimento operário em Lourenço Marques, 1898–1927*. Porto: Afrontamento, 1984.
——. *O vinho para o preto: Notas e textas sobre a exportação do vinho para África*. Porto: Afrontamento, 1973.
Cardão, Marcos. *Fado tropical: O luso-tropicalismo na cultura de massas (1960–1974)*. Lisbon: Unipop, 2015.
——. "Peregrinações exemplares: As embaixadas patrióticas dos clubes metropolitanos ao 'ultramar português.'" In Nascimento et al., *Esporte e lazer*, 109–28.
——. "Um significante instrumental. Eusébio e a banalização lusotropicalismo na década de 1960." In *Esporte, cultura, nação, estado: Brasil e Portugal*, edited byVictor Andrade de Melo, Fábio de Faria Peres, and Maurício Drumond. 172–88. Rio de Janeiro: 7Letras, 2014.
Carreira, Salazar. "A influência social da ginástica de Ling." *Boletim do INEF*, nos. 1–2 (1947): 71–74.
Carvalho, Clara, and João de Pina-Cabral, eds. *A persistência da história: Passado e comtemporaneidade em África*. Lisbon: Imprensa de Ciências Sociais, 2004.
Carvalho, Luís Miguel Carvalho. "Explorando as transferências educacionais nas primeiras décadas do século XX." *Análise social* 40, no. 176 (2004): 499–518.
Castelo, Cláudia. *"O modo português de estar no mundo": O luso-tropicalismo e a ideologia colonial portuguesa (1933–1961)*. Porto: Afrontamento, 2001.

———. *Passagens para África, O Povoamento de Angola e Moçambique com Naturais da Metrópole (1920–1974)*. Porto: Afrontamento, 2007.
Castro, Ruy. *Garrincha: The Triumph and Tragedy of Brazil's Forgotten Footballing Hero*. Translated by Andrew Downie. London: Yellow Jersey Press, 2004.
Clarence-Smith, Gervase. *The Third Portuguese Empire, 1825–1975: A Study in Economic Imperialism*. Manchester: Manchester University Press, 1985.
Claussen, Detlev. *Béla Guttmann: Uma história mundial do futebol*. Lisbon: Paquiderme, 2015 [2006].
Cleveland, Todd. "Following the Ball: African Soccer Players, Labor Strategies, and Emigration across the Portuguese Colonial Empire, 1949–1975." *Cadernos de estudos africanos* 26* (2013): 1–19.
Coelho, João Nuno. *Portugal, a equipa de todos nós: Nacionalismo, futebol e media*. Porto: Afrontamento, 2002.
Coelho, João Nuno, and Francisco Pinheiro. *A paixão do povo: História do futebol em Portugal*. Porto: Afrontamento, 2002.
Cohn, Bernard S. *Colonialism and Its Forms of Knowledge: The British in India*. Princeton: Princeton University Press, 1996.
Comaroff, Jean, and John Comaroff. *Christianity, Colonialism, and Consciousness in South Africa*. Vol.1 of *Of Revelation and Revolution*. Chicago: University of Chicago Press, 1991.
———. *Dialectics of Modernity on a South African Frontier*. Vol. 2 of *Of Revelation and Revolution*. Chicago: University of Chicago Press, 1993.
———. *Ethnography and the Historical Imagination*. Boulder: Westview, 1992.
Connerton, Paul, *How Societies Remember*. Cambridge: Cambridge University Press, 1989.
Cooper, Frederick. *Colonialism in Question: Theory, Knowledge, History*. Berkeley: University of California Press, 2005.
———. "Development, Modernization, and the Social Sciences in the Era of Decolonization: The Examples of British and French Africa." *Revue d'histoire des sciences humaines* 10, no. 1 (2004): 9–38.
———, ed. *Struggle for the City: Migrant Labor, Capital, and the State in Urban Africa*. Beverly Hills: Sage, 1983.
Cooper, Frederick, with Rogers Brubaker. "Identity." In Cooper, *Colonialism in Question*, 59–90.
Coplan, David. "The African Musician and the Development of the Johannesburg Entertainment Industry, 1900–1960." *Journal of Southern African Studies* 5, no. 2 (April 1979): 135–64.
———. *In Township Tonight! South Africa's Black City Music and Theatre*. New York: Longman, 1985.
Coquery-Vidrovitch, Catherine. "The Process of Urbanization in African (From the Origins to the Begining of Independence)." *African Studies Review* 34, no. 1 (April 1991): 1–98.
Coser, Lewis. *The Functions of Social Conflict*. Glencoe, IL: Free Press, 1964.

Costa, Parcídio. "Reflexões sobre o problema da formação: Produtividade e trabalho." *Indústria de Moçambique*, no. 3 (1968): 111.
Craveirinha, José. *O folclore moçambicano e as suas tendências*. Maputo: Alcance Editores, 2008.
Crehan, Kate. *Gramsci, Culture, and Anthropology*. Berkeley: University of California Press, 2002.
Crespo, Jorge. "A educação física em Portugal: Génese da formação de professores." *Boletim da SPEF*, no. 1 (1991): 11–19.
———. "História da educação física em Portugal: Os antecedentes da criação do INEF." *Ludens* 2, no. 1 (1977): 45–52.
Cronin, Mike, and David Mayall. *Sporting Nationalisms: Identity, Ethnicity, Immigration, and Assimilation*. London: Frank Cass, 1998.
Cunha, Joaquim da Silva. *Aspectos dos movimentos associativos na África negra (Angola)*. 2 vols. Lisbon: Junta de Investigações do Ultramar, 1959.
———. "O enquadramento social dos indígenas destribalizados." *Revista do Gabinete de Estudos Corporativos*, nos. 5–6 (January–June 1952): 12–30.
———. *Movimentos associativos na África portuguesa*. Lisbon: Junta de Investigações do Ultramar, 1956.
———. *O sistema português de política indígena: Subsídios para o seu estudo*. Coimbra: Coimbra Editores, 1953.
Damo, Arlei Sander. *Do dom à profissão: Formação de futebolistas no Brasil e na França*. São Paulo: HUCITEC, 2007.
———. "Senso de jogo." *Esporte e sociedade* 1, no. 1 (November 2005–February 2006): 1–36.
Darby, Paul. "African Football Labour Migration to Portugal: Colonial and Neo-colonial Resource." In *Globalised Football: Nations and Migration, the City and the Dream*, edited by Nina Clara Tiesler and João Nuno Coelho. London: Routledge, 2008.
Davis, J. Merle, ed. *Modern Industry and the African: An Enquiry into the Effect of the Copper Mines of Central Africa upon Native Society and the Work of Christian Missions*. London: Macmillan, 1933.
Deniz, Manuel. "'La musique a besoin d'une dictature': Musique et politique dans les premières années de l'État Nouveau (1926–1945)." PhD diss. Paris: Université de Paris VIII, 2005.
Deville-Danthu, Bernardette. *Le sport en noir et blanc: Du sport colonial au sport africain dans le anciens territoires français d'Afrique occidentale (1920–1965)*. Paris: L'Harmattan, 1997.
Dias, Jill. "Uma questão de identidade: Respostas intelectuais às transformações económicas no seio da elite crioula da Angola portuguesa entre 1870 e 1930." *Revista internacional de estudos africanos* 1 (January/June 1984): 61–94.
Direito, Bárbara. "Land and Colonialism in Mozambique: Policies and Practice in Inhambane, c. 1900–c. 1940." *Journal of Southern African Studies* 39, no. 2 (2013): 353–69.

Domingos, Nuno, and Rahul Kumar. "A grande narrativa futebolística." In *Estudos de sociologia da leitura em Portugal no século XX*, edited by Diogo Ramada Curto, 575–638. Lisbon: Fundação Calouste Gulbenkian.

———. *A ópera do Trindade*. Lisbon: Lua de Papel/INET, 2007.

Douglas, Mary, and Baron C. Isherwood. *The World of Goods: Towards an Anthropological Approach to Consumption*. London: Penguin, 1978.

Duarte, Serradas. "O pontapé." *Boletim do INEF* 1, no. 2 (1951): 139–57.

Duffy, James. *Portuguese Africa*. Cambridge, MA: Harvard University Press, 1959.

Dunning, Eric. "The Figurational Dynamics of Modern Sport." *Sportwissenschaft* 9, no. 4 (1979): 341–59.

———, ed. *The Sociology of Sport: A Selection of Readings*. London: Frank Cass, 1971.

———. *Sport Matters: Sociological Studies of Sport, Violence and Civilization*. London: Routledge, 1999.

Dyck, Noel, and Eduardo Archetti, eds. *Sport, Dance and Embodied Identities*. Oxford: Berg, 2003.

Elias, Norbert. *The Civilizing Process*. Oxford: Blackwell, 2000.

———. "The Genesis of Sport as a Sociological Problem." In *The Sociology of Sport: A Selection of Readings*, edited by Eric Dunning, 88–115. London: Frank Cass, 1971.

Elias, Norbert, and Eric Dunning. "Dynamics of Group Sports with Special Reference to Football." *British Journal of Sociology* 17, no. 4 (1966): 388–402.

———. "Folk Football in Medieval and Early Modern Britain." In *The Sociology of Sport: A Selection of Readings*, edited by Dunning, 116–32. London: Frank Cass, 1971.

———. *The Quest for Excitement: Sport and Leisure in the Civilizing Process*. Oxford: Blackwell, 1986.

Epstein, A. L. "Urban Communities in Africa." In *Closed Systems and Open Minds: The Limits of Naïvety in Social Anthropology*, edited by Max Gluckman. Chicago: Aldine, 1967.

Erickson, Bonnie. "Culture, Class, and Connections." *American Journal of Sociology* 102, no. 1 (1996): 217–51.

Eriksen, Thomas. *Common Denominators: Ethnicity, Nation-Building and Compromise in Mauritius*. Oxford: Berg, 1998.

Esteves, José. *O desporto e as estruturas sociais*. Lisbon: Prelo, 1967.

Fabian, Johannes. *Moments of Freedom: Anthropology and Popular Culture*. Charlottesville: University Press of Virginia, 1998.

Fair, Laura. "Ngoma Reverberations: Swahili Music Culture and the Making of Football Aesthetics in Early Twentieth-Century Zanzibar." In Armstrong and Giulianotti, *Football in Africa*, 103–13.

———. *Pastimes and Politics: Culture, Community, and Identity in Post-Abolition Urban Zanzibar, 1890–1945*. Athens: Ohio University Press, 2001.

Fardon, Richard, and Graham Furniss, eds. *African Broadcast Cultures: Radio in Transition*. Oxford: James Currey, 2000.
Faria de Vasconcelos, António. *O que é que deve ser a educação física: Conferência no Ginásio Club Portuguez*. Lisbon: Papelaria Mais, 1928.
Farinha, António Lourenço. *Elementos de gramática landina (shironga)*. Lourenço Marques: Imprensa Nacional, 1917.
Farnell, Brenda. "Moving Bodies, Acting Selves." *Annual Review of Anthropology* 28* (1999): 341–73.
Feio, Noronha. *Plano de trabalhos*. Lourenço Marques: Fundo de Fomento Desportivo, 1972.
Ferguson, James. *Expectations of Modernity: Myths and Meanings of Urban Life on the Zambian Copperbelt*. Berkeley: University of California Press, 1999.
Ferreira, António Gomes. "O ensino da educação física em Portugal durante o Estado Novo." *Perspectiva* 22, special issue (July–December 2004): 197–224.
Ferreira, Eusébio da Silva, *Meu nome é Eusébio: Autobiografia do maior futebolista do mundo*. Lisboa, Publicações Europa-América, 1966.
Filho, Mário. *O negro no futebol brasileiro*. Rio de Janeiro: Mauad, 2003 [1947].
Filho, Wilson Trajano. "A constituição de um olhar fragilizado: Notas sobre o colonialismo português em África." In Carvalho and Pina-Cabral, *Persistência da história*, 21–59.
Forde, Darryl, ed. *Social Implications of Industrialization and Urbanization in Africa South of the Sahara*. London: International African Institute, 1956.
Fortescue, Dominic. "The Accra Crowd, the Asafo, and the Opposition to the Municipal Corporations Ordinance,1924–25." *Canadian Journal of African Studies* 24, no. 3 (1990): 348–75.
Fortuna, Carlos. *O fio da meada: O algodão de Moçambique, Portugal e a economia mundo, 1860–1960*. Porto: Afrontamento, 1993.
Frankenberg, Ronald. *Village on the Border: A Social Study of Religion, Politics and Football in a North Wales Community*. Prospect Heights, IL: Waveland Press: 1999 [1956].
Freund, Bill. *The African City: A History*. Cambridge: Cambridge University Press, 2007.
Freyre, Gilberto. *Integração portuguesa nos trópicos*. Lisbon: Junta de Investigações do Ultramar, 1958.
———. *O luso e o trópico*. Lisbon: Comissão Executiva das Comemorações do Quinto Centenário do Infante D. Henrique, 1961.
———. *O mundo que o português criou*. Lisbon: Livros do Brasil, 1951.
Gabinete de Planeamento e Integração Económica. *IV Plano de Fomento—Ultramar—Relatório Geral Preparatório. Moçambique*. Lisbon: Gabinete de Planeamento e Integração Económica, 1972.
Gallo, Donato. *O saber português: Antropologia e colonialismo*. Lisbon: Editores Reunidos, 1988.

Geertz, Clifford. "Deep Play: Notes on the Balinese Cockfight." In *The Interpretation of Cultures: Selected Essays*, 412–53. New York: Basic Books, 1973.

Giulianotti, Richard. "Between Colonialism, Independence and Globalization: Football in Zimbabwe." In Armstrong and Giulianotti, *Football in Africa*, 80–99.

Gluckman, Max. "Analysis of a Social Situation in Modern Zululand." *Bantu Studies* 14, no. 1 (1940): 1–30.

———. *Custom and Conflict in Africa*. Oxford: Blackwell, 1955.

———, ed. *Essays on the Ritual of Social Relations*. Manchester: Manchester University Press, 1962.

Goffman, Erving. *Asylums: Essays on the Social Situation of Mental Patients and Other Inmates*. Harmondsworth: Penguin, 1968.

———. "The Interaction Order." American Sociological Association, 1982 presidential address. *American Sociological Review* 48, no. 1 (February 1983): 1–17.

———. *The Presentation of Self in Everyday Life*. Harmondsworth: Penguin, 1971.

Gomes, Rui. "Poder e saber sobre o corpo: A educação física no Estado Novo (1936–1945)." Boletim da Sociedade Portuguesa de Educação Física nos. 2–3 (1991): 109–36.

Goody, Jack. *The Logic of Writing and the Organization of Society*. Studies in Literacy, Family, Culture and the State. Cambridge: Cambridge University Press, 1986.

Gramsci, Antonio. *Selections from Cultural Writings*. Translated by William Boelhower. London: Lawrence and Wishart, 1985.

Granovetter, Mark. "The Strength of Weak Ties." *American Journal of Sociology* 78, no. 6 (1973): 1360–80.

Guedes, Amâncio de Alpoim. "The Caniços of Mozambique." In *Shelter in Africa*, edited by Paul Oliver, 200–209. New York: Praeger, 1971.

Guedes, Nobre. "O desporto particular: Forma interventiva do estado." *Boletim do INEF*, nos. 3–4 (1947): 17–18.

Guimarães, Mesquita. "Biotipologia e orientação do desporto." *Boletim do INEF*, no. 2 (1941): 144–54.

Guttmann, Allen. *Games and Empires: Modern Sports and Cultural Imperialism*. New York: Columbia University Press, 1994.

Hammond, R. J. *Portugal and Africa, 1815–1910: A Study in Uneconomic Imperialism*. Stanford: Stanford University Press, 1966.

Hannerz, Ulf. "Thinking with Networks." In *Exploring the City: Inquiries toward an Urban Anthropology*, 163–201. New York: Columbia University Press, 1980.

———. *Transnational Connections: Culture, People, Places*. London: Routledge, 1996.

———. "The World of Creolization." In Barber, *African Popular Culture*, 12–17.

Hargreaves, John. *Sport, Power, and Culture: A Social and Historical Analysis of Popular Sports in Britain*. Cambridge: Polity Press, 1986.
Harries, Patrick. "Christianity in Black and White: The Establishwment of Protestant Churches in Southern Mozambique." *Lusotopie* (1998): 317–33.
———. *Work, Culture, and Identity: Migrant Laborers in Mozambique and South Africa, c. 1860–1910*. Portsmouth, NH: Heinemann, 1993.
Harris, Marvin. "Labour Emigration among the Moçambique Thonga: A Reply to Sr. Rita-Ferreira." *Africa: Journal of the International African Institute* 30, no. 3 (July 1960): 243–45.
———. "Labour Emigration among the Moçambique Thonga: Cultural and Political Factors." *Africa: Journal of the International African Institute* 29, no. 1 (January 1959): 50–66.
———. *Portugal's African "Wards": A First-Hand Report on Labor and Education in Moçambique*. New York: American Committee on Africa, 1958.
Hasse, Manuela. *O divertimento do corpo: Corpo, lazer e desporto na transição do século XIX para o século XX, em Portugal*. Lisbon: Editora Temática, 1999.
Hedges, David, ed. *História de Moçambique*. 2 vols. Maputo: Livraria Universitária de Maputo, 1999.
Henriques, Isabel Castro. "A sociedade colonial em África: Ideologias, hierarquias, quotidianos." In Bethencourt and Chaudhuri, *História da expansão portuguesa*, 5:216–74.
Hobsbawm, Eric. *Bandits*. London: Abacus, 2003.
———. *Primitive Rebels: Studies in Archaic Forms of Social Movement in the 19th and 20th Centuries*. New York: Norton, 1959.
Hognestad, Hans, and Arvid Tollisen. "Playing against Deprivation: Football and Development in Nairobi, Kenya." In Armstrong and Giulianotti, *Football in Africa*, 210–26.
Honwana, Raúl Bernardo. *Memórias*. Porto: Edições ASA, 1989.
Hutchinson, Roger. *Empire Games: The British Invention of Twentieth-Century Sport*. Edinburgh: Mainstream Publishing, 1996.
Ingham, Alan G. "The Sportification Process: A Biographical Analysis Framed by the Work of Marx, Weber, Durkheim and Freud." In *Sport and Modern Social Theorists*, edited by Richard Giulianotti, 11–32. London: Palgrave Macmillan, 2004.
Isaacman, Allen. *Cotton Is the Mother of Poverty: Peasants, Work, and Rural Struggle in Colonial Mozambique, 1938–1961*. Portsmouth, NH: Heinemann, 1997.
———. "Peasants and Rural Social Protest in Africa." *African Studies Review* 33, no. 2 (September 1990): 1–120.
———. "Social Banditry in Zimbabwe (Rhodesia) and Mozambique, 1894–1907: An Expression of Early Peasant Protest." *Journal of South African Studies* 4, no. 1 (1977): 1–30.
Isaacman, Allen, and Barbara Issacman. *Mozambique: From Colonialism to Revolution, 1900–1982*. Boulder: Westview, 1983.

Jackson, Michael. "Knowledge of the Body." *Man*, n.s. 18, no. 2 (June 1983): 327–45.
Jarvie, Grant, and Joseph Maguire. *Sport and Leisure in Social Thought*. London: Routledge, 1994.
Jenkins, Richard. *Pierre Bourdieu*. London: Routledge, 1992.
Jorge, Ismael Mário. "L'éducation physique et le sport." In *Portugal, Colonie de Moçambique*. Paris: Exposition Coloniale Internationale, 1931.
Junod, Henri. *Usos e costumes dos Bantu*. Campinas: Instituto de Filosofia e Ciências Humanas, Universidade Estadual de Campinas, 2009 [1912–13].
Junta de Investigações do Ultramar. *Estudo sobre o absentismo e a instabilidade da mão-de-obra africana*. 3 vols. Lisbon: Junta de Investigações do Ultramar, 1959–60.
———. *Inquérito habitacional realizado no bairro da Munhuana*. Lisbon: Junta de Investigações do Ultramar, Estudos de Ciências Políticas e Sociais, Centro de Estudos de Serviço Social e de Desenvolvimento Comunitário, 1964.
———. *Promoção social em Moçambique*. Lisbon: Junta de Investigações do Ultramar, Estudos de Ciências Políticas e Sociais, Centro de Estudos de Serviço Social e de Desenvolvimento Comunitário, 1964.
Kennedy, Dane. *Islands of White: Settler Society and Culture in Kenya and Southern Rhodesia, 1890–1939*. Durham: Duke University Press, 1987.
King, Anthony D. *Colonial Urban Development: Culture, Social Power and Environment*. London: Routledge and Kegan Paul, 1976.
———. *Urbanism, Colonialism and the World-Economy: Cultural and Spatial Foundations of the World System*. London: Routledge, 1990.
Kirk, David. "Foucault and the Limits of Corporeal Regulation: The Emergence, Consolidation and Decline of School Medical Inspection and Physical Training in Australia, 1909–30." *International Journal of the History of Sport* 13, no. 2 (1996): 114–31.
Kirk-Green, Anthony. "Imperial Administration and the Athletic Imperative: The Case of the District Officer in Africa." In Baker and Mangan, *Sport in Africa*, 81–113.
Kumalo, Simangaliso. "Meeting the Cowboy Turned Renegade Missionary: William Cullen Wilcox." *Studia historiae ecclesiastica* 39, supplement (August 2013): 337–52.
Kumar, Rahul. "A pureza perdida do desporto: Futebol no Estado Novo." PhD diss., Faculdade de Ciências Sociais e Humanas, Universidade Nova de Lisboa, 2014.
Kuper, Adam. *Anthropology and Anthropologists: The Modern British School*. London: Routledge, 1996.
———. *Culture: The Anthropologists' Account*. Cambridge, MA: Harvard University Press, 2000.
Lacharte, Brigitte. *Enjeaux urbains au Mozambique, de Lourenco Marques a Maputo*. Paris, Karthala, 2000.

Leal de Oliveira, António. "Bases para a organização da educação física escolar." *I Congresso da União Nacional: Discursos, teses e comunicações.* 8 vols. Lisbon: União Nacional, 1935.
———. "Construção e conservação dos ginmásios e do respectivo material didáctico." *Boletim do INEF*, no. 1 (1942): 22–55.
———. "Generalidades sôbre o as attitudes e movimento do corpo humano em educação física." *Boletim do INEF*, no. 3 (1941): 273–89.
———. "A lição de gimnástica educativa—1.ª lição de ginástica para o ensino primário." *Boletim do INEF*, no. 2 (1940): 169–81.
———. "Os movimentos." *Boletim do INEF*, no. 4 (1941): 382–401.
———. "A pessoa e a sua educação física." *Boletim do INEF*, no. 2 (1940): 126–32.
Leite, Joana Pereira. "La formation de l'économie coloniale au Mozambique: Pacte colonial et industrialisation: Du colonialisme portugais aux réseaux informels de sujétion marchande, 1930–74." PhD diss., École dês Hautes Études en Sciences Sociales, Paris, 1989.
Leite Lopes, José Sérgio. "Sucesses and Contradictions in 'Multiracial' Brazilian Football." In Armstrong and Giulianotti, *Entering the Field*, 53–86.
Leite Lopes, José Sergio, and Sylvain Maresca. "La disparition de 'la joie du peuple.'" *Actes de la recherche en sciences sociales* 79, no. 1 (1989): 21–36.
Leonard, Yves. "O império colonial salazarista." In Bethencourt and Chaudhuri, *História da expansão portuguesa*, 5:10–30.
Leseth, Anne. "The Use of Juju in Football: Sports and Witchcraft in Tanzania." In Armstrong and Richard Giulianotti, *Entering the Field*, 159–74.
Little, Kenneth. "The Role of Voluntary Associations in West African Urbanization." *American Anthropologist* 59, no. 4 (1957): 579–96.
Lobato, Alexandre. *História da fundação de Lourenço Marques.* Lisbon: Edições da Revista Lusitânia, 1948.
———. *História do presidio de Lourenço Marques.* 2 vols. Lisbon: Estudos Moçambicanos, 1949–60.
———. *Lourenço Marques, Xilunguíne: Biografia da cidade.* Lisbon: Agência-Geral do Ultramar, 1970.
Macagno, Lorenzo. *Outros muçulmanos: Islão e narrativas coloniais.* Lisbon: Instituto Ciências Sociais, 2006.
MacClancy, Jeremy, ed. *Sport, Identity and Ethnicity.* Oxford: Berg, 1996.
Mackenzie, John M. *The Empire of Nature: Hunting, Conservation and British Imperialism.* Manchester: Manchester University Press, 1988.
———. *Propaganda and Empire: The Manipulation of British Public Opinion, 1880–1960.* Manchester: Manchester University Press, 1984.
Maclaren, James. *A Concise Xhosa-English Dictionary.* London: Longmans, Green, 1936.
Magode, José. *Pouvoir et réseaux sociaux au Mozambique: Appartenances, interactivité du social et du politique (1933–1994).* Paris: Éditions Connaissances et Savoirs, 2005.
Mahlo, Friedrich. *O acto táctico no jogo.* Lisbon: Compendium, 1987.

Mangan, J. A., ed. *The Cultural Bond: Sport, Empire, Society.* London: Frank Cass, 1992.
———. "Ethics and Ethnocentricity: Imperial Education in British Tropical Africa." In Baker and Mangan, *Sport in Africa*, 138–71.
Mangan, J. A., and Andrew Ritchie, eds. *Ethnicity, Sport, Identity: Struggles for Status.* London: Frank Cass, 2004.
Mann, Michael. *The Sources of Social Power.* 4 vols. Cambridge: Cambridge University Press, 1986–2013.
Margarido, Alfredo, "Le colonialisme portugais et l'anthropologie." In *Anthropologie et imperialism*, edited by Jean Copans. Paris: Maspero, 1975.
———. *A lusofonia e os lusófonos: Novos mitos portugueses.* Lisbon: Edições Universidade Lusófona, 2001.
———. *Negritude e humanismo.* Lisbon: Casa dos Estudantes do Império, 1964.
Marques Pereira, Celestino. "A educação física na mocidade portuguesa." *Boletim do INEF*, nos. 1–3 (1944): 58–145.
———. *A educação física na Suécia e na Dinamarca: Contribuições para o seu estudo em Portugal.* Lisbon: Ministério da Educação, Instituto para a Alta Cultura, 1939.
———. "A função da ginástica perante o desporto como meio de formação física na juventude." *Boletim do INEF* nos. 1–2 (1947): 13–25.
———. "Necessidade da análise psico-fisiológica e mecânica do comportamento motriz educativo do ser humano: Importância da análise cibernética como hipótese de trabalho e de investigação científica." *Boletim do INEF*, nos. 1–2 (1954): 35–55.
———. "Sur la justification psyco-physiologique de la valeur éducative des compétitions sportives de la jeunesse." *Boletim do INEF*, nos. 1–2 (1950): 83–105.
Martin, Phyllis M. *Leisure and Society in Colonial Brazzaville.* Cambridge: Cambridge University Press, 1995.
Martin, Simon. *Football and Fascism: The National Game under Mussolini.* Oxford: Berg, 2004.
Martins, E. A. Azambuja. *Acção educativa sôbre as populações indígenas de Moçambique, consequente de instrução militar do soldado indígena.* Lisbon: I Congresso da História da Expansão Portuguesa no Mundo, 1938): 16–17.
Marx, Karl. *The Eighteenth Brumaire of Louis Bonaparte.* London: Allen and Unwin, 1926 [1852].
Matias, M. Goretti. "A questão do álcool e a exportação de vinho para o ultramar: O debate de 1902." In *O douro contemporâneo*, edited by Gaspar Martins Pereira and Paula Montes Leal, 233–46. Porto: Grupo de Estudos de História da Viticultura Duriense, 2006.
Mauss, Marcel. *Sociologie et anthropologie.* Paris: Presses Universitaires de France, 1989.
Mayer, Philip. *Townsmen or Tribesmen: Conservatism and the Process of Urbanization in a South African City.* Cape Town: Oxford University Press, 1961.

Medeiros, Eduardo. *Bebidas Moçambicanas de fabrico caseiro*. Maputo: Arquivo Histórico de Moçambique, 1988.
Mellor, Phillip, and Chris Shilling. *Re-forming the Body: Religion, Community and Modernity*. London: Sage, 1997.
Melo, Daniel. "Longe da vista perto do coração: O associativismo regionalista no império português." *Comunicação ao VIII Congresso Luso-Afro-Brasileiro de Ciências Sociais*, 16/17/18 de Setembro de 2004.
——. *Salazarismo e cultura popular (1933–1958)*. Lisbon: Imprensa de Ciências Sociais, 2001.
Melo, Victor Andrade de. *Jogos de identidade: O esporte em Cabo Verde*. Rio de Janeiro: Apicuri/CNP, 2011.
Mendes, Maria Clara. *Maputo antes da independência: Geografia de uma cidade colonial*. Lisbon: Centro de Estudos Geográficos das Universidade de Lisbon, 1979.
——. *Variação especial da densidade de população urbana em Lourenço Marques*. Lisbon: Centro de Estudos Geográficos da Universidade de Lisboa, 1976.
Mitchell, J. Clyde. *Cities, Society, and Social Perception: A Central African Perspective*. Oxford: Claredon Press, 1987.
——. *The Kalela Dance: Aspects of Social Relationships among Urban Africans in Northern Rhodesia*. Manchester: Manchester University Press, 1956.
——. *Social Networks in Urban Situations: Analysis of Personal Relationships in Central African Towns*. Manchester: Institute for Social Research University of Zambia and Manchester University Press, 1969.
Moorman, Marissa J. *Intonations: A Social History of Music and Nation in Luanda, Angola, from 1945 to Recent Times*. Athens: Ohio University Press, 2008.
Morais, João de Sousa. *Maputo: Património da estrutura e forma urbana topologia do lugar*. Lisbon: Livros Horizonte, 2001.
Moreira, Adriano. "Problemas sociais no ultramar." *Estudos ultramarinos* 10, no. 4 (1960): 7–19.
Nascimento, Augusto. *Esporte em vez de política no São Tomé e Príncipe*. Rio de Janeiro: 7Letras, 2013.
Nascimento, Augusto, Marcelo Bittencourt, Nuno Domingos, and Victor Andrade de Melo, eds. *Esporte e lazer na África: Novos olhares*. Rio de Janeiro: 7Letras, 2013.
Nascimento, Augusto, Marcelo Bittencourt, Victor Andrade de Melo, eds. *Mais do que um jogo: O esporte e o continente africano*. Rio de Janeiro: Apicuri, 2010.
Nauright, John. *Sports, Cultures and Identities in South Africa*. London: Leicester University Press, 1997.
Neves, José. "O eterno fado dos últimos 30 metros, nacionalismo e corpo." In *A época do futebol: O jogo visto pelas Ciências Sociais*, edited by José Neves and Nuno Domingos. Lisbon: Assírio e Alvim, 2004.

Neves, Olga. "Em defesa da causa africana: Intervenção do Grémio Africano na sociedade de Lourenço Marques, 1908–1938." PhD. diss., Faculdade de Ciências Sociais e Humanas da Universidade Nova de Lisboa, 1989.
Newell, Stephanie, and Onookome Okome. *Popular Culture in Africa: The Episteme of the Everyday*. London: Routledge, 2013.
Newitt, Malyn. *A History of Mozambique*. Bloomington: Indiana University Press, 1995.
——. *Portugal in Africa: The Last Hundred Years*. London: C. Hurst, 1981.
Nogueira, Rodrigo de Sá. *Dicionário ronga-português*. Lisbon: Junta de Investigações do Ultramar, 1960.
Nóvoa, António. "A Educação Nacional." In *Nova História de Portugal*, edited by Joel Serrão and A. H. de Oliveira Marques, in *Portugal e o Estado Novo* vol. 12 (1930–1960), edited by Fernando Rosas, 455–519. Lisbon: Presença, 1992.
O'Laughlin, Bridget. "Class and the Customary: The Ambiguous Legacy of the Indigenato in Mozambique." *African Affairs* 99, no. 394 (2000): 5–43.
Oliveira, Cândido de. *Football: Técnica e tática*. Lisbon: published by author, 1935.
——. *Relatório da minha viagem a Inglaterra ao serviço do Football Nacional*. Lisbon: Federação Portuguesa de Futebol, 1936.
——. *WM: A evolução táctica no futebol*. Lisbon: published by author, 1949.
Oliveira, Mário. *Problemas essenciais do urbanismo no ultramar*. Lisbon: Agência-Geral do Ultramar, 1962.
Orde-Browne, Granville St. John. *The African Labourer*. Oxford: Oxford University Press, International African Institute, 1933.
Pacheco, António Carneiro. "Notável discurso de sua ex.ª o senhor ministro da educação discurso." *Boletim do INEF*, no. 3 (1941): 257–63.
Parkin, D. J. "Voluntary Associations as Institutions of Adaptation." *Man*, n.s., 1, no. 1 (March 1966): 90–95.
Paulo, João Carlos. "Da educação colonial portuguesa ao ensino no ultramar." In *A história da expansão portuguesa*, edited by Francisco Bethencourt and Kirti Chaudhuri, 5:304–33. Lisbon: Círculo dos Leitores, 1999.
Peel, J.D.Y. "Social and Cultural Change." In *The Cambridge History of Africa*, vol. 8, chap. 4, 142–91. Cambridge: Cambridge University Press, 1984.
Pegado, J. R. "Panorama das investigações efectuadas, até 1961, sobre sociologia urbana em África ao sul do Saara." *Boletim do Instituto de Investigação Científica de Moçambique* 2, no. 2 (1961): 391–97.
Peixoto, Carolina, and Maria Paula Meneses. "Domingos Arouca: Um percurso de militância nacionalista em Moçambique." *Topoi: Revista de História*, 14, no. 26 (2013): 86–104.
Penvenne, Jeanne Marie. *African Workers and Colonial Racism: Mozambican Strategies and Struggles in Lourenço Marques, 1877–1962*. London: James Currey, 1995.

———. "'Here Everyone Walked with Fear': The Mozambican Labor System and the Workers of Lourenco Marques, 1945–1962." In Cooper, *Struggle for the City*, 131–66.
———. "João dos Santos Albasini (1876–1922): The Contradictions of Politics and Identity in Colonial Mozambique." *Journal of African History* 37, no. 3 (1996): 419–64.
———. *Trabalhadores de Lourenço Marques (1870–1974)*. Maputo: Arquivo Histórico de Moçambique, 1993.
———. *Women, Migration and the Cashew Economy in Southern Mozambique: 1945–1975*. Rochester: James Currey, 2015.
Pereira, Rui Mateus. "Conhecer para dominar: O desenvolvimento do conhecimento antropológico na política colonial portuguesa em Moçambique, 1926–1959." PhD diss., Faculdade de Ciências Sociais e Humanas da Universidade Nova de Lisboa, 2005.
———. "Introdução à reedição de Os Maconde de Moçambiques." In *Os macondes de Moçambique*, edited by Jorge Dias, vol. 1, *Aspectos históricos e económicos*. Lisbon: Comissão Nacional para as Comemorações dos Descobrimentos Portugueses, Instituto de Investigação Científica Tropical, 1998.
———. "A 'Missão etognósica de Moçambique': A codificação dos 'usos e costumes indígenas' no direito colonial português: Notas de investigação." *Cadernos de estudos africanos* 1 (2001): 125–77.
Perkin, Harold. "Teaching the Nations How to Play: Sport and Society in the British Empire and Commonwealth." Epilogue to Mangan, *Cultural Bond*.
Pfister, Gertrud. "'Cultural Confrontations': German *Turnen*, Swedish Gymnastics and English Sport: European Diversity in Physical Activities from a Historical Perspective." *Culture, Sport, Society* 6, no. 1 (Spring 2003): 61–91.
Pina-Cabral, João de. "'Agora pode saber o que é ser pobre': Identificações e diferenciações no mundo da Lusotopia." *Lusotopie* (2002): 215–24.
———. "Cisma e continuidade em Moçambique." In Carvalho and Pina-Cabral, *Persistência da história*, 375–93.
Pinheiro, Francisco. *História da imprensa desportiva em Portugal*. Porto: Afrontamento, 2011.
Pitcher, Anne. *Politics in the Portuguese Empire: The State, Industry, and Cotton, 1926–1974*. Oxford: Clarendon Press, 1993.
Polanah, Luís. *O Nhamussoro e as outras funções mágico-religiosas*. Coimbra: Instituto de Antropologia, Universidade de Coimbra, 1987.
Prata, A. Pires. *Dicionário Macua-Português*. Lisbon: Instituto de Investigação Científica Tropical, 1990.
Radway, Janice. *Reading the Romance: Women, Patriarchy, and Popular Literature*. Chapel Hill: University of North Carolina Press, 1984.
Ramos do Ó, Jorge. *O governo de si mesmo: Modernidade pedagógica e encenações disciplinares do aluno liceal: Último quartel do século XIX— meados do século XX*. Lisbon: Educa, 2003.

Ranger, Terence. *Dance and Society in Eastern Africa, 1890–1970: The Beni Ngoma*. London: Heinemann, 1975.

———. "Pugilism and Pathology: African Boxing and the Black Urban Experience in Southern Rhodesia." In Baker and Mangan, *Sport in Africa*, 196–213.

Reis, Ribeiro dos. *Foot-Ball*. Lisbon: Livraria Popular de Francisco Franco, 1927.

Relatório da Missão de S. José de Lhanguene. Lourenço Marques: Tipografia da Missão de S. José de Lhanguene, 1942.

Relatório do governador geral de Moçambique. Lisbon: Divisão de Publicações e Bibliotecas, Agência Geral das Colónias, 1945.

Rigauer, Bero. *Sport and Work*. Translated by Allen Guttmann. New York: Columbia University Press, 1981.

Rita-Ferreira, António. *Os Africanos de Lourenço Marques*. Memórias do Instituto de Investigação Científica de Moçambique / Instituto de Investigação Científica de Moçambique, vol. 9, series C (1967–68), 95–491.

———. "Distribuição ocupacional da população africana de Lourenço Marques." *Indústria de Moçambique* 2, no. 6 (1969): 200–202.

———. "Estudo sobre a evolução, em Moçambique, da mão-de-obra e das remunerações, no sector privado, de 1950 a 1970." *Indústria de Moçambique* 6, no. 5 (1973): 137–52.

———. "Labour Emigration among the Moçambique Thonga: A Comment on a Study by Marvin Harris." *Africa: Journal of the International African Institute* 30, no. 2 (April 1960): 141–52.

———. "A oscilação do trabalhador africano entre o meio rural e o meio urbano." *Indústria de Moçambique* 2, no. 3 (1969): 96–99.

Rocha, Aurélio. *Associativismo e nativismo em Moçambique: Contribuição para o estudo das origens do nacionalismo moçambicano (1900–1940)*. Maputo: Promédia, 2002.

Rocha, Ilídio. *Catálogo dos periódicos e principais seriados editados em Moçambique: Da introdução da tipografia à independência, 1854–1975*. Maputo: Cedimo, 1980.

———. *A imprensa de Moçambique*. Lisbon: Livros do Brasil, 2000.

Rufino, José dos Santos. *Álbuns fotográficos e descritivos da colónia de Moçambique*. 10 vols. Hamburg: Broschek and Co., 1929.

Santandrea, Fr. S. "Evil and Witchcraft among the Ndogo Group of Tribes." *Africa: Journal of the International African Institute* 11, no. 4 (October 1938): 459–81.

Santos, Ana. *Heróis desportivos: Estudo de caso sobre Eusébio: De corpo a ícone da nação*. Lisbon: Instituto do Desporto de Portugal, 2004.

Schieffelin, Edward L. "Performance and the Cultural Construction of Reality." *American Ethnologist* 12, no. 4 (November 1985): 707–24.

Schultz, Jennifer, and Ronald L. Breiger. "The Strength of Weak Culture." *Poetics* 38, no. 6 (2010): 610–24.

Schmitter, Philippe C. *Portugal: Do autoritarismo à democracia*. Lisbon: Imprensa de Ciências Sociais, 1999.

Scotch, N. A. "Magic, Sorcery, and Football among Urban Zulu: A Case of Reinterpretation under Acculturation." *Journal of Conflict Resolution* 5, no. 1, The Anthropology of Conflict (March 1961): 70–74.

Scott, James C. *Domination and the Arts of Resistance: Hidden Transcripts.* New Haven: Yale University Press, 1990.

———. *Weapons of the Weak: Everyday Forms of Peasant Resistance.* New Haven: Yale University Press, 1985.

Serpa, Homero. *Cândido de Oliveira: Uma biografia.* Lisbon: Caminho, 2000.

Shilling, Chris. *The Body and Social Theory.* London: Sage, 1993.

Silva, Astregildo. *Ribeiro dos Reis: Biografia.* Lisbon: Caminho, 2004.

Silva, Teresa Cruz e. *Igrejas protestantes e consciência política no sul de Moçambique: O caso da Missão Suíça (1930–1974).* Maputo: Promédia, 2001.

Simmel, Georg. "Fashion." *International Quarterly* 10, no. 1 (October 1904): 130–55; reprinted in *American Journal of Sociology* 62, no. 6 (May 1957): 541–58.

Soares, A. Castilho. *Política de bem-estar rural em Angola.* Lisbon: Junta de Investigações do Ultramar, 1961.

Sopa, António. *A alegria é uma coisa rara: Subsídios para a história da música popular urbana em Lourenço Marques (1920–1975).* Maputo: Marimbique, 2014.

Steinhart, Edward I. *Black Poachers, White Hunters: A Social History of Hunting in Colonial Kenya.* Athens: Ohio University Press, 2006.

Steinmetz, George. "Le champ de l'état colonial: Le cas des colonies allemandes (Afrique du Sud-Ouest, Qingdao, Samoa)." *Actes de la recherche en sciences sociales* 1–2, no. 171 (2008): 122–143.

Stoddart, Brian. "Sport, Cultural Imperialism, and Colonial Response in the British Empire." *Comparative Studies in Society and History* 30, no. 4 (October 1988): 649–73.

Teja, Angela. "Italian Sport and International Relations under Fascism." In Arnaud and Riordan, *Sport and International Politics*, 147–70.

Telo, António José. *Economia e império.* Lisbon: Cosmos, 1994.

Thompson, E. P. "The Moral Economy of the English Crowd in the Eighteenth Century." *Past and Present* 50, no. 1 (1971): 76–136.

———. "Time, Work-Discipline, and Industrial Capitalism." *Past and Present*, supplement no. 38 (December 1967): 56–97.

Todorov, Tzvetan. *Mikhail Bakthin: The Dialogical Principle.* Minneapolis: University of Minnesota Press, 1984.

Tolleneer, Jan. "The Belgian Catholic Gymnastic Movement in Its International Context, 1908–1940." In Arnaud and Riordan, *Sport and International Politics*, 171–83.

Torre do Valle, Ernesto. *Diccionarios shironga-portuguez e portuguez-shironga.* Lourenço Marques: Imprensa Nacional, 1906.

Torres, Adelino. *O império português: Entre o real e o imaginário.* Lisbon: Escher, 1991.

———. "Pacto colonial e industrialização de Angola (anos 60–70)." *Análise social* 19 (77-78-79), nos. 3, 4 and 5.(1983): 1101–19.
Turner, Bryan S. *The Body and Society: Explorations in Social Theory*. London: Sage, 1984.
———. *Regulating Bodies: Essays in Medical Sociology*. London: Routledge, 1992.
Vail, Leroy, and Landeg White. *Capitalism and Colonialism in Mozambique: A Study of Quelimane District*. London: Heinemann, 1980.
Valente, José Carlos. *Estado Novo e alegria no trabalho: Uma história política da FNAT (1935–1958)*. Lisbon: Colibri, 1999.
Veblen, Thorstein. *The Theory of the Leisure Class: An Economic Study in the Evolution of Institutions*. New York: Macmillan, 1899.
Viana, Mário Gonçalves. "Os problemas da selecção, orientação, preparação e treino do desportista, considerados à luz da pedagogia." *Boletim do INEF*, nos. 1–2 (1955): 29–53.
Vidacs, Bea. "Through the Prism of Sports: Why Should Africanists Study Sports?" *Afrika Spectrum* 41, no. 3 (2006): 331–49.
———. *Visions of a Better World: Football in the Cameroonian Social Imagination*. Berlin: LIT Verlag, 2010.
Wacquant, Loïc. *Body and Soul: Notebooks of an Apprentice Boxer*. Oxford: Oxford University Press, 2004.
Weber, Eugen. "Gymnastics and Sports in *Fin-de-Siècle* France: Opium of the Classes?" *American Historical Review* 76, no. 1 (February 1971): 70–98.
Weber, Max. *Os fundamentos racionais e sociológicos da música*. São Paulo: Editora da Universidade de São Paulo, 1995 [1921].
Wellman, Barry, ed. *Networks in the Global Village: Life in Contemporary Communities*. Boulder: Westview, 1999.
West, Harry G. "Invertendo a Bossa do Camelo: Jorge Dias, a sua mulher, o seu intérprete e eu." In *Portugal não é um país pequeno: Contar o "império" na pós-colonidade*, edited by Manuela Ribeiro Sanches, 141–92. Lisbon: Cotovia, 2006.
———. *Kupilikula: Governance and the Invisible Realm in Mozambique*. Chicago: University of Chicago Press, 2005.
Williams, Raymond. *Culture and Society, 1780–1950*. Garden City, NY: Doubleday, 1958.
———. *The Long Revolution*. Harmondsworth: Pelican, 1965.
———. *Marxism and Literature*. Oxford: Oxford University Press, 1977.
Zamparoni, Valdemir. "Entre Narros e Mulungos: Colonialismo e paisagem social em Lourenço Marques, c. 1890–c. 1940." PhD diss., Faculdade Letras e Ciências Humanas da Universidade de São Paulo, 1998.
———. "Monhés, baneanes, chinas e Afro-maometanos: Colonialismo e racismo em Lourenço Marques, Moçambique, 1890–1940." *Lusotopie* (2000): 191–222.
Zenha, Francisco Salgado. *A prisão do Doutor Domingos Arouca*. Porto: Afrontamento, 1972.

Index

1.º de Maio (Grupo Desportivo), 32, 35, 39, 194, 196, 211, 255

Ágoas, Frederico, 271
Aja, Teresa Gonzalez, 258
Albasini, João, 69, 86, 87, 248, 272, 279
Alegi, Peter, 9, 239, 251, 262, 284, 291
Alexandre, Valentim, 237, 249
Alto Maé (neighborhood), 32, 35, 84, 153, 196, 204, 207, 210
Anderson, Benedict, 36, 99, 185, 205
Anderson, Perry, 235
Archetti, Eduardo, 288
Armstrong, Gary, 241
Associação de Futebol Africana (African Football Association, AFA): end of, 135, 202, 209, 213, 214, 215, 217, 218, 220, 262; foundation, 33, 85–88; and local notables, 87, 90, 97, 98, 104, 105, 280; players, 49, 91, 93, 96, 105, 194, 255, 261; and resistance, 89, 90; and South Africa, 99, 100, 160, 214
Associação de Futebol de Lourenço Marques (Lourenço Marques Football Association AFLM), 32, 34, 200, 201, 201, 213, 252; and local notables, 90, 91; and players 37, 39; and racism, 39, 40, 49, 50, 51, 214, 216, 219; and settlers, 49, 193, 194, 215
athletics, 17, 110, 219
Atlético de Lourenço Marques, 49, 194
Atlético Mahometano (Clube), 87, 88, 90, 95, 108, 150, 280

Barber, Karin, 238
Beira-Mar (Grupo Desportivo), 1, 39, 40, 85, 86, 87, 88, 90, 93, 95, 99, 108, 117, 150, 180, 197, 216, 217, 255, 279, 280, 283, 284, 285, 294
Beirense (Grupo Desportivo), 88, 89, 96, 280, 281, 283, 285
Benfica (Sport Lisboa e Benfica), 56, 57, 73, 83, 189, 154, 156, 172, 186, 187, 189, 195, 221, 291, 292, 295; in Lourenço Marques, 34, 194, 195, 196, 197, 200, 252, 254, 294; and suburban fans, 83, 194, 196, 198, 200, 203, 204, 213, 217, 221
Berger, Peter, 235, 239
Billig, Michael, 265
Blacking, John, 238
body: embodiment, 18, 75, 131, 149, 151, 179, 193, 225, 227, 229, 231, 288, 294; as history, 9, 225–31; and meaning, 4, 13, 43, 102, 114, 117, 125, 127, 156, 162, 181, 183, 184, 217, 218, 220, 243, 244; and motor repertoire, 15, 60, 102, 113, 117, 120, 121, 123, 127, 128, 130, 159, 161, 162, 166, 168, 171, 176, 178, 183, 185, 218, 227; and performance, 9, 13, 44, 49, 67, 115, 130, 132, 146, 156, 159, 169, 181, 188, 228; and practical knowledge, 2, 11, 122, 128, 168, 183, 227, 230, 241, 243; as social and political metaphor, 42–44, 57, 59, 132, 156, 163
Bourdieu, Pierre, 14, 234, 240, 243, 244, 247–48, 288, 289, 298
Brado africano, O, 1, 16, 201, 233, 234; and football, 39, 40, 79, 85, 86, 88, 93, 98, 99, 100, 107–8, 109, 153, 177, 194, 200; and GALM, 27, 100, 155
British: colonialism, 22, 236, 254, 259, 282; in Lourenço Marques, 21, 30, 42, 46, 58, 106, 225, 250

319

Bromberger, Christian, 243
Brubaker, Rogers, 234, 243

Caetano, Marcelo, 67, 269–70
Câmara Municipal de Lourenço Marques (Lourenço Marques City Council), 69, 74, 75, 89, 218, 250, 252, 273, 275
cantinas (canteens), 47, 71, 98, 203, 204, 205, 219
Carreira, Salazar, 260, 264
Carreira de Tiro (Grupo Desportivo), 35, 50–51, 262
Carvalho, Luís Miguel, 259
Castro, Ruy de, 288
Central (neighborhood), 32, 35, 210
Centro de Estudos Políticos e sociais (Center for Political and Social Studies), 67, 270
Chamanculo (neighborhood), 73, 79, 80, 82, 83, 88, 129, 198, 208, 218, 219, 223, 283, 295
Chapman, Herbert, 160, 165, 169, 172, 173, 174
Clarence-Smith, Gervase, 29, 237, 297–98
Cleveland, Todd, 294
Coelho, João Nuno, 265
colonial system: assimilation, 41, 42, 56, 67, 69, 90, 94, 100, 103, 109, 110, 111, 115, 136, 137, 138, 155, 234, 247, 255, 281; Catholic Church, 28, 47, 80, 88, 137, 234, 277; colonial social contract, 3, 29, 61, 65, 67, 68, 79, 128, 208, 227; detribalization, 30, 67, 270; education, 26, 27, 28, 40, 41, 42, 47, 65, 66, 80, 109, 169, 210, 211, 212, 219, 234, 249, 256, 257; indigenato, 3, 18, 27, 29, 55, 59, 61, 65, 66, 67, 70, 73, 75, 76, 135, 201, 209, 226, 248, 276; labor, 8, 22, 25, 28, 29, 35, 53, 64, 67, 69, 77, 78, 84, 91, 96, 100, 152, 163, 184, 207, 208, 215, 223, 227, 229, 246, 269, 270, 271–72; labor, domestic, 25, 68, 72, 77, 96, 226, 271–73; labor, forced, 7, 26, 28, 69, 70, 248, 273; labor stabilization, 49, 56, 67, 133, 137, 227; modernization, 49, 61, 74, 229; racism, 17, 33, 39, 40, 50, 51, 56, 57, 65, 68, 71, 76, 79, 101, 152, 212, 213, 215, 223, 262; resistance, 9, 47, 78, 86, 90, 92, 105; and science, 29, 67, 68, 72–77, 269, 270, 271, 275; social policies, 55, 67, 249, 269, 270, 271; surveillance, 9, 41, 67, 89, 90, 106, 218, 226; violence, 29, 67, 78, 131, 132, 212, 226,
Coluna, Mário, 4, 50, 56, 57, 82, 91, 155, 185, 186, 187, 194, 195, 196, 197, 198, 202, 204, 229, 255, 261, 278
Connerton, Paul, 244
Conselho Provincial de Educação Física de Moçambique (Mozambique Provincial Council on Physical Education), 48, 50, 260, 261, 262, 264, 276
Cooper, Frederick, 234, 236
Coplan, David, 239, 277
Coquery-Vidrovitch, Catherine, 236
Correia, Severiano, 154, 173, 174, 175, 176, 178, 180, 197, 201, 253, 293
Coser, Lewis, 11
Costa Pereira, Alberto da, 156, 186, 195,
Coubertin, Pierre de, 46
Craveirinha, José, 1, 71, 78, 91, 233; and football, 3, 12, 14, 18, 40, 59, 83, 102, 113–22, 126, 128, 134, 135, 137, 140, 155, 162, 169, 178, 181, 182, 215–17, 220, 228, 229, 239, 255, 288, 289
Crehan, Kate, 234

Damo, Arlei Sander, 243
Desportivo (Grupo Desportivo de Lourenço Marques), 33, 34, 35, 39, 106, 145, 179, 182, 194, 195, 197, 202, 211, 215, 216, 217, 221, 251, 252, 254, 295
Dias, Jill, 247
Direcção Geral de Educação Física, Desportos e Saúde Escolar (General Office of Physical Education, Sports, and Scholastic Health), 42, 214
Douglas, Mary, 240
Dunning, Eric, 12, 234, 240, 241, 242, 244, 284, 292

Elias, Norbert, 12, 13, 131, 234, 238, 240, 241, 242, 244, 284, 292
Epstein, A. L., 236, 271

Eriksen, Thomas Hylland, ix, 240
Estado Novo (New State), 27, 28, 41, 237, 245, 249, 256, 257; and sport, 42, 44, 54, 59, 132, 156, 163, 226, 258
Eusébio da Silva Ferreira, 4, 56, 57 62, 83, 155, 179, 187, 189, 195, 196, 218, 221, 229, 265, 266

Fair, Laura, 9
Ferreira, António Gomes, 264
Ferroviário (Clube Ferroviário de Lourenço Marques), 32, 33, 34, 39, 91, 143, 145, 150, 173, 174, 182, 197, 210, 211, 216, 221, 252, 253, 291, 293
field (of activity) 21, 25, 27, 29, 31, 33, 35, 37, 39, 41, 43, 47, 48, 49, 51, 53, 55, 57, 58, 59
Filho, Mário, 265, 296
Filho, Wilson Trajano, 235
football: audiences, 2, 4, 13, 46, 83, 99, 107, 108, 110, 111, 113–15, 118–30, 152, 164, 165, 170, 171, 175, 176, 178, 180, 183, 185, 188, 195, 215, 228; and civilization, 2, 88, 102, 102, 109, 110, 111, 117, 191; and communitarian construction, 4, 11, 79, 84, 92, 93, 99, 103, 105, 108, 109, 119, 129–33, 144, 145, 148, 151, 152, 180, 181, 192, 202, 206, 209, 220, 222, 223, 225, 286; and conflict, 11; as decadence, 110, 191; as a democracy, 104, 118, 121, 127, 131; as language, 2, 12, 13, 14, 18, 19, 134, 164, 166, 168, 169, 182, 188, 197, 213, 227–31, 242, 294; laws of the game, 33, 103, 106, 107, 108, 112, 115, 117, 120, 121, 127–29, 157, 165, 285; and modernity, 127, 149, 151, 177; as moral economy, 14, 18, 127, 131, 152, 162, 188, 218, 229; neighborhood matches, 26, 59, 81, 83, 84, 93, 95, 97, 102, 103, 113, 116, 117, 124, 158–61, 190, 194, 217, 218, 220; professionalization, 39, 42, 54, 59, 163, 164, 169, 177, 185, 186, 188, 196, 209, 229, 264; and social mobility, 4, 19, 27, 42, 158, 208, 215, 221, 230, 231; as social problem, 111–13, 122, 152; as social representation, 14, 20, 65, 85, 193, 194; and violence, 103–8, 111–19, 127, 128, 130–33, 228, 285

football narratives, 10, 36, 55, 144, 190, 222; downtown narrative, 83, 192, 193, 197, 198, 200, 203, 205, 209, 215, 217, 221; and football heroes, 151, 152; and imperialism, 56, 57, 58, 225; as interaction repertoire, 11, 20, 38, 99, 199, 230; international narratives, 83, 158; metropolitan narrative, 192, 193, 197, 198, 200, 203, 205, 215, 217, 221; suburban narratives, 122, 133, 134, 149, 183, 224, 229
Foucault, Michel, 294
French colonialism, 41; and sport, 257, 260
Freund, Bill, 236
Freyre, Gilberto, 28, 57, 249, 265
Fundação Nacional para a Alegria no Trabalho (National Foundation for Joy at Work, FNAT), 257, 260

Gabinete de Urbanização Colonial/do Ultramar (Colonial Urbanization Office), 70, 74, 75, 275
Gallo, Donato, 271
Garrincha (Manuel Francisco dos Santos), 120, 124, 288
Gazense (Clube Vitória), 88, 89, 97, 108, 214, 281
Geertz, Clifford, 239
Giulianotti, Richard, 241
Gluckman, Max, 192, 290, 298
Goffman, Erving, 188, 241, 244, 259
Gomes, Rui, 259
Granovetter, Mark, 11, 241
Grémio Africano de Lourenço Marques/ Associação Africana) (Lourenço Marques African Guild/African Association, GALM), 27, 86, 87, 88, 90, 91, 104, 109, 119, 228, 248, 272, 280, 281, 283
Guedes, Amâncio de Alpoim (Pancho), 24, 73, 248, 275
Guttmann, Béla, 156, 291

habitus, 243, 244, 245, 288; as habitus motor, 14, 47, 57, 60, 105, 110, 121, 131, 142, 159, 162, 168, 169, 177, 179, 181, 185, 186, 188, 218, 228, 244
Hammond, R. J., 235, 236

Index ⇒ 321

Hannerz, Ulf, 282, 298
Harries, Patrick, 289
Harris, Marvin, 236, 271–72
Hedges, David, 236, 248
Hilário da Conceição, 4, 66, 71, 73, 82, 83, 91, 94, 97, 98, 101, 120, 129, 142, 143, 147, 148, 155, 161, 182, 186, 186, 196, 197, 204, 213, 229
Hobsbawm, Eric, 151

Indo-Português (Grupo Desportivo), 32, 49, 154, 211
Inhambanense (Grupo Desportivo) 87, 201
Instituto Nacional de Educação Física (National Institute of Physical Education INEF), 42, 55, 257, 258, 259, 264
Instituto Negrófilo/Centro dos Negros de Moçambique (Negrophile Institute/ Center of the Mozambican Blacks), 88, 90, 191, 195, 218, 274, 280, 282
Interaction Order, 14, 241, 244; in the cement city, 78, 100, 115, 208, 229, 230; in the game, 105, 112, 118, 123, 151, 162, 166, 171, 176, 181, 228; in the suburb, 78, 130, 131, 133, 159, 183, 213
Interaction Repertoire, 10, 11, 15, 121–23, 126, 183, 193, 198–99, 241
Isaacman, Allen, 235, 237, 291
Isaacman, Barbara, 235, 237

Jackson, Michael, 244
João Albasini (Grupo Desportivo), 39, 85, 86, 117, 196, 197, 216, 280, 283, 285
Jorge, Ismael Mário, 31, 250
Juca (Júlio Cernadas Pereira), 196
Junod, Henri, 238–39, 287, 290
Junta de Investigações do Ultramar, 271

Kennedy, Dane, 36
King, Anthony, 236
Kirk, David, 294
Kumar, Rahul, 258
Kuper, Adam, 234

Lagoas (neighborhood), 26, 208, 295
Leal de Oliveira, António, 42, 43, 44, 47, 258

Leseth, Anne, 138
Lopes, José Sérgio Leite, 244, 288
Louis, Joe, 40, 202, 295
Lourenço Marques (Maputo): African petite bourgeoisie, 26, 27, 40, 50, 69, 85, 87, 89, 90, 102, 109, 111, 191, 194, 228, 234, 247, 248, 288; Chinese in, 89; colonial bourgeoisie, 30, 31, 33, 208; English in, 21, 30, 31, 32, 106, 251; history of, 2–4, 6–8, 21–30; Indians in, 21, 32, 33, 49, 84, 89, 98, 154, 211, 251, 278; mestiços in, 33, 35, 49, 50, 85, 89, 129, 194, 212, 261, 287; Muslims in, 71, 84, 86–88, 138, 251, 279; settler population, 7, 21, 27, 31, 33–40, 48, 49, 55, 71, 7, 193, 200, 203, 206, 208, 209, 212, 213, 222, 226, 250, 261; social stratification, 6, 8, 22, 26, 68, 95
Lucas, Vicente, 82, 95, 101, 126, 182, 185, 187, 196, 197, 202, 211, 217, 229, 278
Luckmann, Thomas, 235, 239
Lusotropicalism, 28, 56, 57, 58, 61, 63, 64, 68, 75, 78, 224, 249, 265

Mackenzie, John, 250, 265
Mafalala (neighborhood), 22, 26, 66, 82, 84, 92, 101, 218, 219, 220
Mahafil Isslamo (Grupo Desportivo), 84, 86, 87, 93, 95, 107, 108, 150, 180, 197, 216, 217, 280, 294
Mahlo, Friederich, 292
Malhangalene: Clube da, 35, 211; neighborhood, 22, 26, 75, 116
malice, 1, 2; as body capital, 120, 127, 130, 133, 183, 228; as embodied history, 2, 3, 228, 231; and performance, 117, 120, 122, 123, 157, 160, 184; as strategy, 3, 125, 127, 152, 159, 218, 228; and the suburban community, 132, 135, 212, 228, 231; and survival, 132, 133; and violence, 113, 115, 128
Mangan, James, 241
Maradona, Diego Armando, 121
Margarido, Alfredo, 271, 294
Marques Pereira, Celestino, 42, 46, 47, 257, 258, 259, 260
Martin, Phyllis, 9, 94, 251, 252
Martin, Simon, 258
Marx, Karl, 244

Matateu (Sebastião Lucas da Fonseca), 4, 50, 82, 155, 185, 194, 196, 197, 198, 202, 204, 229, 255
Matine, Augusto, 73, 83, 95, 97, 116, 118, 121, 129, 147, 159, 161, 182, 185, 196, 197, 198, 210, 211, 213, 217, 218
Mauss, Marcel, 15, 245
media, 4, 10, 37, 38, 55–58, 62, 110, 153, 175, 185, 190, 193, 201, 213, 220, 222, 230; and imagined communities, 2, 37, 185, 193, 202; newspapers, 15, 16, 36, 37, 50, 84, 129, 135, 136, 153, 162, 165, 169, 175, 193, 196, 199–202, 205, 230, 272; radio, 37, 193, 198, 199, 199, 201–5, 212, 230, 274, 295; and social networks, 4, 190, 193, 197, 199, 201, 203, 213, 221, 222, 227
Melo, Daniel, 251
Mendes, Maria Clara, 208
military, 4, 9, 22, 33, 38, 40–42, 80, 81, 163, 207, 220
Mitchell, J. C., 236, 239, 298
Mocidade Portuguesa, 17, 41, 44, 118, 260, 269
Mocidade Portuguesa de Moçambique, 41, 47, 48, 53, 262, 263
Moreira, Adriano, 67, 255, 269, 270
Munhuana (neighborhood), 22, 26, 69, 70, 75, 78, 80, 87, 98, 100, 198, 208, 267, 268, 295
Munhuanense "Azar" (Sporting Clube), 87, 98, 179

Nacional Africano (Sport), 85, 86, 89, 214, 215
Nauright, John, 282
Neto, Fréchaut, 136, 139, 153, 289
Newitt, Malyn, 236
Noronha Feio, José Maria, 55, 56, 276
Nóvoa, António, 256

O'Laughlin, Bridget, 236
Oliveira, Cândido de, 165–69, 171, 172, 173, 291, 292
Owens, Jesse, 40, 110

Peel, J. D. Y., 116, 129, 240
Penvenne, Jeanne Marie, 17, 78, 115, 236, 247, 248, 272, 279, 291, 296

Pereira, Rui Mateus, 271
Perkin, Harold, 8, 237
physical education, 40, 168, 214; and state policies, 9, 40–48, 54, 55, 59, 87, 132, 156, 163, 165, 256–61, 264, 277; and women, 17
Pinheiro, Francisco, 292
Polana: Club, 30, 31; Hotel, 32, 187; neighborhood, 26, 207, 208
Polanah, Luís, 139, 209, 289, 290
popular culture: and football narratives, 11, 38, 55, 56, 58, 122, 133, 155, 190–94, 199, 203, 206, 209, 221–24, 229; and identity, 3, 193, 222, 239; as interaction repertoire, 11, 122, 185, 183, 198, 241; and the media, 4, 38, 55, 56, 185, 190, 193, 199, 203, 221, 222, 265; as public space, 84, 122, 190, 199, 212, 223; as representation of the world, 4, 206; as social idiom, 4, 19, 122, 190, 221–23, 230, 240; and social networks, 4, 58, 79, 84, 97, 190–93, 198, 199, 206, 221–22, 224, 229, 241

Rádio Clube de Moçambique, 204, 205, 274, 295
Radway, Janice, 282
Ranger, Terence, 239, 287
religious missions, 38, 277, 278, 282; Catholic, 28, 80, 88, 137, 277–78, 280; Protestant, 28, 81, 86, 89, 248, 277, 279, 281
Rhodesia, 6, 236, 239, 278, 287
Rhodes Livingstone Institute, 236
Ribeiro dos Reis, António, 165, 292
Rita-Ferreira, António, 16, 63, 64, 66, 68, 102, 249, 266, 267, 268, 271–72, 275, 290–91
Rocha, Aurélio, 248, 279
Rocha, Ilídio, 247
Ronga (language), 85, 138, 205, 233, 234, 277, 280, 287–88, 290

Salazar, António de Oliveira, 27, 237
São José de Lhanguene: Club, 80, 88, 153, 191; neighborhood, 22, 80, 88, 277–78
Sarmento Rodrigues, Manuel, 254

Schieffelin, Edward L., 243
Scotch, N. A., 137, 290
Scott, James C., 115, 239, 282, 287, 288
Senghor, Léopold Sédar, 234
Serpa, Homero, 291
Serviço dos Negócios Indígenas (Head Office for the Natives' Affairs), 41, 73, 261, 281–82
Silva Cunha, Joaquim da, 67, 264, 269–70
Simmel, Georg, 242
social stock of knowledge, 4, 38, 193, 197, 215, 239
Sommerschield (neighborhood), 208, 295
Sommerschield, Oscar, 250
South Africa, 9, 28, 34, 158, 214, 223, 248, 270, 272, 279, 284; economic activity, 6, 25, 27, 29, 34, 69, 81, 100, 101, 206, 289; and Mozambican migrations, 7, 22, 27, 29, 65, 69, 80, 89, 96, 178; racism, 101, 296; sport, 9, 37, 40, 80, 85, 99, 159, 160, 174, 226, 252, 254, 262, 278, 282, 283, 291, 293, 296
Sporting Clube de Portugal, 34, 66, 212, 252, 254
Sporting de Lisboa, 66, 200
Sporting de Lourenço Marques, 33, 34, 35, 39, 94, 101, 153, 154, 196, 197, 200, 204, 209, 211, 213, 216, 221
sportization, 12, 58, 145, 158, 160, 229, 242
sports associations, 27, 50, 52, 58, 251, 262; and discrimination, 33, 40, 51, 103, 255, 262; and identity, 21, 34, 58, 86, 87, 89, 99, 193, 251; and notables, 86, 88, 91, 145, 191, 195, 228, 282; and political control, 40–42, 46, 47, 49, 54, 55, 90, 263, 281; and urbanization, 9, 35, 79, 84, 223, 226
style of play: aesthetics, 14, 127–30, 189; and culturalization and nationalization, 3, 57, 165, 166, 235, 244, 288; and historical inquiry, 3, 12, 13, 16, 19; and the public, 118–20; space of stylistic possibles, 15, 133, 141, 173, 188, 227; and the suburbs, 18, 19, 103, 113, 120, 122, 127, 131–35, 141, 146, 149, 151, 157–62, 177, 181–84, 220, 227, 228, 231; and tactics, 14, 16, 153, 164–73

suburbs (of Lourenço Marques): commerce, 26, 58, 77, 79, 88, 96, 98, 204, 205, 207, 226; construction of, 7, 9, 24, 66–70, 228; as a frontier, 100, 101, 129, 178, 206, 213; internal divisions, 87, 95–98, 100, 193; and labor reproduction, 3–5, 8, 68, 78, 112, 133, 163; local elites, 17, 26, 38, 40, 49, 50, 59, 87, 90, 97, 102, 109, 111, 194, 228; local social contract, 3, 15, 17–19, 68, 79, 128, 130, 132, 134, 135, 148, 208, 217, 225, 227, 229; natural disasters in, 63; nutrition, 24, 63, 220; parties at, 82, 98, 119, 180, 276, 283; and poverty, 18, 63, 68, 71, 73, 74, 76, 77, 78, 79, 132, 133–35, 188, 275; and protection, 67, 118, 129, 148, 198; segregated, 3, 33, 38, 74, 76, 80; suburban habitus, 3, 18, 79, 130, 132, 180, 227, 228, 245; workers, 24, 78, 95–97, 211

tactics (football), 156; and aesthetics, 127, 166, 189, 243; classic formation, 165, 171–73, 292–93; coaches, 164–67, 170, 174–76; and creativity, 162, 185–89; and efficiency, 163–69, 184–86; and interaction order, 118, 159, 162, 171, 181, 183, 229; intimidating, 118, 121, 124, 130, 156, 159, 184; in Lourenço Marques, 173–77; and motor habitus, 158, 186; in the suburbs, 161–63, 177–82; WM, 160, 161, 164–66, 169, 171–74, 178, 181
Teja, Ângela, 258
tennis, 8, 31, 33, 82
Thompson, E. P., 239, 286, 291
Torres, Adelino, 29

Vasco da Gama (Grupo Desportivo), 49, 87, 98, 107, 118, 119, 194, 195, 200, 261, 280, 283, 285
Veblen, Thorstein, 240
Vidacs, Bea, 9, 238, 241

Wacquant, Loïc, 244
Weber, Eugen, 238, 256

Weber, Max, 164, 242, 243, 245, 291, 292
Wellman, Barry, 296
West, Harry G., 236, 271
Williams, Raymond, 241, 242
Wilson, Mário, 33, 39, 65, 72, 196, 204, 235, 255, 261
witchcraft (vovô), 1, 111, 130, 135, 290; in the cement city, 136, 152–56; and ritual innovation, 139–41; as a suburban right, 19, 67, 148, 149, 156, 157, 180; and urban adaptation, 137, 143, 145, 157, 184, 229

Xipamanine: neighborhood, 69, 78, 80, 84; pitch, 84

Zambeziano (Grupo Desportivo), 88
Zamparoni, Valdemir, 236, 245, 246, 247, 248, 251, 272, 276, 278, 279, 280, 281, 283, 286, 296

www.ingramcontent.com/pod-product-compliance
Lightning Source LLC
Chambersburg PA
CBHW020639300426
44112CB00007B/173